The Piratization of Russia

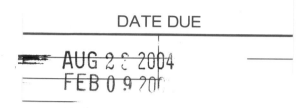

In 1991 a small group of Russians emerged from the collapse of the Soviet Union to claim ownership of some of the most valuable petroleum, natural gas, and metal deposits in the world. This resulted in one of the greatest transfers of wealth ever seen. By 1997, five of those individuals were on *Forbes Magazine*'s list of the world's richest billionaires. These self-styled oligarchs were accused of using guile, intimidation, and occasionally violence to reap these rewards.

Marshall I. Goldman argues against the line that the course adopted by President Yeltsin was the only one open to Russia, since an examination of the reform process in Poland shows that a more gradual and imaginative approach worked there with less corruption and a wider share of benefits.

The Piratization of Russia is an accessible, lucid, and timely book that is required reading for those with an interest in the debâcle of Russian reform, from the interested lay-reader to students, academics, economists, and politicians who want to understand the problems facing Russia and how they could have been avoided.

Marshall I. Goldman is Davis Professor of Russian Economics, Emeritus at Wellesley College, and Associate Director of the Davis Center for Russian and Eurasian Studies, Harvard University, USA. He has appeared as a commentator on *Good Morning America* as well as *Nightline* and McNeil Lehrer *News Hour* and is a regular commentator on National Public Radio in the USA and the BBC in Britain.

The Piratization
of Russia
Russian reform goes awry

Marshall I. Goldman

Routledge
Taylor & Francis Group
LONDON AND NEW YORK

First published 2003
by Routledge
11 New Fetter Lane, London EC4P 4EE

Simultaneously published in the USA and Canada
by Routledge
29 West 35th Street, New York, NY 10001

Reprinted 2004

Routledge is an imprint of the Taylor & Francis Group

© 2003 Marshall I. Goldman

Typeset in Baskerville by Taylor & Francis Ltd
Printed and bound in Great Britain by TJ International, Padstow,
Cornwall

British Library Cataloguing in Publication Data
A catalogue record for this book is available from the British Library

Library of Congress Cataloging in Publication Data
Goldman, Marshall I.
The piratization of Russia : Russian reform goes awry / Marshall I.
Goldman. p. cm.
Simultaneously published in the USA and Canada.
Includes bibliographical references and index.
1. Russia (Federation) –Economic policy – 1991–2 2. Oligarchy – Russia
(Federation) 3. Commercial crimes – Russia (federation) 4. Businessmen –
Russia (Federation) – Political activity. I. Title.

HC340.12.G653 2003
330.947–dc21   2002037158
ISBN 0–415–31528–X (hbk)
ISBN 0–415–31529–8 (pbk)

To Jessica, Samuel Todd, Jacob, Sam, Jonah, David, Elie, Nathan, Lauren, and Isaac, so that we may learn from the past

Contents

Illustrations

Tables

Figures

Acknowledgments

Let me begin by thanking the Indiana University Press and the journals *East European Jewish Affairs*, *Eastern Economic Journal* and *Challenge Magazine* for allowing me to reprint portions of my articles that they had published earlier. Beyond that I am as usual indebted to a platoon of institutions, colleagues, assistants and friends for their advice and support. First and foremost are Wellesley College and the Davis Center for Russian and Eurasian Studies at Harvard University. My interaction with Wellesley students has allowed me to test run chapters and ideas for this book and the research facilities at Harvard's Davis Center have provided me with an ideal writing environment with always stimulating and supportive colleagues, especially the Wednesday economic seminars. It has been a wonderful and fruitful combination.

Equally important, I am grateful to the dozens of scholars, businessmen, oligarchs, journalists and government officials in Russia who have allowed me to visit them in their offices, homes and factories. I have more access there than I sometimes have here. Forgive me however if my criticism sometimes appears to be ingratitude. It is meant to be constructive.

As for individuals in this country, my first thanks go to my assistants, most recently to Daniel Gurvich and Robert Price. Given my computer and typing skills, there would be no manuscript without their efforts. I should also thank Susan Gardos in the Davis Center library and her assistant Helen Repina and my students who have fine-tuned my manuscript, especially Inna Poliakova and Jessica Goldman. But the one whom I must thank more than anyone else is my wife Merle. It is hard to imagine a more supportive partner. Her encouragement comes with insight and criticism that only a caring and thoughtful colleague could provide. We are lucky in that we not only share four children and ten grandchildren, but common interests in related fields. Comparing and contrasting reforms in Russia and China has stimulated and provoked both of us. Our arguments are not for the faint of heart or weak of will. However, as painful as it almost always is, there has been nothing more helpful than her editing of this, and for that matter all of my previous books. If there ever has been a labor of love, this must be it.

1 Russia's financial buccaneers

The wild and woolly East

The battle for Sviazinvest would never pass as soap opera. Who would believe it? But the 1997 struggle for ownership and control of Russia's largest and potentially most profitable telecommunication company among one-time allies highlights the perverted and seamy nature of Russia's economic reform. The battle sparked not only a scurrilous, semi-violent struggle over ownership of valuable corporate assets, but also a battle for influence over Boris Yeltsin, then the president of Russia. J.R. Ewing in *Dallas* never reached so high in his battles. However, within a year, on August 17, 1998 when the Russian stock market crashed and their paper holdings fell to almost one-tenth of their original value, the winners also became losers.

The bitter combatants in the 1997 Sviazinvest fight had agreed just a year earlier to set aside their previous quarrels to stage-manage the June 1996 presidential election campaign. Together they worked to manipulate the Russia electorate into voting for Boris Yeltsin. This small but influential band of thirteen businessmen–or "oligarchs" as they came to be called–mobilized themselves into a Yeltsin for President campaign committee headed by Anatoly Chubais. Yeltsin had just fired Chubais from his post as First Deputy Prime Minister, but everyone agreed that he had been a very effective administrator who almost single-handedly pushed through the government's privatization effort. Until Chubais and the businessmen took over, the opinion polls showed that Yeltsin's opponent, Gennady Zyuganov, the head of the Communist Party, would be the most likely winner, a prospect the oligarchs feared would lead to a return to a Soviet-style economy. On a personal level that meant that such a born-again communist state might not only seize the hundreds of millions of dollars worth of property they had accumulated since 1991, but might imprison or execute them as well.

In gratitude for his come-from-behind victory, Yeltsin gladly acquiesced as seven of the participants, Peter Aven, Boris Berezovsky, Mikhail Fridman, Vladimir Gusinsky, Mikhail Khodorkovsky, Vladimir Potanin, and Alexander Smolensky, divided up some of the country's most valuable raw materials,

businesses, and media outlets. In addition, he also appointed two of them–
Potanin and Berezovsky–to senior government posts; Potanin as First Deputy
Prime Minister and Berezovsky as Deputy Secretary of Russia's Security Council.
Insensitive to the issue of "conflict of interest," their government appointments
enhanced their business dealings. Thus by late 1996, Berezovsky was able to boast
that these seven influential bankers had gained control of 50 percent of the
country's assets.[1] An exaggeration perhaps, but not too far from the truth.

They grabbed an even more important hold on the media. This "Big
Seven," or *Semibankirshchina*, as the Russians began to call them, came close
to controlling 70 percent of the Moscow press and radio and 80 percent of
the nation's TV. (The *Semibankirshchina*, a play on words, alludes to the
seven Boyars (Semiboyarshchina) who acted as the government of Russia
after Czar Vasily Shuisky was overthrown in 1610.)

That should have been enough power and influence, but as Grigory
Yavlinsky, the leader of Yabloko, the main democratic party in the Russian
Duma, said, "Russia's financial oligarchy knows no limit to its greed. They will
never be satisfied."[2] As the state continued to sell off its enterprises, these
bankers established holding companies or, as they described them, financial-
industrial groups (FIGS) with which to acquire more and more. There were
minor squabbles and accusations that this or that auction of an oil company or
an aluminum smelter was rigged, and even reports of a beating or assassination, particularly among the bankers and directors involved with the
aluminum smelters. But generally these natural rivals agreed that by working
together there would be enough for all. Equally significant, the close if not
incestuous relationship between government leaders and corporate directors
and bankers allowed for insider deals, golden parachutes, corporate jets, villas
in Cyprus and Spain, and instant millionaire status for those who played along.

By contrast to this narrow elite, 80 to 90 percent of the rest of the population found themselves cast off, many in very dire straits. In 1999, for
example, almost 38 percent of the population was declared to be below the
poverty line.[3] Even those who had earlier put aside savings ended up with
almost nothing to show after the 26-fold inflation of 1992. This looting of
the country–all in the name of privatization and a move to the market–was a
form of piratization. Yet despite the open and blatant seizure of what had
been public property and the accompanying deterioration in the status of
the overwhelming percentage of the population, there was relatively little
protest or reaction from the ever-patient, long-suffering Russian people.

I

What brought the Sviazinvest matter to a head and resulted in the collapse
of this harmonious looting of the country was Yeltsin's decision to bring in

an outside reformer, Boris Nemtsov, as one of the country's two First Deputy Prime Ministers. Nemtsov previously had been the appointed and subsequently elected governor of Nizhny Novgorod. As governor, Nemtsov toiled and lobbied relentlessly to bring the market to his region in an open, relatively transparent way, an anomaly in Russia where so much was done covertly. His record was not perfect, and once he assumed power in Moscow, rumors and accusations abounded. Nevertheless, except for two or three governors in regions such as Samara or Velikii, Novgorod, few others had managed the economic reform process as effectively as Nemtsov did in Nizhny Novgorod.

Summoned to Moscow by Yeltsin in March 1997, Nemtsov moved immediately to institute the same level of integrity that he had sought in his province. As he put it, "I will promise three things: I will not steal. I will not take bribes. I will not tell lies."[4] Few believed him. As they saw it, there was no way to work and breathe the air of Moscow without becoming similarly infected by the all-pervasive greed and graft. As one of his critics told me, "You don't go into a brothel unless you expect to sample the wares."

As he himself anticipated, Nemtsov's arrival in Moscow sparked a tidal wave of accusations and charges of past, hidden or imagined indiscretions, most of them false (the Russians call this *kompromat*).[5] This was a throwback to the Soviet era when slander and half-truths were used to discredit rivals. Accusations of prostitutes and financial manipulators against Nemtsov (some broadcast on television) were largely initiated by those fearful that Nemtsov's crusade might impinge on their own interests.

Nemtsov's initial attempts at a cleanup sparked fierce resistance and as a consequence produced rather trivial results. His opponents realized that if Nemtsov succeeded in forcing all government officials to replace their foreign-made cars with those made in Russia and to declare their income and wealth, Nemtsov might yet cause real damage. Thus, in the very first auction of the government's foreign cars very few were sold off, and while a large number of officials did file income and wealth declarations, most of these reports bore little relationship to actual income or wealth. Moreover the decree did not cover family members, many of whom became the beneficiaries of assets put in their names.

II

Nemtsov insists that he was serious. He was also determined to clean up what was called the "Loans for Shares" program. This involved the auction to private buyers of some of the country's most valuable holdings of petroleum and other raw materials. Until his arrival in Moscow almost no auction under the Loans for Shares program had brought the government more than a fraction of the real value of those properties. This was because in almost all cases the "high" bidder turned out to be affiliated with the auction organizer. For that matter, the idea for the Loans for Shares program came from Vladimir Potanin, the head of Oneximbank, who outlined it on March 30, 1995. Not surprisingly, by the time most of the auctions had been held, Oneximbank emerged as the biggest beneficiary of the program.

The pretext for the Loans for Shares scheme was that the bankers wanted to do something to help the government reduce its budget deficit.[6] Because almost no one, including the banks, was paying much in the way of taxes, the government could not generate the revenues it needed to underwrite its expenditures. Therefore in a gesture that proved too good to be true, the Big Seven *Semibankirshchina* offered to lend money to the government to substitute at least temporarily for the uncollected taxes. All the bankers asked in exchange was that the government put up collateral for these loans in the form of shares of government-owned stock from some of the larger enterprises the state was planning to sell. Ostensibly that was no cause for alarm. After all, once the government found a way to collect those taxes, it could repay its loan. The banks would then return the government's collateral. Of course if the loans were not repaid (and no one thought they would be) the banks would then be free to sell off the collateral so they could recoup their money. Moreover, these were shares of stock that the state in any case intended to sell.

The original plan specified that to generate as much revenue for the state as possible, the bank holding the collateral would conduct an auction on the state's behalf for the purchase of that collateral. This was thought to be the best way to attract additional bidders. If done properly the resulting competition would yield funds sufficient to repay the banks and would go on to generate for the state a considerably larger amount than the initial loan. But by holding the auction in remote locations, closing the airport on the day of the auction, or specifying terms that only the auctioneer himself could meet, the auction rarely generated more than a few dollars above the original offering price. And in virtually every instance, the winner of the auction was an affiliate of the bank that held the auction.

Determined to break this pattern and end the collusion between what under different circumstances should have been fierce rivals, Nemtsov promised that he would see that Sviazinvest, which was the next state enterprise to be privatized, would be auctioned at full value. Not only would this be a means to restore confidence in government procedures, but also the government desperately needed the proceeds from this sale in order to pay the back wages of government employees, particularly the military. At one point the government was behind by as much as $4.4

billion in overdue wages.[7] It did not take a Machiavelli to realize that the timely payment of military wages was of particular urgency. In mid-1997, angered by a host of grievances, several former generals began to call openly for "action" by the military. Eliminating their salary backlog would dissipate some of that anger.

Set for July 25, 1997, there was considerable uncertainty as to just how much interest the Nemtsov-organized auction for Sviazinvest would attract. This was not the first time an effort had been made to privatize Sviazinvest. In late 1995, the government reached a tentative agreement with STET, the Italian telecommunication company, to pay $1.4 billion for 25 percent of the company's shares.[8] At the last minute, however, STET withdrew its offer, complaining that the Russian authorities had refused to allow it access to long-distance markets as well as important financial data.[9] Subsequently the privatization authorities called in N.M. Rothchild and ING Barings, Western financial advisors, for guidance in finding additional foreign investors.[10] However, some of the Big Seven banks, particularly MOST-Bank, began to complain that Sviazinvest was too important to Russia's national security to allow it to be sold to foreign investors. Succumbing to pressure, the government then severed its work with N.M. Rothchild and ING, Barings and announced that only a company with Russian majority control could bid for Russia's telecommunication network. Everyone understood that this meant MOST-Bank had an inside track.

As the time for the auction approached, it became clear that other bids would also be submitted, including one from Oneximbank. When the plans to auction off Sviazinvest were drawn up, the founder of Oneximbank, Vladimir Potanin, was serving as First Deputy Prime Minister. He had taken a leave of absence from his bank, and he had made it clear that as a member of the government it would be unwise for his bank to submit a bid.[11] But when he was removed from office in March 1997, he quickly decided to enter a serious offer.

In an attempt to avoid a real competition that would be costly for the winner, the two lead bidders, Potanin of Oneximbank and Vladimir Gusinsky, the founder of MOST-Bank, sought a meeting in France with the vacationing Anatoly Chubais to see if they could work out a sweetheart deal in advance. After all, they had all worked together so well the previous year during the presidential election. And after Yeltsin's victory, Chubais had been brought back into the government and was serving as First Deputy Prime Minister along with Nemtsov. Potanin, Gusinsky, and Chubais were joined on the French Riviera by Boris Berezovsky, the founder of Logovaz bank, also one of the *Semibankirshchina*. Potanin had been accumulating more and more state property and Gusinsky and

Berezovsky were worried that, if left unchecked, Potanin and his bank would soon become so dominant as to threaten their own business empires. Therefore the two decided to unite despite the fact that only a few years ago they had been bitter enemies. Berezovsky was present not openly as a banker but ostensibly in his official capacity as Deputy Secretary of the Security Council; he justified his presence by explaining that he wanted to insure there would be no foreign or criminal control of Sviazinvest. That, he insisted, would threaten Russia's national security.

As the original architect of the privatization drive, Chubais had subsequently developed close relations with all three–Gusinsky, Potanin, and Berezovsky–during Yeltsin's successful 1996 presidential campaign. Having been one of the leaders of the reform movement in Leningrad, Chubais had been regarded as Mr. Clean when he arrived in Moscow in 1991 to organize the privatization effort. But when he was fired by Yeltsin in late 1995 and no longer a government employee, Chubais felt free to work the private sector. He worked fast. Within four months he had accumulated a taxable income of at least $300,000. According to an article in *Izvestiia*, that was in part income earned from a $3 million interest-free loan provided by Alexander Smolensky's Stolichnyi bank, one of the Big Seven.[12] Chubais then used the loan to invest in high-yielding government securities.[13] Later, Chubais would also acknowledge that $538,000 in laundered dollar bills found in a suitcase being carried out of Yeltsin's election headquarters by two of Chubais' assistants was also ill gotten and, until its discovery, was intended also to be disposed of illicitly.[14] Had they not been confiscated, the funds would have been used secretly to attack Yeltsin's opponents.

Given Chubais' involvement with the Big Seven, it seemed to Gusinsky, Potanin, and Berezovsky that if anyone would be sympathetic to their concerns, it would be Chubais. For that reason they requested a meeting with the First Deputy Prime Minister, who appeared to be amenable to a "sensible" settlement, unlike his colleague, the uncompromising Nemtsov.

The meeting was arranged for two nights before the auction. But despite Gusinsky's and Berezovsky's best efforts, Chubais refused to intervene. Upon their return to Moscow several other last minute meetings were called to seek some compromise. None were successful, and the auction was held as planned.[15]

Nemtsov had provided fair warning. Gathering the bankers together at an April meeting several weeks before the auction, he announced that henceforth there would be uniform treatment for everyone in the way government tax money from the budget was allocated to the banks to hold temporarily until spent by the government. In other words, the banks could no longer count on their connections to divert the government's money to their bank as if it were their own.[16] Furthermore, he added,

"Guys [*rebiata*], enough! That's it. Let's live honestly," by which he meant that henceforth the state auctions for government businesses would be transparent and that the highest bidder, not the highest briber, would be the winner. As he subsequently put it, there would be no more rigged deals where, "based on personal connections," state property would be sold off "for free or at a discount."[17]

True to his word, the sale of 25 percent of the shares plus one share of Sviazinvest went to the highest bidder, which turned out to be a group headed by Potanin's Oneximbank.[18] Potanin's team included participation by the German Deutsche Morgan Grenfell Bank, as well as the American Bank Morgan Stanley and the investor George Soros' Quantum Fund. Their bid was for $1.875 billion. This substantially exceeded the government's starting price of $1.18 billion, as well as the losing bid of $1.71 billion from a Gusinsky-coordinated partnership consisting of the Alfa Bank, MOST-Bank, Credit Suisse First Boston, and the Spanish telephone company Telefonica de España S.A. As critics of the Potanin victory came to note, the losing side was the only one to include among its partners one with technical skills.

To outsiders the deal appeared to be fair and above board. To the losers and to some skeptics, it was anything but. For starters, the winners were only speculators with no technical know-how. Then there was controversy about the way payment was made. It was supposed to be in rubles but the money came in dollars instead. Others complained that because potential bidders were given only two weeks between the time the auction was announced and the time the auction was held, they were denied the time and access they needed for a due diligence search of the company's records. These restrictions undoubtedly deterred some investors from bidding. Not only that, but the money that Oneximbank put up in advance of the bid was partly government money, some of which was said to have been embezzled in a scheme involving the sale of government military equipment.[19] It also included customs taxes that had been collected by the government but deposited with Oneximbank. In addition, Potanin and the head of the privatization agency responsible for the auctions, Alfred Kokh, were good friends. While that in itself was not enough evidence of collusion, it was later disclosed that a Swiss company that served as a front for Potanin had arranged to pay both Kokh and Chubais $100,000 as a book advance, an amount that would never be earned by the sale of a book from either of the two men. All of this gave the strong appearance that, despite Nemtsov's best efforts, the Sviazinvest auction was just one more example of insider trading.

Having lost the bid, Gusinsky, abetted by Berezovsky, attacked Potanin, Nemtsov, Kokh, and Chubais in their respective newspapers, radio and television networks. Potanin responded in kind through his newspaper *Komsomolskaia Pravda*. The Big Seven coalition had come apart at the seams and the media owners who were once united behind Yeltsin for political purposes now divided up to protect their own business interests. (That would not be the last instance where one-time allies found themselves desperately fighting each other.) Each side called the other a crook, a liar, and immoral.[20]

Gusinsky's attacks on Kokh in particular undoubtedly help explain why in 2001 Kokh took such pleasure in seizing control of NTV and Media-MOST from Gusinsky, previously the source of the latter's power. At the time however, Gusinsky appeared the most aggrieved. He had wanted badly to add the telecommunications company to his media empire (a natural combination). Reflecting his hurt, his newspaper, *Segodnia*, ran a story headlined "The Money Stank."[21] MOST-Bank's defeat was particularly galling to Gusinsky because he assumed that since MOST-Bank and Alfa Bank had been advising the privatization ministry on how to conduct the transaction, they would have the inside track. Based on past experience, the bank that acted as the consultant almost always ended up as the winner in the subsequent auctions. Moreover, they had already been instrumental in sidetracking STET, the Italian firm, and limiting the sale to Russian bidders. That made the winning bid by the Western bankers and George Soros all the more painful. Their loss in the Sviazinvest tender made them suspect that someone had changed the rules or revealed their bid to the other contenders. The close relationship between Potanin's Oneximbank, the winner, and Alfred Kokh, the head of the privatization office, did nothing to dampen such suspicions. The fact that the winners offered a higher bid was immaterial.

To defend himself, Potanin's paper *Komsomolskaia Pravda* arranged for Nemtsov to give a press conference. Headlined "Enough of Bandit Capitalism," the article printed Nemtsov's warnings that Gusinsky, aided by Berezovsky and his papers and TV programs, were playing into the hands of an unholy coalition of communists and nationalists who were bitterly opposed to the whole privatization and economic reform effort.[22] *Izvestiia* printed a similar warning.[23]

Nemtsov added to these criticisms when a few days later he publicly attacked Berezovsky for meddling in the dispute.[24] Gusinsky had been very careful to distance Berezovsky from any commercial interest in his own quest. As he put it, Berezovsky's presence at the French tryst with Chubais was in his capacity as Deputy Secretary of the Russian Government Security Council. After all, Berezovsky had promised to set aside his business interest in his Logovaz bank while working in his government post. But Nemtsov suggested that Berezovsky lacked the ability to differentiate between what was his and what belonged to the state. Berezovsky's presence in France with Gusinsky, Nemtsov charged, was simply another case where Berezovsky had abused his government post in order to protect his and not the state's interest.

That Berezovsky and Gusinsky should join together was somewhat of a surprise, not because Berezovsky was supposed to absent himself from business activities benefiting his "former" companies, but because the two bankers were often literally at each other's throats. (This feuding was repeated in 1999, before the election to the Duma. They became allies again in 2000.) In his insider-tells-all book, the one-time chief bodyguard and confidant of Boris Yeltsin, Alexandr Korzhakov, charged that Berezovsky considered ordering a contract killing of Gusinsky.[25] For good measure, Berezovsky was also said to have debated whether or not to add Mayor Yuri Luzhkov as a target. Korzhakov also reports that Berezovsky offered him $5 million not to publish the book. Rumors and reports of this sort underlay the claim by *Forbes Magazine* that Berezovsky headed the Russian Mafia.[26] Although Berezovsky finally managed to convince a London judge to hear a libel suit against *Forbes*, there is no doubt that the players in this privatization drama were gambling for big stakes. According to one report, in reaching for some papers in his briefcase, one of the bankers involved in the bidding for Sviazinvest "accidentally" dropped a pistol on the table.[27] Since several government officials responsible for privatization have been shot at and, in a subsequent incident in St. Petersburg, one was actually murdered, such "accidental" displays were not to be taken lightly.

Despite some criticism of the Sviazinvest auction from then Prime Minister Viktor Chernomyrdin, both the Sviazinvest sale and another auction for the nickel and non-ferrous metal facility at Norilsk, which Oneximbank also won, were agreed to by the government. This meant that the rather sudden resignation of Alfred Kokh, the head of the privatization agency, the November 5, 1997 dismissal of Berezovsky from his government post at the Security Council, the subsequent attack on Chubais and his removal as Minister of Finance, and the eventual criticism by President Yeltsin of what he said was the overly intimate relationship between Kokh and Potanin, were not reasons enough to invalidate the auction. But injustice has its own reward. By August 1998, barely a year later, the Russian stock market crashed and the Russian government ordered a moratorium on the payment of all government debt, both domestic and foreign. In the aftermath, Potanin's bank had to close its doors, and both Berezovsky and Gusinsky, once again enemies, found their financial and media holdings badly in debt and worth a fraction of their previous value. As for George Soros, his near $1 billion investment collapsed to a bare $100 million; as he put it, "the worst investment he had ever made."[28] After a time, Sviazinvest stock regained some of its value, but belatedly. Only Chubais emerged better off. After leaving the government, he won an appointment as CEO of UES, Russia's electrical monopoly, thus becoming an oligarch in his own right.

III

This vignette of undue influence and self-dealing, all in the name of reform, is a typical and far from unique example of how messy the effort by Russia to privatize and switch to a market system has been. What were "the initial conditions" as Joseph Berliner has phrased it with which the reformers– President Mikhail Gorbachev and his successors, Boris Yeltsin and Vladimir Putin–had to deal? In a stimulating article, Berliner looks at both the communist and Gorbachev legacies, the economic, political, and social conditions that prevailed as their regimes came to an end. Building on that essay, our study attempts to examine what led to such outrageous crimes as the Loans for Shares program and the Sviazinvest auction. We will begin with a look at the "initial conditions," that is, the economic, political, and social state of the Soviet Union prior to its collapse.[29] But to understand the conditions with which Mikhail Gorbachev, Boris Yeltsin, and Vladimir Putin had to contend, we have to go back to the czarist era. Indeed so much of what is happening in the economic and business world in Russia today is an echo not only of the communist era (Chapter 4) but of the czarist period as well (Chapter 3).

Against this political and economic backdrop, in Chapter 5 we will discuss what led the reformers to adopt the tactics they did, specifically their approach to privatization. Given how unsuitable these "remedies" were for Russia, it was all but inevitable that there would be the massive self-dealing and theft that helped set the stage for widespread corruption and the seizure by a few oligarchs of what had been state and public assets. Even officials in the Kremlin and the Russian Central Bank schemed to help themselves. This self dealing will be the focus of Chapters 6–9.

Some argue that given the legacy of seventy years of communism, central state planning and ownership, and at best a weak market infrastructure, there was no chance that the Russian economy horse, as Berliner would put it, would be able to reach its destination. Others insist however that, as unfit as the horse might have been, the real problem (continuing with Berliner's metaphor) was with the jockey, the country's leaders. None of the leaders or reformers was capable enough of implementing a successful package of reforms. Such critics may have a point.

Those studying what happened in Russia are usually unaware that–as we shall see in Chapter 10–not all privatization efforts in the former communist world turned out so badly. Just why Russian privatization was such a failure and why then the term "piratization," rather than privatization, is a more appropriate description shall be the focus of our attention in what follows.

In addition to the usual written materials, the chapters that follow incorporate over ninety personal interviews, conversations, and seminar presentations involving senior Soviet and Russian officials, including prime ministers, several of the oligarchs, and about twenty-five factory directors, primarily in Novosibirsk, Yaroslavl, Podolsk, Moscow, and St. Petersburg. Many of the discussions also took place at the World Economic Forum annual meetings in Davos, Switzerland, and Salzburg, Austria. A list can be found in the 'Meetings, interviews, seminars, and discussions' section in the Bibliography.

2 Setting the stage

The Russian economy in
the post-communist era

The struggle over Sviazinvest is just one example of the chicanery associated with privatization in Russia and the reform process in the 1990s. Why did Sviazinvest, along with almost all the other privatization efforts in Russia, become so encrusted with scandal and become so badly mismanaged? What, if anything, could Russia have done to spare itself some of these misadventures? Digging even deeper, why did Russian reformers choose a shock therapy strategy and by extension a program of rapid privatization, a mistake that will take years to correct? Why didn't they move gradually? Why is it that some post-communist countries, particularly Poland, have succeeded in avoiding most of those difficulties?

What follows will be an attempt to answer these questions. By no means is this analysis the first to raise such issues or criticize the privatization process.[1] But going beyond some of the earlier studies, we will also seek alternative scenarios that might have involved fewer aftercosts. We also consider what, if anything, can be done now, after the initial miscues, to redress some of the mistakes of the past.

Our first task in this chapter will be to describe the initial conditions, that is, the state of the economy as Mikhail Gorbachev, Boris Yeltsin, and Yegor Gaidar found it and how they left it. As Joseph Berliner would have put it, how healthy was the horse (the initial conditions) and how effective were the jockeys or the country's leaders in guiding that horse?[2] Did Russian leaders do all they could to guide Russia to a successful transition or were reforms in Russia doomed to fail? We shall then inquire as to why the reformers chose to follow the path that some have come to call shock therapy. Finally we will consider some of the more important factors which have made reform in Russia, any kind of reform, so difficult to implement.

I

After seven decades of central planning, the Soviet economy in 1985 was in need of serious repair. When Gorbachev came to power in 1985, the horse (the economy) was already incapacitated. The initial conditions were not favorable for reform. Also, Gorbachev, despite his skills as a statesman, was a poor jockey, at least when it came to designing and implementing a good economic policy. By December 25, 1991 when Yeltsin helped push Gorbachev out of office, the economy was in even more desperate straits. During Gorbachev's last years in office, economic growth, which had begun to slow, actually turned negative (see Table 2.1). According to calculations by the US Central Intelligence Agency, in 1990 GNP for the whole Soviet Union fell somewhere between 2.4 and 5 percent. The following year, in 1991, the GDP for just Russia also fell 5 percent.

But Yeltsin got what he wanted: Gorbachev was gone and the Soviet Union was no more. What counted now was just Russia. Yeltsin was to find, however, that Russia alone was more of a mixed blessing than he anticipated. Once the Soviet Union disintegrated, one-quarter of the land mass and one-half of the population was split off from Russia to form fourteen other independent countries. Moreover a region or two, such as Chechnia which remained within Russia, threatened periodically to join the exodus. As for the economy, in the years that followed it was wracked by runaway inflation, collapsing industrial production, empty shops, and massive flights of capital. There were times when Russia was close to

Table 2.1 Changes in annual Russian GDP

	GDP as a % change of preceding year	*Change in %*	*Index of consumer price as a % of preceding December*
1989	–	–	?
1990*	97.6 to 95.0	-2.4 to 5.0	?
1991	95.0	-5.0	+260
1992	85.5	-14.5	+2,610
1993	91.3	-8.7	+940
1994	87.3	-12.7	+320
1995	95.9	-4.1	+230
1996	96.6	-3.4	+122
1997	100.9	+0.9	+111
1998	95.1	-4.9	+184
1999	103.2	+3.2	+137
2000	107.7	+7.7	+120
2001	105.0	+5.0	+119

Source: Goskomstat Rossii, *Rossiiskii Statisticheskii Ezhegodnik* (Russian Statistical Report), Moscow: Goskomstat, 2000, pp. 16, 559; *Economic Newsletter*, Davis Center for Russian Studies, Harvard University, February 19, 2002, p. 12.

* 1990 is for GNP of USSR: Directorate of Intelligence, Central Intelligence Agency, *Handbook of Economic Statistics*, 1991, Washington, September 1991, p. 6.

insolvency. By some measures, such as the measly $2 billion of currency and gold reserves in the Russian Central Bank in 1991, it already was.[3] That Russia did not implode is a testimony more to the stoicism or perhaps inertia of the Russian people than to wise leadership.

Much to their disappointment, the drop in GDP that began under Gorbachev rapidly accelerated under Yeltsin and Gaidar. The GDP fell every year until 1997 when it rose by somewhat less than 1 percent. The drop resumed however, in 1998, even before the August 17, Black Monday financial crisis.

Having hit bottom, the GDP began to increase again in 1999. This continued in the years immediately thereafter, including a relatively robust 7.7 percent in 2000. But the damage to both economic growth and the institutional structure from the early 1990s was massive. Official Russian statistics indicate that from 1991 to 1998, Russian GDP fell by more than 40 percent (some say 50 percent). This drop exceeded America's economic collapse during the Great Depression. But unlike the US in the 1930s, Russia also suffered from simultaneous hyperinflation. In 1992, for example, Russian prices rose twenty-six-fold (see Table 2.2). As a result, by December 1999, 1,602,658 rubles were required to buy the same basket of goods that theoretically only 100 rubles would have purchased in December 1990.[4] The effect of this hyperinflation was to wipe out almost everyone's savings.

This was an inauspicious environment in which to begin the reform process. The "initial conditions" inherited by Yeltsin from Gorbachev were daunting but the reform agenda pursued by Yeltsin and his subordinates, rather than alleviate the situation, aggravated it. Neither Yeltsin nor Gaidar turned out to be much better jockeys than Gorbachev.

Table 2.2 Equivalent of 100 rubles after inflation (based on December 1990 consumer prices)

	Rubles	*Rate of inflation*
12/90	100	
12/91	260	2.60
12/92	6,786	26.10
12/93	63,788	9.40
12/94	204,123	3.20
12/95	489,483	2.30
12/96	572,769	1.22
12/97	635,733	1.11
12/98	1,169,823	1.84
12/99	1,602,658	1.37

Source: Table 2.1.

As welcome as the beginning of economic growth in 1999 was, the results for the decade as a whole since 1990 came nowhere close to initial expectations. This was despite countless and repeated predictions as early as 1992, by a determined group of officials, inside investors and Western spin doctors that economic growth would begin at any minute.[5] To the contrary, despite its raw material and human riches, Russia seemed unable even to match the growth achieved by most of its one-time satellites in Eastern Europe, the majority of which reported positive growth as early as 1993 (see Table 2.3).

Yet some argue that the criticism of Russian economic performance in the 1990s and, by extension, the economic policies and the transition strategy Yeltsin pursued at the time is unjustified because the Russian economy did not in fact suffer as much as some critics say. That is because the official statistics did not capture Russia's economic turnaround. Visitors to Moscow, especially those who attended its 850th Anniversary in September 1997, were struck by how dynamic the city had become. If Moscow were any indication, the country as a whole had come out of its slump, argued Martin Feldstein, the President of the National Bureau of Economic Research.[6] This was but eleven months before the August 1998 financial collapse. Estimates differ, but some reports indicate that in 1996 and 1997 Moscow's economy did grow by as much as 6 percent.[7] But Moscow has always done better than the rest of the country. Yet just as New York City is not the United States, so Moscow is not Russia. While Moscow was doing well, the Deputy Governor of the Novosibirsk Oblast in June 1997 told me that his region's economic output fell 15 percent in 1996, in part because of decisions taken in Moscow. He went so far as to imply that because as much as 80 percent of the country's financial resources flow through Moscow, and it absorbs 57 percent of the country's foreign investment, Moscow's growth at least to some extent came at the expense of the provinces, such as Novosibirsk.[8] Yet even Moscow could not escape its own meltdown in the fall of 1998, made worse by the over-building that preceded it.

Those who question the accuracy of Russian statistics point out that the official statistics did not reflect what was happening in the private or unofficial economic sectors. Some believe that official state statistics may not even have fully encompassed what was happening in the state sector. This is a twist because in the Soviet era, most Western observers agreed that it was necessary to deflate Soviet growth statistics because of official pressure to exaggerate industrial and agricultural output. The rapid economic growth that the Soviet Union experienced was also hard to determine precisely because of technical statistical reasons arising from the nature of index numbers. Depending on which set of weights were

Table 2.3 Annual percentage change in GDP for countries of Eastern Europe and the former Soviet Union

	1991	1992	1993	1994	1995	1996	1997	1998	1999	2000
Bulgaria	-12.7	-10.7	+0.8	+4.2	+2.4	-10.1	-6.9	+4.5	+2.4	+5.4
Czech Republic	-11.7	-4.1	+1.0	+5.6	+5.0	+4.4	-0.9	-1.2	-0.8	+3.1
Hungary	-6.8	-0.6	+1.3	+6.1	+1.5	+0.6	+4.6	+4.9	+4.5	+5.3
Poland	-7.6	+5.3	+6.1	+8.3	+6.5	+6.0	+6.9	+5.3	+4.1	+4.2
Romania	-12.9	-4.9	+4.3	+8.6	+5.4	+4.1	-6.6	-5.5	-3.2	+1.6
Slovakia	-14.6	+0.8	-2.5	+8.4	+6.0	+6.9	+6.5	+5.0	+1.9	+3.0
Estonia	-11.0	-14.2	-8.5	-2.7	+2.9	+4.0	+11.4	+5.0	-1.1	+6.6
Latvia	-10.4	-34.9	-14.9	+6.0	-1.6	+2.8	+6.6	+4.0	+1.1	+5.7
Lithuania	-5.7	-21.3	-30.4	+1.0	+2.6	+3.6	+5.7	+5.5	-4.2	+2.9
Armenia	-11.7	-41.8	-8.6	+5.4	+6.9	+5.8	+3.1	+6.9	+3.2	+5.9
Azerbaijan	-0.7	-22.6	-23.3	-19.7	-12.0	+1.3	+5.9	+10.1	+7.3	+11.1
Georgia	-21.1	-44.9	-29.3	+8.7	+3.3	+11.2	+10.5	+2.7	+3.0	+1.9

Belarus	-1.2	-9.6	-7.6	-12.6	-10.4	+2.6	+11.3	+8.4	+3.4	+5.8
Kazakhstan	-11.0	-5.3	-10.6	-12.6	-8.2	+1.1	+1.7	-1.5	+2.8	+9.7
Kyrgyzstan	-7.8	-13.9	-15.5	-20.1	-5.4	+5.6	+9.8	+2.2	+3.6	+5.0
Moldova	-17.5	-29.0	-1.2	-30.9	-1.9	-8.0	+1.7	-6.6	-3.5	+2.1
Russia	-5.0	-14.5	-8.7	-12.7	-4.1	-3.4	+0.9	-4.9	+3.2	+7.7
Tajikistan	-8.5	-32.3	-17.3	-12.7	-12.4	-16.7	+1.7	+5.6	+3.4	+8.5
Turkmenistan	-4.8	+15.0	+7.8	-24.0	-10.0	+0.1	-11.3	+5.1	+16.0	+17.6
Ukraine	-8.7	-9.9	-14.2	-22.9	-12.8	-10.0	-3.2	-1.5	-0.4	+7.5
Uzbekistan	-0.5	-11.1	-2.3	-4.2	-1.2	+1.6	+5.4	+2.8	+4.4	+3.9

Sources:

World Bank, *World Development Indicators, 1999*, Washington: World Bank, 1999, pp. 184, 186.

World Bank, "Studies of Economics in Transformation," *Statistical Handbook 1996, States of the Former Soviet Union*, Washington: World Bank, 1996, p. 11.

Internet Securities, Economies of Countries of CIS in January, May, June, 1997; July 11, 1997.

Directorate of Intelligence, Central Intelligence Agency, *Handbook of International Economic Statistics, 1998*, Washington: CIA, 1998, p. 18.

NB: There is not always agreement among the sources listed above as to the percentage of change in GDP each year for each country. When there is a difference, the World Bank or *Internet Securities* figure is used.

Ekonomika i Zhizn', January 2000, no. 4, p. 30.

Goskomstat Rossii, *Rossiiskii Statisticheskii Ezhegodnik* (Russian Statistical Report), Moscow: Goskomstat, 2000, p. 16.

European Commission, *Economic Reform Monitor*, issue 2001/2, April 2001; European Commission, *Economic Survey of Europe 2001*, no. 2, p. 162.

used in the calculations, the results would show very high or very low growth.[10]

The situation today is very different. Since one of the chief goals of managers in both private business and state-owned enterprises in the post-Gorbachev era of private ownership and ineffective state economic control is to hold down taxes, output, sales and profits are understated or masked. Until 1997, Russian statistical authorities offset the resulting distortion by adding on an additional 20 percent to their results, which they felt reflected economic activity in the private sector. Without an official announcement, however, in early 1997 they increased their estimate and markup of the size of the unreported private sector in the economy to 23 percent.[11] Since the private sector of 1997 with its larger base was measured against the smaller base figure of 1996, it created the appearance of more vigor in the economy than may actually have existed.

While not condoning the mishandling of the statistics, others reason that the unofficial sector in the Yeltsin years actually accounted for as much as 43 percent of the economy, and if properly incorporated into the GDP and industrial output figures, this more appropriate statistic would show a considerably smaller drop in GDP and/or an earlier and more substantial recovery.[12]

Goskomstat seemed to imply as much in 2001 when it again changed the way it calculated its index of industrial production. Industrial output according to the new calculation showed that industrial output was on average about 3 percent higher each month than stated previously.[13] Thus when it was originally reported, the increase in industrial output in February 2001 compared to February 2000 was only 0.8 percent. However, after the recalculation, the increase was said to be 3.1 percent, hardly a trivial adjustment (see Table 2.4).

Those who insist the official statistics have understated growth and that a higher rate is warranted also point to the fact that since 1993 the Russian economy has consistently generated a very healthy foreign trade surplus. Russia's exports increased every year from 1993 to 1996 (see Table 2.5). While imports also increased, that still left a trade surplus which usually amounted to $15 billion or more.[14] Petroleum and natural gas make up about 40 percent of Russia's exports, as they have done traditionally. But beginning in the early 1990s Russia also began to export increasing quantities of ferrous and non-ferrous metals. The United States, for example, imported almost $1 billion worth of Russian processed aluminum in 1995 and 1996. Previously Russia exported only minor quantities of such metals because most metallurgical production, especially non-ferrous metals, was commandeered for military production.

Table 2.4 Changes in industrial output

	1999 as % of 1998	2000 as % of 1999		2001as % of 2000		2002 as % of 2001
		Original index	New index	Original index	New index	New index
January	97.6	110.7	114.1	105.3	107.8	102.2
February	97.0	113.7	116.7	100.8	103.1	102.0
March	100.4	109.6	112.3	103.6	104.7	103.7
April	100.6	105.5	109.5	105.2	107.0	104.3
May	106.0	110.6	114.2		107.0	102.8
June	109.0	109.8	112.4		103.7	
July	112.8	108.5	111.9		104.5	
August	116.0	110.2	113.2		105.1	
September	120.2	107.2	110.7		103.8	
October	110.3	110.4	113.9		105.1	
November	112.9	107.6	111.6		104.7	
December	111.1	102.5	103.9		102.6	

Source: *Goskomstat* – monthly reports provided by internet securities.

At the same time, others insist that the surplus is not really that large because, even though the statistics in Table 2.5 are said to include what is referred to as "non-organized trade," the customs and statistical authorities cannot accurately record the amount of consumer goods brought into the country by so-called "shuttlers." These are individuals who move in and out of Russia carrying several suitcases and bundles filled with clothing and food products from such places as China, Turkey, and India, which they re-sell in kiosks and markets throughout the country. Some estimate that at its peak the shuttle trade amounted to as much as between $14 billion and $20 billion a year.[15] While that might reduce the trade surplus, at the same time the fact that the public could buy so much does suggest a more robust picture than the falling GDP would indicate.

Table 2.5 Russian foreign trade ($US millions)

	1992	1993	1994	1995	1996	1997	1998	1999
Export	53,605	59,646	67,542	81,096	88,599	88,252	74,200	84,346
Import	42,971	44,304	50,518	60,945	68,828	73,460	59,000	52,288
Surplus	10,634	15,342	17,024	20,151	19,771	14,792	15,200	32,058

Sources:
Goskomstat Rossiiskoi Federatsii (Russian Statistical Agency), *1998 Sotsialno-Ekonomicheskoe Razvitie Rossii* (The Socio-Economic Development of Russia), August 1999.
Goskomstat Rossii, *Rossiiskii Statisticheskii Ezhegodnik* (Russian Statistical Report), Moscow: Goskomstat, 1999, p. 563; 2000, p. 577.

To buttress their insistence that the Russian economy did not suffer as much as the Goskomstat statistics would imply, other critics have argued that because GDP figures are so difficult to compile, perhaps a surrogate such as changes in electricity generation might be a better measure of economic expansion.[16] As they see it, it may be relatively easy to conceal profits from state authorities, but there are few who can operate their business without the use of electricity supplied by easily monitored central sources. It follows therefore that when business activity slumps, electricity generation should also decline and vice versa. There may not be unit elasticity or a one-for-one change between increase and decrease in electricity usage and business volume, but there is probably no better gauge of what is actually happening in the underground, gray or unofficial economies. Yet electricity generation fell every year from 1991 to 1998 (see Table 2.6). So even if electricity output fell only 5.7 percent in 1992, considerably less than the official GDP drop of 14.5 percent, it nonetheless fell. This decline in electricity generation thus undermines those who argue that if the unofficial sector of the economy could be measured, it would show that Russian GDP began to expand as early as 1995 and certainly no later than 1996.

Finally, and equally puzzling, if the Russian GDP and its industrial production really dropped so precipitously, why did the Russian stock market from mid-1996 to October 1997 register such phenomenal growth? According to the RTS index of the Russian stock exchange, Russian stocks rose threefold over an eleven-month period from November 1996 to October 1997.[17] As a result, the Lexington Troika Dialog Russian Fund, which bought only Russian securities, registered gains larger than any other investment fund in the world in the year ending October 31, 1997.[18] Why would investors be so bullish about the operations and prospects of Russian enterprises if the economy were in such a calamitous state? The weekly chart ranking the stock markets and GDPs in twenty-five emerging countries published by *The Economist* magazine highlighted this paradox. In August 1997, of all the twenty-five countries covered by the chart, the

Table 2.6 Percent change in electricity usage and official GDP, Russia, 1991–98

	1991	1992	1993	1994	1995	1996	1997	1998	1999	2000
Electricity usage	-1.3	-5.7	-5.1	-8.5	-1.8	-1.5	-1.6	-1	+2.2	+3.5
Official GDP	-5	-14.5	-8.7	-12.6	-4.1	-3.4	+0.9	-4.9	+3.2	+7.7

Sources:
Goskomstat Rossii, *Rossiiskii Statisticheskii Ezhegodnik* (Russian Statistical Report), Moscow: Goskomstat, 1998, pp. 47, 395; 2000, p. 19.
Ekonomika i Zhizn', January 2000, no. 4, p. 30.

Russian stock market recorded the highest percentage growth, 134.7 percent, for the preceding twelve months. By contrast, except for Venezuela, Russia was the country with the poorest GDP record–a drop of 0.6 percent–in the second quarter of 1997. What was going on? According to *The Financial Times*, "The real economy and the financial world seem to have parted company."[19]

The answer came soon enough. After hitting a peak of 571 in October 1997, just twelve months later, the RTS index hit a low of 39. A dollar invested in October 1997 was, by October 1998, only a year later, worth not quite 7¢!

In sum, try as they might, there is scant justification for such economic revisionism by those who want to whitewash the reform policies of the early Yeltsin years. Nonetheless, such divergent tendencies are confusing. As one astute observer put it, "The economic system of Russia has undergone such rapid change that it is impossible to obtain a precise and accurate account of it … almost everything one can say about the country is true and false at the same time." That seems rather obvious now but it was written in 1925 and the observer was John Maynard Keynes.[20] But even if the Russian economy is healthier than its official statistics indicate and the growth that finally began in mid-1999 is sustained, it is hard to deny that at the least, the Russian economic reforms did not measure up to the optimistic predictions of those who thought that Russia would embrace the market and make up for lost time with rapid economic growth. Moreover, in no case, and even after the beginning of economic expansion in 1999, have the results been robust enough to warrant papering over the social monstrosities that the reforms spawned such as the Russian Mafia, a business oligarchy, capital flight and inflation. These have saddled Russia with not easily remedied dysfunctional patterns of behavior.

II

In defense of their actions, those in charge, such as Yegor Gaidar and Anatoly Chubais, rationalize what they did by insisting that in 1992 the fate of the reform movement, even the rejection of communism, was in doubt. Therefore they felt it was essential to adopt a strategy which would reinforce the public's initial determination after the failure of the coup in August 1991 to reject the communist system. Whenever challenged, Chubais insists that, whatever the consequences of the ill-fated reform process, preventing the Communists from regaining power was justification enough for what has happened since.[21]

But is this a valid defense? Had reform–particularly privatization–followed a different or more gradual course, would that have meant a return to central planning and communism? Based on what has happened in Poland, which we will examine in more detail in Chapters 4 and 10, a case can be made that while price liberalization, legal reform, and facilitation of business startups should have been instituted, a more gradual and somewhat more delayed process of privatization need not necessarily have led to the return of communism. If anything, a more gradual approach toward privatization as in Poland might have made possible a healthier market economy without the distortions that have come to characterize the market in Russia, and without the coterie of newly entrenched owners and stakeholders who now make it all the more difficult to adopt remedial measures.

Of course, not all privatization has been perverted or violent. Nonetheless, in the extreme case there have been a multitude of assassinations, and at one time it was charged that the Mafia controlled as much as 70 percent of the country's private sector.[22] (For a fuller discussion of the Mafia, see Chapter 9.) Yet, most of the Russians I have met, particularly those who are not in business for themselves, do not feel directly threatened by organized crime. But that overlooks the fact that because of the Mafia's efforts to create cartels and monopolies, the price of most products is higher than it would otherwise be. Thus the public is indirectly affected. However, even that is in dispute. Some argue that because the Mafia usually took only between 10 and 20 percent off the top of profits, the cost of doing business in Russia might actually be cheaper this way than if the state were stronger and was able to push out the Mafia. Without the Mafia and with effective state control, presumably the state would then be able to collect more of the almost 200 different taxes that were in effect at least through 1998. Indeed, by the late 1990s more and more businessmen began to tell me that state corruption and extortion had become more of a problem than the Mafia. Many businesses reported that until President Vladimir Putin instituted his series of tax deductions in 2001, the combination of bribes and official tax rates, if paid, would approach 100 percent of profits and sometimes more.

There is no doubt that the faulty privatization process is responsible for many of Russia's present-day problems. The oligarchs who are a product of that privatization are responsible for much that has gone wrong. President Vladimir Putin was at least partially correct when he taunted a group of oligarchs (see Chapters 6 and 7) who had come to call for more favorable treatment from the government, with the following warning, "When you demand political guarantees for yourselves and your businesses from the government, I want to draw your attention to the fact that you built this state yourself, though a great degree through the political or semi-political structures under your control. So don't blame the reflection on the mirror."[23] In other words, don't blame the mirror when you see your own face.

III

While the oligarchs should not be immune to criticism, they were just one of the factors which all but guaranteed the failure of the reforms. Other obstacles we will examine in detail include the absence of a consensus among the public as to whether the country should move to the market or continue with central planning and state control. No wonder the country's politicians found themselves at loggerheads and unwilling to work together. But even if there had been a consensus, Yeltsin and his close advisors would have had a hard time. The initial conditions, as we noticed, were anything but favorable. After seventy years of vertical control and what was misleadingly called democratic centralism, the country lacked a cadre of skilled and experienced leaders who could think for themselves. Such leaders were necessary to deal with not only the switch to the market but also with the disruption that followed from the breakup of the USSR into fifteen different countries. Another hurdle was the need to adjust to the sudden end of the Cold War. Few anticipated it, but the end of the arms buildup brought with it some major economic headaches. Some of the adjustments necessary might have been facilitated if there had been a well-developed market infrastructure to fall back on. But the few market institutions that evolved in the czarist era were all but destroyed in the communist era, which meant that everything had to be invented anew. Finally, it might not seem like it would be a problem, but Russia's enormous natural wealth turned out not to be an advantage but a disadvantage.

Let's begin with the inability of the leaders to work together. The honeymoon following Yeltsin's defeat of the putsch ended quickly. After a few months, the country's Supreme Soviet (as the Parliament was called until 1993) began to quarrel continuously with President Yeltsin and his staff. In other words, the jockeys couldn't agree about which direction to steer the horse. These battles were climaxed by an attempted coup by a group including Alexander Rutskoi, Yeltsin's hand-picked Vice President, and Ruslan Khasbulatov, the Chairman of the Supreme Soviet. Despite a vicious tank attack on the Russian White House, which then served as Russia's Parliament building, ultimately Yeltsin prevailed. Yeltsin won, but his run for reelection as President a few years later in June 1996 looked uncertain for several months. The Communists after all managed to win more votes than any other party in the December 1995 battle for the Duma, as the renamed parliament came to be called. To compound the uncertainty, by June 1996 Yeltsin's handlers could no longer disguise the fact that Yeltsin was suffering from a severe heart condition. Despite the orchestrated effort to reassure the public, the eventual acknowledgment that Yeltsin had to have a quintuple bypass only added to the government's credibility problem.

Under the circumstances there were not many in Russia who had much faith in the economy. There were of course some who did, more often foreigners than Russians. But the overwhelming majority of Russians who had money did all they could to smuggle it out of the country, much as their counterparts in Latin America or Asia do. Confronted by runaway inflation, random and pervasive violence, an intrusive Mafia, government corruption, and uncertain political stability, theirs was a natural reaction. In many instances overseas bankers reported that it was a common occurrence for Russians to walk into their banks, open up their suitcases, and empty out wads of $100 bills. One reporter witnessed a Russian carrying a suitcase with $500,000 stuffed inside.[24] Real estate brokers had similar experiences. In other cases, exporters of Russian oil, gas and other minerals simply instructed their customers to remit their payment to their overseas accounts in Western banks. Many politicians, including some large-city mayors, opened similar accounts, collected a percentage of the revenue owed the city from real estate sales and tax collections, and diverted it to these accounts.

Those who were neither politicians nor in the export business sought some way in which they could similarly protect their assets. In one of the more ingenious strategies, importers discovered that they could also benefit. This involved placing large orders overseas for the purchase of foreign goods. The prospective importer would then direct his bank to transfer his funds to an overseas account but then never actually take delivery or import the specified goods.

Naturally there are no precise data as to the exact total of such transactions, but it is widely accepted that on average at least $1 billion a month was secreted out of the country from 1991 to 2000.[25] But as share prices on the stock market rose after Yeltsin's election in 1996, fueled disproportionately by foreign investors, Russian investors became envious and some decided that they should share in the bounty. Thus, periodically in late 1996 and early 1997 and again in 2000 after Putin's election, some Russians returned their funds from such places as Cyprus, Switzerland, the United Kingdom and the United States.

Given such economic and political turmoil, it would have been a surprise if the state's decision to privatize had not been dominated by controversy and scandal. Moreover, the breakup of the Russian empire into fifteen parts and the abandonment of central planning was also disruptive.

Long-time buyers and sellers to each other in these now-independent countries not only had to fend for themselves without the guidance and dictate of central planners, but they also had to arrange trading access across country borders and over tariff and foreign currency barriers. Certainly not everyone was happy with the way Moscow and Russia dominated trade and money relationships in the old USSR, but there were advantages in being able to sell within such a large market. To dissolve that arrangement overnight was inevitably terribly confusing and costly.

To add to the chaos, the breakup of the Soviet Union coincided with the end of the Cold War. For those concerned about preserving world peace or triggering accidental nuclear war, this was like an impossible dream come true. But for the economy it was yet another devastating blow. The success and achievements of the Soviet economy depended very much on the stimulus provided by the purchases of the Soviet military-industrial complex. Former President Mikhail Gorbachev writes that military expenditure amounted to 20 percent of GNP.[26] That was serious enough, but in cities such as Irkutsk, Perm, Novosibirsk, and even St. Petersburg, an estimated 70 percent of their industry was directed to military production.[27] Therefore the impact of a significant cut in the military budget was profound. The politicians promised each other a peace dividend. But when an economy is so heavily addicted to military production, the easing of tensions is more likely to yield a production disaster and, if the bankruptcy laws were enforced, lead to widespread bankruptcy. Under the best of circumstances conversion from military to civilian output is difficult. If on top of that the economy is also moving from central planning to a market system, it is all but inevitable that there will be massive unemployment and factory shutdowns. Few governments, even those that are undemocratic, can survive such radical surgery. The Russian public is noted for its ability to endure enormous pain and suffering, but cutting back military expenditures so sharply and imposing hard budget constraints (no subsidies) risked massive street protests and likely violence. This was hardly the time to initiate other far-reaching social experiments such as the privatization of large state industries. But reformers such as Gaidar and Chubais concluded that it would be even more dangerous to wait.

The reformers' efforts at privatization were further handicapped not only by the seventy years of anti-market indoctrination and repression imposed by the Communists, but also because markets had never taken firm root in the czarist era. As we will examine in more detail in Chapter 3, business under the czar bore at best a superficial resemblance to what we would consider viable market competition. Not surprisingly, therefore, many of the market anomalies that distinguish Russia from today's Western businesses originated under the czars. Thus many notions such as the state's control of raw material resources and the all-powerful role played by the country's *chinovniki* (bureaucrats) may trace their origins back to the czarist era but they were enhanced under communism. Richard Pipes, for example, argues that we in the West are so imbued with the market system and the checks and balances that over time have evolved around it that we take them all for granted. By contrast, the Russians, in the same way, automatically assume a much more dominant role for the state. Pipes called the Russian approach "patrimonialism." As he sees it, the sovereign of a patrimonialist state not only considers himself the ruler of the country, but also its proprietor.[28] Thus not only are the people at the czar's disposal but so is the country's land. This was because the czar considered himself the owner of the country's raw materials and soil and he parceled out economic privileges to his subordinates on condition that they in turn support him. These powers of the czar were delegated to the *chinovniki*, who then implemented them to their own personal advantage. Not surprisingly, then as now, it became nearly impossible for Russian businessmen to do business without having a well-paid patron at court. Those less well connected would have to resort to the payment of outright bribes and widespread graft and corruption. While corruption and patrons at court are not unknown in Western Europe or in the United States, such overarching state dominance by the country's chief executive is anathema to most market economies and offers opportunities for both the corrupters and the corruptees.

The "patrimonialist state" helps explain the Russian public's acceptance of communism. If anything, the Communist Party imposed a more extreme form of patrimonialism than the czar. In the Soviet era the state and the Party, and through them the General Secretary, controlled and owned all means of production including the land, and relied on the Party and state bureaucracy to administer and supervise those resources. Admittedly there were times during the Stalinist era when corruption was less of a problem because of the brutality of the Stalinist repression. But even in the most draconian times, there was corruption, crime, and privileges for the favored few. The economic reforms begun by Nikita Khrushchev and extended by Boris Yeltsin, and even Vladimir Putin, were predicated on many of the same assumptions held by the czars, namely that the state authorities had the power to parcel out stewardship if not ownership of valuable assets to vassals who pledged allegiance in one form or another to the party leader and his closest advisors. This privilege included not only the ostensible ownership of factories, but also tax and tariff exemptions, access to state funds, and the issuance of permits and licenses. And just as in the days of the czars with their *chinovniki*, or the General Secretary with his *apparatchiki*, the post-communist Russian government has been administered by modern-day bureaucrats masquerading as civil servants. The byproduct, corruption, and the need for a protecting patron high in government ranks, is much the same as it has always been. As Yeltsin put it, "Corruption is an old problem of ours … corruption is like weeds. No matter how hard you try to get rid of them, they keep reappearing."[29]

Many of the advisors who worked on economic reform in Russia refused to accept the proposition that Russia and Russians might deal with economic situations differently than their counterparts in the West. There is no such thing, these advisors argued, as a special Russian economic man.[30] Those of us who insisted that Russian history and culture did not prepare the Russians for a market economy were often dismissed as special pleaders.[31]

But even if some Russians do respond to identical stimuli in the same way as Americans or Germans, the problem is that the institutions that have been sculpted by seventy years of communism and by centuries of czarist rule were very different from those that have evolved in the West. Thus, the response may be the same but because the institutions in place in Russia are so different, the impact of the response may well be channeled in a different direction. In other words, "culture" makes a difference. But as we shall see in Chapters 4 and 5, "culture" became a fighting word for many economists who insisted that economics overrides such considerations.

One need not be a Marxist economic determinist to acknowledge that there are indeed occasions when long-held cultural traditions succumb to the superior temptations of new economic incentives. However, the greater the differences in the makeup of the institutional environment, the more likely it is that the reactions will vary. For example, many Western advisors have reasoned that it makes no difference if in the process of privatization, unsuitable and incompetent managers, including those with a Mafia connection, end up as chief executive officers of a new enterprise. If something similar happened in the West, profits would drop, the stockholders would be upset, and the board of directors would mobilize to vote out the incompetent and bring in new management. The problem is that while this may happen with some regularity in the West, even in the United States this is not always the result. More to the point, it is an even rarer occurrence in Russia where, as we shall see in Chapter 7, disputes over Mafia or rival control of an enterprise were and still are often resolved instead by contract killings.

Many Western reformers have failed to appreciate that even when the Mafia is not involved, it is rare that stockholders and directors are able to oust enterprise officials in a Russian proxy fight. The reason for that is that the Western state and national corporate governance rules and laws which are also backed by the self-imposed regulations and codes of behavior voluntarily imposed by the securities markets are only just being introduced in Russia. Moreover the laws being adopted are inconsistent. In some cases bits and pieces of a legal code have been taken from one legal system and some from another. Often this was done without anticipating that there might be contradictions, but on occasion Russian officials have knowingly created such ambiguity. The more uncertain the meaning of a law, the more likely it is that bureaucrats must be sought to adjudicate what must be done, and the more likely that this will mean a bribe for the bureaucrat. For that matter, even if the laws are consistent there is no guarantee they will be observed and enforced. This is a distinction that many advisors fail to appreciate, particularly because most of these advisors come from Western countries where the security markets and stockholders' rights are zealously guarded.

Finally, it is Russia's misfortune to be very richly endowed. This may seem strange to leaders in most of the other countries in the world, who are envious of Russia's vast deposits of gas, oil, gold, and other precious and non-ferrous metals: if only they could be so lucky! The problem, however, is that the very magnitude of Russia's riches means that this wealth brings out the worst forms of Russian life. Announcing that most of the country's richest resources are suddenly to be tossed up for grabs to the highest or most conniving bidder is too much for most buccaneers to pass up. A few were willing to take greater than normal risks including resorting to more criminal or brute-force tactics, to obtain such resources. By contrast, in Poland and China the natural endowment is considerably less abundant and therefore the rewards generally not worth the risk of violence or even murder.

IV

It has been a painful lesson. With time, however, more and more observers have come to acknowledge that something more than economics must be involved in designing a reform strategy. That does not mean that all are convinced. For example, those who drew up the official privatization strategy have been slow and reluctant to concede their responsibilities for these misbegotten measures; that would mean that they might have been wrong.

Thus even now attacking Russia's method of privatization risks a frenzied response from some former advisors. Take the attack on Joseph Stiglitz, the chief economist of the World Bank until January 2000. In an unusual critique of a sister institution, Stiglitz challenged the conditions imposed by the International Monetary Fund (IMF) on those countries seeking loans from it.

He also criticized the so-called "Washington Consensus" for economic transformation, which in part underlay some of the ideas put forward by the Maxim Boycko, Andrei Shleifer, and Robert Vishny trio.[32] In particular Stiglitz criticized "...the West's best and brightest," who ended up relying on what he called "simple textbook models or naïve ideology." Evidently feeling himself caught in the act, Anders Aslund responded that "Stiglitz is a striking embarrassment to himself and the World Bank. Without knowing anything, he mouths any stupidity that comes to his head."[33] Of course, Aslund wrote this before Stiglitz was awarded the 2001 Nobel Prize in Economics. Stiglitz's critique has also been disputed by many Western economists as well as Russian reformers, although in more gentlemanly fashion.[34]

As fierce as the attacks on Stiglitz have been, by no means is he the only observer who has been dismayed by the Russian reforms and the advice and processes they evoked. In fact, one of the most thoughtful critics of how the Russian reforms were implemented is Alan Greenspan, Chairman of the Board of Governors of the Federal Reserve Bank of the United States.[35] Credited by many with the remarkable success of the record economic American boom in the mid-1990s and therefore immune at the time to the type of criticism directed at Joseph Stiglitz, we do not usually think of Greenspan as a specialist on the Russian economy. But in a lecture at the Woodrow Wilson International Center for Scholars, June 1997, Greenspan pinpointed the reasons why the Russians have had so much difficulty with privatization. To Greenspan the major problem was the difference in "culture," a word that, as we saw, other economists sometimes have trouble pronouncing in public. In his words:

> Much of what we took for granted in our free market system and assumed to be human nature was not nature at all, but culture ... The dismantling of the central planning function in an economy does not, as some had supposed, automatically establish a free-market entrepreneurial system. There is a vast amount of capitalist culture and infrastructure underpinning market economies that has evolved over generations: laws, conventions, behaviors, and a wide variety of business professions and practices that have had no important functions in a centrally planned economy.[36]

If only Russia's economic reformers Yegor Gaidar and Anatoly Chubais and their Western economic advisors such as Andrei Shleifer, Jonathan Hay, Anders Aslund, Jeffrey Sachs and after he became a senior official in the U.S. Treasury, Laurence Summers had been more cognizant of such differences before they began designing their programs in late 1991. But except for a small number of Sovietologists who tried to explain

Russia's lack of appropriate institutions and culture, few pointed out these differences. Greenspan was one:

> Little contemporary thought had been given to the institutional infrastructure required of markets. [Nor, notes Greenspan, does experience with black markets fully qualify.] Black markets by definition are not supported by the rule of law. There are no rights to own and dispose of property protected by the enforcement power of the state. There are no laws of contract or bankruptcy or judicial review and determination, again enforced by the state. *The essential infrastructure of the market economy is missing.*[37]

This last sentence is critical for much that will follow.

V

Without concern for the lack of such preconditions, the reformers plowed quickly ahead with privatization and prided themselves initially at least on the fact that 60 to 70 percent of Russian state enterprises were privatized in just three or four years.

Such an approach made sense in dealing with the country's small shops, although even here, many of those shops continued to operate much as they had under state ownership for a number of years. Most of the new owners failed to inject new capital into their businesses. Even fewer bothered to give much thought to altering the way they delivered their services to the consumer. The only notable change was that once price regulations ended on January 2, 1992 and reasonable profit margins could be earned, most goods became more readily available, and most store owners were able to expand the assortment of goods they could offer for sale.

As we shall see in what follows, while it made good sense to move forward with other reforms such as price liberalization and the demise of many state controls, privatizing the larger enterprises was fraught with difficulties. In many cases the resulting unintended and unfortunate consequences shaped the nature of Russia's economy for years and perhaps generations to come. The insider enrichment and self-dealing that took place was an inevitable consequence of Chubais' decision to launch an immediate privatization campaign before an adequate infrastructure had been put in place.

Oddly enough, initially the directors of state enterprises were none too eager to go private. They feared that they would lose their power, prestige, and perks. Only later did they come to appreciate that they might end up even better off as the owners of those enterprises that Chubais wanted to privatize.

Normally the Russian bureaucracy can frustrate or at least slow down any project it chooses, but with his unique skills as a political administrator, Chubais was able to override the resistance. It also helped that, after some initial resistance, Gaidar and Chubais agreed to subsequent legislation proposed by members of the Supreme Soviet that made it easier and virtually cost free for enterprise directors to gain access to a controlling share of their enterprise's stock. Acting as if he were a Soviet administrator, Chubais steam-rollered his privatization campaign, allowing for few if any exceptions.

He moved so quickly, in fact, that at times his critics, including the then Prime Minister, Viktor Chernomyrdin, compared him to Stalin and his drive to collectivize agriculture. Overreacting to Stalin's edict, Party and state officials began to collectivize everything in sight, creating enormous chaos.[38] This led Stalin in March 1930 to pull back. As he put it, "We are dizzy with success." Of course Stalin was imposing state control and Chubais was trying to undo it, but as is so typical in Russia, both Stalin and Chubais insisted on instantaneous, non-evolutionary transformations. Inevitably this resulted in excess and distortion.

By imposing political goals and ignoring economic imperatives, Chubais, inadvertently created structural deformities in the economy that will not be easy to remedy. He chose to overlook the fact that there was no market or competitive infrastructure in place to absorb and temper these newly privatized monopolies. Nor were there essential controls such as audited accounting procedures and accountability to stockholders and boards of directors. (As we have discovered in the United States, even reputable accounting firms may not be entirely reliable.)

Privatization under the best of circumstances is a complicated and complex affair. Even Margaret Thatcher encountered problems when she sought to privatize some of England's state-owned businesses. This should have alerted Chubais to the hazards involved, especially because in Margaret Thatcher's case she was dealing with only a hundred or so enterprises, many of them small.[39] Moreover, she had the advantage of working in a developed market economy with an experienced and well-regarded banking and credit infrastructure, and competing enterprises. England also had a stock market and well-endowed investors who were accustomed to playing by a carefully designed set of rules and regulations. The contrast with Russia, where Chubais decreed that thousands of enterprises were to be privatized in two or three years without any comparable infrastructure, evoked a very different response.

Admittedly, Russia in the early 1990s already had several thousand stock markets and commodity exchanges.[40] Market specialists might find that surprising, even alarming. That was many more than a normal market system could sustain. In fact, the large number reflected the abnormal conditions then prevailing in the country. That so many markets developed was a consequence of the need to fill the vacuum created by the sudden demise of central planning. Without central planning buyers and sellers suddenly found themselves at a loss as to how to link up with their suppliers and customers. There were no Yellow Page directories or established guides to consult, not even a phone book. Thus finding someone with a truck or ten trucks to buy or sell, or concrete or timber or wheat, was often an impossible task. Commodity markets dealing in day-to-day products, not futures, became a necessity. Most of these markets became superfluous and disappeared as a more normal market infrastructure came into being, but by then much of the damage from the premature and over-ambitious privatization had already been done.

Another difference between Margaret Thatcher's United Kingdom and Russia was that Russia lacked a middle class with savings that they could use to buy newly issued stock. Whatever savings most Russians had, as we saw, were wiped away by the twenty-six-fold inflation in 1992. Nor was there a class of investors or well-established investment funds eager to buy up the newly issued securities of these just-purchased enterprises. The only ones with control over capital at the time were members of the Mafia, Party and government *nomenklatura* who had begun to divert or usurp government and Party funds and gold, and factory directors who were treating enterprise assets as personal property. Some enterprise directors combined their enterprise funds in order to create commercial banks. These banks in turn provided loans to these directors so they could finance their personal purchases of stock as the enterprises they had been managing became their own private entities.

The scale of the corruption and insider theft that developed in Russia was a match for anything seen previously. But given the legacy of both czarist Russia and the communist Soviet Union, such a result was probably inevitable regardless of the makeup of the reform package. In Chapter 3 we will see why.

3 The legacy of the czarist era
Untenable and unsavory roots

Adopting market business codes and institutions will not be easy in today's Russia. Not only has the first decade of privatization left Russia with a deformed, rather than reformed, set of institutions and values, but it has also implanted a powerful set of stakeholders who are determined to sustain the status quo and frustrate change. Furthermore, there is no historic business code to reclaim or build on that is appropriate for today's Russia. The small number of czarist era business practices and institutions that were suitable for a market economy and that would have been useful today were almost all destroyed with the Bolshevik takeover and the seventy years of communism that followed. Moreover, most businesses in the czarist era were in an early stage of development, with only weakly defined rights and enforced rules of law. The czarist government controlled commerce and manufacturing and only gradually did it agree to liberalize so that few of the operating procedures and codes were comparable to those applicable in the West at the time. Even then that was more than eighty years ago. In the interim, the Soviets had no interest in keeping up with the way the market evolved in the West.

Given the eight-decade absence of normal market development, when the Yeltsin government tried to revive some of their pre-Revolutionary institutions, the czarist era market infrastructure and associated attitudes they tried to reintroduce seemed as if they had been taken from a time warp. It was inevitable therefore that there would be many similarities between the way business was conducted before the revolution in Russia and today. In an effort to close the gap, many well-intentioned consultants and advisors sought to transplant foreign legal and business codes, which they believed would foster a market economy in Russia.

Unfortunately, an unusually large number of such efforts have so far proven to be futile or even counterproductive. Like a liver transplant that is rejected, without some organic support from within the system itself, alien business codes are likely to remain just that. Given Russia's traditional hostility to foreign mores and institutions, it was hardly likely that Russian authorities would readily adopt and implement a full and nuanced package of Western practices.[1] At best, Russian officials might go through the motions of embracing some limited changes, while omitting other more objectionable but often essential components. On occasion, rather than improve things this can and has created enormous damage, particularly if those changes are made without incorporating any provision for feedback or self-correcting mechanisms. It is reminiscent of what happened when conservation authorities in the Florida Everglades decided that they had to do something to stop the erosion and dry out parts of the swamp that at the time were considered useless. Looking around to see if anyone had a similar problem, they found that the Melaleuca tree seemed to accomplish much the same thing in its native habitat in Australia. Therefore, in 1900, the decision was made to transplant several of the trees to Florida.[2] The Floridians neglected, however, to bring the Melaleuca's natural predators with it. With nothing to check its growth, the Melaleuca soon spread rapidly and widely. By the late 1990s the Melaleuca covered more than 7.6 million acres and was expanding at fifty acres a day. It had become more of a menace than the erosion it was intended to check.

Transplanting foreign legal and commercial practices such as privatization and bankruptcy into a heretofore communist Soviet Union created similar unanticipated distortions. In the West, bankruptcy laws, for example, are used to facilitate the restructuring of failing businesses so that they can be revived and again become productive entities. In this way, they can best satisfy creditors equally and fairly with whatever proceeds the banks and businesses are able to generate. Sometimes this is accomplished through liquidation, but just as often through restructuring and reopening the business. In Russia however, until some supplemental reforms were introduced in 2002, bankruptcy proceedings have frequently produced just the opposite effect. By taking advantage of inexperienced judges, avaricious oligarchs in cahoots with complicit local governors have learned how to use such laws to seize not only struggling businesses but also what in other societies would be considered healthy and even profitable enterprises.

Here is how it works. In the simplest scheme, local authorities at the behest of various oligarchs initiate some trumped-up criminal charge against an enterprise. By doing so, or by sending in the tax police, the government officials can then freeze the enterprise's bank accounts. At that point, the oligarch arranges for a creditor of the enterprise to demand the payment of some outstanding debt. But since the enterprise's funds are frozen, the enterprise can not gain access to its bank account and so it is forced into bankruptcy. The oligarch buys up the debt and then, as the controlling voice in the bankrupt company, demands the right to install new management and take over control. Tyumen Oil seized Chernogorneft from Sidanko (not itself a model of integrity) in just this way. The judge who made the decision in the case was appointed by the governor, Leonid Roketsky, who just happened at the time to be the Chairman of Tyumen Oil.[3] This is not how the bankruptcy laws were intended to operate. (We will return to this topic in Chapter 7.)

I

The similarity between Russian business–government relationships in the pre-Revolutionary era and today is largely a legacy of the czar's commanding ownership and control of not only the land, but much of its business activity. As Richard Pipes notes in his book *Property and Freedom*, in the early feudal era in Western Europe, the kings, just as the czars, determined land use *de facto* by allocating land and villages to local vassals.[4] But there was an important difference between Russia and Western Europe. In Western Europe, individuals gradually came to own property. In Russia, as we saw in Chapter 2, the czar continued to own all the land. He also collected all the rents and claimed the services of his subjects. This power meant that he did not have to impose taxes on the nobility or provide them with various services in exchange (except for defense) as did the kings of Western Europe.[5] But whereas as early as 1215, with the signing of the Magna Carta, the Western kings began to encounter challenges from increasingly independent regional barons determined to protect "their" land and an increasingly rich and independent cohort of merchants determined to protect their property, the czar had no such problems. He did eventually grant land titles to the nobility in 1762, but continued as absolute ruler for most of the following century.

This absolute power perpetuated itself. As Thomas Owen, in a remarkable study of business life under the czars, put it, "Oppressive censorship and a ban on representative institutions prevented any single social group or coalition of forces from seeking to impose restraints on the autocracy."[6] Thus, because they might serve as a rallying point for opposition to the state and czar, chambers of commerce were banned in Russia until the end of the czarist regime.[7] In Marc Raeff's view, "the state remained in command and retained the initiative until the end of the nineteenth century."[8] Even then, efforts to reduce the czar's powers were, at best, marginally effective. R.M. Guseinov points out that it was only in 1870 that Russian cities became self-governing.[9] Not only was that long after the monarchs in Western Europe had been forced to cede similar powers to city burghers, but unlike the struggle that was necessary to win such rights in Western Europe, in Russia the czar extended such powers voluntarily.

The few burghers in Russia at the time did not seem to be in any particular rush to exercise such prerogatives. Extending rights to the city was done almost as an afterthought by the czar following the emancipation of the peasants in 1861.

Those limited rights never blossomed into a sustained effort to limit czarist authoritarianism. Not having had to fight for such privileges, Russian town fathers and officials never fully exercised or appreciated them as did their counterparts in Western Europe. Moreover, until late in the nineteenth century, the czars (especially Peter the Great) and not businessmen were the main initiators of industrial activity, primitive as it might have been. As Michael Karpovich points out, in the nineteenth century, the initiative to establish a new factory almost always came from the government, and then the factories they encouraged were almost always expected to enhance military means or state revenue.[10] Under these circumstances, few industrialists were willing to criticize the state.

This reticence was not because the peasants, merchants, and artisans fully supported Peter the Great, his successors, or the Russian militarists' emphasis on war and other empire-enhancing priorities.[11] In fact, there were many attempts, most half-hearted, to dilute the czar's power.[12] Such efforts came to naught, however, because, unlike the West European businessmen and merchants, the Russian business community was weak, generally discredited, and thus unable and unwilling to generate sustained political opposition or wide support.[13] This weakness reflected the relative absence of successful merchants and industrialists whose businesses did not depend upon state contracts. For much the same reasons, most Russian cities except for St. Petersburg and Moscow were administrative, not commercial or industrial centers.

This domination by the czar also had a negative effect on the growth and competitiveness of Russian industry. Because business depended so much on the czar there was no built-in feedback mechanism to generate essential upgrading from the bottom up or innovation. Thus, when Peter the Great decided to build up Russia's military and naval power, rather than wait for someone to set up a private metal industry, he took the initiative himself and commissioned several blacksmith-type operations in the Ural Mountains. On the basis of Peter's efforts, until 1805 Russia along with Sweden was the world's largest producer of iron and steel. Since the plants were commissioned by Peter and dependent on state owners, there was no doubt that they were beholden to Peter and his successors and produced only at the czar's command.[14] For a time that proved to be an advantage. But while private producers in other countries, especially Great Britain, began to experiment with new production technology, Russia's steel-making technology remained until the mid-nineteenth century much as it had been when Peter initiated the first production efforts in the Urals in the early eighteenth century.

Not surprisingly, by the latter part of the nineteenth century a need for some flexibility and accommodation between the czar and the business community became increasingly evident. But as Owen points out, despite pleas from the business community, the czar and his court had difficulty understanding and adjusting to the inherent dynamism and needs of the modern corporation. The czar refused to relax his strict regulation of business and reduce the role of the state. Thus Russia in the pre-Revolutionary era was never able to develop a culture or set of institutionalized forces that might have contained or restrained the state. Even in 1598 during the Time of Troubles when there seemed to be no clear successor to the czarist line and governing authority had all but disappeared, the Russian people seemed incapable of "challenging the state and preventing the reassertion of autocracy."[15]

The inability to curb the powers of the czar has been attributed to many factors. Unlike Western Europe, Russia did not benefit from the enlightening aspects of the Renaissance and the intellectual currents that derived from it. Similarly, there never was any effective challenge to the Russian Orthodox Church.[16] The Old Believer movement did attract a few adherents, but they never threatened the dominance of the Orthodox Church and its absolute hold on power and dogma, as did Martin Luther in his attack on the Catholic Church. The alliance between czar and patriarch remained unassailable. Until almost the twentieth century both the Church and the business community were heavily dependent on state patronage. That explains why there were so few calls to check the powers of the czar and Church and why the few efforts there were proved to be ineffective.

Jozef Kaczkowski, a legal historian, described in 1908 how inadequate reform efforts had been. "To be sure, we see efforts to introduce reforms; commissions and subcommissions are appointed and bills written; but these never reach the point of confirmation and implementation. This is the characteristic feature of Russian bureaucracy: that bills prepared on every aspect of the law subsequently pass [directly] into the archives."[17] All of this added to public cynicism about the legitimacy of those laws that did exist.[18]

The "by your leave" domination by the czar continued through most of the nineteenth century. As the sociologist Natalya Evdokimova Dinello put it, "One's economic capital" depended rigidly upon "the civil service and the benevolence of the tsar." Should the czar cease to smile on you, that would mark the end of your business. Dinello points out that the same "friend of the court" atmosphere carried over into the communist era, although then it was the General Secretary, not the czar, who exercised the powers.[19]

Historically, Russia's rulers, czars, general secretaries, and now presidents have had little regard for those who have gone into business. Good Russians ("our kind of people") simply did not do that kind of thing. Beginning with the czars, Russians of the upper class served in the court or in the army. In a pinch, they occupied some honorary post in the bureaucracy, while theoretically supervising a landed estate. This mentality carried over into communism where it was reinforced with the Marxist depiction of businessmen and bourgeoisie as exploiters of the working class. More recently, even in the market economy, Vladimir Putin has attacked the oligarchs for stealing money, manipulating the public, and lying about the state of the Russian economy and the military.[20]

Making money as a merchant or even a manufacturer has always been considered grubby, gross, and exploitative. Underlying all such activity was the assumption that businessmen were inherently dishonest. Of course, such attitudes in the nineteenth century were not unique to Russia. The British aristocracy also regarded businessmen with some contempt. They opted instead for positions in the court, army, navy, colonial service, as country squires. Many British elite also served in the hierarchy of the Church of England. As for the French, they were no different. The writer Honore de Balzac spoke for them when he stated, "Behind each great fortune there is a crime."[21]

Unfortunately, the perception of shady dealing, speculation, and outright corruption was often not far from the truth. There were some businesses, such as munitions manufacturer N.I. Putilov's company in St. Petersburg, that were notable for the relatively little corruption associated with them.[22] Yet on the whole, dishonesty was so widespread that Nikolai Kh. Bunge, later to become the Minister of Finance, actually delineated four ways in which corporate officials defrauded investors:

1   Transform an unsuccessful private business into a corporation and sell the worthless stock to gullible investors.
2   Pump up the real value of the company's property.
3   Poor management.
4   If there are no profits, pay dividends from capital.[23]

The Soviet economic historian Peter Lyashchenko has described some of the stock flotation swindles of the 1890s.[24] These schemes, along with those listed by Finance Minister Bunge, compare nicely with American speculative swindles of that time, not to mention present-day hoaxes. Watering the stock was a favorite tactic. In one case cited by Lyashchenko, the substantial sum of 8.5 million French francs was turned over by the investors, but the promoters put only 1.5 million Francs of that into the business. The rest went into the promoters' personal pockets.[25] Even more common, new business ventures almost always began with a government contract and the government agreeing to pay almost ten times more than the market price for the purchases. Just as it does today, this necessitated influential contacts at court and in the bureaucracy as well as kickbacks for those contracts and handsome rewards for the promoters. As contemptuous as the czarist aristocracy might have been about engaging in business and dealing with the *nouveaux riches*, they were not above accepting such gratuities.

Honesty and compliance with the letter of the law was considered to be more of a hindrance than a virtue. This misuse of the law is reflected in Gogol's play *The Inspector General*, where it is assumed that the only way to do business is to bribe, lie, and cheat. Foreigners were assumed to be especially easy targets: "West European capital finds it very hard to work in Russia. This is due both to the pseudo-patriotic outcries about foreigners' occupation of Russia and customs and regulations enabling all manner of parasites to suck the blood out of any business."[26] This statement was originally published in the journal *Industry & Trade* in 1908, but it could just have easily been written today.

There were many explanations for the primitive state of Russia's business practices. To some extent, it was due to the fact that so few members of the "better classes" deigned to participate actively (that is, not superficially or merely as decorations). Nor did it help that at least 40 percent of the population were serfs, illiterate and, for the most part, excluded from anything but menial activities until their emancipation in 1861. Eventually, some of Russia's more successful businesses were created by former serfs. But as impressive as such upward mobility was, it did nothing to enhance the social standing of the business class as whole, who were treated generally as *déclassé* or *nouveau riche*. That same attitude explains in part why Russians, despite or maybe because of their distrust of foreigners, were happy to relegate business activities to foreigners and minority groups. Poles, Germans, Jews, Armenians or Georgians were particularly active at the time. Given their traditional prejudices, this only increased the contempt Russians had for business.

While it was accepted that foreigners were better suited than the Russian aristocracy to handle business matters, there were nonetheless limits to their autonomy, particularly if there was lots of money to be made. For that reason, Russian law required that the number of Russian directors on a company's board exceed the number of foreigners and that only Russian engineers could serve as intermediaries between the company

and its Russian directors.[27] Nonetheless, by the end of the nineteenth
century, foreign investors had come to play an increasingly prominent
role.[28] Lyashchenko reports that 42.6 percent of the capital stock of the
largest eighteen corporate banks in 1914 came from foreign investment.[29]
There was also extensive foreign control of industrial enterprises. As of
1900, foreign companies accounted for 28 percent of all the registered
capital of the 1,600 or so corporations that were in existence.[30] By the
onset of World War I, foreign companies made up one-seventh of the
country's corporations but they accounted for one-third of the country's
corporate capital. Foreign investors were particularly active in the
petroleum, chemical, mining, metal, and metal processing industries.[31]

But while foreigners began to have a growing financial and physical
presence, they had to cloak most of their efforts with token Russian figure-
heads. Such nationalist behavior reflected concern about foreign economic
dominance and control. But it also underscored Russia's historic ambiguity
toward foreigners. Recognizing that some Western notions might be worth
adopting, a group called the "Westernizers" sought to bring Western institutions and behavior to Russia. But there was also a strong strain of
xenophobia. These nationalists were called Slavophiles, and they feared
that too much contact with the West would contaminate Russia with
disruptive ideas and practices. It is this xenophobia and distrust that also
led Russian authorities to seal off foreigners from ordinary people. For
example, during the czarist era Moscow officials restricted visiting foreign
merchants to a walled-in area called Kitai-Gorod, remnants of which can
still be seen. Because they were so constrained and because Russian
authorities continued to fear Western ways, foreigners had a relatively
minor impact on Russian business practices, commercial codes, and operating mores.

This fear of foreign contamination was also evident during the Soviet
years when foreigners in the Soviet Union were again required to live in
special compounds and guarded twenty-four hours a day by Soviet police.
Intellectual contact was similarly restricted. Russians were required to
report unauthorized contact with foreigners to the KGB, and normally
only specially entrusted "big brothers" were authorized to meet with
foreigners whether inside or outside the USSR. That insecurity has even
carried over into the twenty-first century under Putin. In the spring of
2001, the Russian Academy of Sciences issued a decree ordering all its
affiliate members to report any contact with foreigners to intelligence
authorities.

More than anything else, however, what distinguished business practices
in Western Europe and the United States from those in czarist and present-
day Russia is the response to the discovery of shady practices. Typically,

when dishonest or unethical practices such as the Arthur Anderson-type accounting abuses have come to light in the West, serious efforts have been made to prevent their reoccurrence. President Theodore Roosevelt was particularly responsive. Such measures seldom succeed 100 percent, but usually there is an improvement. The pressure for reform requires, however, the prevalence of a consensus that such corrupt practices are and should be the exception, not the general rule.

There must also be a self-policing mechanism, as well as external watchdogs or public goads such as a free press, watchdog commissions, and a civil society that is allowed to expose the corruption. Until the late 1980s the Russian press was very much controlled. After a period of *glasnost* under Presidents Gorbachev and Yeltsin, President Putin began to clamp down on the press and a growing number of journalists were denied access to news developments. Again some have come to find it necessary to work under formal or self-imposed censorship. In addition, watchdog commissions established in the Yeltsin years to deal specifically with business practices, such as the Anti-Monopoly Committee, or the Federal Securities Markets Commission, have so far proven ineffective.

Thomas Owen contrasts czarist practices with nineteenth-century Victorian England.[32] Fraud and speculation were rife in England at the time, but by 1860 both business and government leaders came to recognize the need for some kind of objective standard. Failure to ensure transparency would certainly have deterred future investors. Without transparency, everyone would have suffered, including those who, in the short run, were prepared to cheat. It was decided, therefore, to institute strict certified accounting standards that businesses would have to accept.[33] Those who failed to accept such audits would be denied certification. Such practices were agreed to by British accountants as early as 1860 and were adopted as law in 1918.

Nothing of the sort occurred in pre-Revolutionary Russia. In fact, there were no pre-Revolutionary accounting professionals to speak of. Without something comparable, there was no way to rein in corporate dishonesty.[34] In response to the continuing dishonesty and fraud, the authorities refused to encourage self-policing and certification by the business community. Instead the remedy pursued by the czar and his bureaucracy was to tighten controls.

This emphasis on authoritarian control in Russia is not something limited only to the business community. Again, whether it be the czar, the general secretary, or the president, whenever in doubt, the response has been to promulgate rigid laws and controls. And because the laws usually end up being so all-encompassing, contradictory businesses must beseech the bureaucrats for exceptions.[35] This opens the door for bribes. It also means that while it may look like there is the rule of law, the exceptions for favorites and bribe payers makes it anything but. As an illustration, Soviet officials used to boast that they had the most comprehensive and demanding set of environmental laws in the world. True enough, but these laws were ignored more than they were honored.

This insistence on control and regulation, combined with the distrust and disdain for the business world and businessmen, more than anything explains why, beginning in 1836, businesses operating in Russia had to obtain specific approval from the czar before they were allowed to incorporate.[36] Russia was not the only country to institute such control. But unlike other countries, which gradually began to systematize, simplify, and facilitate the process as incorporation became a more common practice, Russia continued to demand individual approval by the czar and, more importantly, his bureaucrats. If anything, rather than institute automatic registration for incorporation as became the practice in the West, Russian laws and stipulations became even more onerous and cumbersome.[37] Thus, instead of facilitating economic modernization and growth, Russian bureaucrats hampered it. Owen put it succinctly, "What is most striking about the history of czarist economic policy in general and corporate law in particular is that it demonstrates the inability of czarist bureaucrats to accept, or even acknowledge the axioms of modern capitalist culture."[38]

Despite numerous pressures to change and accommodate world commerce and the Industrial Revolution, the czar and his advisors found themselves at odds with the dynamic of the evolving corporation and the move to self policizing in late nineteenth- and twentieth-century economic life.[39] And it was not just the czar who was resistant to change. As long as the laws were so rigid, the bureaucrats were able to continue to find a role for themselves and benefit financially from the opportunity to extort. By determined control and supervision, they prevented or deterred the business community from organizing effectively to force the kind of political and economic change brought about by their West European counterparts.

II

Many Russian business practices of the nineteenth century and early twentieth century were different from what they are today. Nonetheless there are a remarkable number of similarities. Admittedly, when Russia moved to the market in the late 1980s and early 1990s, there were not many who were still around from the pre-Revolutionary business community. Russia was very much unlike Poland, which endured only forty-five years of communism and where communism had been imposed from outside of Poland, not from within. Still, it has to be more than coincidence that

Russian business practices today so much resemble behavior of ninety years ago. It is easy to conclude that there is something in Russian culture and history (a desire for control and collective restraint, as well as a fear of individual initiative) that works to lead Russian businesses back to where they started. This brings to mind the traditional Russian doll. Wooden, with the weight in its rounded bottom, no matter which way you push it, it always reverts to its standing position.

Strange as it might seem, there are also behavioral similarities in the way private business is conducted today and the way communist leaders ran the economy in the communist era when there was no private business. For example, cheating and stealing from the state was considered a normal response to state ownership of the means of production. Bribes were commonplace and by the Brezhnev years, some Party officials even began to open secret overseas bank accounts. In the provinces, then as now, local party secretaries (modern-day governors) worked hand-in-hand with the local factory directors, protecting and supporting each other.

In another example, today as in the days of communism, foreigners are generally treated as ripe for the plucking. Take the example of Andrew Fox, the honorary consul of Great Britain in Vladivostok and the principal of Tiger Securities, an investment fund set up to invest in the Primorie region. In December 1999, Yevgeny Nazdratenko, then the governor of the region, summoned Fox to his office. "There was the head of the local police, the head of the Interior Ministry force in the region, the governor, the vice governor, and the chief executive of..." Far Eastern Trading Company (FETC), the profitable shipping company in which Fox had become a major stockholder.[40] Nazdratenko demanded that Fox turn over most of his shares in FETC to the regional administration. If not, Fox was told, he "would be sent to prison."[41] Such incidents were not limited to misbehavior by wayward governors. In an equally grievous case that we will examine in more detail in Chapter 8, the head of the Russian Central Bank and a former First Deputy Prime Minister were instrumental in misleading the IMF, as well as members of the London and Paris Clubs of international creditors, about the size of the reserves available to repay Soviet–and later Russian–debts.

These similarities are all the more remarkable given that during the seventy-five years or so of communism, market activities and private ownership of the means of production were basically prohibited. But just as in the days of the czar, it is virtually unthinkable that a businessman can today rise to significant power and wealth without a patron at court. Whether that patron operates under the czar or president matters not. Further, as then, senior government officials and leading businessmen move back and forth between positions in the government and in the private sector. Thus, Peter Aven, once the Minister of Foreign Economic Relations, is today President of Alfa Bank and partner with Mikhail Fridman of the Alfa Group. Vladimir Potanin, then and now the head of Oneximbank and Interros, served for a time as the country's First Deputy Prime Minister, while Boris Berezovsky, the founder of Logovaz and the behind-the-scenes controller of Sibneft, Aeroflot, and the TV network ORT, was appointed for a time as Deputy Secretary of the Security Council. Similarly, most of the banks have served mainly the credit needs of their principals, so that at least during the Yeltsin years almost the only loans these banks provided were used to finance the acquisition of the owner's industrial conglomerate. Of course there have been some changes since the days of the czar, but it is eerie to find that the economic historian Lyashchenko used the word "oligarch" to describe the rich businessmen of the czarist era just as it is used today.[42] Before we explore how the modern-day oligarchs became so rich and powerful in such a short time, we will explore more closely the legacy of Soviet central planning.

4   It's broke, so fix it

The Stalinist and Gorbachev legacies

Overextended by its war with Germany in 1917, the czarist government began to disintegrate. None too strong to begin with, the Russian economy could not supply both the country's military and civilian needs. On the political side, Russia was wracked by corruption and intrigue. In this weakened and vulnerable state, the unthinkable happened. In late February 1917, the heretofore all-powerful czar Nicholas II ordered the members of the parliamentary Duma to go home, but they did not. This was the first 1917 revolution. The Provisional Government under Alexander Kerensky, which was formed shortly after those events in February, was, however, unable to restore order and economic growth. Thus, the country's economy and political structure continued to weaken. In November (October of the old calendar) the Bolsheviks seized power, promising a new order.

What followed was unprecedented. After a prolonged Civil War and a New Economic Policy (NEP) retreat to markets and private trade, Josef Stalin ordered the collectivization of agriculture and the nationalization of the means of production. With the state in control of agriculture, industry, and trade, he then instituted central planning, imposing on the country procedures that heretofore had been utilized by only a few of the world's largest corporations.

Boycotted by most of the governments of the rest of the world, the Soviet Union stood apart, determined to prove that central planning was a more effective way to bring about economic growth than the market and private enterprise. Moreover, the Soviets would do all of this, they promised, in an equitable way, by abolishing exploitation of labor and private property as well as interest and rent. Given that by 1930 the rest of the world found itself in the grip of the Great Depression, the Soviet experiment attracted many believers. Unemployed engineers from all around the world gladly signed up for jobs in the Soviet Union, often the only place in need of such skills. No wonder idealists such as Lincoln Steffens, George Bernard Shaw, and Sidney and Beatrice Webb proclaimed their belief in this new approach. For Steffens it was, "I have been over into the future and it works."[1] A softened and sanitized version of the Soviet model became the prototype for many Western theories of economic development.[2]

Whatever its shortcomings, even its critics agreed that one thing the Soviet model did well was extract resources and savings for future investment in poor, even impoverished countries. It was not always done in the gentlest ways, but that those following such a model were able to generate any savings in such very poor countries was regarded as a major achievement unattainable in other, more traditional market economies.

In addition, the Soviet model seemed well suited for utilizing those assets. As Stalin and his planners saw it, the first priority in this triage effort was investment in heavy industry and machine tool production. By contrast, resources in a market economy first go to the production of consumer goods. Then as demand increased, suppliers of consumer goods would order machinery and equipment to make more consumer goods, which in turn would lead the producers of the machinery to order more steel and other machinery. Only after a passage of time would steel and machine tool production expand. Soviet leaders concluded that by reversing the sequence they could eliminate the middleman and expedite the whole process. As they began to report annual economic growth rates of 10 to 12 percent, it looked as if they might be right.

A downside of the Soviet system was the political repression that seemed to be an accompanying and thus inevitable part of the process. Some radicals today argue that the political trials and gulag camps were more a function of Stalin's paranoia than of the economic system that he adopted, but if so, why was it that virtually all leaders in those countries such as Mao Zedong in China or Nicolae Ceauşescu in Romania which adopted the Soviet model, behaved in just the same way? Stressing machine tools and steel production rather than consumer goods and luxuries meant postponement of an immediate improvement or even a deterioration in the standard of living. In the interim, there were bound to be housing and food shortages, and often even hunger. (That was one of the reasons why Marxists argued that communism should follow, not precede, capitalism. That way the hardships of industrialization would have already occurred and be attributed to capitalism, not communism.)

Since not everyone living in the Soviet Union was willing to endure short-term deprivation for long-term promises, there were sure to be many who would not find Stalin's scenario appealing. To prevent them from protesting and jeopardizing the whole effort, the Soviet leaders decided it was necessary to suppress not only actual but potential dissidents. Such suppression and preemptive restraint are all but inevitable in societies where the leader is able to gather in his hands not only all the economic controls, but all the political controls as well: in other words, where there are no restraining checks and balances within the government or between the government and the public.

A byproduct of this political repression and crackdown on dissent was the suppression of almost anything having to do with the market and the old regime. While the czarist market economy was underdeveloped, those few market institutions and professions that did exist had to be attacked and destroyed. This was to make it all the more difficult to resurrect a market system. They burned their institutional bridges behind them. Should there ever be an effort to return to the market, future reforms would first have to rebuild those bridges (institutions).

Those targeted included lawyers and accountants as well as entrepreneurs, commercial codes, and the judges who interpreted those codes. Anyone caught engaging in private trade or manufacture ran the risk of being charged with an economic crime, which was punishable by death. After sixty years of such repression, not only Pavlov's dog but the average Russian was afraid to set up his own business or treat a share of stock or a voucher as a piece of paper worth valuing. The Stalinist model repressed all aspects of the market and its institutions.

I

Western experts still cannot agree about how fast the Soviet Union grew between the late 1920s and 1991. Ten years after the collapse of communism and the Soviet Union, even present-day Russian economists and historians have begun to challenge the earlier estimates of the Soviet Central Statistical Agency (TsSU). All agree, however, that in the 1960s the Soviet rate of industrial growth had begun to decline.[3] For some industries such as steel production the rate on occasion was negative. While the Soviet economic model might facilitate growth in an underdeveloped economy, it turned out to be increasingly inappropriate for a developed economy. By the time Leonid Brezhnev had become General Secretary, the Soviet economy had become considerably larger than it had been in the early 1930s, and the challenge of incorporating an expanding assortment of planning needs became increasingly more complex and cumbersome. The number of interconnections grew geometrically. This was bad enough, but complicating matters even more, Gosplan held back on introducing computers into its operations. Furthermore, because the Soviet model eschewed the use of market prices as a governing guide for enterprise managers, it became increasingly difficult to arrange the most effective, least wasteful use of raw materials.

With its abundant reserves of raw materials, Russia could probably have continued to grow economically for several more decades. It had become clear, however, that such growth would entail an ever higher price. Even in a country as large and rich as the Soviet Union, there were limits to how much oil and gas the country could extract at reasonable cost. Moreover, because of a decline in population growth and increasing difficulties in extracting savings, by the 1970s there was a diminishing flow of labor and capital input into the economy. Eventually this would put a brake on growth because, unlike many market countries, the Soviet Union's economic growth was almost entirely a result of increasing those inputs of labor and capital in the production process. By contrast, market economies also derived growth from increased factor productivity. That meant they were able to produce more output using the same amount of labor and capital. This additional output was usually the result of technological developments in the production process. Soviet planners were not as adept as the market in finding the most productive uses of inputs. Thus, Soviet factor productivity seldom, if ever, was anything but negative. Most Soviet manufacturers did not add value to what they manufactured–they subtracted. So if instead of processing them they had exported those raw materials directly, they would have earned more money and generated more product. In other words the Soviet Union's GDP would actually have been higher without manufacturing than with it.[4]

If these developments did not sufficiently alert Soviet leaders to the fact that the Soviet planning process had outlived its usefulness, the increasing pace of technological innovation elsewhere should have. Remember why the Soviet model was initially so attractive. There were two advantages to this process. First, it worked well (if ruthlessly) to accumulate and extract savings from a poor and generally unwilling public, most of whom were peasants. Second, it then became adept at funneling that capital into steel mills and similar heavy industrial products providing Soviet industry with what were expected to be enormous economies of scale. This worked as long as the Soviet Union could compensate for the failings of its system, for example falling productivity and food shortages, by exporting sufficient quantities of oil and gas.

Despite such shortcomings the Soviet system functioned well for many decades, at least as long as there were few, if any, major changes in technology. By mobilizing its vast resources it gradually began to build up its industrial output. However because the planning procedures of the central planning bureaucracy were so long and cumbersome, the Soviets had difficulty adapting to rapid alterations in production procedures. Soviet planners had an especially hard time mastering advanced technologies.

Even with an effective espionage system, the Soviets often experienced considerable difficulty in reproducing what others had already done. There were several reasons why the planning system could not keep abreast of rapid technological change. A hallmark of the technological revolution in the West has been that a large number of innovations have come from small, often startup entities. Since small companies usually do not have to bother with large bureaucratic structures, they are able to make quick decisions and act upon them, something a large bureaucracy such as Gosplan (or even a large U.S. corporation) had trouble doing. Moreover, existing large corporations and state-owned enterprises often have a vested interest in maintaining the status quo because they have so much already invested in machinery or servicing customers with what were once advanced products and systems.

Large and established corporations such as IBM, if they are to survive, must also innovate. Many that at one time were sophisticated companies–such as RCA, Polaroid, and Digital Equipment–did indeed fail. Even when they survive, they often find that they must share the market with dynamic newcomers.

What is striking about the high technology sector is how many of the late twentieth century's most successful innovators, such as Microsoft, Intel, and AOL, did not exist thirty-five or, in the case of Microsoft, twenty-five years ago. According to Lester Thurow of MIT, three of the nine most highly capitalized corporations in 1999 did not exist in 1960. Of the largest twenty-five corporations, eight were not in existence then.[5] Such life and death in the corporate world is considered to be an essential characteristic of the market system. Like pruning a tree, periodically it is necessary to allow the death of obsolete machines, products and business techniques in order to make way for the new.

By contrast, the central planning system, which had worked so well in an era of slowly changing technology, found itself unable to keep up with such rapid change. In particular, Soviet planners viewed bankruptcy and the resulting unemployment as inherent shortcomings of the capitalist system. By contrast they assumed that as planners they could prevent such suffering by anticipating gradual adjustments. But this was predicated on the notion of slow-moving changes in technology, not the rapid innovation in large part anticipated by Joseph Schumpeter and his concept of "creative destruction."[6]

Soviet central planners apparently never anticipated having to deal with rapidly changing technology and rapid economic growth. While there would be new inventions, Soviet leaders assumed that Soviet engineers and scientists were equal if not superior to those in the West and, if properly supported, they would put Soviet science and technology in the lead.

Certainly that seemed to be a reasonable assumption in the depression of the 1930s when, as already noted, the best job opportunities for scientists and engineers were usually in the Soviet Union.

Stalin and later Khrushchev devoted significant resources to research and education in Russia. They both believed that sooner or later Soviet science and technology would lead the world. In part, Stalin's conviction that Soviet scientists would soon be outperforming their Western counterparts fed his sense of paranoia and secrecy. He had a deep fear that Soviet research efforts would fall into the hands of foreigners. As a result he instituted unprecedented secrecy over almost all economic activity. Wherever possible, the Soviet Union masked its scientific and economic activities. Numerous secret scientific cities (some built underground) were established to prevent Western theft of Soviet technological secrets. And truth be told, the Soviet Union did lead the world in several areas of science, especially in space and military technology. Occasionally, of course, the secrecy also served to shield Soviet incompetence or shortcomings, as well as its efforts to buy, copy, or steal Western technology.[7] In an extreme case, Anthony Sutton argued that virtually all of the Soviet Union's space achievements were borrowed or stolen from the West.[8]

While cutting themselves off from the rest of the world behind the "Iron Curtain," as Winston Churchill came to call it, had costs, these were tolerable so long as the Western countries were periodically caught in economic crisis and technology was slow moving. There was relatively little new to be learned from interaction with the West. But as economic conditions in Western Europe, Japan, the United States and even East Asia continued to improve and technological breakthroughs became a daily occurrence, the Soviet Union's isolation made less and less sense. While ideas and technology began to move rapidly and back and forth in the non-communist world, not only among different corporations and scientific centers within a country but around the world–what came to be called "globalization"–the Soviet policy of isolation prevented it from enjoying the stimulus of such interaction. Espionage was no substitute for regular commercial intercourse.

By the 1970s and 1980s, the Soviets began to see that their so-called advantage in the economic race (that is, their ability to extract investment funds and use them to expand output in traditional heavy industries) had become less and less relevant in the new technological age. The Soviet Union was no longer just a poor agrarian society; it had become a poor industrial consumer economy as well. Whereas in the early days forced savings had come from the peasants through collectivization, now they came almost entirely from the pockets of the urban population. In fact once Khrushchev abandoned Stalin's confiscatory tactics in the countryside, the government found it necessary to provide the peasants with larger and larger subsidies. Agriculture was no longer a well, pumping out investment funds for the country. It had instead become a sinkhole.

II

By the 1980s the disparity between the pace of technological investment and innovation in the Soviet Union and the outside world began to threaten not only the Soviet Union's economic growth but its ability to mount a credible military threat. Given state ownership of the means of production, the Soviets denied themselves the innovation spawned by the growing number of private startup corporations. Dominating the growth process in the United States, these were generally less capital-intensive operations, at least initially, and were financed by adroit and highly flexible venture capital entities–what might be called the antithesis of central planning, or even the traditional Western investment banking model.

With the pace of technological investment in the rest of the world accelerating, by the 1980s the Soviets found themselves falling further and further behind. Instead of protecting Soviet technical secrets from the West, the Iron Curtain served more and more to deny Soviet scientists and engineers access to the outside world's scientific and technological breakthroughs.

Dealing with this challenge would become one of Mikhail Gorbachev's major tasks.[9] Gorbachev's mentor, Yuri Andropov, was probably the first General Secretary to sense the change in dynamics. He commissioned several studies to examine the Soviet economy's growing malaise. Tatyana Zaslavskaya, a sociologist at the Siberian division of the Academy of Sciences, wrote a particularly critical and candid analysis that was leaked to the West. It was a devastating critique that could just as well have been written at the then Russian Research Center at Harvard. She depicted the Soviet economy as wasteful and nonresponsive to the public's needs.

Because Andropov died only a short year and a half after becoming General Secretary, we will never know whether he would have acted on Zaslavkaya's diagnosis. Gorbachev, however, did consult with Zaslavskaya several times and was well aware of her analyses. Several of her colleagues, particularly Abel Aganbegyan, also voiced similar concerns and worked closely with Gorbachev.

But criticizing a system and curing its problems are two different matters. Gorbachev was quick to discover that the former is a lot easier than the latter. He agreed that Russia could not long continue its wasteful ways. While most products were in short supply, Soviet factories were also producing other goods, which were piling up in warehouses because no one had ordered or wanted them. Factor productivity remained negative while labor and capital productivity were low; and as we saw, it became harder and harder to recruit new members of the workforce and find new sources of capital.

As long as it could extract and export its oil and gas, the Soviet Union could continue to squander its resources, at least for a time. It might be unable to avail itself of the startup technology companies that had become so important in the West, but there was no reason why it could not sustain its traditional industries that supplied the military sector. Since the days of Stalin these have been the main driving forces of the Soviet economy. There may have been no use for all that steel or those machine tools in the commercial market but they did feed in nicely to the Soviet military buildup.

As a measure of just how important the Soviet military complex was, Gorbachev, as noted earlier, has acknowledged that 20 percent of the country's GDP was set aside to finance the production of military equipment, as well as space and related expenditures. Whatever the estimate for the country as a whole, in some regions of the country the percentage of military-industrial production amounted to much more. For example, while visiting Irkutsk I was told that 70 percent of all the city's factories had been dedicated to the production of armaments.[10]

Gorbachev himself told me that he never knew precisely how much was being spent. While a member of the Politburo's inner circle under Yuri Andropov, Gorbachev asked about the size of the Soviet Union's military expenditure relative to its GDP. Andropov responded that there was no need to know or worry about it.[11] This was despite the fact that Gorbachev had just been assigned by Andropov to examine future economic policies, which he could not do without including some study about the importance of the military-industrial complex, the largest component of the country's economy. In our conversation Gorbachev acknowledged, however, that even when he became General Secretary himself, he lacked precise data. This was because of the arbitrary way prices were set, particularly for armaments. Since the prices of military equipment relative to consumer goods seemed to be low, it was likely that the share of the military-industrial complex as a percentage of GDP was probably understated and exceeded 20 percent, but no one knew for sure.

Whatever its precise size, the country's expenditures on the military-industrial complex served an economic, as well as a military purpose. As John Maynard Keynes would have put it, they served as an enormous stimulus to the economy. Producing those airplanes and tanks generated a need for aluminum and steel. However when the Cold War came to an end, there was no longer a need for any of those products. Thus the producers of aluminum found that instead of the 4 million tons that had been produced and consumed by Soviet industry each year, in 1992 after the collapse of the USSR, domestic demand fell to only 200,000 tons.[12]

Moreover, given the peculiar nature of the Soviet incentive system, there was no reward for economizing on the usage of such materials. On the contrary, because Soviet factories produced a varied mix of products most factories could not be evaluated simply by the total number of tons or meters of a product they had produced. Instead, to evaluate managerial performance, they added up the ruble value of all the goods that an enterprise produced. This was called the VAL system (gross ruble value of output). For the manager this meant that the larger the ruble value of his output, the higher his bonus in rubles. But the price of each good was determined by adding up the costs of the inputs it used; economists call this a "cost plus" system. In other words, the more spent on raw materials, the higher the gross ruble value of output. Profits are not important. As a result, managers were encouraged to increase costs as much as possible because the higher the costs, the higher the value of the output. The result was enormous waste.

Since the Soviet Union was so rich in raw material resources, cost concerns and, by extension, profit did not play a governing role in determining enterprise effectiveness. Should there be a shortage of an essential item, supplies could quickly be replenished with imports, paid for by oil and gas or other desired Soviet minerals. Granted it might have been wasteful, but with the idiosyncratic Soviet pricing system, no one could tell for sure. There was no problem as long as there were adequate supplies of oil and gas. But that was what Gorbachev was beginning to fear. Besides, even if more raw material deposits would someday be found, Gorbachev believed that squandering Russian resources would penalize future generations of Soviet citizens.

Gorbachev realized that he had to do something quickly, but he was unsure what. Although he did not want to dismantle the Soviet system nor the Communist Party, the unintended consequences of his actions were to lead to just that.[13] As a firm believer in what he considered the socialist system of the USSR, Gorbachev thought that he could accomplish the necessary changes by fine-tuning the system: just a few improvements here and there. The fine-tuning included a cutback in military expenditures in order to spend more on consumer needs. At the same time, he sought to supplement the incentives for managers in order to induce them to seek a more effective utilization of their capital and raw material inputs.

What Gorbachev did not anticipate was that once he started moving in this direction his economic reforms, when combined with his political reforms such as *glasnost* and secret elections, would set off demands for even more far-reaching measures. As a result, Gorbachev undermined the whole framework of the Soviet system. Once he began to shrink military expenditures and seek an end to the Cold War, he eliminated at least 20 percent of the country's GDP. Military conversion to civilian industries is hard even in a market economy, where there are alternate opportunities. While the U.S. record after World War II and the Korean War was better than it had been during World War I, it still took several years to absorb the excess capacity. Such a transition is even more difficult when the military sector is much larger and there is no meaningful market system in operation to accommodate alternate uses of such a large percentage of the economy.

It was like the death-defying motorcyclist act at the carnival. He races around a wooden cylinder. Eventually, he builds up enough speed so he can move perpendicular to the wall of the cylinder and end up parallel to the ground. As long as he maintains that speed, he defies gravity. Should he hit a bump, however, or momentarily break that momentum, he will crash to the ground. Gorbachev, by reducing the emphasis on military spending and introducing semi-market-type incentives, broke the momentum of the Soviet economy and, by 1991, it had crashed.

Gorbachev began slowly, first introducing *perestroika* (economic restructuring) and *uskorenie* (acceleration). Initially his reform involved a campaign to produce more machine tools in a more intensive fashion. He also consolidated several ministries in the expectation that this would lead to a reduction in the bureaucracy. As part of his early efforts, Gorbachev also attempted to emphasize work discipline and curb the consumption of alcoholic beverages. This crackdown made sense in terms of fighting alcoholism, but it immediately alienated most of the male workforce. Gorbachev would never recover their support.

His treatment of private business was similarly contradictory and also confusing. In 1986, he embarked on a crackdown on private trade. Vendors in collective farm markets where private trading was permitted had to show that they themselves had produced everything they were selling. There were to be no middlemen. When this disrupted the flow of goods, Gorbachev reversed course in 1987 and permitted the establishment of cooperatives and private business. He also launched a whole series of liberalizing reforms such as price flexibility that served as a prelude to Boris Yeltsin's even more far-reaching changes. Not since the NEP (New Economic Policy) of the mid-1920s had private traders and state enterprises in the Soviet Union been allowed so much leeway. Before the year was out, Gorbachev also authorized the legal formation of joint ventures between Russian and foreign companies as well as the establishment of private farms.

Though stopping short of a voucher and privatization program, Gorbachev also shook up the country's state enterprises. He understood that something had to be done to make the country's industries more responsive to consumer demand. He attempted to do this by extending more decision-making authority to enterprise directors. Toward that end, he put through the 1987 "Enterprise Law" that was designed to wean state enterprises from complete dependence on Gosplan and other state planning entities. This was intended to be an ingenious way to move gradually away from complete dependence on the state and toward increased market behavior and its institutions. While he wanted to preserve state ownership and central planning, he believed the best way to shake up the state enterprise sector was to allow for a parallel but competitive structure. After all, in the United States the federal government purchases more than 10 percent of GNP a year and the Pentagon alone spends about 3 percent of this. In Gorbachev's plan, spending in Russia by state enterprises would be a considerably higher percentage, but the principle should be the same–state entities should be made to compete in the market. That way, Gorbachev aimed for a more efficient use of the country's resources.

Under the Enterprise Law, once managers of state enterprises had fulfilled their planned target, they had free rein to sell whatever else they could produce on the open market. There was one hitch however; if they needed more inputs to produce those extra goods, those inputs had to be procured on the open market. Much to Gorbachev's dismay, most managers did not want to take such risks. They had been trained to be engineers, not salesmen and entrepreneurs.

As part of another measure intended simultaneously to increase production and energize state enterprises, Gorbachev authorized such structures to lease out their premises during off-peak hours.[14] The presumption was that members of the staff would come back on weekends or work overtime at their regular jobs. This form of intensification was designed as a way to increase output capacity without having to increase existing capital stock. All the revenues earned, minus of course the leasing fee, would be divided up among the lessors. As we shall see, these leasing agreements and the spontaneous seizing of state enterprise assets by factory directors which began to occur were to have a much more significant impact on privatization than was initially anticipated.

III

In addition to the intentional set of institutional changes implemented under Gorbachev, there were other largely unintended byproducts of the transition process that had a negative impact. Unlike market economies, fiscal and monetary policies were not what mattered in the Soviet centrally planned, state-owned economy. Decisions to increase production were made by Gosplan and the ministries. In the Soviet Union there were no corporate executives anticipating, for example, increased demand because of a cut in taxes, an increase in government expenditures, or a reduction in interest rates. Equally important, price increases in the Soviet Union had always been the prerogative of the Ministry of Prices, which usually fixed prices for periods of five to ten and sometimes more years. It was the direct plan that mattered–not indirect or roundabout incentives. Moreover, until 1976 government revenues generally exceeded or balanced government expenditures, so fiscal policy would have been dampening, not expansive.[15] As for investment, when it was decided to expand factory capacity or build a new one, Gosplan instructed the necessary ministries to set aside construction materials and machinery from the factories under their jurisdiction. This decree was accompanied by a parallel order to Gosbank to fund the purchase and delivery of those supplies. The level of interest rates had no significance either for the savers or the lenders.

This arrangement worked as long as the Soviet system remained intact. Even when expenditures exceeded revenues, as they began to in the mid-1970s, the impact was muted because all commerce and production was in state hands, as was price-setting. Occasionally, there were signs of suppressed inflation, but that had been a persistent characteristic since the 1920s and 1930s, when the decision was made to accelerate economic growth and sacrifice consumer goods production in favor of heavy industry. Inflation was also a real problem during World War II and immediately thereafter, when budget deficits could not be controlled, but after a currency reform in 1947, inflationary pressures diminished and, while never absent, were not a source of serious concern until the 1980s.

The yearly series of deficits which were only acknowledged a decade later in October 1988, combined with the decision to allow the formation of cooperative and private businesses, created a brand new set of challenges. The cooperatives and private businesses began to act more and more independently of the state, and even began to set prices. Previously, whatever inflationary pressures a deficit might have created were masked by the inability of the managers of state shops to raise prices. At most, queues at the state stores grew longer. But with the advent of cooperative and private businesses, store managers could and did raise their prices.

The reluctance of the budget authorities to acknowledge that the federal budget was no longer in balance meant that very few were informed about the growing annual deficits or potential problems. After all, these had not been matters of concern in a planned economy.

As unprepared as the Soviet government was to deal with budget deficits and inflation, it was even less prepared for an end to the Cold War. Though many dreamt that someday there would be an end to the Cold War, the arms race, nuclear confrontation, or threats of preemptive strikes, when that day actually arrived no one knew what to do.

The end of the arms race, as we saw earlier, also had important economic consequences. As we discovered in the United States, after the Cold War came to an end there was no longer any need for such an extensive buildup of missiles, munitions, airplanes, and submarines. For the producers of those weapons however, whether American or Soviet, the end of the arms race was no excuse for halting production. As the beggar in *Fiddler on the Roof* might have said, "Just because you have no use for those weapons is no reason why I should not produce them." Lest they be accused of not protecting their constituents' jobs, even the most committed "peaceniks" among U.S. Congressmen became ardent advocates of increased, or at least sustained spending on those advanced submarines, planes, and missile systems produced in their districts.

Theoretically a central planning system should have been better suited for such a transformation. However that assumes that the process would have been gradual enough to allow the planners to work through the necessary changes. But the arms race ended so suddenly that there was little time to plan. For that matter, even if the end of the Cold War had been preceded by several years' notice, the Soviet planning authorities would still have had difficulty coping. There was simply too much to absorb.

Problems like this occur for ecologists all the time. Nature can easily absorb limited amounts of pollutants. However, when there is a massive spill, the system is overtaxed and crashes. This was analogous to the problem confronting Russia at the end of the Cold War when it suddenly had to convert 20 percent or more of its industrial output.

Transforming itself into a consumer-oriented economy was further hampered by the fact that the existing Russian enterprises already producing consumer goods were hardly noted for their market savvy or responsiveness to consumer needs. In addition Soviet consumer goods were notorious for their poor quality. Compounding the problem, Soviet factories were protected by the Ministry of Foreign Trade against competition from foreign imports. At the same time, the Soviet incentive system provided no incentives for the Soviet factory directors who might want to try to compete in foreign markets. No wonder that when the Soviet Union collapsed and import curbs were abolished, Russian consumers seized the opportunity to gorge themselves on foreign imports. By 1995, imports comprised as much as 70 percent of the goods sold in some of Russia's largest cities. The loss of sales and markets for Russian industry was on par with the collapse of armaments production. Thus, production of Soviet color television sets (especially those that had been notorious for catching fire, even when turned off) fell from 2.7 million in 1990 to 102,000 in 1996. Production of watches fell by a comparable amount.[16]

The loss of these markets for the most part stirred little change in behavior among Russian managers. Some, such as those at Wimm-Bill-Dann, Russia's leading food processing company, did reinvent themselves, but most did not.

I discovered this first-hand in 1996 when I met with Nikolai Rychkov, the Director of the Elektrosignal factory in Novosibirsk. As the head of what had once been one of the military's main suppliers of advanced electronics and a factory noted for its electronic sophistication, Mr. Rychkov seemed unable to recognize that with the end of the Cold War his vaunted status had come to an end. When I visited his nearly shuttered factory, he seemed unconcerned that it was operating only two days a week, and even then only partially. He was convinced that sooner or later Russian consumers would come to their senses and opt for his radar and radio equipment, rather than the foreign-produced alternatives. Whatever Russian consumers might think, as far as he was concerned, his products were world-class. As proof, he boasted that a Japanese company had approached him about forming a joint venture. But convinced of his company's capabilities, Rychkov had rejected the offer. To a foreigner, the proposed joint venture seemed to be an answer to his problems, but he regarded the Japanese offer as a ruse to gain a foothold in his factory and seize control from him. He insisted that he did not need such foreign involvement, and that eventually the Russian public would become nostalgic for good old Soviet products. They had been good enough for the Soviet army so it was just a matter of time before his factory would be once again fully employed.

The combined effect on Russia of the end of the Cold War, the switch from central planning to the market, and the shunning of domestically produced goods in favor of accessible imports, induced a collapse of production far greater than even that experienced by the United States during the Great Depression of the 1930s. According to the official statistics, by 1998 Russian GDP was barely 60 percent of what it had been in 1990, a collapse of at least 40 percent (see Table 2.1).

IV

Embarking on his program of reform in 1992, Boris Yeltsin did not envisage a depression of this magnitude. But he never seemed to concern himself much with the details of his economic reforms. In October 1991 Yeltsin decided to delegate such matters to his economic advisors. He chose Yegor Gaidar over both Yuri Skokov, a longtime associate of Yeltsin who had been his economic advisor in the 1990 campaign for President, and the economist Grigory Yavlinsky, who later became the head of the Yabloko Party. The choice of Gaidar had as much to do with politics and Yeltsin's determination to avenge himself against Gorbachev as with Yeltsin's views on economics. In the fall of 1991, after Yeltsin led the fight to defeat a coup effort to oust Gorbachev, he understood that Gorbachev's days were numbered. In his mind, the future lay with Russia, not the USSR and the other fourteen republics, many of which were pressing for secession from the Union. Dissolving the Union, even though it meant dumping historically Slavic regions such as Ukraine and Belarus, would accomplish two objectives. It would leave Yeltsin free to run Russia as he wanted, without having to worry about being second-guessed by Gorbachev. And if there were no USSR, there would be no necessity for a President of the USSR, leaving Gorbachev jobless, the perfect revenge with no fingerprints. As arcane as it might seem, this scheme worked in favor of Gaidar, who more than any other had become a strong advocate of an independent Russia separate from the other republics.

Gaidar was a strong proponent of a market system. He was an even stronger advocate of privatization and, for that matter, a whole package of near-simultaneous reforms that came to be known as "shock therapy," and today is called the "Washington Consensus." Gaidar had come to this concept as a result of his studies as well as from a series of discussions with economists from both Eastern Europe and the United States. Among those interacting with Gaidar at one stage or another were Jeffrey Sachs, Andrei Shleifer, Jonathan Hay, all of Harvard University, Anders Aslund of Sweden, and, later, the Carnegie Endowment and Richard Layard of the London School of Economics. IMF officials and Stanley Fischer in particular had long advocated something similar, that is, simultaneous and far-reaching economic liberalization (that is, micro policy reforms combined with determined macro restrictions to curb inflation).

Gaidar acknowledges his interaction with such advisors, some of whom had official and semi-official appointments at various levels of his government.[17] Janine Wedel, an outspoken critic of the role played by foreign advisors, blames most of them, especially Jeffrey Sachs, for almost everything that went wrong.[18] She faulted them not only for poor advice, but, in the case of Shleifer and Hay, for alleged conflict of interest, self-aggrandizement, and insider dealing. The U.S. Department of Justice has expressed similar concerns. Federal prosecutors convened a grand jury to investigate personal misbehavior (that is, insider dealing) by Andrei Shleifer and Jonathan Hay. They recommended jury-level civil charges. The U.S.

Department of Justice sought $102 million in damages from Harvard, the main contractor, because of charges that both men "invested in (Russian) companies directly affected by advice they gave the (Russian) government."[19]

Despite some excessively emotional, even reckless attacks by Wedel on Sachs, he has never been accused of similar behavior. Ms. Wedel seems obsessed with attacking the man. Among other charges, she also insisted that Professor Sachs was never in fact an official advisor, something also asserted by Viktor Chernomyrdin, who replaced Gaidar as Prime Minister in December 1992.[20] Here as elsewhere she seems blinded by her anger at Sachs, who did have an official relationship with Boris Fedorov, at least, while he was Minister of Finance. Nonetheless, some of her criticisms of Sachs and the others, especially about several misguided policy recommendations, are very much on target. But it is only fair to point out that the flaws have become clearer with hindsight. Now that he has had a similar chance to look back, Sachs, unlike Aslund, has also come to acknowledge many of the same concerns.

When I asked about the role of Western advisors, Gaidar acknowledged that Sachs and the others were advisors and that Sachs joined Gaidar in September 1991, when Gaidar's team was preparing its reform proposals for Yeltsin. However, to the extent that Sachs and some of the others did play a role, they did so, as Gaidar put it, "only on marginal matters."[21] Gaidar takes full responsibility for the policies that were introduced, not in an effort to shield others but because he insists that, given his belief in and devotion to the market, he would not have supported any other course of action.[22]

V

Gaidar's strategy was relatively simple: remove as much government control and involvement as possible from economic decision-making. He quickly discovered, however, that implementation of such a policy, especially in the former Soviet Union, was incredibly complex. Heretofore, when other countries adopted a shock therapy policy, this usually meant returning the power to determine prices and output to individual decision-makers in the market. That was usually because in most of these countries much of the market infrastructure was still in place. Abolishing price controls and the Ministry of Prices was likely to be disruptive and inflationary, but only briefly. He was convinced that once prices were deregulated, private business would kick in and stimulate higher production.

In advocating such reforms, he took for granted that private businesses and farms as well as commercial codes and markets, even if dormant, were ready to spring to life. But after seventy years of Communist rule, anything resembling market institutions in Russia had almost certainly been destroyed. In addition, the memory of those institutions and the resulting practices had also faded.

The absence of such critical institutions was an all but insurmountable obstacle to meaningful reform. Only when basic structures such as commercial and accounting codes, courts, startup private businesses, anti-monopoly laws, and private property are in place or have been restored will shock therapy work. As enumerated by specialists in the IMF, successful economic reform presupposes the following:

1 Price liberalization.
2 Foreign trade liberalization and current account convertibility.
3 Enterprise reform–privatization.
4 Creation of a social safety net.
5 Development of an institutional and legal framework for a market economy, including market-based financing.

Those are the microeconomic changes.

The IMF economists, like most Western-trained economists, also assumed that these changes would be accompanied by or give rise to the "rule of law" as well as a strong government.[23] Unfortunately, in Russia and most of the rest of the USSR, this did not happen.

What the reformers failed to understand is that when market institutions are not already in place, it may take not months but years or decades to create them. Given how far removed Russia was at the time from typical market conditions and behavior, under the best of circumstances it would have taken considerable extra time to put in place such essential market institutions. For example, before Yeltsin began his reforms, not only was the ruble inconvertible outside Russia, it was not even fully convertible within Russia itself. That meant holders of rubles had no guarantee that they could spend those rubles to buy what they wanted. Many products, both for consumers and especially manufacturers, were allocated according to what the Russians called "funds," in effect, ration coupons. And not everyone had them. Thus, members of the Central Committee of the Communist Party had access to "special stores," which sold goods unavailable in regular stores open to the general public. Commodities used in manufacturing were also distributed using such special funds.

Overriding market forces in this way almost always leads to more and more distortion. In a typical scenario, the process begins when a government leader finds himself with public pressure to do something about rising prices. The usual reaction is to impose price controls. Invariably, that leads to shortages. In an effort to induce manufacturers to maintain production, the state then finds it necessary to step in with subsidies to offset the inadequate revenue.

The way bread was distributed in the Soviet Union is a good illustration. Bread has always played a central role in Russian life, often constituting the only lifeline between the Russian peasant and starvation. When bread prices began to rise in 1955, riots broke out and the Soviet authorities agreed to hold prices constant. To do this, however, they had to subsidize the collective farms to cover their costs of operation. These subsidies ultimately grew to about 100 billion rubles, at that time over $100 billion a year. Eventually this subsidy became a major cause of the Soviet Union's budget deficit. The policy also had an impact on the demand side. Russian peasants quickly saw that it was more profitable for them to sell the grain they harvested to the state at the higher subsidized price rather than feed that grain to their own livestock. They would then buy the heavily subsidized bread at the bakery and feed it to their livestock. Approximately 15 percent of the bread baked each year was wasted in this way.

Eventually, when the waste becomes too obvious to hide, political and economic leaders come to recognize how shortsighted such policies are. Shock therapy has been a traditional cure. Price controls are abolished. Producers then raise their prices and the government, in turn, eliminates the subsidies. With an end to subsidies, the government is better able to reduce its deficit and the printing of money, which is likely to reduce inflationary pressures. At the same time, the higher prices force some previous consumers out of the market. Higher prices mean higher profits which attract more production. The queues disappear, as do inflationary pressures.

This scenario assumes, however, that there is already in existence a solid core of producers ready to respond to the higher prices with increased production. Other producers may also decide to open up new businesses to compete for sales, or switch production from other, less profitable lines. However, if there are only a few producers, many barriers to entry, or if there is a monopoly, shock therapy may not work. It will take too long for the new startups to come on line and, in the interval, the monopolists may move to intimidate potential competitors or bribe government officials to impose comparable restrictions.

The analogy that proponents of shock therapy used to make their case was that "One doesn't jump over an abyss in two leaps." You must do away with all economic restraints and do it all at once. Gradualism in their eyes was a prescription for chaos. For example, if producers were allowed to produce whatever they wanted but prices remained fixed, the producers would start to manufacture the wrong products. Similarly, if startups were restricted, profits would end up being too high.

But the "single leap over the abyss" analogy only makes sense if the system is merely dysfunctional. In Russia it was destroyed. The "initial conditions" (Joe Berliner's horse) were not well suited for too radical reform. In Russia's non-competitive markets it was a mistake to expect that price liberalization would perform miracles. Since private businesses and farms were completely outlawed until 1987, and the businesses that did become private in 1992 were predominately state enterprises only recently transformed into private businesses, Russia's markets were not competitive; monopoly behavior still prevailed. Soviet planners intentionally assigned a low priority to opening retail outlets. This was at least partly a deliberate consequence of the Soviet government's determination to reduce the duplication and overemphasis on consumption they saw in the capitalist world. Even more important, under Yeltsin private startups were discouraged, if not officially, then unofficially, as they had to register with corrupt and extorting bureaucrats, fire marshals, and tax officials. Because of the Soviet de-emphasis on consumption and retailing, even after the privatization of the existing state network there were only six businesses per 1,000 Russians in 1999; the comparable number was forty-five in the European Union and seventy-four in the United States.[24] After a decade of reform, private small businesses in Russia generate only about 6 to 10 percent of the country's output, whereas in Western countries the comparable figure is generally 50 percent or more.

With time, there has come a growing understanding that with its weakly developed institutions and business codes (both formal and informal) Russia in 1992 was not ready for the full set of shock therapy measures.[25] But given the unfamiliarity with Russia's history and culture, it did appear to many foreign advisors at the time, superficially at least, that shock therapy might well be the best approach. In an indirect way even Anatoly Chubais, the architect of the privatization program, acknowledges that in 1991 and 1992 Russia was in such a chaotic state that almost any reform would have gone awry. He concludes however that this made it all the more urgent to move forward with privatization because all the alternatives would have resulted in even more damage.[26]

Even now proponents of shock therapy, such as Anders Aslund, insist that countries which used shock therapy and rapid reform have prospered, whereas those which moved gradually or held back have not.[27] Poland is cited as a good model whereas Ukraine, or sometimes Russia, model what not to do (this despite the fact that Aslund was a consultant to both of the latter). But those who argue this way may have reversed cause and effect. An equal if not more persuasive argument could be made that those countries with the essential institutions already in place or those which took time to build the missing institutions before the full force of the reforms was unleashed did better.[28] To go back to the "one leap over the abyss" analogy, that lesson should be amended to say that one leap makes sense only if the leaper is able to leap from one cliff to another–that is, when the necessary institutions are already in place and able to respond to the reforms. If the leaper is in a pit and needs to jump to the opposite cliff without the necessary institutions in place, he risks disaster unless he takes the time to make two leaps; the first from the pit to the cliff above him (he takes the time to build up the market infrastructure by encouraging start-ups and relaxing price controls), and a second leap from the cliff on his side of the abyss to the opposite cliff (and only then does he apply the full range of shock therapy, including privatization).

The rush to adopt shock therapy, especially large-scale privatization rather than a more gradual step-by-step approach, gave rise to whole series of dysfunctional institutions in Russia. That is not to argue that moving slowly from stone to stone as was done in China would have guaranteed a successful economic transition; seventy years of Soviet central planning were far too devastating to permit a quick resurrection of a market economy. Nevertheless, in Russia the shock therapy approach exacerbated conditions more than alternate courses of action would have done. Moreover, it helped to produce the emergence of the oligarchs, the Mafia, the theft of state resources, and the resulting money laundering. On the micro side, without a competitive infrastructure in place, shock therapy, the liberalization of most prices and the failure to precede price liberalization with a currency reform fueled the inflation (twenty-six-fold in 1992 alone) as well as the collapse of industrial production (by over 40 percent) above and beyond that resulting from the end of the Cold War and the shrinking military-industrial complex. On the macro side, the insistence of advisors, both within and outside the IMF, that strenuous efforts be made to curb inflation and institute macroeconomic stabilization in turn created a credit crunch. This subsequently resulted in higher interest rates, a reluctance to pay bills, wages, and taxes, in cash or at all, and the sudden predominance of barter, what Clifford Gaddy and Barry Ickes called the "virtual economy" and I called the "barter economy."[29]

In his book, Yegor Gaidar insists that by early 1992 when he was put in charge of the economy, he had to act quickly because the country was running out of foreign currency and even food. He had no choice.[30] But he did; he could, and he should have moved ahead with price liberalization, convertibility, a currency reform, and the encouragement of startup businesses, but held back on privatization. It was the latter that has caused the problems.

Some advisors, including Anatoly Chubais, Maxim Boycko, Andrei Shleifer, and Robert Vishny insist that the overall program, despite its flaws (some even refuse to acknowledge there were flaws), was a success.[31] The most important achievement in their eyes was that the Communists did not regain power, a market took shape, and privatization occurred and was not undone. Much of their argument for immediate privatization was predicated on the Coase Theorem.[32] Coase argued that once property rights became private, regardless of how irrational the initial allocation, those property rights would ultimately be traded until they found their highest and most productive use. Therefore, even if the "wrong" people became owners of privatized assets that had once been state property, ultimately these owners and their inept directors would be fired in favor of better-trained, more competent owners and managers. If the stockholders of the company settled for something less, other investors would sooner or later seek a takeover by more efficient managers, as often happens in the capitalist world.

A few held such notions right up to the August 17, 1998 collapse.[33] Anders Aslund and Jeffrey Sachs argue that the shock therapy strategy was not to blame because shock therapy was never really implemented in Russia and anticipated foreign financial aid was never sufficiently provided.[34] In other words, don't blame us when our suggestions were never fully implemented. If only Russian political leaders had exerted more political will and foreign governments had been more supportive, the reformer's programs would have been instituted and would have produced the results that Sachs and Aslund had predicted.

While insisting that on the whole he would have acted no differently on the major issues in 1991 and 1992, Yegor Gaidar, the chief designer of the Yeltsin economic reform package, does now acknowledge that he might have made some technical changes in his program. He concedes, for example, that he should not have waited until the spring of 1992 to liberalize oil prices. Had he acted sooner, that would have obviated the need for the government to institute a set of complicated controls intended to regulate exports of raw materials, especially oil, and capture the rent from some of those sales. But as for the overall design of the reforms, he insists, "I would have acted approximately the way I did. But I would be surer of undertaking the right measures and less ready to make compromises."[35]

VI

Despite the justifications of the various reformers, they still seem unable to recognize that the failure of economic reforms was also due to the fact that the Russian public was unwilling to go along with shock therapy. Given the lack of consensus among the Russian people about switching to a market system, shock therapy was politically unrealistic. Gaidar now says that he never should have allowed the Communists to push through legislation that allowed factory managers to seize ownership of their factories. But if his reforms are to occur in something resembling a democracy, he cannot ram through his ideas, regardless of how they might appear to others. This belated realization is why Gaidar now acknowledges that had he been czar instead of prime minister, he indeed would have acted differently.[36] The point is, however, he was not czar, Boris Yeltsin was. Capable as he may have been, Gaidar could only push so hard; in other words, there were significant restraints on the "jockey's" freedom to act. And in an aspiring democracy even Yeltsin could only push public opinion so far. That is why Gaidar was pressured by the Supreme Soviet to appoint Viktor Gerashchenko as Chairman of the Russian Central Bank. He was someone more beholden to the Supreme Soviet, which wanted an easy credit policy, than to the IMF and a Gaidar-type money regime. That also explains why, when it became clear that Gaidar's policies were not working, Yeltsin responded to the demand of the Supreme Soviet that he bring in someone more acceptable to the factory directors who had a very strong presence in that body. That led to the appointment of Viktor Chernomyrdin as Deputy Prime Minister. Yeltsin would then promote that same Chernomyrdin to the post of Prime Minister at the end of the year, something he tried but could not do for Gaidar. True, shock therapy was not fully implemented in Russia, but that was because major components of that policy were anathema to the public. Unfortunately, the fragments of shock therapy that did make it through gave birth to economic distortions.

That a different approach which took into consideration Russia's cultural heritage might have produced a less dysfunctional result is suggested by the way reforms evolved in China and Poland. As noted earlier, China, unlike Russia, moved slowly, as Deng Xiaoping put it, by crossing a stream a stone at a time. The Chinese set up the contract responsibility system in agriculture, which effectively meant decollectiviza-tion and a return to pre-revolutionary family farms. In the same way, the government authorized–even encouraged–individuals to form cooperatives and individual enterprises. Initially, the Chinese government limited the number of employees that private business could hire, but gradually they lifted restraints. They also allowed joint ventures with foreign firms and set up a series of special economic zones along the coast. Some price controls were also removed gradually, although on occasion reinstituted when it looked like prices might rise too rapidly.

It was not a perfect transition, and today corruption is rampant throughout the system as Chinese government officials as well as ordinary people seek to share in the new wealth that the country has generated. Nonetheless, a competitive market system has taken shape as some of the smaller enterprises have moved beyond the mom and pop level. Some have even become significant factors in the export market. Most important of all, unlike the near decade-long collapse of the Russian economy, the Chinese economy took off after reforms began in December 1978, and grew an average of 9 to 10 percent a year for nearly twenty years.

That is not to say that Russia should have copied everything done by China or Poland. However, for differing reasons, neither China nor Poland instituted immediate privatization. This is the one sector where the Chinese, like the Poles, have moved slowly. Fearing civil unrest if large numbers of workers were fired from unprofitable factories, China continued to underwrite these factories with subsidies into the late 1990s. In the case of Poland, political quarrels forced delay but in the interim, as we will see in Chapter 10, this allowed the Poles to think through the procedure and design a more intelligent process. Without the premature privatization that took place in Russia, both Poland and China avoided the Russian-type scandals. By moving gradually they also facilitated the growth of market institutions that have tempered the powers of potential oligarchic hierarchies.

There is no denying that the continued monopoly of the Chinese Communist Party and the corruption of local party cadres has produced distortions and abuses. Yet the fact remains that the non-state sector in China is much more vigorous and less prone to oligarchic control than in Russia. Gradualism in China, while flawed, at least with respect to privatization has produced a much more responsive economy and a much greater improvement in the overall economic wherewithal of the ordinary person than the reforms in Russia.

The contrast with Poland is equally striking. After a bad year or two, the Polish economy began to grow in 1992. For a time during the last half of the decade, it became the fastest growing country in all of Europe. For that reason, Poland is often cited as proof that shock therapy works, and that if it worked in Communist Party Poland, it seemed only sensible to follow the same strategy in Communist Party Russia.

Digging deeper however, it turns out there were significant differences between Poland and Russia on the eve of their reforms. This should have alerted the reformers to the fact that the approach to reform in Russia would have to vary significantly from the strategy adopted in Poland. For example, Russia's communism was self-generated; Poland's was imposed from the outside by the Soviet Union. Poland had endured communism for only forty-five years, not seventy as in Russia, a full generation less. There were still Poles who remembered how a market system operated. All of this meant there would be less ambiguity among the Poles about abolishing central planning.

There was also a much broader consensus in Poland than in Russia as to where their respective countries should head. For the Poles, it was to look West to the market and democracy. This orientation differed from the Russians, who split along historic lines–the Slavophiles versus the Westernizers. By no means was there agreement in Russia about a westward shift. As reflected in the 30 percent of the population that continued to vote for the Communist Party with its traditional hostility toward the market and the West, a large percentage of the population seemed to prefer central planning and state control. By contrast, although many Poles continued to vote for what had been the Communist Party, and even a Communist president, by the 1990s the Polish Communist Party had changed its name as well as its program. It had become more Social Democratic, not only in name but behavior, which meant that it did not advocate a return to central planning nor a recreation of the Warsaw Pact.

Finally, there were some geographic and institutional differences. Poland was closer (less than a day's drive) to West Berlin and access to Western goods that could be brought back to Poland and sold. About 90 percent of the farms in Poland had never been collectivized; in Russia they all had been. Similarly, unlike Russia, Poland had always had a small private service sector and even some private manufacturing. Thus a change in prices was very likely to trigger a supply reaction from at least some producers.

In preparing for their reforms, the leaders of the Polish Solidarity Movement who had just taken control of the government recognized that some segments of their economy had been more severely deformed by forty-five years of communism than others. Thus they adopted a strategy that combined both shock therapy and gradualism. Prices and currency convertibility were liberalized in shock therapy fashion in January 1990, as was the opening of new private businesses. But since Poland never collectivized most of its farms and since it had permitted a degree of private business, there was less reason for a full institutional overhaul of the sort needed in Russia. Most important of all for our analysis, while Poland moved immediately to privatize its small shops, it did not initially privatize its larger enterprises. As we shall see in Chapter 10, by the time it got around to that in 1995, the government had had sufficient time to think through the process with considerable care and design a strategy intended to anticipate and prevent oligarchic control of the sort that characterized privatization in Russia. The four- or five-year delay also provided the time needed to build up an impressive number of startup companies, not only in services, but in manufacturing. These new businesses combined with the recently privatized small shops constituted a critical mass that was vigorous enough to form a competitive market. Thus, by the time that the larger Polish state enterprises were privatized, there was in place a new set of "initial conditions," and as a result, the factory directors and potential oligarchs were not able to dominate the economy as did their counterparts in Russia, where there was no such emphasis on startups and no resulting competitive formation.

VII

Whether it was the different approach to reform or the underlying difference in cultures, or a combination of both, there is no doubt that the reforms in Poland and in Russia produced two very different results. Not only did the rates of economic growth differ, so did institutional behavior. This is reflected in some fascinating interviews conducted by Timothy Frye and Andrei Shleifer.[37] They surveyed fifty-five small shops in Moscow and fifty in Warsaw in the spring of 1996. Whereas 45 percent of the shopkeepers in Moscow said they needed to use the courts but did not because they did not trust them, only 10 percent of the Warsaw managers said they had need to use their courts but did not. In other words, in Warsaw there was more trust in the judicial process as well as a system of informal codes of behavior that eliminated the need for such adjudication. Reflecting the lawlessness that accompanied the collapse of the communist system and the breakup of the USSR, in Moscow 76 percent of the respondents said they could not operate their businesses without a "roof," or Mafia protection. In Poland, only 6 percent felt such a need. Moreover, 39 percent of those in Moscow acknowledged that they had been contacted by the Mafia within the last six months. By contrast, in Warsaw only 8 percent of the respondents had been so contacted. Muscovites reported that they had to deal with over eighteen inspections by government agencies during 1995, compared to nine in Warsaw.[38] The likelihood of being fined after such an inspection in Moscow was 83 percent, compared to 46 percent in Warsaw. Finally, in Moscow it took an average of 2.7 months to register a business, but only 21 days in Warsaw. Frye and Shleifer concluded from these results that in Russia rents were being extracted by the bureaucrats and Mafia, whereas in Poland rents were being divided among the business competitors.

VIII

The approach to markets and economics of the czars, the Soviets, as well as Gorbachev and Yeltsin, created a legacy (the initial conditions) that was not conducive to markets and structural competition. It may be that culture and historical legacies were so deeply rooted that no other outcome was possible. However, the examples of China and Poland, where there was also a weak bourgeoisie, suggest that with other reformers (Berliner's "jockeys") other outcomes and gradual changes in the initial conditions might have been possible.

Certainly, there were many factors that explain why the reforms in Russia produced results so different from those in Poland and China. But in particular, the approach to privatization stands out. The way the process was conceived and implemented cast a shadow over the whole reform effort. In some sense, privatization was a keystone for the rest of the reforms, and influenced or infected them as well. In the chapters that follow, we shall examine the rationale behind the strategy that was adopted, and what groups emerged as the winners and losers.

5 Privatization

Good intentions, but the wrong advice at the wrong time

Gaidar's reform strategy–in our analogy, the jockey's game plan–was to remove price controls and move ahead with the privatization of state enterprises. Given that in early 1992 the newly empowered Russian government had virtually no foreign currency reserves left in the Russian Central Bank (RCB), barely adequate food stocks, and no way to halt the unauthorized and spontaneous privatization of one-time state enterprises, Gaidar's decisions at first glance are hard to fault.[1]

Gaidar knew that raising prices *à la* shock therapy would discourage wasteful use and, more important, induce more production and reduce stockpiling and hoarding. But because so many rubles had been printed by Gosbank during the waning days of the USSR and by the central banks of what had once been the Soviet republics, Gaidar feared that market-determined prices would soar, making it impossible for the public to purchase some essential goods such as bread and gasoline. Thus he retained controls on a few priority prices such as petroleum.[2] In fact, he should have been even bolder and also decreed a currency reform. This would have absorbed much of the excess money supply and in all likelihood prevented the twenty-six-fold increase in prices that took place in 1992. That would have allowed him to avoid those energy price controls since there would have been less of a price disparity between domestic and foreign oil prices. With a smaller difference in prices, there would have been less temptation to divert so much petroleum to foreign markets where the price was sometimes as much as ten times higher than prices at home. In turn, Gaidar could have avoided much of the corruption that ensued when those with petroleum fought to win export permits.

Gaidar felt however, that he could not support such a currency reform because he feared that those who had kept their money in rubles would accuse his government of confiscating the savings of those who played by the rules–that is, those who kept their money in rubles, not dollars or other currencies. If their trust were destroyed, how could he expect them to hold rubles in the future? In the end, of course, the twenty-six-fold increase in prices resulted in much the same confiscation.

As much as the Russian public was upset by the inflation, Gaidar's determination to move ahead immediately with the privatization of state enterprises made them even angrier.[3] Gaidar and Anatoly Chubais, the architect and implementor of the privatization process, insist that at the time they were convinced that emergency measures had to be taken. They had to act not only to halt the ongoing disintegration of the economy and spontaneous privatization that had begun to mushroom during the waning years of the Gorbachev administration, but to prevent the still influential supporters of communism from attempting to reassert state control and reinstitute communism, central planning, and state ownership.[4] Equally important, given the disintegration of state control and the increasingly chaotic business climate, it had become harder and harder to discipline the workforce and enforce what laws remained. The two believed that as long as an impersonal government was the owner, the workforce would feel free to help themselves to the enterprise's property. By contrast, a private owner would more likely take steps to protect his property.[5] This convinced Gaidar and Chubais that if industrial enterprises were not immediately converted to private ownership, their assets would be stripped.[6]

To prevent the vaporization of their industrial infrastructure and to hold off what they were convinced would be a communist resurgence, they concluded that they had to create widespread public support for their reforms. Therefore, they decided to issue a share of stock (a voucher) to every Russian citizen and in that way transform not only the workers and management, but the public-at-large into stakeholders as well as stock-holders in the country's industry. As direct owners and beneficiaries of a minute portion of Russia's now-private enterprises, the public would then resist efforts to renationalize "their property."

Gaidar and Chubais were also influenced by the arguments, long associated with the University of Chicago, that the de-politicization of enterprise ownership and its privatization results in greater efficiency and is preferable to state ownership.[7] Having seen firsthand the effects of sixty years of nepotism and political patronage resulting from state ownership, Gaidar and Chubais believed there was no other feasible approach. In the early 1990s, reform economists in Eastern Europe were often among the most fervent advocates of a private market economy—more so than many Western economists.

Though reformers such as Gaidar and Chubais were committed to the idea of the market, their experience with actual markets and private ownership was relatively limited. They had read a good deal and engaged in many discussions, especially with East Europeans, but their exposure to the market was more theoretical than hands-on. For that reason, they welcomed foreign economic advisors. But as Russia suddenly found itself inundated with economists and pseudo-economists from across the ideological spectrum, the country's leaders were overwhelmed with contradictory advice. Proposals included adoption of a gold standard, market socialism, input–output systems, a foreign currency exchange board, and radical laissez-faire capitalism.

In late 1991, Gaidar committed himself to shock therapy and assigned Anatoly Chubais to carry out the privatization effort. To assist him, Chubais sought guidance from Andrei Shleifer, a young Harvard University professor of economics who specialized in corporate finance and governance. Shleifer was introduced to Chubais that November by his Harvard colleague Jeffrey Sachs, who had worked with Gaidar and Chubais when they were formulating their overall strategy a few months earlier in September.[8] Shleifer, in turn, brought in Maxim Boycko, a young Russian economist, as well as Jonathan Hay, a recent graduate of the Harvard Law School. Hay eventually became a specialist in security legislation and "wrote many regulations governing Russia's privatization."[9] Everyone involved supported the privatization effort and its urgent implementation. Shleifer, Maxim Boycko, and Robert Vishny, an economist at the University of Chicago, helped design the voucher program. In 1995, after the voucher program had been completed, they set out the rationale for such a program and explained why they considered their program a success.

As they saw it, privatization, or de-politicization, was not only a way of creating stakeholders (in effect bribing them), but it would also lead to the more efficient operation of the economy. Resources would be utilized more productively and decisions would be made for economic, not political reasons. Thus, if a plant director was unable to operate at a profit, or if it appeared that he was not taking full advantage of the profit opportunities open to the company, the board of directors could replace him. Obtaining the highest return on one's investment would become the governing principle. This followed from the Coase Theorem referred to in Chapter 4.[10]

This scenario is predicated on several crucial assumptions.

Property right holders in Russia would act no differently than their counterparts in other market economies (that is, there was no such thing as a special Soviet economic man). Russians, like Americans, are "economic men" (Homo Economicus) who respond rationally to incentives.[11] Supporters of such a notion cite a public opinion study by Robert J. Schiller, Maxim Boycko, and Vladimir Korobov in the *American Economic Review* which found that New Yorkers and Muscovites share similar attitudes toward markets and private property.[12] Building on these findings, they assumed that what was true about Moscow would more or less hold for the rest of Russia and that the Coase Theorem was applicable. Given the commonality of these attitudes, Russian stockholders would act like their U.S. counterparts.

Boycko *et al.* also took for granted that the existence of property rights automatically guaranteed that the state and the society would enforce those rights. This assumed that there was something like the "rule of law" and that the state would not be in a condition of near anarchy.

While events in Russia were to disprove these assumptions, the authors denigrated "a group of scholars commonly known as Sovietologists" who challenged their assumptions. They refer specifically to the book *Lost Opportunity* by Marshall I. Goldman and my reference to Schiller's study on page 18.[13] We skeptics had cautioned that the Moscow telephone sample conducted by Schiller, Boycko, and Korobov should not have been used as an example of public opinion because far fewer than 25 percent of the people living in Moscow at the time had access to telephones.[14] As of March 2000, the telephone penetration rate for Russia as a whole was still below 20 percent.[15] Nevertheless, Boycko *et al.* still insisted that "The experience of Russian privatization demonstrated how misguided…" those people were who warned that Russians were unaccustomed to a market economy.[16] Ironically, as Boycko *et al.* themselves say, for the Coase Theorem to work, there must be "an appropriate institutional structure in place."[17] In addition, as the economist Douglass North points out, it is not only formal institutions such as impartial courts, police and commonly practiced commercial laws that must be in place, but also informal norms and conventions.[18] But none of these institutions and norms were in place when Russia began its reforms.

Nevertheless, the belief of Gaidar and Chubais in the importance of creating private property and severing the link between the state and the economy led them to think that even though all of the necessary institutions were not in place, it was necessary to move forward quickly with the privatization effort. They argued that the best way to create the institutions necessary for an efficient market economy, and the ensuing benefits brought by the optimality of the Coase Theorem, would be to create private property owners out of the state managers and blue collar workers.[19] Shleifer and Vishny explained that "The architects of Russian privatization were aware of the dangers of poor enforcement of property rights." But the reformers predicted that institutions would come into being after private property was created rather than the other way around.[20] That is, the new owners would then fight to put in place the institutions they found missing. The proponents of privatization, explains Joseph Stiglitz, assumed that "Once restructuring had occurred, political pressures for competition and regulation would succeed. More broadly, privatization would set in motion a process of legal reforms that would eventually lead to an efficient system of corporate governance."[21] In a typical market economy that might indeed happen, but because Russia's transition has come slowly and the newly privatized factories had the same monopoly power that they had when they were fully state-owned, it did not. Georgy Skorov, formerly of the Institute of the United States and Canada of the Soviet Academy of Sciences, pointed out in 1996 that 75 percent of Russia's 6,000 most basic goods were supplied by a single producer.[22] In addition, in 1993 the Russian Mafia and other criminal groups were said to dominate over 50 percent of the country's enterprises–and liked it that way.[23] In other words, there were neither private nor state mechanisms in place to insure the protection of property rights.

As the founding oligarchs die, retire or begin to worry that someone less noble than they may muscle them aside, it might well be that they and the next generation of business people will begin to demand institutions and practice norms that will regularize laws and establish codes to protect their empires and their successors. But as we shall see in Chapter 11, while demands for such reforms are now beginning to appear, there is still something less than a groundswell, and many of the reforms that have been introduced have also been sidetracked.[24]

I

While outside advisors to Chubais may have been concerned with economic efficiency, to Chubais the overriding consideration was political–preventing a return to communism.[25] Moreover, privatization of Russian industry was influenced by the Russian underlying attitude to land reform–that is, the land belongs to the tiller or peasant. The corollary here would be that the factory belongs to the workers and managers. What this assumption ignores is the communist notion that both the land and the factories belong to the public at large. Land development and the industrial infrastructure created in days of the Soviet Union came into being as a result of the savings and investment that came involuntarily from the entire population. It was assumed, therefore, that privatization would provide immediate and ongoing benefits to everyone. However, unlike privatization in Poland, the Russian reforms failed to insure that, once in place, there would be substantial and continuing benefits for the country at large. (As we shall see in Chapter 6, few of the privatized enterprises with partial state ownership paid dividends and shared profits with the state.)

For privatization to succeed, various conditions have to be put in place. Joseph R. Blasi, Maya Kroumova, and Douglas Kruse enumerate some of them and we have added others:[26]

1 Privatization should facilitate further reform and build a constituency opposed to a return to communism.
2 Reform should be fair, honest, and as devoid of corruption or corrupting opportunities as possible.
3 Reform should lead to a more efficient operation and, if need be, restructuring and changes of management.
4 The reform should be simple and easy to implement.
5 All major interest groups should share in the distribution of property–that includes the general public and the state at large as well as the employees and the managers.
6 The market should be enhanced by privatization.
7 Privatization should be accompanied by an effort to facilitate the creation of new businesses and startups.
8 While sharing in the proceeds, the directors should not necessarily end up as the owners, and stock shareholders should not be too diffuse a group.
9 Provisions should be made for attracting new investment and possible foreign advice.
10 Foreign stockholders and advisors should be welcomed, but they should not be allowed a widespread takeover of ownership.
11 There should be a reduction in public sector borrowing.
12 The role of government in decision-making should be reduced.[27]

II

The actual privatization program fell far short of most of these goals. In part this was because of faulty design and inadequate understanding of the Russian economic environment. But in fairness to the architects of privatization, almost any design would have fallen short. The Russian social, political, and economic climate at the time was simply not ready. Seventy years of communism had created a setting that was hostile and likely to distort any privatization process.

In fact, initially, there seemed to be relatively little interest in the privatization effort. The first reactions to Gorbachev's decision in 1987 to allow cooperative and private businesses were unenthusiastic. Many Russians were wary; others feared a trick. Just a few months earlier Gorbachev had passed another decree proclaiming just the opposite–a crackdown on those who were selling goods they had not produced themselves. Some feared that if they came out from the shadows and traded openly as a private or cooperative business they might fall victim to yet another ideological shift in direction, something that had happened in Russia all too often.

This hesitancy was widespread. Interviewing both private and state taxi drivers at the time, we found that there was general agreement that only a few would opt to set up their own companies. Those who did we subjected to tire-slashing and other forms of harassment from the drive of the state-owned companies, who were determined to prevent new forms of competition. They called this the "red eye disease." Similarly, as I found when I visited a private farm in Sakhalin in June 1992, some peasants who attempted to set up their own farms experienced property damage and arson in the countryside and in urban areas.[28] Apartment dwellers were similarly hesitant, at least initially, to accept ownership of their apartments, even when the state offered them free of charge. Why would anyone assume responsibility for covering the expenses of common hallways and roofs? As one Muscovite told me, as long as he stayed as a rental tenant, the municipality or the factory would continue to bear such costs in exchange for a paltry rent. Moreover, if most of the other tenants in the building refused to become owners, the whole burden would then fall on only a few shoulders: a real-life version of game theory and the Prisoner's Dilemma.

In the beginning, factory directors and the workforce were equally hesitant. More than anyone else, the factory directors and the labor force knew how ill equipped most of the Russian industrial infrastructure was to compete in a market economy. Designed for a Cold War environment, the economy's overemphasis on machine tools and metallurgy and its concentration on the production of armaments and military hardware meant that few Soviet-era factories would be viable without the subsidization and support that came with central planning and an arms race. Who would want to assume financial responsibility for rust-belt-type assets? As the former Minister of Privatization in Poland put it, "It would not be easy to sell enterprises that nobody owns and nobody wants to people who cannot pay."[29]

Yet a small number of individuals saw that, in some cases, massive fortunes could be made overnight from Russia's plentiful natural resources, especially from its exportable raw materials such as petroleum and natural gas. It mattered not if the refineries were inefficient and the pipelines primitive. Oil and gas were tradable commodities for which the demand was great. And with the end of the Cold War, suddenly there were vast quantities of other items such as aluminum, titanium and steel available in Russia at prices far below those prevailing in world markets. Disregarding complaints about dumping, some of the more savvy operators, both domestic and foreign, came to appreciate that such exports could earn $1 billion or more a year. With costs low (the factories were basically free to the new owner and fewer and fewer factories bothered to pay wages to their workers and bills to their suppliers on time) most of the revenue earned was virtually pure profit. Even more tempting, since payment for the goods, especially exports, was coming from overseas purchasers, these funds were easily kept outside Russia.

Those who took advantage of these opportunities were a variety of groups. In some cases, this allowed those who had been operating underground in the Soviet Union to come out into the open and effectively launder the money that they had earned in the past but had been forced to hide. For example, while visiting Sakhalin I met a man who had been selling furs illegally out of the basement of a government building prior to 1987, but who had opened a street-level operation once it became legal to do so. Others came to appreciate that, if nothing else, some of the working capital and equipment could be stripped and resold. Failing that, they could always find some benefit in selling or leasing some of the underlying land. But at the time, there were still probably more skeptics than enthusiasts for the privatization process.

III

Gaidar and Chubais' task was to figure out how best to take these factories out of the hands of directors who were subordinate to the state and make them available and, indeed, desirable to private owners. It was a slow and not always linear process. As we saw, it began with Gorbachev making it legal for individuals to set up private and cooperative businesses. In the midst of the crackdown on middleman trading in 1985 and again on July 1, 1986, the Enabling Decree Authorizing Private and Cooperative Trading was passed by the Supreme Soviet on November 19, 1986, and became effective as of May 1, 1987.[30] In November 1989, the government authorized the leasing of state factory facilities to their employees during off-peak hours. By the time Gorbachev had left office, almost 30,000 such leases had been arranged,[31] and by 1992 13 percent of the country's industrial output was produced in leased factories.[32]

Although most of the privatization of state enterprises occurred while Chubais was Minister of Privatization and Boris Yeltsin was President, many of the initial laws were actually put on the books during the Gorbachev era. Most analysts commenting on Russian privatization only focus on what happened after late 1991, but the regulations passed by Gorbachev were instrumental in shaping the parameters and the environment in which the actual privatization took place. Initially, however, there was more legislation than action. The Supreme Soviet of the USSR, for example, passed a key law on "destatization" and privatization in July 1991.[33] The law authorized the various republics of the USSR to move at their own speed toward privatization. Responding, the RSFSR (which was later to become Russia) then adopted much the same statute, and also established two implementing agencies: the State Property Committee (Goskomimushchestvo, or the GKI), and the Russian Federal Property Fund (Rossiiskii Fond Federalnogo Imushchestva).[34]

The GKI moved immediately to create subordinate agencies in all of the republic's eighty-nine *oblasti* and regions. Their task was to divide the enterprises among the federation, the regions, and the local municipal authorities. More important, they were to prepare these enterprises for ultimate privatization. Before that could be done, however, the state enterprises were transformed into corporations; that is, they were converted into joint stock companies. However, since the state remained as the owner of the stock this step was just an enabling act. For the time being, that stock was turned over to the Property Fund to act as custodian for the state. From time to time the Property Fund was instructed to sell off or auction shares in various enterprises. In a number of cases, it disposed of all the shares, but more often the state retained some–in many cases, enough to control central management. Thus, the Ministry of the Gas Industry was transformed into Gazprom. Only gradually were some of its shares sold to staff members and ultimately to the general public. Even as late as 2002, the state retained 38 percent of the corporation's shares.

All of this legislation was on the books before November 1991 when Anatoly Chubais came on the scene and was made Chairman of the GKI, as well as the Minister of Privatization. By then it was clear that the USSR and Gorbachev's days were numbered and that Russia, with Yeltsin as president, would emerge as the dominant but independent member of whatever new entity evolved after the USSR's disintegration.

Effective doer that he was, Chubais moved quickly. Under his guidance Yeltsin issued a series of decrees on privatization in late December 1991 and January 1992. He was also instrumental in establishing the Russian Privatization Center in 1992,[35] that was designed to process technical assistance from international agencies such as AID (Agency for International Development), the World Bank, the European Bank for Reconstruction and Development, and the European Union, as well as process foreign grants and credits.[36] (Maxim Boycko, who worked closely with Chubais, served as the Center's managing director until July 1, 1996, during its most active years).

In his role as Chairman of GKI, Chubais designed and carried out the privatization effort. One of his first steps, during the first part of 1992, was to dispose of the state's small shops and restaurants. By late 1995, 60 percent of the country's retail stores had been privatized and, for the most part, turned over to the staff, often at no charge.

Disposal of the larger enterprises posed a greater challenge. Some of the more valuable enterprises, such as raw materials producers (petroleum), natural monopolies (electric utilities and telecommunications), and some of the armaments factories were excluded from the initial privatization program. That still left thousands of large enterprises. The task was to determine how to satisfy the qualms of the enterprise directors and staff and, at the same time, to provide some benefit or compensation for the public at large.

To reconcile these somewhat contradictory goals, Chubais operated on two separate tracks–one for the enterprise staff and the other for the public at large. Initially, on the principle that the land should go to the tiller, it was decided that the employees and directors (the insiders) would be entitled to a substantial share of their enterprise's assets. Once they had been taken care of, the remainder would be divided up among the general population. That division was done to insure support not only from the insiders, but also from the average man on the street: a form of "people's capitalism."

It was important, therefore, to limit how much ownership was allocated to the director and staff. As set out in the basic July 2, 1991 legislation of the RSFSR, the enterprise staff–both managers and regular employees–were to be provided with 25 percent of the enterprise's non-voting preferred stock free of charge.[37] Under Variant One, as this came to be called, a manager could also buy another 5 percent of the voting shares at book value, as well as 10 percent more of the voting shares at a 30 percent discount.[38] By taking advantage of these concessions, the staff would be able to control 15 percent of the voting and 25 percent of the non-voting stock.[39] Whatever was not claimed by the employees would be offered to the public at auction by the Property Fund, which could also buy some of the shares for itself. Thus, Variant One left open the possibility that outsiders could seize control, something not appreciated by the enterprise's insiders. This explains why only 17 percent of the country's managers and employees elected this procedure.

Concern about outsider takeovers sparked protests and lobbying by enterprise directors. Under the leadership of Arkady Volsky, the head of the Russian Union of Industrialists and Entrepreneurs and its strong representation in the Russian Supreme Soviet, opponents mobilized enormous pressure to expand the possible options. Volsky even joined forces with the Federation of Independent Trade Unions. As a result, Chubais faced criticism from groups representing both labor and management.[40] On March 31 Volsky warned that the country's workers would go out on strike unless the reforms were refashioned more to Volsky's liking.

These protests resulted in the passage by the Supreme Soviet of an expanded privatization law on June 11, 1992. It provided for two new options. Variant Two, the most widely adopted (by about 75 percent of the enterprises), was a surrender to the plant directors, a price Gaidar apparently had to pay for support in the Supreme Soviet for the passage of his privatization legislation.[41] The workforce was allowed to purchase 51 percent of the enterprise shares before those shares were made available to the public. Thus, as long as the staff remained united, this meant that no outside buyers could take control.

Theoretically, this could be rationalized as a tougher requirement than Variant One; in Variant Two, no shares were issued free of charge. That meant that both manager and staff would have to exercise their options, which entailed paying for the stock, which was offered not at the initial par value, but at 1.7 times book value as of July 1, 1992.[42] While this option might appear to be out of reach, once the twenty-six-fold price inflation of 1992 was factored in, the par value of stock prices was much understated. Moreover, payment could be made in cash or up to 50 percent and later 80 percent of the total in vouchers that were issued to the population.[43] Either way, it was argued that Variant Two was the best way of privatizing and, at the same time, assuring continued worker control. This satisfied both the Communist Party and the factory director faction in the Supreme Soviet.

Gaidar admits that the concession on Variant Two was a mistake. While generally insisting he would have not done things differently, he acknowledges that, were he to retrace his steps, he would have fought harder against such a measure. In retrospect it is clear that Variant Two ultimately allowed the factory directors to grab control and effective ownership of most of the country's factories at minimal cost to themselves, as well as minimal benefit to the public at large.[44] The managers were able to do this by buying up shares and vouchers of the workers, who sometimes sold them voluntarily and sometimes because of coercion. Since they were unaccustomed to coordinating their efforts even when the workers held on to the stock, most managers were able to prevent them from organizing against management.

Given the pressures on President Yeltsin at the time over what was regarded as a flawed set of reforms, it is probable that neither Gaidar nor Chubais would have been able to prevent authorization of Variant Two. At about the same time, Yeltsin, as we saw in Chapter 4, yielded to pressure from the Supreme Soviet and agreed reluctantly to appoint Viktor Chernomyrdin as Deputy Prime Minister. Chernomyrdin, a former industrial minister (Minister of the Gas Industry), was closely associated with Gazprom and other enterprise directors. His appointment was seen as a sop to Volsky and the other industrialists. At the same time, Gaidar himself, again against his better judgment (even though Gaidar told me earlier there is very little he would have done differently, he nonetheless has acknowledged that this was "the most serious of my mistakes in 1992"), agreed to fire Georgy Matyukhin, head of the RCB, regarded as a tight money man. He replaced him with Viktor Gerashchenko, who quickly accommodated the factory directors and the Supreme Soviet's demands for easier access to money.[45]

While Variant Two was the option of choice for most of the managers of larger enterprises, the June 11, 1992 law added a Variant Three intended mainly for small businesses. Variant Three also provided up to 20 percent of a company's shares of stock to the staff at no charge. If they wanted more, they could buy another 20 percent at a discount of 30 percent below par value, that could be purchased over a three-year period.[46] Because Variant Two seemed so much more advantageous, less than 5 percent of those firms being privatized chose Variant Three.[47]

IV

The three variants for privatization, as well as the decision to allow managers to buy businesses they had leased at pre-inflationary prices, were in essence a surrender to the country's factory directors. Although Chubais had sought to include the general public in these enterprises, if for no other reason than to generate political support for his program, his effort basically failed. Once Variant Two became an option, it was all but impossible to prevent a national buyout by factory directors since a voting majority of stock was guaranteed to them and the rest of the staff.

There was an additional advantage for those factory managers who had the foresight after 1989 to lease the factories back to themselves. The reason that lessors had an advantage was that the regulations authorized the lessors to acquire enterprise assets at the capitalized value of their annual lease payments. Since most of these leases had been arranged prior to the onset of the twenty-six-fold hyperinflation in 1992, capitalizing the leases at the pre-inflation rent was an enormous windfall. It meant that if the lessors decided to buy the property that they had been leasing since January 1, 1992 they would only have to pay the capitalized value of the January 1, 1992 rent, not the capitalized rent that on December 31, 1992 would have been at least twenty-six times higher. In 1993, about 30 percent of the businesses privatized had previously been leased.[48]

Whichever method of privatization was used, the new owners still had to find some way to fund their purchases. In the capitalist world, most managers seeking funds to buy up their companies would turn to their local bankers for a loan. Until 1987 however, all the banks in Russia were part of the state-owned network under Gosbank. There was no such thing as a loan for private entrepreneurs. Moreover, since such funds were provided automatically by Gosbank to meet the plan determined by Gosplan, few enterprise directors had much experience borrowing money on behalf of their enterprises. Almost overnight, individuals and organizations found that there were very profitable opportunities but only if they had access to some cash or funds.

While generally there was a severe shortage of funds, some individuals did have cash, if only for short periods of time. Many of these were traders who had found some way to import consumer good computers. Once they acquired those funds they began to look for put those funds to work. Matching up those with funds to tho... needed them occurred almost spontaneously out of the imperative of the moment. It turned out that virtually none of the reformers had anticipated there might be a need for such financial intermediation.[49]

That there were virtually no surplus funds available for use by prospective borrowers in the Soviet economic planning system was not unintentional. Like so much else in the Soviet era, it was a byproduct of the Soviet effort to prevent unauthorized activities that might lead to theft or private manufacturing or agriculture. The money supply was tightly regulated. In effect, it was divided into two categories. The first category was cash (*nalichnie*), which was turned over to enterprises so they could put rubles into the pay envelopes for their workers' wages and so the workers, in turn, could use those rubles for shopping or as payment for services and other daily life needs. The bulk of the country's money, however, was in the form of clearing accounts (*beznalichny*), money which could not be taken out of the Gosbank system; it was a form of virtual money. Enterprises simply instructed their branch of Gosbank to deduct the necessary amount from their clearing accounts and transfer it as payment to their suppliers. Since everything was produced according to plan (in theory at least), it allowed Gosplan and Gosbank to keep track of the plan and money flow–both cash and clearing accounts.

Gorbachev's attempt to encourage enterprise managers to show more initiative and depend less on the plan proved in retrospect to be a massive undermining of the Soviet economic system. As we saw, enterprise managers, beginning in 1987, were told that once they had fulfilled their planned targets, anything more they produced could be sold wherever they wanted, conceivably at a higher price. Nonetheless, few accepted such a challenge. While the manager could theoretically profit from producing more than called for in the plan, the state did not accept responsibility for finding the extra inputs and the extra skilled (or more expensive) workers that might be needed. Moreover, the few willing to take the risk had not only to find a supplier willing to sell and laborers willing to work, but also a lender willing to lend cash. (Clearing accounts on occasion could be used, but cash was clearly the preferred approach because it allowed for so many more possibilities.)

Despite these difficulties, these new opportunities gradually allowed the cash ruble (*nalichnie*) to come into its own. Ruble holders found that goods whose disposal was heretofore determined by the planners now could be purchased using those rubles. In effect, the ruble gradually became convertible–not just into foreign currency but into ordinary domestic goods, something taken for granted in the capitalist world but long denied Russian consumers.

Under the Gosplan and Gosbank system, enterprises were generally indifferent as to whether they had positive clearing accounts or cash balances.[50] There wasn't much that they could do with them, and the banks paid only a fraction of a percent interest on what they held for their depositors. Once the enterprise law was enacted, this was no longer the case. Those with positive cash balances (not only state enterprises but the newly authorized cooperative and private ventures that conducted most of their activities on a cash basis) and even those with clearing balances began to discover that they had something that others wanted and would even pay for: eventually this would be called interest.[51] Intermediaries came to see that they could play a role bringing together those with cash surpluses and those with cash needs. Some of the more sophisticated among them even began to take a more entrepreneurial function by offering to transform clearing accounts into cash balances, albeit at a substantial discount.[52]

For those of us born in a market economy and who take it for granted, the fact that this intermediation began to occur may not seem at all unusual. But given that the state remained in control of most of the country's assets, and that there were very few businesses and individuals with large disposable sums of money or goods, few people were willing or able to put together such transactions. Nevertheless, as we saw, beginning in the late 1980s, a series of commodity markets began to spring up all over the country to do just that. By 1993 Russia had over 1,000 such exchanges.[53] These stock exchanges, as they were sometimes called, were often nothing more than meeting places where individuals possessing something in excess could interact with individuals in need. The items exchanged ranged from nuts and bolts to trucks and food or access to rubles.

The intermediaries who were able to lend or re-lend rubles bore a strong family resemblance to bankers. So it was probably no coincidence that various cooperative groups with access to surplus rubles sought to set up their own banks. In turn, Gosbank issued new regulations that authorized the legal establishment of cooperative and commercial banks. In fact, some of the first commercial banks began to operate in 1988, even before the laws came into existence.[54] In May 1988, the law on cooperatives authorized cooperatives to form banks. Though there was no provision for non-cooperative groups to do so, according to Joel Hellman, Gosbank allowed it anyway. Finally, in August 1988, banks formed by something other than a cooperative were able to register and operate legally. Formal guidelines for doing so were issued on January 3, 1989.[55]

For those with ambition and ingenuity, it was a time of great opportunity. Opening a bank was relatively simple and cheap. Initially, each group forming a bank had to negotiate a specific arrangement with Gosbank (which inevitably meant bribes and connections). The capital requirements were only 500,000 rubles for a cooperative bank, the equivalent of about $750,000 in 1989, but because of inflation and devaluation of the ruble, only $75,000 in early 1990.[56] The minimum for a commercial bank was 5 million rubles ($7.5 million in 1989 and $750,000 in 1990), considerably more.

Where did this capital, even if relatively modest by Western standards, come from? Much of it came from the profits earned by the newly created cooperatives, some of which earned enormous sums of money quickly in an era of suddenly unleashed consumers. One of the first banks to be formed was the KIB NTP Zhilsotsbank (Commercial Innovative Bank) which was created on December 29, 1988. The founders were the Zhilsotsbank, which was a special state bank under Gosbank, and Menatep Associates, a cooperative made up of Young Komsomol League members who were graduates of the Mendeleeva Chemical Technical Institute.[57] A year earlier, in December 1987, this group of graduates had formed a cooperative which they called the Intersectoral Center of Scientific Technical Progress. In August 1988, after having become quite prosperous from selling computers and designing software, they set up the Interbank Organization for Scientific Technical Progress, Menatep for short, which in 1990 was adopted as the name of their bank.[58] Rumors abound that Menatep profits were supplemented by funds controlled by various Komsomol, Central Committee or even KGB groups which were eager to divert and thus privatize state funds for their own personal purposes.[59] Similar rumors ascribed fund laundering and reshuffling to almost all the newly funded banks.[60] Yevgeniia Albats at Harvard's Davis Center has provided me with a copy of a letter from Mikhail Gorbachev to V.V. Kulikov seeking suggestions for "transforming" Central Committee assets.

Anxious to share in the wealth of the new order, the directors of many state enterprises as well as their colleagues in the industrial ministries joined in this bank-creation frenzy. In 1994, while visiting Podolsk outside Moscow, a city officially closed to foreigners during the Cold War, we were taken to see Lutch, at one time an important factory in the Soviet Union's military-industrial complex. In the race for a missile defense system, Lutch had been a center for research on a Star Wars-type laser.[61] With the end of the Cold War, the management of Lutch attempted to involve itself more in the civilian sector, but it had trouble doing so. As part of their shift to commercial activities, Lutch agreed to join with other Soviet-era factories in establishing six different commercial banks. Among the banks it helped create were Commerzbank, an offshoot of the Ministry of Atomic Energy, for which Lutch had put up 11 percent of the capital. It also provided almost 10 percent of the capital for Inkombank and 35 percent for the Russian Bank for Reconstruction and Development. Rosbusinessbank, however, was their main interest. Lutch contributed 40 percent of that bank's capital, and the chairman of Lutch at that time devoted most of his attention to his new job as Deputy Chairman of that organization.[62]

Having created and staffed these banks, the founders naturally expected that they would address their needs, especially those generated by the privatization program. To finance their purchase of the newly issued stock in their companies, the enterprise directors relied heavily on the loans issued by these banks. In fact, given the inflation and instability of the times, few banks actually operated as normal commercial banks, soliciting deposits and issuing two- or three-year commercial loans. Russian banks seldom extended loans for more than six months at a time, except to insiders who used the funds to seize control of the enterprises they managed. Once the enterprise assets were privatized, the new owners would then use the enterprise's cash or assets to repay their loans. Consequently these banks were dismissed as "pocket banks" in the fashion of Gilbert and Sullivan, a reference to "pocket borough" seats in Parliament.[63]

V

While privatization ended up as a plum pudding delight for the factory directors and insiders, it must be said for Chubais that in late spring 1992 he also sought to include the general public in the giveaway. But how does one provide the general public with a share of the country's industrial and commercial wealth? Chubais did just that—he calculated the value of the country's industrial and commercial assets and divided it by the number of citizens in the country. He then issued each of them with vouchers worth their proportionate share. Essentially, this was the format of what became the country's voucher program. Gaidar and Chubais assumed that once the inside managers and workforce had purchased their stock, the remaining assets would be divided up and offered to the voucher holders. The calculation was relatively simple. Their expectation was that they would transform about 16,500 medium and large enterprises and that 35 percent of the book value of these enterprises would be set aside for the voucher holders.[64] Using very conservative estimates, they then calculated that the face value of each voucher should be set at 10,000 rubles.

Setting such a low value for the voucher was a mistake. Inflation continued to eat away at real values so that within a year or two 10,000 rubles was worth only about $25, and for a time voucher holders sold their vouchers for less than $10. Furthermore, most Russians viewed the 10,000-ruble voucher as an insult, even a swindle. The Soviet Union, in its rhetoric at least, had insisted that it was a proletarian society that supposedly belonged to the people, not to a few wealthy businessmen. Though, not everyone took such assertions seriously, after nearly six decades of five-year plans, with rich deposits of gas, oil, and other raw materials, and a GNP reported to be the world's second largest, it was hard to see how an individual's share in that wealth could be a mere 10,000 rubles. Just as after the various currency reforms that they had been subjected to since World War II, the Russians once more saw themselves as the victims of another scam.

The use of vouchers was not unprecedented. The Czechs had issued them in the first wave of voucher privatization from October 1991 to December 1992, a year before Russia adopted them. Larisa Piiasheva, then in charge of privatization in the City of Moscow, attempted to do something roughly comparable earlier, in 1990.[65] In her version, however, the vouchers were only intended for the employees of the specific firm. Prior to that, at the beginning of the Gorbachev era in 1985, the economist Vitaly Naishul was one of the first to design such a scheme.[66] Advisors to Solidarity in Poland subsequently discussed a similar concept in December 1988.[67]

After considerable planning and debate, Yeltsin announced Russia's voucher program on August 18, 1992. Ultimately, 146,064,000 Russians out of 148 million, over 98 percent of the population, ended up with a voucher.[68] The procedures were relatively simple.[69] From October 1, 1992 to December 31, 1992, those who wanted to could pick up a voucher from a branch of Sberbank, the country's savings bank system, for a nominal fee of 25 rubles. The subscription period was eventually extended to January 31, 1993. In the same way, the life of the vouchers, which was due to expire on December 31, 1993, was also extended through to June 30, 1994. Voucher holders were offered a variety of options. Because the vouchers were not registered, they could be sold on the market or exchanged for stock in newly privatized enterprises previously owned by the federal or regional governments and, eventually, even municipal governments.

After seventy years of being told that financial assets such as vouchers and shares of stock were worthless pieces of paper distributed by capitalists to create the illusion of wealth, most Russians had no idea of how much their vouchers were really worth or what they should do with them.

Recognizing that, several promoters, who promised immediate high dividends, convinced large numbers of holders to trade in their vouchers for a new share in what they called "voucher funds." The voucher funds then traded in the vouchers for shares of stock in the privatized enterprises and assumed they could then take the dividends they expected to receive as shareholders to pay their own promised dividends to their voucher fund shareholders. Holding shares in a voucher fund was also a way for the average Russian to diversify his or her investment. If one company failed, the voucher fund might suffer a bit, but the voucher fund would still hold shares in a variety of other companies, not all of which were likely to fail.

As of late February 1994, 620 such funds had been created, attracting 60 million vouchers.[70] But, within a few months, almost one-half of these funds had collapsed, leaving their shareholders with little to show for their original vouchers. A few, along with some mutual funds established at the same time, such as Chara or MMM, squandered their assets or were outright scams; the founders simply ran off with the assets.

The MMM Fund was one of the most flagrant examples. Through the use of skillful TV advertising, Sergei Mavrodi and his two brothers enticed 5 million people to invest in MMM by promising them that with high yields on their investment, they could fly off to exotic places like the tropical islands.[71] By taking the investment fund proceeds paid in by the most recent investors, he was able to pay high yields to earlier investors, "proving" that his promises were real. This of course served to attract even more investors eager to share in this "proven investment opportunity"–in the West this is called a Ponzi Pyramid. It works only as long as new investors can be found whose funds can be used to pay the high returns to the early investors at the top of the pyramid. According to some estimates, as many as 25 million Russian investors were swindled by such schemes.[72]

Even those that tried to operate honestly had a difficult time. Given the desperate state of the economy, few companies earned profits and those that did often masked their earnings to avoid paying taxes. Thus, there were few dividends for the voucher funds to redistribute. Moreover, because the managers were able to buy so much of their stock for themselves, by the time the first phase of the privatization effort had been completed, voucher funds were only able to gain control of about 5 percent of the stock issued by the Russian companies.[73] For most Russians, therefore, the voucher funds were another example of how ordinary Russians can be abused by the state and financial manipulators. This result helps explain why so many Russians (37 million) ignored the voucher funds and sold their vouchers for cash or a bottle of vodka. It also explains why so many Russians became increasingly distrustful of investment projects, whether initiated by private firms or by the government.[74]

VI

Once Chubais and Gaidar launched the voucher program, they then had to find an enterprise which would agree to be privatized for vouchers.[75] The GKI (The Property Committee) would in turn then organize an auction so that those with vouchers could bid for control. This would then serve as a model for similar auctions throughout the country, and also demonstrate that the vouchers did have a value. The challenge was to find managers in a state enterprise who were willing to allow their enterprise to be transformed by such a process and a group willing to organize the auction.

Chrystia Freeland describes Chubais' effort to hold such an auction before the December 1, 1992 Seventh Congress of People's Deputies, where the conservatives and communists were expected to undo the entire effort.[76] The Russian reformers turned for guidance to the European Bank for Reconstruction and Development (EBRD) which had been established to facilitate privatization and the development of markets in Russia and Eastern Europe. Acting on their advice, the reformers decided they should seek the talents of Western investment bankers who could draw on their considerable experience in privatizing companies in places such as the United Kingdom.[77]

Officials from the EBRD approached Credit Suisse First Boston (CSFB), asking them to help identify state enterprises that might be willing to serve as guinea pigs in the voucher privatization program. CSFB on its own was already deeply involved in the Russian market. Recognizing how grossly underrated and undervalued shares in Russian companies were, CSFB under Boris Jordan began to buy up those unappreciated vouchers in order to exchange them for that cheap stock. Jordan, then only twenty-six years old and a graduate of New York University, had grown up on Long Island in a family of former military officers and civil servants for the czar.[78] His family had fled Russia shortly after the Revolution.

Taking advantage of the millions of Russians eager to swap whatever they could get for their vouchers, CSFB managed to buy anywhere from one-eighth to one-fifth (7.5 to 14 million) of the newly issued vouchers.[79] With these vouchers, CSFB had already managed to gain control, or at least a voice in several of the properties set aside for privatization.

With only five weeks to find a volunteer enterprise and draw up auction procedures, both the GKI and CSFB moved quickly and ultimately successfully. They convinced the managers of a Moscow bakery, founded originally by the Swiss in 1855 and later renamed the Bolshevik Cake and Biscuit Factory, that privatization would materially reward them. The main inducement other than profit was that privatization would also free them from meddling by government agencies which continued to issue orders to its still partially state-owned subordinate.

Finally, on December 13, 1992, CSFB held the country's first voucher auction.[80] They sold 44 percent of the shares in what was reported widely as a success. Factory staff as well as outsiders were among the buyers. For example, under the direction of Mikhail Fridman the Alfa Fund purchased 10 percent of the shares. The completion of the sale paved the way for future voucherization auctions, and the Supreme Soviet did not reverse its commitment to privatization.

VII

While the GKI was struggling over the broad outlines of privatization, several municipalities decided to move on their own. They did so, but not always in step or agreement with the GKI. One of the first to act was Nizhny Novgorod. Boris Nemtsov, its young reform governor, called in Grigory Yavlinsky for advice. Rejected by Yeltsin as his economic czar in favor of Gaidar, Yavlinsky was eager to demonstrate that he could be an implementor and doer, not just a designer of economic plans. Working together, Nemtsov and Yavlinsky turned for help to the International Finance Corporation (IFC), an agency of the World Bank. Eager to advance the privatization effort with technical and financial support, the IFC readily accepted Nizhny Novgorod's invitation.[81]

Nizhny Novgorod moved quickly. The city council published its privatization regulations on March 3, 1992, several months before the Supreme Soviet agreed to its June 11, 1992 resolution. It announced that it would auction off retail, transport companies, and several small service organizations in the second half of 1992.[82] Whereas the Gaidar and Chubais design focused on privatizing existing state-owned enterprises, Nizhny Novgorod also encouraged brand new startups.[83]

The Moscow program also differed from the Chubais and Gaidar model. In fact, the differences later triggered a personal feud between Chubais and Moscow Mayor Yuri Luzhkov. But the differences also reflected Luzhkov's conviction that the new owners of these businesses should pay for their purchase and should not be given valuable property for such cheap vouchers. Because Luzhkov had supported President Yeltsin in the standoff with the Supreme Soviet in October 1993, Yeltsin eventually agreed in May 1994 to let Luzhkov carry out privatization in his own way in Moscow, exempt from Chubais' control.[84]

Moscow was filled with rumors about Mayor Luzhkov's cutting of corners and use of the privatization process to favor family and friends. For example, Luzhkov ordered all the city's soccer stadiums to equip themselves with plastic seats made by Inteko, his wife's plastics factory.[85] Luzhkov was also said to have a significant interest in Sistema, one of the country's most successful conglomerates with vast holdings in the telecommunications and electronics industry.[86] Protesting his innocence, the mayor successfully sued many of those who made such assertions. Moreover, he proudly noted that in 1994 the City of Moscow collected 1.5 trillion rubles (about $344 million) from the privatization process, whereas privatization in all the rest of Russia brought in only 1 trillion rubles.[87] So he asked, who, Chubais or Luzhkov, was guilty of the most giveaways?

VIII

On paper, the results of the privatization drive were very impressive. The architects of the program, particularly Chubais and his advisors, Boycko, Shleifer, Vishny, Treisman, Layard, Parker, and Aslund, have pointed with pride at what they considered to be the most impressive achievement of the whole reform package.[88] To them, privatization was impressive not only in terms of the number of enterprises privatized, but because privatization made the market in Russia a permanent fixture. Is their enthusiasm warranted?

There is no doubt that economic reform and privatization have made Russia very different from the Soviet Union. At a minimum, the shelves are full, the stores are more solicitous of customers, foreigners are a substantial presence, and there are more private businesses than state businesses. However different it might be from markets in the West, Russia is a market economy. Central planning and Gosplan are relics of the past.

Once set in motion, the transformation from state enterprise to private enterprise took place rapidly; some might say too rapidly. Joseph Stiglitz has likened it to "the Bolsheviks" who "tried to impose communism on a reluctant country in the years following 1917."[89] Over 46,000 businesses were privatized in 1992, almost half in the fourth quarter of the year.[90] The pace in 1993 was almost as fast. By late 1995, 122,000, or more than one-half of Russian businesses, had become private (see Table 5.1).

Table 5.1 Number of privatized businesses by public sector and year

	1993	*1994*	*1995*
Municipal	26,340	11,108	6,960
Regional	9,521	5,112	1,317
Federal	7,063	5,685	1,875
Total	42,924	21,905	10,152

Source: Goskomstat Rossii, *Rossiiskii Statisticheskii Ezhegodnik* (Russian Statistical Report), Moscow: Goskomstat, 1996, p. 702.

Since the change was so rapid there were bound to be abuses. The early 1990s saw the creation of the very new and very rich. Enormously valuable assets were theirs for the taking. With so much upheaval and relatively little control, it was not surprising that there would be theft on a massive scale, or, as I call it, "piratization." The reformers were so busy patting themselves on the back for fulfilling their goals; they failed to notice that in actual fact they had created a monster.

Chubais and his fellow reformers believed they had accomplished their most important goal–the prevention of a return to communism. Part of that effort involved creating as many stakeholders as possible. Moreover, because of their faith in the Coase Theorem, they continued to believe that even if unsuitable managers ended up as directors or owners, sooner or later they would be swept aside in the desire for a higher return on assets.

Chubais had good reason to fear there would be efforts to abort the privatization process. For example, Gennady Zyuganov, the head of the Communist Party, did all that he could to obstruct the reforms and, along with Arkady Volsky, he demanded a larger role for the workforce and managers. But a case can also be made that while there might have been some threat of counterrevolution and a return to communism, the odds of that happening after the implosion of the Soviet Union were not as high as Chubais and others imagined. Most of the hostility to the reform process, especially in the attempted takeover of the White House in October 1993, was due in a much greater degree to the sharp drop in production and consumption and the runaway inflation.

In December 1992 opponents of reform managed to convince Yeltsin that he should fire Gaidar. Unhappy with the collapse of the economy, they ridiculed Gaidar's efforts, characterizing him and his team as "urchins in pink shorts and yellow sneakers."[91] But that was primarily a response to Gaidar's refusal to relax credit restrictions and provide more state support. After a steady drumbeat of such criticism, in December 1992 Yeltsin decided to replace Gaidar with Chernomyrdin. Nonetheless under Chernomyrdin the pace of privatization was almost as fast in 1993 as it had been in 1992.

While the number of privatized firms was taken as a measure of success, a closer look suggests that behind that facade many problems persisted which privatization did not eliminate or resolve. It was assumed, for example, that with privatization, enterprise managers would give more serious attention to economic efficiency and profits. But nothing was done to break up the monopoly of power that was an integral feature of most Soviet-era enterprises. Since the state owned all of the means of production, Soviet planners assumed they could gain economies of scale by concentrating production in extraordinarily large enterprises. "Gigantomania," they called it. In 1988, for example, 16.6 percent of all Soviet factories had a workforce of 1,000 or more employees compared to 2.4 percent in all of West Germany's factories.[92] Not surprisingly, private monopolies did not behave much differently from state monopolies, particularly when the state continued to hold shares in the now ostensibly "private" entity. Yet, it is unfair to attribute the drop in production in the first half of the 1990s only to the monopolization of so much of the privatized sector. There were other macroeconomic problems, such as the inability to offset the collapse of the country's military-industrial complex and curb galloping inflation. For all of these reasons, in mid-1996 over 40 percent of the country's enterprises operated at a loss.[93] Privatization alone was evidently not enough to ensure efficiency.

Another shortcoming in the first round of privatization was that it generated very little in the way of revenue, either for the government budget or the firm's balance sheet and capital. Based on my unofficial estimates, the state collected a mere $160 million during the first three years of privatization (see Table 5.2).[94] Only in 1997, long after the expiration of the voucher program, was any effort made to make the new owners pay for what they acquired. Still, complaints about giveaways and inside dealings persisted and were widespread.[95] Despite the privatization of some of the country's most valuable assets (see Table 5.2), according to my calculations, from 1992 to 1999, the government managed to collect only about $6 billion. In effect, two-thirds of the country's companies were given away or seized at prices far below their market value.

The looting was not limited to the privatization process. For almost a decade the state received little in the way of dividends or rent on the stock that it continued to hold in the five most important companies–Gazprom, UES, LUKoil, Almazy Rossii-Sakha, and Transneft. Nonetheless, compared to the country's other companies, these five were relatively generous. They provided 86 percent of the state's dividends. Another twenty-four companies paid 10.3 percent of the dividends, and 244 others generated a mere 3.7 percent.[96] Combined, this amounted to a shocking total of only $113 million in 1998, and about $250 million in 1999 (see Table 5.2).[97] Measured against what we set out as the goal of privatization, the Russian effort was not very successful.

Of all the shortcomings, however, the failure to prevent Soviet-era or "red" factory directors from taking over ownership and control was probably the most serious long-term failing. This takeover, which all but precluded structural change, especially of management, was a direct consequence of the agreement to add Variant Two to the privatization options. This option essentially allowed insiders to seize control of the

Table 5.2 Receipts from privatization of federal enterprises, dividends, and rent from government-owned shares (millions, 1998 Rubles and U.S. Dollars)

	1992		1993*		1994		1995		1996		1997		1998		1999	
	Rubles	*$US*	*Rubles*	*$US*	*Rubles*	*$US*	*Rubles*	*$US*	*Rubles*	*$US*	*Rubles*	*$US*	*Rubles*	*$US*	*Rubles*	*$US*
Privatization	18	80	60	26	114	52	5,700	1,253	1,100	198	18,078	3,172	15,443	813	8,486	333
Rent on Federal Govt. property	–	–	–	–	–	–	96	21	223	40	305	54	1,672	139	2,165	85
Dividends on Federal Govt.-owned shares	–	–	–	–	–	–	115	25	119	21	271	48	1,357	113	6,510	255
Total	18	80	60	26	114	52	5,911	1,299	14,412	259	18,654	3,274	18,472	1,065	17,161	673

Source: Ekonomika i Zhizn', December 2000, no. 49, p. 3

*Estimated

enterprises they managed, and they were not going to fire themselves. Precise data about shareholdings are not available, but according to one survey, non-government outsiders held only 13 percent of the shares of 312 privatized companies and just one-quarter of those shares was owned by individual private citizens.[98] Another survey reports that "When voucher-based privatization ended (and the ministries of the Former Soviet Union disbanded), half of the enterprises had no outside shareholders at all, and two-thirds of them had no outside shareholders on their boards of directors."[99] An official study by the Federal Securities Committee, theoretically Russia's counterpart of our Securities and Exchange Commission, reported that as of 1996, 65 percent of Russian companies were owned by insiders–that is, staff or managers.[100] Only 17 percent was effectively owned by outsiders with a controlling majority, and in 16 percent of the country's enterprises, there were no majority owners. Along the same lines, Blasi, Kroumova, and Kruse found that management controlled 25 percent of the companies' stock in 1994, 15 percent in 1995, and 18 percent in 1996.[101] In addition, non-managerial employees owned about 40 percent. All combined, insiders controlled about 60 percent of the stock. Since the non-managerial staff was generally unorganized, this usually meant that in addition to controlling operations, the managers acted as *de facto* owners.

As for the state, it remains the majority owner in 2 percent of the companies. Moreover, the state held on to 10 percent or more of the stock in most of the newly privatized companies. In some of the largest companies, however, the state retained a substantially larger share. Thus, as of 1999, it maintained 100 percent ownership in 382 companies, over 50 percent in 470, 25 to 50 percent in 1,601, and less than 25 percent in 863.[102] Since the state seldom took an active role in management, the directors usually had an easy time running the company as they saw fit. As a consequence, there was little incentive to seek efficient operation. Such behavior was not anticipated by believers in the Coase Theorem.

Gazprom, Russia's largest producer of natural gas, is one of the prime examples of how this absentee government ownership and lack of outside directors allowed the management to treat a company as a cash cow for their personal projects. As the government with its 38 percent ownership stood by passively, the management set up numerous sister entities reportedly owned by relatives.[103] One such company, ITERA, with headquarters in Jacksonville, Florida, of all places, became the third largest natural gas producer in Russia and the main supplier of natural gas to Ukraine and several other former Soviet republics. ITERA bought gas from Gazprom at the low transfer price of $2.20 to $5.20 per 1,000 cubic meters–a loss for Gazprom–and sold that same gas for $40 to $80 per 1,000 cubic meters, thus providing enormous profits for ITERA and the pockets of its owners, whoever they may be.[104] (For more about ITERA, see Chapter 6.)

This stripping of assets from Gazprom through transfer pricing is not atypical and undercuts the proponents of immediate privatization who argued that privatization would prevent asset stripping. In fact, asset stripping, or "spontaneous privatization," as it was called, was set in motion by the Gorbachev-era reforms, especially leasing and the legalization of "semi-private cooperatives."[105]

Supporters of the privatization plan, such as Daniel Treisman, defend themselves along the following lines: "Yeltsin's lieutenants might have tried to control prices and hold off privatization for another year or two, *as Ukraine did* [emphasis added]. But Ukraine's subsequent inflation and asset stripping were even more severe than Russia's."[106] Fair enough, but it is not just that Ukraine wasted a year or two. The Ukrainians waited longer and, for that matter, showed no real commitment to reform any time during the 1990s. That meant not only no privatization but no price reform. More to the point, what is never mentioned in these comparisons is Poland. There they did wait four or five years, with very little in the way of asset stripping, and when they finally began to privatize they were remarkably successful: a model for what Russia should have done (see Chapter 10).

One of the reasons that Russia's economic reforms failed while Poland's succeeded may be due less to plan design or leadership and more to the fact that Poland is relatively poor in resource endowment, while Russia is incredibly rich. Except for coal, which was not very much in demand, Poland had much less to steal or, as an economist might put it, much less rent to seek. By contrast, with all its natural gas, oil and ferrous and non-ferrous metals, Russia had much to steal. Certainly there were other factors, but with all that wealth suddenly set aside for the taking, there were a small number of perceptive Russians who saw what was happening and decided that they better take their share and become rent seekers before someone less deserving decided to do the same thing.

It is ironic, but more often than not Russia's wealth has been a curse rather than a blessing. In contrast to countries like Japan and Switzerland which do not possess such endowments, the Russians with their wealth of resources felt less need to work intensively. The Swiss and the Japanese had no choice but to work hard.

IX

Measured against the goals we set out earlier in the chapter, what kind of judgment can we make about the Russian reform? There were only a few observers at the beginning of the twenty-first century who would describe Russia's economic reforms as effective or fairly carried out, or as an honest process devoid of corruption. Whatever restructuring or new investment that occurred prior to 1998 was modest at best.

True, as the jockeys Chubais and Gaidar intended, the role of the government in decision-making has been reduced and the market, or what passes for the market in Russia, has more impact today on economic behavior than state planners. Nor has Russia reverted to communism. Moreover, after a turbulent decade and countless lost opportunities, the Russian economy in 1999 did finally begin to grow. However even then this growth was due more to a tripling in the price of Russian oil exports and a radical devaluation of the ruble (effectively cutting imports by 50 percent and thus providing an opportunity for domestic producers) than to shock therapy reforms and intentional policy choices.

But even with this belated growth, by most every other economic measure, privatization has failed. Equally important, the move to the market has been tainted by the corruption and emergence of a dishonest oligarchy that probably still controls over 50 percent of Russia's economic activity.[107] (Allegations that two of the main U.S. consultants to the privatization officials were actively lining their pockets with insider information did nothing to enhance the effort to lessen corruption and curb political influence. See *The United States District Court, District of Massachusetts, United States of America, Plaintiff v. The President and Fellows of Harvard College, Andrei Shleifer, Jonathan Hay, Nancy Zimmerman, and Elizabeth Hebert, defendants*, Civil Action 00cv11977dpw, September 26, 2000.) Admittedly, there is no sure way to determine whether, in the absence of the privatization effort, the communists would have again seized power and brought back five-year plans and state ownership. Granted communists were returned to power in Poland for a time, but Poland continued with the privatization effort. In any event, there are few who would insist that there was no room for improvement in Russia's privatization effort. Nor did the reforms do much to advance the cause of further reforms. If anything, for many years they sullied the reform process, impeded other reform efforts, and gave rise to a multitude of dysfunctional economic and anti-social behavior.

6   The *nomenklatura* oligarchs

In any other country it would be a paradox. As Russia's Boris Yeltsin and Prime Minister Sergei Kiriyenko pleaded with world leaders in July 1998 to pressure the IMF to lend it $20 billion for a financially strapped Russia, *Forbes Magazine* released its list of the world's wealthiest 200.[1] For the first time it included five Russian businessmen. Even more unprecedented, ten years earlier none of these new rich had a net worth of any significance.

Four of the Forbes Five plus ten of Russia's richest and most influential "oligarchs," which they also called themselves, were summoned to a series of meetings with Kiriyenko on August 15 and 16, 1998. He felt it necessary to ask their help in dealing with Russia's economic problems, which were on the verge of metastasizing into a financial meltdown. Ironically this was just a few weeks after Kiriyenko had vowed that he would not involve himself with the oligarchs that everyone had come to call "the third government." Who were these oligarchs, and how did they become so wealthy in such a short time? The emergence of these new billionaires is all the more impressive given the fact that as recently as 1987 anyone in Russia engaging in private business risked arrest for committing an economic crime.[2] Table 6.1 provides examples of oligarchic empires.

Considering how quickly the various oligarchs accumulated their wealth, it was inevitable that there would be rumors about involvement with criminal activities and Mafia-like tactics. A CIA study, for example, asserted that ten of Russia's twenty-five largest banks owned by the oligarchs including Menatep were linked to organized crime.[3] At the other extreme, some were alleged to be linked to the KGB. Vladimir Gusinsky, who was particularly sensitive about such allegations, successfully threatened suit against several publications for reporting that he had an unusually large number of former KGB agents on his staff.[4] (For a time, he also threatened me with a related suit.) Some also wondered why a former Deputy Minister of the Petroleum Industry such as Vagit Alekperov or the

Table 6.1 Business holdings of selected Russian oligarchs

	Oligarchs	Primary financing institutions	Primary industries	Primary subsidiaries
Gazprom	Rem Vyakhirev, until May 30, 2001	Gazprombank, National Reserve Bank, Imperial Bank, Sovfintrade Bank, Olympic Bank, Sogaz Insurance Company, Gazfond Pension Fund, Gorizont Investment Co.	Gazprom, Gazexport, Mezhregiongaz, ITERA, Gazmash Corporation, Ascot Corporation (Cherepovez)	Newspapers: *Rabochaya Tribuna* and *Trud*; Magazines: *Profile, Companiya, Oil and Gas Vertical, Factor.* Telecommunication companies: *NTV Network*
LUKoil	Vagit Alekperov	Imperial Bank, Petrokommertz Bank, Nikoil Investment Co., LUKoil-Garant Pension Fund, LUKoil-Reserve Investment Co., CK-LUKoil Insurance Co.	LUKoil, Arkhangelsk Geology	Newspapers: *Izvestiia*; Magazines: *Russian Oil*; Telecommunication companies: TV-31, REN-TV, TV-6, TCN
Interros-Onexim	Vladimir Potanin	Oneximbank, MFK Bank, Baltoneximbank, Alfa-Alliance Bank, Renaissance Capital Investment Co., East Investment Co., Swift Investment Co., Interrossoglasie Insurance Co., Renaissance Insurance Co., Interros-Dostoinstvo Pension Fund	Sidanko, Russia-Petroleum, Norilsk Nickel, Holding Corp. Oboronitel'nie Sistemy, Severnie Ver, Baltiskii Zavod, Permskie Motory, OKB Sukhogo, Novolipetskii Steel Plant Co., Northwest Shipping	Newspapers: *Izvestiia, Komsomolskaia Pravda, The Russian Telegraph Newspaper*; Magazines: *Expert*

Continued

	Oligarchs	Primary financing institutions	Primary industries	Primary subsidiaries
Khodorkovsky	Mikhail Khodorkovsky	Menatep Bank, "Menatep St. Petersburg" Bank, "Russkie Investory" Investment Co.	YUKOS, Eastern Piping Co., Omskshina Tire Factory, Apatit Voskresenskie Mineral Fertilizers, Volzhskii Pipe Factory, Nitron Corp., Murmansk Ocean Steamliners, Volgotanker	"Independent Media" Publishing House
Inkombank Group	Vladimir Vinogradov	Inkombank, Reso-Garantia Insurance Company	Bakery Holding Babayevskii, Rot-Front Corp., Novosibirskii Fat Processing Factory, Omskii Bacon, Sameko Magnitogorskii Semi-Precious Metals Co., Sukhogo Corp., Baltiskii Zavod, Severnie Ver Morskaya Tekhnika Corp.	Newspapers: *Novaya Gazeta*, *Vek*
Berezovsky and Smolensky	Boris Berezovsky, Alexander Smolensky	SBS/Agro Bank, Agroprombank, Zolotoplatinabank, Obiedinennyi Bank, KOPF Bank, STS Insurance Company, Dobroe Delo Pension Fund	"Sibneft" Corp., Eastern-Siberian Oil and Gas Company, Aeroflot, "Dragotsennosti Urala" Corp.	Kommersant Publishing House; Newspapers: *Nezavisimaya Gazeta*, *Novie Izvestiia*, *Rossiiskie Vesti*, *Obshchaya Gazeta*; Magazines: *Ogoneok*; Telecommunication companies: ORT, TV-6, NSN

Continued

	Oligarchs	Primary financing institutions	Primary industries	Primary subsidiaries
"Rossisky Kredit" Bank Group	Dmitry Lyubinin	Rossiiskii Kredit Bank, Metalex Bank, PK-Garant Insurance Company, NPF Banka Rossiskii Kredit Pension Fund	Mikhailovskii State-Owned Enterprise, Smolenskii State-Owned Enterprise, Lebedinskii State-Owned Enterprise, Tulachermet, Orlovskii Steel Rolling Factory, Beshetskii Steel Rolling Factory, Plitspichprom, Krasnoyarskii Aluminum Factory, Achinskii Brick Plant, TANAKO Corp.	n/a
"Consortium Alpha-Group"	Mikhail Fridman, Peter Aven	Alpha-Bank, "Alpha-Kapital" Investment Firm	Tyumen Oil, Holding Alpha-Cement, Holding Kyban'-Sakhar, Nikitin Corp., Akrikhin Pharmaceutical Company, Borovskii Glass Factory, Western-Siberian Steel Plant, Achinskii Brick Plant	n/a

	Oligarchs	Primary financing institutions	Primary industries	Primary subsidiaries
Group MOST	Vladimir Gusinsky	MOST-Bank, Insurance Group "Spasskie Vorota"	Moscow Fuel Company, "MOST-Development"	Newspapers: *Segodnya, Sem' Dnei, Obshchaya Gazeta;* Magazines: *Itogi;* Radio station: "Echo Moskvy;" Telecommunication companies: NTV, NTV+; Film Companies: NTV-Profit, NTV-Mir Kino
AFK "Sistema"	V.P. Evtushenko, Yuri Luzhkov	Moscow Reconstruction and Development Bank Insurance Company, Leader Insurance Co., Inkastrakh Insurance Co.	Electronic Industrial Enterprises in Zvenigorod (including Micron, Kvant, and possibly Angstem, Elion Elaks), Mobilnie Telesistemy, Rosiko, Radiopager, MTU-Inform, Nedra, Kedr-M, Businovskii Meat Processing Plant, Intourist Hotel, Sputnik Hotel	Newspapers: *Vechernaya Moskva, Literaturnaya Gazeta;* Radio stations: "Rossiia," "Kultura," "Govorit Moskva," "M-radio," "Avtoradio," "Sportivnoe Radio;" Telecommunications companies: TV-Center, TV-Stolitsa

Source: Ia. Sh. Pappe, *Oligarchs, Economic Chronicle 1992–2000,* Gosudarstvennyi Universitet, Vysshaia Shkola Ekonomiki Moscow, 2000, pp. 206–10.

former Deputy Minister of the Gas Industry, Rem Vyakhirev, should end up owning so much of what they formerly supervised.

This transfer of so much wealth from the state into the hands of so few in such a short time seems unprecedented. The bulk of this new wealth came from the expropriation of what had been state property. Relatively little oligarchic activity led to the creation of new productive entities. The Russian oligarchs, unlike America's Andrew Carnegies, Henry Fords, Bill Gateses, or even John D. Rockefellers, did not give birth to new enterprises or technologies.

The collapse of communism and the start of privatization precipitated a chaotic and potentially explosive time. Without any government regulations in place for dealing with private businesses and markets (all existing regulations were designed for state enterprises), and with no already entrenched business competitors, there were no limits to what entrepreneurial buccaneers could achieve, assuming of course that they could find ways, both legal and illegal, to provision themselves. But this is something that several of the future oligarchs had learned to do well in the environment of shortage that characterized the planning era. That experience helps to explain how in addition to those who simply privatized the whole or part of a government ministry, a few individuals could start out with so little and accumulate so much in such a short period of time. Of course, the absence of effective state regulation also meant that they had to fend for themselves against criminal and Mafia groups as well as the limited number of rival marauders who embarked on the same path of acquisition.

I

There were three main categories of new Russian oligarchs: former factory managers, former senior members of the communist-era *nomenklatura*, and those who prior to 1987 were on the margin of Soviet society. Though a few in this third category were university-trained, at the time they would generally have been characterized as being more outside than inside the establishment and in several cases outside even the law. Some indeed had been charged with economic crimes and a few had even served time in jail. That they grew so wealthy so rapidly, despite or because of their previous low social standing, provides us with some fascinating insights into the privatization process.

The most common "New Russians," as they were also called, especially those who assumed ownership in medium and smaller businesses, were factory and business managers in the Soviet era. This put them in positions in the post-Soviet era to acquire a majority of their enterprise's shares. Taking advantage of the fact that their employees, with their newly issued shares of stock, were seldom well organized, most factory directors were able to manipulate proxy contests so that they could dominate the makeup of the board of directors. In some cases, the factory directors simply bought up the shares from their employees. On occasion, some directors coerced their employees to sell them their shares with threats to fire those who didn't.

Vladimir V. Kadannikov and **Nikolai A. Pugin** are examples of factory directors who became the principal stockholders in their companies. After graduating from the Gorky Polytechnical Institute, Mr. Kadannikov went to work for the Gorky Automobile Plant (GAZ). In 1967, Kadannikov moved to the Volga Automobile Plant in Tolyatti, which produced the Zhiguli, or Lada. After privatization, he became the President and Chair of the Board of what was to become the Avtovaz Joint Stock Corporation. In much the same way, Mr. Pugin, also a graduate of the Gorky Polytechnical Institute, served as the Director of GAZ from 1981 to 1983. He subsequently served as the Minister of the Automobile and Agricultural Machinery Ministry in Moscow from 1986 to 1988, but returned to Gorky, renamed Nizhny Novgorod, where he again took over GAZ, but that time as President of the GAZ Joint Stock Company. Although he was in Moscow during the privatization process, and thus did not partake in the initial allocation of enterprise stock, he made up for his absence when he returned as Plant Director and by 1995 he was, he told me, the enterprise's largest stockholder.[5]

As owners they had the opportunity to run a productive enterprise and, when opportune, strip assets from their own factories and divert them to build up their personal net worth. On the whole, their wealth was localized. Most former factory directors limited themselves to their specific factories and did not qualify to enter the ranks of the super rich. Some also joined together to create regional banks which were then used as personal loan funds to provide the money they needed to buy up the workers' shares. Since they lacked banking skills or failed to bring in those with banking skills, many of these banks and their oligarch owners failed quickly or were absorbed by larger Moscow banks in the aftermath of the various financial panics, such as Black Tuesday, October 11, 1994, or Black Monday, August 17, 1998. By 2002, GAZ had come under control of another oligarch, Oleg Deripaska.

II

The second category of oligarchs consists primarily of former members of the Communist elite, the so-called *nomenklatura*. Typically they had been senior officials in a government ministry or regional industrial administration. Sensing the opportunity, these officials arranged for the transformation of several state enterprises into non-state joint stock companies and then appointed themselves as managing officers. On the surface, this was not much different from the factory directors who gained control of enough vouchers to make themselves the effective owners. The difference, however, is that these former *nomenklatura* were able to gain control of Russia's rich resource endowments, even though for a time at least the state retained a significant equity. In some cases the state continued to be the controlling stockholder. But because the state usually did not exercise its rights, the managers generally could disregard the state's interests as a stockholder and act as they pleased. In the case of Gazprom, for example, the state was passive until 2001. In these circumstances, most of these managers quickly realized that they could benefit more by stripping the parent company's assets and diverting them to companies owned more directly by these insiders and their relatives. As a result, the executives of these newly and partially privatized companies often ended up among the country's richest oligarchs.

Two prime examples of one-time bureaucrats turned oligarchs are **Rem Vyakhirev** and **Viktor Chernomyrdin**. Of all the oligarchs, Mr. Vyakhirev and Mr. Chernomyrdin are perfect prototypes of what were Soviet *apparatchiki*. They not only acted the part, but with their slightly overweight demeanor, they looked the part. They were also the two main oligarchs who were born before World War II. With the exception of Boris Berezovsky, who was born in 1946, all the others we will discuss were born after 1950.

The influence of Vyakhirev and Chernomyrdin derived from their stewardship of the former Ministry of the Gas Industry, which they subsequently privatized into Gazprom. This natural gas monopoly at the time controlled not only the production fields but also the natural gas pipelines in Russia. Overall Gazprom held at least one-quarter and perhaps one-third of the world's natural gas reserves. This exceeded the energy reserves controlled by Exxon Mobil eight-fold and its natural gas output nine-fold.[6] Gazprom generated 7 percent of Russia's GDP, one-fifth of Russia's export revenues and 20 percent of the country's tax revenue.[7] It supplied 24 percent of all the gas sold in Western Europe. That total included $3.5 billion a year in sales to Germany representing 37 percent of the gas it consumed annually.[8] In 1999, 28 percent of Gazprom's exports went to Germany, 16 percent to Italy and 11 percent to France.[9] In 2001, total yearly revenues exceeded $20 billion, of which $15 billion came from exports outside the former USSR.[10]

Born in 1934 in the Samara region to obviously dedicated Communists (his first name, REM, stands for Revolution, Engels, and Marx), Rem Vyakhirev ran Gazprom from 1992 until 2001. After graduating from the

Kuibyshev Polytechnical Institute, he went to work at oil and natural gas drilling sites in Samara (then called Kuibyshev), Orenburg, and Tyumen. Moving up through the ranks, Mr. Vyakhirev became First Deputy Minister of the Gas Industry in 1983 and served under Chernomyrdin, then Minister of the Gas Industry.[11]

Four years younger than Vyakhirev, Viktor Chernomyrdin was born in 1938 in a small village near Orenburg. He worked as a fitter at the Orsk oil refinery in 1957, and after his army service, he also entered the Kuibyshev Polytechnical Institute, graduating in 1966.[12] After another stint at the Orsk refinery, he moved into party and administrative work, where he was assigned to the industrial department of the Orsk City Communist Party. After completing an engineer-economist correspondence course offered by the Kuibyshev Polytechnical Institute in 1972, Chernomyrdin in 1973 was appointed Deputy Engineer of the Orenburg gas refinery and promoted to Director in 1978. He then moved to Moscow and served as an instructor at the Central Committee of the Communist Party from 1978 till 1982, when he was appointed Deputy Minister of the Gas Industry and then, in 1985, Minister.

Given the trend of the Gorbachev reforms in the late 1980s, Chernomyrdin realized that he had better transform the Ministry into a single joint-stock company before someone else broke it up into several entities. He wanted to avoid what subsequently happened to the country's petroleum sector. In August 1989, he took the Ministry of Gas Industry's assets involved in the production, processing and shipping of natural gas and created a separate state entity, which he called Gazprom. This was the first hybrid state–corporate enterprise. The state was still the sole owner, but ownership now took the form of shares of stock, 100 percent of which remained with the state. Accordingly, Chernomyrdin switched his title from Minister of the Gas Industry to Chairman of Gazprom's Board of Directors and its CEO.

Under pressure to add someone to his government with more practical experience in industry, Yeltsin made Chernomyrdin Deputy Prime Minister in May of 1992, under the then Acting Prime Minister Yegor Gaidar. With the continuing decline of the economy, Yeltsin ousted Gaidar and in December 1992 put Chernomyrdin in his place as Prime Minister. When Chernomyrdin was appointed Deputy Prime Minister, Vyakhirev moved up as the Chairman of the Board of the Council of Directors and Chairman of the Management Board of Gazprom.

Without concern for issues of conflict of interest, Chernomyrdin continued to promote the well-being of his former company. Unlike the oil-producing companies, which were divided into several entities, Gazprom remained a monopoly, controlling both its pipelines and producing fields. With Chernomyrdin serving as his Deputy Prime Minister, it must have been something more than coincidence that in November 1992 Boris Yeltsin issued a decree converting Gazprom from a wholly state-owned joint stock company into an independent and private joint stock company, some of whose shares the state continued to own. This allowed Gazprom to sell a substantial portion of its stock to its officers and friends.[13] By 1994, 15 percent of Gazprom shares had been sold to its employees and 33 percent to 747,000 members of the public for vouchers.[14] Some allege that both Mr. Chernomyrdin and Mr. Vyakhirev benefited from this denationalization, although for a long time Chernomyrdin denied that he personally owned any shares. Another 10 percent of the stock was kept by Gazprom itself. When added to the 40 percent of the stock then owned by the state, 35 percent of which was assigned by proxy to Vyakhirev this was more than enough to give Vyakhirev effective operating control. As a result he ran Gazprom as if it were his own company and, by 1998, *Forbes Magazine* included him in their list of the world's 200 richest.[15] Under a secret 1993 trust agreement thought to involve First Deputy Prime Minister Oleg Soskovetz and Chernomyrdin, Vyakhirev, and some of his friends were also issued options to buy 30 percent of the government's Gazprom stock at its cheap pre-inflation face value.[16] Under pressure from the then reformist Deputy Prime Minister Boris Nemtsov, this sweetheart deal, or "theft," as Yeltsin put it, was revoked in December 1997. Nevertheless, until 2000, Gazprom management, under Vyakhirev, managed to exercise the proxy on that 38.37 percent of Gazprom stock owned by the state.[17]

To protect its control, Gazprom regulations allowed its management the right to deny permission to potential purchasers of its stock if it deemed them undesirable. It also sought to prevent foreigners from purchasing or owning Gazprom stock sold within Russia. Foreigners could own stock in Gazprom but that stock had to be purchased outside the country and at a price that was double, at a minimum, and often more than that of the same shares of stock sold within Russia.[18] Given the windfall profits to be made, there were many schemes whereby foreigners sought to buy up domestic Gazprom shares. In one such arrangement, Ruhrgaz of Germany in December 1998 bought 2.5 percent of the Gazprom stock for $660 million and another 1 percent in May 1999 for $200 million.[19] Ruhrgaz also indirectly ended up controlling another 1.5 percent through its 49 percent ownership of Gerogaz, a joint venture with Gazprom.[20] Thus, as of the time of writing, Ruhrgaz owns or controls about 5.5 percent of Gazprom's stock.[21]

Eager as they were to run Gazprom as their own protectorate, Vyakhirev and Chernomyrdin appear to have been even more determined to treat Gazprom as a suckling pig, spinning off resources and assets to several hundred new subsidiaries. Until 2001 when President Putin tried to put a stop to it, most of these entities seem to have been created for the benefit of a few favorite insiders and family members at the expense of the country as a whole. According to Boris Fedorov, who served as an outside director on the Gazprom Board, company executives stripped Gazprom of $2 billion a year for almost a decade.[22] William Browder, another Gazprom critic, estimates that Gazprom engaged in what he describes as seven dubious transactions that led to the disappearance of $5.5 billion, or 10 percent, of Gazprom's total natural gas reserves.[23] As if all this were not notable enough, what distinguishes their asset stripping from similar cases elsewhere in Russia and other countries is that Chernomyrdin was either Russia's prime minister or deputy prime minister when this asset stripping occurred. This was a blatant example of conflict of interest.

Several of the subsidiaries and spin-offs of Gazprom put through in the 1990s resembled a Vyakhirev and Chernomyrdin family business. Chernomyrdin's son Vitaly was appointed First Vice-President of Stroytransgaz, a company involved with pipeline construction and gas exploration work. Vitaly's brother, Andrei, and Vyakhirev's daughter, Tatyana Dedikova, also became major stockholders.[24] They, along with the children and relatives of the Gazprom managers Arngolt Bekker and Vyacheslav Sheremet, owned nearly 60 percent of Stroytransgaz (see Figure 6.1).[25] What is particularly noteworthy is that thanks to then Prime Minister Chernomyrdin, the state authorized the sale of 4.8 percent of the shares of Gazprom to Stroytransgaz for only $2.5 million. Others estimate that if outsiders, not relatives, had been the buyers, they would have had to pay at least $80 million.[26] According to Boris Nemtsov, as part of this asset stripping and diversion of holdings, Gazprom established 300 subsidiaries, including banks.[27] Not only did these subsidiaries facilitate money laundering, it also made it easier to strip assets from Gazprom and divert its profits from the state, despite the fact that the state ostensibly controlled the largest batch of Gazprom stock.

Not to be outdone, Yuri Vyakhirev, Rem's son, was made the managing director of Wingas, a joint venture set up in 1993 by Gazprom with Wintershall, a subsidiary of the German BASF chemical group. Wingas in 2001 supplied 12 percent of all Germany's gas and competed with Ruhrgaz, which has the largest share of the German market and is the largest customer of Gazprom.[28] Until January 2002 when he resigned under pressure from Putin, Yuri was also the general director of Gazexport, a subsidiary that bought gas cheaply from Gazprom and sold it at a much higher price to exporters in Eastern Europe.[29]

Much of what has happened within Gazprom during the Yeltsin years remains secret. Periodically, small revelations have been made public which

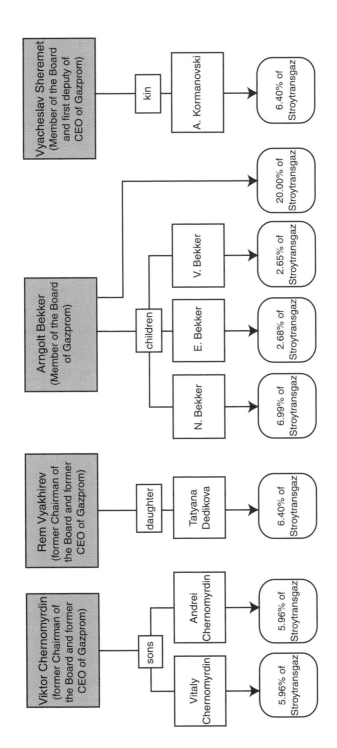

Figure 6.1 Stroytransgaz shareholders

unmask how uninhibited and brazen executives in the ministries were. What is yet to be determined is how much more is out there that is yet to be uncovered.

It turns out that the seizure of state property began early. As far back as June 15, 1989, while Gorbachev was still in control and before Chernomyrdin converted the Ministry of the Gas Industry into Gazprom, Mikhail Rakhimkulov, an official in the Soviet Ministry of the Gas Industry, created a corporation called Interprocom. Although initially it was partially owned by the state, in a short time it became wholly private and Rakhimkulov and his deputy Oleg Vaynerov ended up with majority control.[30] On October 15, 1997, Interprocom was turned over as a gift to Khorhat, a company created in Moscow in 1991, which was owned at the time by Rakhimkulov's wife Galina and Irina Kravtsova, a woman living with Vaynerov. A year later on November 2, 1998, 90 percent of Khorhat stock was transferred equally to five individuals. They included Chernomyrdin's son Vitaly, Vyakhirev's daughter Tatyana Dedikova, Rakhimkulov's son Ruslan, and Vyacheslav Sheremet's daughter Yelena Dmitriyeva.[31] Sheremet at the time was Vyakhirev's closest and most trusted assistant. Kravtsova, Vaynerov's friend, kept 10 percent of the shares without any charge. The others had to pay only a total of $2.50 for their stock. They paid little or nothing but their stock became very valuable. Over the decade, Interprocom's holdings came to include

- a 10 percent share in Panrusgas which contracted to supply Hungary with $23 billion worth of gas over a fifteen-year period;
- a 1.5 percent share in Gaztelecom which operates Gazprom's fiber optic network;
- a 38 percent share in Interprocom/LAN, a computer company;
- and a large share of Intergazkomplekt, an importer of gas distribution equipment.

Rakhimkulov became general manager not only of Panrusgas but of Altalanos Ertekforgalmi Bank (AEB), which handles all the payments to Gazprom for its gas exports to Eastern and Central Europe. In 2000 that amounted to $2.3 billion. AEB was regarded as the major channel which Gazprom used to move its capital outside Russia. Valuable as AEB might be, Gazprom has been stripping itself of ownership of most of AEB, which it once wholly owned. By 2000, it owned only one-quarter of AEB. Family friends have been given most of the rest.

The prize for asset stripping from Gazprom, however, probably belongs to ITERA (International Energy Corporation). Who owns ITERA remains murky, but all signs indicate that relatives of Gazprom managers are again the key stockholders. ITERA executives have long denied such connections. In response to an audit by PricewaterhouseCoopers, 219 Gazprom managers denied they or their families had any affiliation with ITERA.[32] However nineteen, including apparently Viktor Chernomyrdin, failed to answer the question. The auditing firm also acknowledged that it had not been able to gain access to all the information it sought. This obstruction seems to add to the circumstantial evidence that such ties exist.[33] After mounting complaints from investors and possible foreign lenders such as the European Bank for Reconstruction and Development, ITERA ultimately published a list of its shareholders. But the report stated that 87 percent of the stock was held in trust, which means that we still don't know who the owners are.[34]

Headquartered as we saw in Jacksonville, Florida, ITERA was founded with twelve employees in 1992 to trade consumer goods with Turkmenistan.[35] Two years later, in 1994, it broadened its mandate to handle natural gas and trade with Gazprom. In May 1996, an affiliate of the ITERA Group in Ireland and Gazprom established the International Energy Limited Liability Company under Delaware law. But the Jacksonville, Florida, office became the group's principal operating company, and Igor Makarov, a former Olympic cyclist, became the Chief Executive Officer of the entire ITERA Group of Companies.[36] And in yet another bizarre twist, as an ostensible American company, ITERA applied for and received a $868,000 grant in February 2002 from the United States Trade and Development Agency. The rationalization was that the funds would be used to help ITERA, as an American company, gain contracts overseas (that is, to convince Russian companies to buy American-made gas turbines for use on Russian pipelines). After complaints from minority stockholders of Gazprom about the way ITERA was stripping assets, the U.S. government suspended the grant.[37]

In 1997, Gazprom authorized ITERA to take over some of its output in the Yamal Nenets Autonomous District in Siberia.[38] In a sweetheart deal with its governor, who by chance also happened to be on Gazprom's Board of Directors, the Yamal Nenets District agreed to take natural gas as payment for Gazprom's taxes.[39] In lieu of cash, Gazprom paid its taxes with 66 billion cubic meters of its gas (one-tenth of its total output in the region) valued at the low price of approximately $2 to $5 per 1,000 cubic meters.[40] On behalf of the region, the Governor then sold this gas to ITERA at the same price, but ITERA resold it at between $40 and $80 per 1,000 cubic meters. Some of the difference was absorbed by pipeline shipping costs, but this unquestionably was transfer price abuse. In 2001 the Federal Audit Chamber of the Duma banned such arrangements.[41] Moreover, almost no other companies besides ITERA are allowed access to Gazprom's gas pipelines.

In 2000, ITERA sold over 85 billion cubic meters of natural gas worth $3 billion.[42] ITERA itself produced only 18 billion cubic meters of that while 34.3 billion cubic meters of ITERA's sales originated in Kazakhstan, Turkmenistan, and Uzbekistan. In the Gazprom pattern, ITERA had 130 subsidiaries with operations in twenty-four countries.

Not only ITERA , but offshoots of ITERA, shared in Gazprom's asset stripping. In 1998, ITERA set up two straw companies called ZAO STISigma and OOO Lanka-Promkomplekt. Lanka-Promkomplekt and ITERA have the same Moscow address.[43] These two companies bought a 51 percent share of a company called Rospan from Gazprom. Vyakhirev ordered Gazprom to sell that equity for just $284.[44] What angered non-insiders in Gazprom is that Rospan had a license to work two national gas fields with reserves exceeding 300 billion cubic meters of gas, which have been valued at $345 million.[45] To justify this sale Gazprom officials argued that Rospan at the time had been declared bankrupt, but it was widely assumed that this was just another devious use of the bankruptcy law to seize assets at a cost far – in this case, very far – below their market value. Lanka-Promkomplekt also purchased 40 percent of the shares in Sibneftegas from Gazprom in 1999, at a cost of $1.8 million. Independent estimates at the time indicated that the shares were really worth $80 million. Other insiders who made purchases in Sibneftegas included senior managers of Gazprom, as well as a company owned by Vyakhirev's brother Gennadi Vyakhirev and son.[46]

The financing of these various purchases was facilitated by loans from other Gazprom subsidiaries.[47] Among its 300 subsidiaries, Gazprom also controls or has an interest in several banks, most notably Gazprom Bank, as well as Imperial Bank, the National Reserve Bank and MOST-Bank. As a measure of how sophisticated and manipulative Gazprom executives have been, Enron in the United States with its 3,500 subsidiaries is one of the few corporations which has had more subsidiaries than Gazprom–not exactly something to boast about.[48]

Controversy has surrounded many of those other Gazprom subsidiaries. For example, it looked for a time that Gazprom was about to lose control of Sibur, a major petrochemical producer. Initially Gazprom remained inactive when Sibur announced that it planned to increase its capital base from 4.3 billion to 52 billion rubles. That would have meant Gazprom would no longer control 51 percent of Sibur's stock. At the last minute, Gazprom decided to pay $800–900 million for some of the new stock issue in order to sustain its majority control.[49] In similar fashion, Gazprom was criticized for selling 32 percent of its stock in Purgaz to ITERA for a mere $1,300.[50] Given that in 2000 Purgaz produced 14 billion cubic meters of natural gas, the price failed to reflect Purgaz's value. Indeed, when Gazprom subsequently decided to exercise an option it had to repurchase Purgaz, the stated price was $188 million and the value of the gas reserves was estimated to be at least $300 million.[51]

Despite widespread skepticism, Chernomyrdin has insisted that while Prime Minister he owned no shares in Gazprom. After being forced out as Prime Minister in August 1998 however, he was selected as the government's representative on the Gazprom Board of Directors, and in mid-1999 he was voted Chairman of the Board of Directors. While his function was to vote the government's shares, now that he was no longer Prime Minister, presumably Chernomyrdin was able to purchase shares for himself.

In early 2001, Gazprom authorized the conversion of 1.44 percent of the company's shares sold within Russia into its foreign shares or ADRs (American Depository Receipts). While foreigners at the time were prohibited from buying domestic shares of Gazprom, they could buy the ADRs. For that reason the price of Gazprom ADRs was typically double the price of its domestically sold shares. Thus, those who were authorized to transform their shares of Gazprom stock into ADRs instantly doubled the value of their stock. Only a very few holders of Gazprom stock were allowed to participate in this transaction. Demands by minority stockholders to learn the names of the beneficiaries of this inside deal were ignored, although it was assumed they were Gazprom executives or relatives.[52]

Against this backdrop, where the children, relatives and associates of Vyakhirev and Chernomyrdin have siphoned off such valuable assets, it probably didn't matter whether Chernomyrdin was correct when he asserted that he was not a major stockholder in Gazprom. Nor did it seem to matter much if there seemed to be occasional tension between Vyakhirev and Chernomyrdin, particularly after Chernomyrdin was removed as Prime Minister. Both families, for a time at least, held hundreds of millions of dollars worth of assets that used to belong to Gazprom.

In order to ensure that public opinion remained supportive of its operations and continued to allow Vyakhirev a free hand, Gazprom became an active participant in the media business. Its message was that since Gazprom controlled what might be considered Russia's most valuable asset, nothing should be done to jeopardize the company's viability. This campaign, along with liberal financial support for Communist Party projects, helps explain why the Communist Party was for many years one of Gazprom's strongest supporters in the Duma.[53] To make sure that the message was heard, Gazprom gained control of major media outlets by buying shares or lending money to newspapers such as *Rabochaya Tribuna* and *Trud*, and the television networks NTV and ORT.

Gazprom played a particularly important role in financing NTV and Media-MOST, and amidst considerable controversy, ultimately became its largest stockholder and creditor. Gazprom Media was set up in 2000 to administer its media properties. In 2001, its head, Alfred Kokh, launched and won a fierce battle to seize control from Vladimir Gusinsky as head of Media-MOST. Some assert that Kokh was motivated in large part by his desire to seek revenge for the way Gusinsky's media attacked Kokh's ethics when Kokh did not award control of Sviazinvest to Gusinsky in 1997 (see Chapter 1).[54] Others speculate that this attempt to seize NTV was due to pressure on Gazprom from President Putin, angered by NTV's criticism of his policies, especially in Chechnia.

When President Yeltsin removed Chernomyrdin as Prime Minister, Gazprom lost its protector. Mr. Vyakhirev came under increasing pressure to run Gazprom not so much as his own honey pot but as the custodian of a valuable entity with substantial state ownership. The asset stripping was bad enough but there was also anger over the blatant waste and extravagance diverted to resorts and other benefits for the staff. Gazprom's new glass headquarters alone was said to cost $150 million.[55]

Given the extent of the asset stripping, extravagance and waste, eventually some of the stockholders, both individuals and representatives of the state with its 38.37 percent interest, began to demand independent audits and changes in management. Vyakhirev did not take kindly to such efforts, particularly those of Boris Fedorov of the United Financial Group, a Moscow brokerage firm. Fedorov, who once had served as the head of the Russian Tax Office as well as the Minister of Finance, had managed to line up enough shares to win a seat on Gazprom's Board of Directors. From there he began to insist that Gazprom hire an accounting firm other than PricewaterhouseCoopers to conduct an independent audit of ITERA's relationship with Gazprom, something the Duma's Audit Chamber decided to do in February 2002.[56] He also began to agitate for a change in management, especially in early 2001 before Vyakhirev's contract was due to expire.

Vyakhirev reacted so aggressively to Fedorov's efforts that Fedorov began to fear for his life. Among other forms of intimidation, Fedorov was threatened with jail, visited by intimidating members of the Mafia and sued to invalidate (the Russians say "arrest") his voting shares in Gazprom. To drive home the message, his dog was poisoned.[57]

In addition, beginning in January 2001, as if by command, over fifty newspapers published articles attacking him. After some investigation, Fedorov ascertained that there was such a command and he discovered how much each newspaper charged to print such attacks.[58] For example, *Vedomosti*, which is a joint venture involving Dow Jones and *The Financial*

Times, published four such attacks. Given its parentage and respectability, it was among the most expensive at $6,000 per article. That this was all coincidence as some might argue is refuted by the fact that once Vyakhirev was removed as CEO, such articles ceased and some of the newspapers then published retractions.

One of Fedorov's chief complaints about Vyakhirev's management was that Gazprom rarely paid any dividends to stockholders, including the Russian government. Critics also began to demand that Gazprom pay its taxes. In 1995 and 1996 combined, for example, Gazprom paid only $3.5 million as dividends to the state for its 38.37 percent equity despite earnings of almost $2 billion or more.[59]

It was hard to tell exactly what was happening behind Gazprom's opaque accounting practices. According to official Russian accounting standards, Gazprom said it had a profit of $1.3 billion in 1999. Yet according to international accounting standards, it had a loss of $3.2 billion for that same year.[60] Furthermore, a government audit discovered that Gazprom had lent $788 million to outside firms in 1999 largely interest free as well as guaranteeing a total of $2.2 billion in loans including many to Gazprom directors and relatives. None of this was mentioned at the time by Gazprom's auditor, PricewaterhouseCoopers.[61] At the same time it borrowed $1 billion at up to 15 percent interest, as Gazprom officials explained, to pay Gazprom's taxes and finance investments. Some of these investments had nothing directly to do with Gazprom. For example, Gazprom funds were used to finance some of Mayor Yuri Luzhkov's pet projects in Moscow.[62] After three years of losses (as defined by Western accounting principles) Gazprom reported profits in 2000 of $9.9 billion. Even then, actual profits were said by some to be only $2 billion; the remaining $7 billion was the result of creative accounting.[63]

The pressure to pay dividends and taxes to the state and to stop spinning off assets to insiders increased in 2000 when Vladimir Putin became president. In June of that year, the state used its shares to force Chernomyrdin out as Chairman of the Board of Directors. He was replaced by Dmitri Medvedev, a trusted deputy of Putin and the head of the Kremlin administration.[64] As more became public about how Vyakhirev had siphoned off assets for his family and friends, pressure also mounted to replace him when his term expired on May 31, 2001. Putin seemed particularly incensed to learn that Russian gas was sold to East and West European importers "at prices two or three times higher than our export prices." "Where," he wanted to know, was "the money?"[65]

But because he had so much power and wealth, as well as influence and support in the Duma, and because Vyakhirev decided to switch his allegiance from Gusinsky to Putin and agreed to foreclose on Gusinsky's loans, it looked for a time that, out of gratitude, Vyakhirev's term would be extended if not renewed. It was somewhat of a surprise therefore when on May 30, 2001 the Gazprom Board of Directors voted unanimously (meaning that Vyakhirev also voted to fire himself) to replace Vyakhirev with the relatively unknown Alexei Miller. Miller, who was nominated by Putin, had been serving as Deputy Minister of Energy since 2000. Aged only thirty-eight and with little administrative experience Miller had also worked as an assistant to Putin when he ran the Committee for Foreign Relations in St. Petersburg.

Putin pressured Miller to rein in Vyakhirev, but to soften the blow Vyakhirev was allowed for a time to remain as Chairman of the Board of Directors. Nonetheless there were some immediate changes. In June 2001, the Board of Directors decided to pay out approximately $230 million in dividends. That was seventy times more than the previous amount paid out by Vyakhirev. Moreover, Miller pledged that henceforth, Gazprom would pay out 15 percent of its profits as dividends.[66] In similar fashion, Miller seemed to be supportive of the effort by the Prosecutor General's office to recoup some $85 million from an alleged illegal sale of company assets by Sibur. Those called in for questioning included Sibur's president Yakov Goldovsky and Vyacheslav Sheremet, who had been Vyakhirev's number two man at Gazprom. Goldovsky and Sibur Vice President Yevgeny Koshchits were even put in jail and new managers put in their place.[67] At Miller's behest, the new management also sought to collect $932 million that Sibur owes Gazprom. Even more important, Gazprom sought to reclaim its stake in Sibur which would have fallen from 51 percent to 4 percent if the old Sibur management had been allowed to move ahead with a new stock issue.[68] Gazprom also moved to retake 32 percent of the Purgaz Gas Field stock it sold to ITERA for a mere $1,026.[69] It also managed to win a Russian Court decision to force Stroytransgaz to return a 4.8 percent share of ownership in the firm to Gazprom. As we saw earlier, those shares had been sold in 1995 for $2.5 million to the children of Vyakhirev and Chernomyrdin. They were thought to be worth $1 billion.[70] In August 2002, Gazprom pressured the stockholders in Stroytransgaz–most likely Bekker, the former president, and the Vyakhirev children–to sell another 25 percent of their stock to Gazprom.[71] These were promising signs, but Miller's health is uncertain and he has had little experience with such a large company. Moreover, because some of Vyakhirev's people remain in place within the company and the scope of the asset stripping was so monumental, it will still take some time before Gazprom will be able to purge itself of all its misdoings.[72] Still, by November 2002, Miller claimed that "absolutely all the core assets" worth billions of dollars had been recovered.[73]

The story of **Vagit Alekperov** is similar to that of Chernomyrdin and Vyakhirev. He too was listed as one of *Forbes Magazine*'s five richest Russians; he also headed a Soviet raw material ministry–petroleum. Born in Baku, Alekperov graduated in 1974 from the Azerbaijan Institute of Oil and Chemistry and went to work in the nearby Caspian Sea oil fields. In 1979 he moved to the Tyumen oil fields in Siberia. One of his first administrative positions came in 1984 when he was appointed general director of Kogalymneftegaz which he managed until 1990. He then moved to Moscow, where he became Deputy and then First Deputy Minister of Fuel and Energy and finally, in August 1991 after the coup attempt, Acting Minister of Fuel and Energy. He was now in a position to influence the breakup and privatization of the Soviet petroleum industry.

Unlike the gas industry, which was kept intact as a monopoly before and after privatization, the petroleum industry was divided into a dozen or so independent entities.[74] Among them they controlled thirty-one drilling companies, twenty-eight refineries and seventy-eight joint ventures. In late 1991, Alekperov assumed the presidency of LUKoil, the largest of the dozen, which encompassed seven drilling subsidiaries and eighteen joint ventures. Patterned after the vertically integrated oil companies of the West, LUKoil initially consisted of three production fields, the initials of which spell out the company's name. They were Langepaz, Urengoi, and Kogalym (where Alekperov had been general director). LUKoil was formally privatized in November 1992 and then transformed into a joint stock corporation in April 1993. The state however remained for a time the dominant shareholder. As of May 1995, the state still held 80 percent of the stock.[75] Eventually much of that stock was sold off, and by January 1996 state-held stock had fallen to 21 percent of the total.

After further sales, including a 9 percent share that was sold to Reforma, an obscure group, in 1999 for a mere $200 million (only $5,000 above the asking price) and a 5.9 percent stake that the state tried to sell in 2002, the state announced that it planned to cut back its shares to 8 percent.[76] Assuming that the state is successful, it will own less than Alekperov. After insisting a month previously that he owned only 3 percent of its stock, he acknowledged on July 28, 2002 that he owned 10.4 percent of LUKoil's shares. This provided him with a net worth exceeding $1 billion.[77] As part of the ongoing privatization effort, on August 15, 1995, Prime Minister Viktor Chernomyrdin transferred what had been the state-owned oil fields of Permneft, Kaliningradmorneftegaz, Astrakhanneft, and Nizhnevolzhskneft to LUKoil. In addition, LUKoil acquired some other distribution and service companies. By 2000, its reserves were said to match or exceed those of Exxon.[78] LUKoil also has its own refineries and filling stations–including 1,300 in the United States that it purchased from

Getty Oil–and is participating in the development of the Caspian Sea fields.[79] Having bought 6 percent of LUKoil stock for $250 million, ARCO became one of LUKoil's largest shareholders. After some unfortunate experiences with Sidanko, another Russian oil company, BP/Amoco, which acquired ARCO in 2001, sold all of its inherited LUKoil shares and some bonds.

Along with the other oligarchs, Mr. Alekperov also moved into banking and the media. There have also been allegations that his company has had links with organized crime and the seizure of a diamond mine from the Arkhangelsk Diamond Corporation, a Denver-based company.[80] He and LUKoil control Imperial Bank (in which Gazprom also has an interest), several television stations and the newspaper *Izvestiia*.

The takeover of Getty Oil reflects the natural inclination of the Russian oligarchs to extend their operations to other countries. In principle, it is a tendency to be applauded. The more involved Russian businessmen become with the West, the more likely it is that they will come to adopt Western business practices, presumably good ones. But there is no guarantee. Given how deeply ingrained some of the less desirable practices are among Russian administrators (past and present) it is only to be expected that some of the more nefarious behavior we have encountered inside Russia will also surface outside.

LUKoil's treatment of Getty Oil seems to be one instance of such seamy behavior, at least as viewed through the eyes of the gasoline service station owners and the tank truck drivers. The owners for example report that LUKoil immediately began to squeeze and coerce them. In the words of one dealer, "we are told to either get out of the business or sue–Getty [LUKoil] has enough money and legal power to keep us in court until we are bankrupt or out of business. Our contracts have become worthless pieces of paper. We feel we are being 'Enron-ized'."[81] LUKoil raised the wholesale price of the gasoline it delivers to the old network of dealers while cutting the wholesale price to the new dealers, most if not all of whom were rumored to be Russian. As a result, a growing number of the old dealers have purposely been forced into bankruptcy. What is equally disturbing is that appeals to the Attorney General of Delaware have gone unanswered. The Russians were supposed to adopt our ways, not bring their ways to the United States. It may be that the addition to LUKoil's Board of Directors of respected and experienced Western businessmen such as Mark Mobius of Templeton Asset Management and Richard Matzke, the former Vice Chairman of Chevron Corporation, will bring an end to such behavior, at least outside Russia. It will not be easy. As we will see in Chapter 11, there are numerous examples of such strong-arm methods affecting Western investors inside Russia, the greater involvement of Western directors and senior executives notwithstanding.

Not all of the *nomenklatura* oligarchs evolved out of the raw material and energy sectors. The president and founder of Oneximbank, **Vladimir O. Potanin**, came out of the foreign trade sector. He was listed by *Forbes Magazine* in July 1998 as the richest Russian, with an estimated net worth of $1.6 billion. Somewhat prematurely, *Forbes* also selected him as one of the world's top ten "smartest" businessmen. A month later, on August 17, 1998, Russia's financial crisis hit, and much, but certainly not all, of Potanin's wealth seemed to vaporize. He was dropped from the *Forbes* list in 1999 and 2000 but reemerged in 2001 and 2002 with an estimated $1.8 billion as well as a seat on the Board of Trustees of the Guggenheim Museum in New York.[82]

Born in 1961, Mr. Potanin attended the Moscow Institute for International Relations, an elite school for those headed for the Ministry of Foreign Affairs, Foreign Trade, or the KGB. His father, who had been a senior official in the Ministry of Foreign Trade, helped prepare his way. In 1983, like his father, he went to work in the Ministry of Foreign Trade. The younger Potanin worked in Soiuzpromexport, a foreign trade organization where he dealt primarily in the export of non-ferrous metals. He stayed there for eight years. In 1991, somewhat belatedly (not in 1987, when the first new cooperatives were established), he created Interros, a cooperative foreign trade association, which also traded in non-ferrous metals. In effect, Potanin privatized Soiuzpromexport. With the capital he accumulated at Interros, he went on to create MFK (or, in English, the International Finance Company).[83] Drawing on his connections, in 1993 he utilized some funds from Vneshekonombank, the foreign trade bank, for the capital of his new start up Oneximbank (this is the acronym for United Export/Import bank) of which he became president. Although Oneximbank was founded later than most of the other big banks, Mr. Potanin quickly made up for lost time. While Oneximbank focused on commercial banking activities, MFK became its investment bank affiliate, along with Renaissance Capital, a new startup put together by Boris Jordan (until then, the head of the Credit Suisse First Boston office in Moscow) and several other one-time employees of CSFB.

In appreciation of Potanin's help in winning the 1996 presidential election, a few months later in August 1996 Yeltsin appointed him First Deputy Prime Minister. This made Potanin the number two man in the government. For appearances' sake, he agreed to take a leave of absence from his business, which he did until he left the government in March 1997. He had trouble, however, divorcing himself from his business interests, and there were many complaints that he used his government authority to enhance his investments.

Most significant, he created the country's largest industrial empire. Bundled under Interros, his original cooperative, Mr. Potanin ultimately acquired control over twenty formerly state-owned enterprises. Interros acquired some of these enterprises through the bitterly attacked "Loans for Shares" program that, conveniently enough, was suggested to the government by Mr. Potanin himself (see Chapter 1).

As we noted earlier, the Loans for Shares program was intended to help the government fund a shortfall. Since the government was not collecting enough tax revenue to cover its expenditures, Potanin suggested that it make up the deficit by borrowing money from banks such as his. As collateral for the loans, the government could put up shares of stock in some of the companies that it still controlled. The banks agreed that if the loans were not repaid, the government would still benefit because the banks would auction off the stock. Only the naïve, however, were shocked when in almost every case, the auctions turned out to be a charade. Invariably the banks holding the collateral and conducting the auctions emerged as the winner at a price that seldom exceeded the price of the initial loan.[84] When others did try to bid, they found either that the airport at the site of the auction was closed for the day or that the bidders were disqualified for some other reason.[85] This was larceny on a grand scale. Potanin eventually ended up controlling thirty major properties including Sidanko Oil, Sviazinvest, a telecommunications company, and a number of other industrial and metallurgical firms including holdings in Perm Motors, Northwest Shipping, Magnitogorsk Steel, the GAZ automobile plant, various metallurgical plants and newspapers including *Izvestiia*, *Komsomolskaia Pravda*, and the magazine *Expert*. In 2001, Potanin's group began to invest in agriculture and the food processing business. Through Agros, its agricultural subsidiary, it bought a $1 billion stake in Roskhleboprodukt.[86] Agros' goal is to gain control of 7 percent of the world's grain market.

Potanin's biggest catch, however, was Norilsk Nickel, which reported profits in 2000 of $1.5 billion: Potanin bid a mere $170 million for its control.[87] Interros is said to account for approximately 3 percent of the country's GDP. It alone controls one-fifth of the world's nickel, two-thirds of its palladium and one-fifth of its platinum. Moving offshore, Interros has also purchased mines in Australia and Montana.[88]

After the August 1998 crisis, Potanin's bank fell into bankruptcy. But Potanin, like several other oligarchs, managed to end up in something less than poverty. He did this by stripping Oneximbank of what viable assets it retained and transferring them to a new banking entity he created, Rosbank. Simultaneously, he transformed Interros' holdings into

Interrosprom which became his holding and operating entity. He also himself managed to divert considerable sums to his personal account outside of Russia–more than enough to throw a party for over a hundred of his closest friends at a reserved nightclub in Courchevel, a French ski resort.[89]

Russians were not the only ones affected by Potanin's manipulations. In addition to the ordinary Russian citizens who put their money in his bank, foreigners also bought his bank's Eurobonds and ended up with worthless paper. Also, because of his management of Sidanko, BP/Amoco was forced to write off $200 million of the $500 million or so stake it had paid in November 1997 for its 10 percent equity in Sidanko.[90] After a series of complicated legal moves including some in the bankruptcy court fighting Tyumen Oil, BP/Amoco managed to recover at least part of its investment, and after a good deal of struggle BP/Amoco and Tyumen Oil worked out a new arrangement that allowed BP/Amoco to assume management of Sidanko.

Vladimir V. Vinogradov was one of the few oligarch bankers who had previous banking experience during the Soviet years. Born in 1955, Mr. Vinogradov graduated from the Ordzhonikidze Moscow Aviation Institute. He then went to work as a senior economist in Promstroibank, a Soviet-era state bank. In October 1988 he founded Inkombank, one of the country's first wholly private commercial banks with shareholders drawn from such diverse groups as the Plekhanov Economic Institute, the state insurance company Gosstrakh, Magnitogorsk Steel, and over fifty other groups including technology-driven state enterprises such as the laser company Lutch.[91] Inkombank was established as a private limited partnership, a status authorized the year before as part of Gorbachev's reform efforts. Vinogradov became its chairman of the board of management and then its president. Subsequently Inkombank was converted into a joint stock bank on March 25, 1991. Several of the country's larger enterprises (at the time state-owned) provided most of the bank's initial capital and, in the Russian way, many of the same enterprise shareholders also became subsidiaries of the bank–among them Magnitogorsk Steel, the Babayevskaia candy factory and Sameko metallurgy. Inkombank also had substantial control of timber operations, Transneft oil pipeline, and the Sukhoi aircraft design bureau.

For reasons that probably have to do more with personality than experience, Vinogradov was sometimes excluded from the inner circle of the big bankers, none of whom had ever previously worked for a bank. Vinogradov was the Vice President of the Association of Russian Bankers, yet he was not among the Big Ten who met with Prime Minister Kiriyenko and President Yeltsin in August 1998 to discuss the country's economic crisis.

Inkombank, Vinogradov's bank, was also attacked by, among others, the Russian Central Bank in June 1996 for what was claimed to be its inadequate reserves. In effect, the Central Bank tried to create a run on the bank for what seemed to be extraneous reasons, and Inkombank lost $39 million in assets in a few days.[92] Conversely, following Black Thursday on August 24, 1995, the Central Bank did the opposite and helped Inkombank with a temporary loan so that it could continue to service its depositors. Nevertheless after the August 17, 1998 crash, with $238 million owed to Russian depositors and about $2 billion to foreign lenders, Inkombank was forced to close its doors and lost its banking license.[93] As bankruptcy proceedings dragged on for several years, Vinogradov, unlike most of the other oligarchs, was unable to reestablish a new entity with assets stripped from his pre-1998 bank. Eventually most of his enterprises were seized as collateral. In December 2001, the Audit Chamber of the Duma (their counterpart of our General Accounting Office) accused Inkombank managers of fraud. They were charged with diverting $1.5 billion in assets before declaring bankruptcy.[94] Vinogradov's empire disintegrated and he all but disappeared from public view.

III

For the most part, none of these *nomenklatura* oligarchs added much to the state properties they seized, nor did they restrict themselves to the management of their new businesses. Of course not all the *nomenklatura* oligarchs behaved in this way. For example, **Vladimir Bogdanov**, a former Soviet oil executive, who took over Surgutneftegaz is sometimes credited with limiting himself to the effective operation of his oil company. On the whole, though, until 2001, the most valuable properties were milked, not nourished. Most oligarchs who were former Soviet officials, both at the *nomenklatura* and below *nomenklatura* level, stripped and did not reinvest in their enterprises.

There is another breed of oligarch however, one that did not spring from the former Soviet official class. To the contrary, many of them in fact were regarded as ne'er-do-wells in the Soviet era. They tend to be more colorful, but as we shall see in Chapter 7 most of their business practices were equally shady.

7 The upstart oligarchs

That privatization should give birth to new owners who previously had been the factories' directors or senior government ministers is not surprising. It was merely a matter of seizing what was already there. Of course this made them very different from the robber barons in the United States who built their empires by building steel mills, railroads, and refineries. These Russian oligarchs did not build. They simply purloined what previously belonged to the state and in the process became instant millionaires, if not billionaires. As colorful as these oligarchs are, it is the third category of oligarch that is the most interesting. The people in this group are generally not ethnic Russians nor members of the main *apparatchik* cadre of the Soviet era. Moreover, they acted more outside than inside the law during the communist era. Several had been charged earlier with economic crimes and some even served time in jail. We shall explore here how they grew so wealthy so rapidly. What makes them so intriguing is that their rise to affluence may have been because of–not despite–their previous low social standing.

To understand how people of such humble, even despised, origins were able to acquire wealth so quickly, it is necessary to look at Soviet economic and ethnic policies in the 1970s and 1980s. During Soviet times, except for the sale of food grown in the peasants' small garden plots, all private business activity was officially prohibited. Those who violated this law were charged with an economic crime. Even though the punishment, as noted earlier, could be death, some were willing to run such risks. Some (*fartsovshchiki*) engaged in selling banned foreign and black-market goods. A particularly popular item was blue jeans. Others engaged in currency speculation (*valiutchiki*), and still others provided private services and repairs (*deltsy*). Most of those involved in such endeavors were members of non-Russian ethnic groups such as Jews, Armenians, Georgians and Muslims who, with rare exceptions, were excluded from mainstream positions of authority within the party, the military, the KGB, the Foreign Service, or even as factory directors. With such opportunities precluded, and unwilling to accept low-level work, some of the more ambitious among them set up their own underground businesses even if it meant violating the law and risking death. They catered to Russian consumers unable to satisfy their needs through the state sector.

Consumers were not the only ones who sought goods outside the inflexible centrally planned system. Factory managers frequently were short of crucial supplies. Sometimes, this was the fault of suppliers who failed to keep commitments or who were unable to deliver because of breakdowns in the railroad system or other channels of supply. In other cases, needs arose which were not anticipated when the plan was conceived. This could have been a consequence of any manner of events, including miscalculation, bad weather, and faulty specifications.

Rather than watch their enterprises underfulfill their plans and suffer penalties, many factory directors added a *tolkatch* (a "pusher", or "expeditor") to their staffs. These *tolkatchi* arranged for the supply and delivery of components "off the books"; that is, not provided by Gosplan, Gossnab, or the ministries. While socially more acceptable than the *deltsy*, *tolkatchi* functioned in much the same way as the *fartsovshchiki*, but more openly. A *tolkatch* was one of the limited number of occupations open to non-Russians eager to show initiative. Yet they were always on or beyond the fringe of society.

The perestroika reforms of Mikhail Gorbachev, his ultimate ouster, the decline of the Communist Party, the disintegration of the USSR, and the displacement of the centrally planned system by a market system with private ownership also meant a radical upheaval–a reversal–in the country's mores and values. When Gorbachev in May 1987 decided to allow the operation of cooperatives and private businesses, it marked the first time Soviet citizens could legally operate their own private businesses since the New Economic Policy period of the 1920s. Virtually overnight, what had once been treated as an economic crime became legal and standard operating procedure. Engaging in market activities was no longer illegal. Suddenly, the *tolkatchi* and *fartsovshchiki* found themselves with skills and knowledge that gave them an advantageous position relative to those establishment Russians who were unaccustomed to creating a business from scratch. (Of course, those members of the communist *nomenklatura* who could grab what had been state and party assets for themselves also ended up in an advantageous situation, though for very different reasons.)

Gorbachev's new policy, however, was not accompanied by a change in mainstream social attitudes. Most Russians, just as in the czarist and communist eras, continued to look down on wheeler-dealers engaged in business. As a result, Slavic Russians without extensive experience in seeking out commodities in short supply and bartering without the use of money found themselves at a disadvantage. Few had the experience necessary to operate in the chaotic economic and social conditions of the early 1990s. By contrast, ethnic "businessmen," including many Jews, had been carrying on such operations for decades on a daily basis. In the post-1987 climate, many of them flourished.

By 1991, the Soviet system that had prevailed for sixty years was suddenly superseded. Central planning was dead, as were its controlling and decision-making institutions, Gosplan, Gossnab, and the ministries. Store shelves were empty. As yet, no effective market system had come into being to replace the Soviet government's planning agencies. In such near-anarchic conditions, those who had developed skills searching out and selling scarce supplies had an enormous advantage.

A typical first step was to create a cooperative, which often was just a legitimate cover for an earlier underground operation. The profits from the cooperative frequently provided the capital needed to open a bank since the capital requirements for opening a bank at the time were quite modest–as little as $75,000 in early 1993. These banks, in turn, underwrote loans to their directors, in order to finance the purchase of former state-owned enterprises that were being privatized. Many of these banks were little more than personal ATM machines.

I

Alexander P. Smolensky is an archetypal model of how these once ne'er-do-well "buzinessmen" rose to the pinnacles of finance and political power–at least until the August 17, 1998 financial meltdown. In the Soviet era, Smolensky attempted early on to operate outside the bounds of the centrally planned system. In effect he created his own business.[1]

Mr. Smolensky began conventionally enough. Born in 1954, he graduated from the Dzhambulski Geological Technical Institute in Kazakhstan, where he also met his wife.[2] Forsaking his training as a geologist, he became a typesetter. To make some additional money, he managed to secure a second job at a bakery. To do this he had to have a permit, which he obtained illegally.

His trouble with the authorities began when he decided to use his position as a typesetter to begin publishing bibles on the side. For this he was arrested in 1981 for stealing government ink and paper (an economic crime) and sentenced to two years of hard labor on a construction brigade.[3] (Paul Klebnikov and Jonas Bernstein speculate that in exchange for his release, Smolensky agreed that he would keep tabs on some of the other "buzinessmen" for the KGB and allow himself to be used as a conduit for state, Party and KGB funds.)[4]

Smolensky claims to have served only one day in jail after his brush with the KGB, and afterwards began to work in construction. Construction was a more freewheeling sector of the economy even in the Soviet era because of the universal need for emergency repairs, especially in individual apartments, homes and dachas. Moreover since there were so many construction teams, and they were so scattered, the teams, referred to as *shabashniki*, were hard to police, especially among do-it-yoursleves. Several of the other "new" oligarchs also began in this way.

Responding to Gorbachev's 1987 legalization of cooperatives, Smolensky brought his construction work out in the open and founded the Moscow No. 3 Construction Cooperative. He started by sawing up logs into lumber, which he then used through his position as a contractor to build dachas.[5]

This was at a time when there were no readily available supplies including simple things such as nails and lumber. It was a situation made to order for someone with Mr. Smolensky's ingenuity. With his trading experience, he was able to avail himself of the unavailable supplies. Making great profits quickly, he searched for a place to put his money. Rather than trust state banks which were unaccustomed to dealing with large private accounts, he created his own bank, the Stolichny Bank, on February 14, 1989. His bank was one of the first to take advantage of the new laws. In an interview with *The Washington Post* on October 17, 1997, Mr. Smolensky acknowledged that he knew nothing about commercial banking. His main consideration was "to evade the state banks and become as independent of state authorities as he could."

As an oligarch Mr. Smolensky was applauded for his charitable contribution of 116 pounds of gold for the cupolas of Mayor Yuri Luzhkov's Cathedral of Christ the Savior, as well as for his business savvy. Nonetheless, allegations about his past continued to haunt him. The newspaper *Rossiiskaia Gazeta* ran an investigative article on March 14, 1995, which charged that he participated in a forgery scheme to smuggle $25 million in cash out of Russia to Austria, the home of his grandfather, where Mr. Smolensky is also a citizen and his wife has a home and office. *The Wall Street Journal* on October 4, 2000 ran a follow-up piece detailing Smolensky's sale just before the August 1998 crash of $500 million in bonds that were not legally his to sell.[6]

Unlike many of his fellow risk takers Mr. Smolensky did not actively seek to build up a large industrial empire. His bank did come to control the newspapers *Kommersant* and *Novaia Gazeta*, and he shared in the ownership of the Sibneft oil company and the television network ORT with Boris Berezovsky. But for the most part, he focused instead on developing a large network of bank branches. In November 1996, he won a controversial bid for what had been the state-owned Agroprombank, which had some 1,250 branches in rural areas. Several critics have charged that Smolensky won the bid with the help of Anatoly Chubais.[7] Suspicions were heightened after President Yeltsin fired Chubais in January 1997, when Mr. Smolensky cushioned Chubais' fall by extending an interest-free $3 million loan to an organization run by Mr. Chubais.[8]

After acquiring Agroprombank, Smolensky then changed the name of all of his banks to SBS/Agro (which stands for Stolichny Bank Savings Agro). Until it was crippled by the financial collapse in August 1998, Mr. Smolensky's bank had the largest number of private branches in the country and was second only to the government's Sberbank in terms of number of branches.

The devaluation of the ruble, the crash of the Russian stock market, and the moratorium on the repayment of Russian treasury bills on August 17, 1998, was a devastating blow for most Russian bankers, including SBS/Agro. Because of its many outlets, SBS/Agro was especially vulnerable in a time of panic. Technically, Smolensky's bank became insolvent, but now an insider, he called on his ties with Viktor Gerashchenko, the head of the Russian Central Bank (RCB). Somehow Smolensky was able to pressure the RCB into providing him with a series of large loans, including one for $450 million.[9] Nor did it hurt that the Deputy Chairman of SBS/Agro at the time was Arkady Kulik, the son of the then Deputy Prime Minister.[10] Smolensky used the loans to reassure the bank's depositors that he had sufficient funds to remain solvent and to prevent a further run on the remaining deposits. But he needed more loans to postpone bankruptcy. On October 2, 1998, the RCB opened a 7 billion ruble credit line for SBS/Agro which equaled about $1 billion.[11] This provided some breathing space, but rather than pay back his depositors and creditors in full, Smolensky used the time for more asset stripping. Like several of the other oligarch bankers, he set up a new banking shell and shifted most of his viable assets out of SBS/Agro to the new banking entities Soyuz and Pervy, the First Mutual Society. As part of that "shell game," in December 2001 Alexander's twenty-one-year-old son Nikolai Smolensky was made chairman of the Pervoye OVK Bank. This made Nikolai the youngest board chairman in Russia.[12] But such efforts failed to revive Smolensky senior's empire; he never fully recovered from the 1998 crash.

Smolensky's creditors also did not recover. SBS/Agro left behind approximately $1.2 billion in debts, including $700 million in loans owed to Western banks, such as Société Générale S.A. of France, the EBRD, J.P. Morgan Chase, Bank of America, ING Group, and Lehman Brothers Holdings, Inc.[13] Smolensky's bank offered to settle its debts at one cent on the dollar. Russian depositors did a little better; they received up to approximately

$800, which often meant about 10 cents of every dollar they had deposited. Much of the remaining $1 billion of missing money is thought to be hidden somewhere, mostly offshore.[14]

Vladimir Gusinsky emerged from the underground economy much as Smolensky did. But even in this group, he is probably unique. Born in 1952, Gusinsky attended not only the Gubkin Institute of Petrochemicals and Natural Gas (he says for four years; the Institute says for one) but also Gitis, a school for theatrical directors.[15] He then became a theatrical producer in the provinces. After a two-year term in the army he returned to Moscow and drove a cab on the side to earn money. Some say that he also became involved with under-the-counter street trading involving, among other products, the conversion of copper wire into copper bracelets, something highly sought after for what many believe to be its beneficial medicinal effect.[16] One newspaper, *Rossiiskaia Gazeta*, reports that he engaged in other questionable activities and was charged with embezzlement.[17] Gusinsky denies such accusations and has successfully sued several of his accusers and critics.[18] (As noted in Chapter 6, in August 1994 he also had his lawyers threaten me because of an article I published on August 5, 1994 in the *International Herald Tribune*. Not surprisingly he took offense when I wrote that his bank, MOST-Bank, "is widely thought to be under Mafia control." A few months later, in December the CIA did indeed publish a secret report asserting that "half of Russia's 25 largest banks ... are linked to Russian organized crime groups or involved in other illicit financial activities."[19] But because the report was classified, despite my best efforts I was never able to determine if MOST-Bank was one of those banks. Gusinsky's lawyers in the meantime threatened to move ahead with a libel suit in a London court where the libel laws are more protective of those libeled than in the United States. It did not help my nerves when *The Wall Street Journal* and *The Wall Street Journal Europe* published retractions on April 11, 1995 (pp. A2, A14) for an article that made a somewhat similar allegation. In the end, Mr. Gusinsky turned to other concerns and although I lost my umbrella insurance coverage, he did not pursue the lawsuit. In fact, he and I subsequently have had several civilized, even pleasant and forthright discussions. Because I admired his efforts to provide critical news coverage about Russia's policies in Chechnia and Putin's behavior after the sinking of the submarine *Kursk*, I have worked to support his unsuccessful efforts to retain control of Media-MOST, and his TV and press operations.)

At one point Gusinsky attended the University of Virginia where he studied financial management but he also continued with his theatrical work in Russia, which helped him make important connections. He worked with the Komsomol in Moscow, for example, to organize "mass events." *The Washington Post* has reported that he did some work for Ted Turner and his Goodwill Games as well as the International Youth Festival in 1986, although, in an interview, Gusinsky denies this.[20]

Gusinsky opened his first cooperative in 1987 with $1,000. It was the second cooperative approved in Russia and the first in the Moscow region. It produced women's clothing.[21] Two years later in 1989, he opened a second cooperative called MOST, a consulting firm which offered to help foreigners seeking to invest in Russia. According to Gusinsky, the name MOST, which also means "bridge" in Russian, was inspired by a bank's ATM machine that he saw while visiting Washington, D.C. MOST initially was a fifty–fifty joint venture with APCO, an offshoot of Arnold and Porter, a prominent Washington, D.C. law firm. At the time, APCO was looking for a Russian contact which could provide guidance and advice to prospective foreign investors. By 1992 Gusinsky had bought out APCO's shares and MOST then became a wholly Russian-owned company.

Gradually, MOST branched out into providing office supplies, items unavailable in state stores. And like so many of the non-establishment oligarchs, Gusinsky also engaged in construction work and the procurement of construction supplies. Just as had Smolensky, Gusinsky found that there was a ready market for tools and supplies.

With the profits that he earned from his various business activities, Gusinsky, again like Smolensky, next moved in 1992 to open his own bank, MOST-Bank. As we have seen, at that time capital requirements to open such cooperative banks were minimal.

It was his construction work, however, that put Gusinsky in touch with Yuri Luzhkov, then Deputy Mayor of Moscow. The two became allies. Luzhkov turned over key properties to Gusinsky to manage and renovate. In January 1993, by then Mayor of Moscow, Luzhkov made MOST-Bank one of the banks authorized by the city to accept city deposits and allowed Gusinsky to benefit from the float generated by the use of funds held by the city of Moscow.[22] Consequently, MOST-Bank had control of much of the city's money from the time that it was deposited until the money was used to pay a bill. In the meantime, MOST-Bank could use the funds for its own purposes, including currency speculation or investment in high-yielding national government securities; on occasion, these securities yielded as much as 200 percent interest. This was how most of the banks at the time became so profitable. By 1994, MOST-Bank had become one of the country's largest banks.

Bored with banking, Gusinsky fell back in 1992 on his original training as a theatrical producer and decided to branch out and create his own media network. He created an independent newspaper in 1993 called *Segodnia* and hired away some of the best journalists from other newspapers, while issuing threats on occasion to those newspaper editors who had refused to join him.[23] Using his connections with Mayor Luzhkov, he also managed to gain control of TV Channel 4 in Moscow and was able to begin broadcasting a few hours a day in 1994. With the beginning of the Chechen War in 1994, his station became increasingly critical of Yeltsin and his policies. However, when it looked like the Communist candidate Gennady Zyuganov might defeat Yeltsin in the 1996 election for president, Gusinsky suspended criticism. Indeed, Igor Malashenko, one of Gusinsky's chief aides, became head of Yeltsin's media efforts. As a reward for helping Yeltsin win, Gusinsky was awarded broadcast channels throughout the country, thereby allowing him to set up the NTV network ("nezavisimost TV," or "independent"), the country's first and, for a time, only private TV network.

Gusinsky's Media-MOST became a media conglomerate that at its peak encompassed the country's largest private television network, NTV, a satellite communication network, a series of radio stations such as Ekho Moskvy, newspapers such as *Segodnia*, and magazines such as *Itogi*, which was jointly published with *Newsweek*. Unlike most of the first and second categories of oligarchs, whose wealth came from taking over former state-owned state industrial projects, Gusinsky created new enterprises. Some, including Gusinsky himself, regarded him as the Rupert Murdoch of Russia.

NTV may have been officially independent of state control, but periodically Gusinsky would be reminded that there were still limits to the network's criticisms and Gusinsky's autonomy. Yeltsin's bodyguard, Aleksandr Korzhakov, described how in December 1994, Yeltsin complained to him that Gusinsky had become too self-important, inconveniencing his daughter Tatyana and wife Naina on the highway, but also that NTV had become too presumptuous and obnoxious (an allusion to its coverage of the Chechen War).[24] The next day Korzhakov and his Kremlin guards intercepted Gusinsky's convoy and harassed them as they drove into town. Barely avoiding a gunfight outside Gusinsky's office, Gusinsky's bodyguards were forced to lie in the snow in what came to be known as "the faces in the snow" incident. NTV remained critical of the fighting in Chechnia, but a few days after Korzhakov's escapade, Gusinsky and his family fled to England.

Angry as he may have been about Yeltsin's effort to intimidate him, by 1996 and the real possibility that the Communist candidate Gennady Zyuganov might win the election for president, Gusinsky easily shifted direction and used his "independent" media to campaign for a Yeltsin victory. But that was not to last for long. By 1999, Gusinsky had switched again and as before adopted a critical attitude toward the Yeltsin government. Some allege his change in attitude was triggered when Alexander Voloshin, Yeltsin's Chief of Staff, refused to provide Gusinsky with a large loan.[25] Immediately thereafter NTV carried a series of reports about Yeltsin's daughter, the Yeltsin family's favorite oligarch Roman Abramovich, and the doings of the "Yeltsin Family," the entourage running the Kremlin. NTV's investigative journalism of Yeltsin and his staff continued with its critical coverage of Putin. In particular, NTV produced *Kukly*, a devastatingly satiric puppet show that ridiculed the Russian political and business establishment. It was irreverent toward everyone but Gusinsky. Though Yeltsin was not happy about the program, he did nothing to force it off the air. By contrast, Putin did all he could to terminate it. But Gusinsky persisted in protecting *Kukly*. When NTV was exceptionally critical of Putin's passive response to the sinking of the *Kursk* submarine in August 2000 and of his government's inability to provide heating and electricity for freezing residents in the Russian Far East, especially Vladivostok, Putin stepped up the pressure and set in motion through others a string of attacks on Gusinsky's empire and staff. Beginning in June 2000 Gusinsky was arrested on charges of embezzling some $10 million from the St. Petersburg firm Russkoye Video, in which he was a partner. He was jailed then for three days in Moscow. After a promise to turn over some of his stock in Media-MOST and NTV to Gazprom, from whom he had earlier borrowed $261 million, Gusinsky was allowed to go to Spain. However, shortly thereafter a warrant was again issued for his arrest, and he was jailed for another thirteen days, this time in Spain.[26] In the meantime, as part of this harassment, there were over thirty raids on Media-MOST headquarters and offices by everyone from masked tax police to deputies of the Prosecutor General. The Media-MOST treasurer was also jailed for over two years on the flimsiest of charges, and two of NTV's news anchors were called in for interrogation.

Admittedly Gusinsky had vastly overextended himself by hundreds of millions of dollars and could not repay his debts. But Gazprom's demand that Gusinsky repay his loan was probably politically motivated and attributable to Putin and the state's ownership of 38 percent of Gazprom's stock. The other TV networks, RTR and ORT, which were uncritical of Putin, also had overdue debts, but no one pressured them to pay up.[27]

Despite many questionable transactions Gusinsky was not an easy target for Putin. By casting himself as the last defender of an independent media in Russia, Gusinsky had to be handled with extreme care. In addition, part of his international support derived from Gusinsky's establishment in 1996 of the Russian Jewish Congress, an umbrella group of Jewish religious, social welfare, and communal groups. When I asked him why he had created an organization that made it more likely that he would become a target in a country with such a long history of anti-Semitism, he responded half-seriously, half-facetiously, "My mother made me do it." Undoubtedly she did. But Gusinsky must also have realized that by creating and heading such a group, he could establish valuable contacts around the world. This was especially so in the United States, where there has been a century-old concern about the well-being of Jews in Russia, be it czarist or Soviet. It was much the same thinking that led Gusinsky to seek dual citizenship by becoming a citizen of Israel. Undoubtedly, it was reassuring to know that if need be, he could also seek asylum there.

Gusinsky's involvement with the Jewish community created a serious problem for Putin. Given Russia's history of anti-Semitism and Putin's desire to participate in world affairs, it would damage his reputation were he to harass–let alone imprison–the head of the Russian Jewish Congress. Since almost all factions in the Jewish community were deeply devoted to Gusinsky, it would have been very difficult to take over the existing Russian Jewish Congress. Gusinsky had not only brought them out of the closet and provided them with respectability; he also subsidized their efforts with a $10 million annual contribution.[28] The alternative was to create a wholly new umbrella group, even if the leadership had to be brought in from outside Russia. The choice was Rabbi Berel Lazar, who was not a Russian citizen. Born in Italy, he was actually an American citizen who had lived in Russia only nine years, and his command of the Russian language was relatively weak. To remedy that, on May 26, 2000 Putin extended Russian citizenship to thirty-one individuals. While most were Uzbeks and Azeris, the final candidate was Rabbi Lazar.

Lazar belongs to the Orthodox Lubavitch Hassidic movement, or Chabad, headquartered in Brooklyn, New York. He had been sent, along with several dozen other adherents, to establish Hassidic communities all over the former Soviet Union. It was the Jewish equivalent of a missionary movement. By coincidence, one of Putin's favorite oligarchs, Roman Abramovich, attended Lubavitch services and provided financial support to Rabbi Lazar's movement.[29] Thus Abramovich may have inspired the strategy of the challenge to Gusinsky. Abramovich was also allied with Lev Levayev, a one-time official in the Russian Jewish Congress, who was a major supporter of the Lubavitch Hassidic movement in Israel and Russia, and a man eager to win favor with President Putin.

Levayev became the president of the new umbrella group, which instead of the Russian Jewish Congress they called the Federation of Jewish Communities in the Commonwealth of Independent States.[30] An Israeli citizen born in Uzbekistan, Levayev was a controversial diamond dealer who has allegedly used his access to President Putin to encroach on

De Beers' exclusive rights to Russian diamonds.[31] He has also been involved with the one-time aluminum oligarch Mikhail Chernoi, accused by the Israeli police of being deeply involved with the Russian underworld and international money laundering, charges denied by Chernoi.[32]

On June 13, 2000, two weeks after becoming a citizen and a day after meeting in the Kremlin with Putin, Lazar convened a meeting of his fellow Hassidic rabbi emissaries from forty-five Russian regions. They voted unanimously to make Rabbi Lazar the Chief Rabbi of Russia. This was somewhat awkward since there was an already existing Chief Rabbi, Adolf Shayevich, who was recognized by the Russian Jewish Congress. Undeterred the Russian government immediately decreed Lazar's Federation of Jewish Communities of Russia the official representative of Russian Jews, thereby superseding Gusinsky's Congress.

With the new Jewish Federation in place, Putin moved quickly. Once Gusinsky's Jewish communal group was no longer officially recognized as the official voice of Russia's Jews, there was less concern that pursuing Gusinsky would provoke charges of anti-Semitism. Thus, five hours later that same evening, June 13, 2000, Gusinsky was called in for questioning and put in prison. During a visit to Spain, Putin insisted that the Russian judicial system was completely independent and it was beyond his authority to influence the courts to release Gusinsky. Yet, after protests of several world leaders, the charges were dropped, and Gusinsky was freed. Nevertheless, there ensued a series of raids on the main Moscow synagogue and harassment of not only Gusinsky and Media-MOST, but Pinchus Goldschmidt, a Swiss citizen who had been the Chief Rabbi of Moscow under Shayevich. When Goldschmidt refused to shift his allegiance to Rabbi Lazar, it looked for a time that the Russian government would not renew his visa, and thus he would have to leave Russia. Moreover, while harassing Gusinsky's Russian Jewish Congress, Putin attended the dedication of the expanded Lubavitcher synagogue and community building. He also invited Lazar to a special dinner at the Kremlin during the January 2001 visit of the President of Israel, Moshe Katsav. To insure that Rabbi Lazar would have access to kosher food, Putin ordered a special cleansing (or koshering) of the Kremlin kitchen, the first time that this had happened in Russian history.

Speaking with both Rabbis is like watching the Japanese film *Rashomon*; witnesses to the same event describe sharply conflicting reports. Rabbi Lazar reports for example that Levayev was not only a founder and supporter of the Russian Jewish Congress with Gusinsky, but that Gusinsky had also been a supporter of the work of the Lubavitch movement. Rabbi Lazar says the Russian Jewish Congress became too political while his Federation was more involved with religious and cultural concerns. He denies charges by Reform rabbis that Hassidic rabbis go around asserting that the Reform movement "is not a religious organization" and therefore should be denied funding from Jewish groups. He also objects to those in the Russian Jewish Congress who complain that Putin's attack and harassment of Gusinsky was anti-Semitic. Moreover, when Gusinsky was arrested Rabbi Lazar said he wrote a letter of strong protest.[33]

By contrast, Rabbi Goldschmidt, whose father was a heroic Swiss Rabbi who helped to rescue Jews from Hitler's Germany, questions Rabbi Lazar's insistence that Lazar was not invited to Putin's inauguration as President.[34] Goldschmidt also argues that the Russian Jewish Congress is a more democratic group where the leaders are elected by the membership, in contrast with the Chabad, whose leaders are determined in Brooklyn and subservient to Putin's wishes. Rabbi Goldschmidt felt that Rabbi Lazar was too accommodating to Putin when he adopted what many said was a too nationalistic national anthem. In response, Rabbi Lazar insisted that the national anthem was not a matter for rabbinical criticism. At the same time, Rabbi Lazar asserted that he was the first to criticize Vladimir Zhirinovsky when he refused to join other members of the Duma in a moment of silence on Holocaust Day in 2001.

What all this demonstrates is how just as in the days of the czars, business in Russia is as much a matter of political and social intrigue as competence. Putin had no hesitation playing off factions in the Jewish community to achieve his political ends. Equally disturbing is the way members of the Jewish community allowed themselves to be used. These events echo back to Stalin's manipulation of the Jewish community in the 1940s and 1950s. While both Rabbis Lazar and Goldschmidt have left the comfort of the West to help Russian Jews practice their religion, anyone who allows himself to be manipulated in a country long noted for its anti-Semitism will discover that short-term gains are unlikely to be without cost. This was reflected in the spontaneous response of yet another Rabbi, Yachov Ben Haim, the head of the Reform Movement in Moscow. When I asked "What are your relations with Putin?" he replied just as the Rabbi in the play *Fiddler on the Roof* might have, "Baruhk Ha Shem (Praise be to God), I don't have any relations with Putin!!"

As for Putin, he has skillfully rid himself of this most outspoken media critic while deflecting charges of anti-Semitism. He proudly points to his struggle with Gusinsky as an example of his determination to crack down on the oligarchs and his visit to the synagogue and koshering of the kitchen as a demonstration of his support for the Jewish community.

For the first two years he was in power, Putin's attack on the oligarchs was limited to two specific targets, Gusinsky and **Boris Berezovsky**. It was more than coincidence that Berezovsky also controlled a major television network. Like Gusinsky, he used it to support Yeltsin, but when he criticized Putin for his failure to respond quickly enough to the sinking of the *Kursk*, as did Gusinsky, Berezovsky also quickly discovered that criticizing Putin is not without its risks.

All the oligarchs have been controversial, but perhaps none more so than Berezovsky. Also included among the initial Forbes Five top Russians as noted earlier, Berezovsky, born in 1946, was described in an earlier December 30, 1996 issue of *Forbes* as the head of the Russian Mafia.[35] Berezovsky took exception to this and has been attempting to sue Paul Klebnikov, the author of the article, and *Forbes* for slander. Klebnikov, among others, had inquired into Berezovsky's accumulation of wealth.[36] They point out that a number of those who opposed Berezovsky in one way or another, including the TV journalist Vladislav Listyev, died prematurely.

In a sense such charges are surprising because, unlike the other oligarchs, Berezovsky had not been involved in shady deals such as currency speculation or the second economy (underground or illegal) during the communist era. On the contrary, his was an academic background; he earned his Ph.D. in mathematics and physics in 1983, becoming an expert on systems control and operations research at the Moscow Forestry Institute, a research center that Stephen Kotkin of Princeton has called a cover for the Soviet Space Program.[37] Some Russians question the authenticity of his work, but he founded the Central Science Institute, which became affiliated with the Russian Academy of Sciences. He also became a corresponding member of the Academy.[38] He did some research work at the Harvard Business School in the 1970s and California Institute of Technology (Cal Tech) for one month in 1988.

Like the other oligarchs, however, Berezovsky also began his move to the market by creating a cooperative, called Logovaz, a consulting firm, in 1989. In the late 1980s he also imported and resold computer software from the West and worked as a management consultant to Avtovaz, the Soviet Union's largest automobile manufacturer and the producer of the Zhiguli, or Lada as it was called in Western Europe.[39] As Gosplan began to weaken in the late Gorbachev era, Berezovsky worked out a marketing arrangement between Logovaz and Avtovaz to help Avtovaz sell its automobiles. Without Gosplan or the help of economic ministries, most factories were at a loss as to how to sell their products. Berezovsky's earlier consulting work with Avtovaz provided an entry for Berezovsky to the company's managers who were seeking a way out of the twilight zone created by the collapse of the centrally planned system. Since most of those in authority at Avtovaz were engineers and production specialists, virtually no one there had any experience in selling, as opposed to manufacturing, automobiles. Berezovsky helped them obtain automotive parts and find customers for the automobiles. In the chaos of the early transition period, as we saw in Chapter 4, most transactions were done through barter. Because barter can be very complicated, Berezovsky convinced Avtovaz to transfer its cars to him and Logovaz–the cooperative trading company he created for this purpose–at a very low price. The low transfer price comes at the expense of the manufacturing enterprise and its workforce, although not necessarily the factory directors, who, in instances of this sort often worked out kickback schemes with the barterer, in this instance Berezovsky.

Since almost all the oligarchs either operated originally as trading companies or used trading companies, it might be helpful to explain why trading companies came to be so important in post-Soviet Russia. Historically, most enterprises in the Soviet era often found themselves with a need to procure and sell products not provided for by the official state plan. To do this, as we saw, they traditionally relied on a *tolkatch*. In the post-Soviet era, these *tolkatchi* converted themselves into "trading companies." For that matter, trading companies are not unique to Russia. Some of the largest businesses in Japan are trading companies. Unlike present day Japanese trading companies, however, the post-Soviet Russian version operated at first primarily through barter, not cash (the "virtual" or "barter" economies mentioned in Chapter 4).

Because it is so hard to find perfect matches in a barter deal, the *tolkatchi*'s skills in complex trading and their familiarity with possible sources of supply and demand made them indispensable in the immediate post-Soviet economy. The extra trouble and transaction costs involved were warranted because buying and selling for cash, which is cheaper and faster, was not an option in the near anarchy that characterized Russia in the early 1990s. It also helped that the *tolkatchi* trading company procedure was used by many factory directors as a way to line their own pockets with kickbacks.

Few Western analysts have paid much attention to the role of the trading companies in the transition process. Yet as Logovaz shows, understanding how the trading company worked is essential to explaining how many of the oligarchs rose to power. While I was unable to gain access to Logovaz, I had ample opportunity to familiarize myself with a similar operation, the Verkhne Volzhsk Shina (VVSh), a tire trading company in the city of Yaroslavl. It was established in 1994 in the wake of the privatization of the Yaroslavl Tire Factory, which had been one of the largest state enterprises in the city. As a state factory, it had no need to worry about the acquisition of raw material supplies or disposal of the tires produced. That was the responsibility of Gossnab, the state supply organization. After privatization, however, these acquisitions and sale functions became the responsibility of the tire company executives. Given their lack of experience with basic commercial market activities such as buying and selling, mastering such new procedures quickly was not easy. Furthermore there were no well-established markets to provide guidance as to what prices to charge. In addition, because of the tight money policy adopted to curb inflation, almost no one had cash to pay for large tire orders.

The Yaroslavl Tire Factory is also an example of the crime that sometimes accompanied the use of barter. On a 1997 visit to the factory making tire molds for the Yaroslavl Tire Factory, we noticed that there was a wreath hung over a picture in the main display room. When we asked about it, we were told that this was a picture of the manager who had privatized the tire mold factory. As payment for the tire molds, he was provided with tires. He then sold the tires at a price that upset the manager of the adjacent tire factory. After refusing to charge more, the manager of the tire mold factory was murdered. Of course, such crimes can occur in more conventional business transactions, but it is an example of how the Russians sometimes "eliminated" competition.

To avoid additional incidents, the commercial director of the tire factory suggested to some associates that they set up the VVSh Tire Trading Company. Under this new arrangement, since neither the tire factory customers nor its suppliers had cash, the trading company was to be given first call on the tires produced by the factory. It was understood that the barter that resulted would entitle the commercial director of the factory to a kickback. Initially dependent on the Yaroslavl Tire Factory for its tires, the VVSh Trading Company soon began to branch out, so that by the time of my visit it had ventured into real estate, textiles, and the conversion of a nuclear submarine shipyard.

The commercial director of VVSh explained to me that similar trading companies very quickly sprouted all over the country. As we saw, most large Russian factories found it hard to adjust to the market. Moreover, this was a convenient way for the executives of the tire company to supplement their incomes, something they became eager to do when outside bankers and investors sought to assume control of their factories.

While not always visible to outsiders, these trading companies became a key element in the operation of the Russian economy. Their influence has not always been benign. In many instances they became the tail that wagged the dog, and were responsible at least in part for the poor economic performance of a number of businesses. That there was a problem is suggested by the fact that while 50 percent or more of the state enterprises newly privatized during the 1990s ran at a loss, most of the trading companies did quite well.

The near bankruptcy of the Magnitogorsk Steel Mill typifies how trading companies operated to strip a manufacturer's assets. Since the plant managers dealing with the trading company were not the majority owners of the plant, they were not particularly concerned that the trading company was siphoning off the steel mill's assets. The trading company, like the one in Yaroslavl, also found ways to reward those with whom it worked. Thus, Profit, the trading company that supplied Magnitogorsk with the scrap steel it used as a raw material input, purchased the scrap at a very cheap price and sold it to the same Magnitogorsk at six times the prevailing market price. Moreover, because the brother of Magnitogorsk's general director ran Profit, he had relatively little concern about the high prices. Magnitogorsk also overpaid for its coal swaps in much the same way. Similarly, it bartered the steel that it produced at a low price for a small quantity of natural gas. Reflecting the lack of concern for whether or not Magnitogorsk's management made a profit for the enterprise as a whole, in the second half of 1997 the plant exchanged 280 billion rubles worth of steel for 75 billion rubles worth of natural gas.[40]

Berezovsky's trading company arrangement with Avtovaz operated in much the same fashion. It was profitable, though considerably more dangerous. In mid-1994, an assassination attempt was made on Berezovsky. He escaped, but his driver was killed. Despite the dangers, Berezovsky's trading company established strong control over the automobile market in Moscow. Paul Klebnikov, the reporter for *Forbes*, asserts that Berezovsky did this with the help of the Chechen mafia.[41] Klebnikov also notes that almost everyone who attempted to horn in on one of his business activities somehow met a tragic and unexpected death. Coincidence or not, Berezovsky's empire grew to include the sale of foreign cars such as Fiat and Mercedes, and eventually he took over the management, although not necessarily the stock or ownership, of Aeroflot, the oil company Sibneft, most of Russia's aluminum industry, and ORT, the state's largest and most influential television network.

Berezovsky also profited from an investment scheme called AVVA (The All Russian Automobile Alliance) that he created with Alexander Voloshin in October 1993.[42] They sold shares to the general public and promised to use the proceeds to create a joint venture with Avtovaz and General Motors. This joint venture would then produce 300,000 automobiles a year. Once GM agreed to the deal, over 100,000 Russians rushed to buy shares, which brought in $50 million. But that was not sufficient to carry out the joint venture, which fell through. By the fall of 1994, AVVA securities had become worthless.[43] Berezovsky, however, did not suffer. He reportedly retained some of the proceeds. Moreover, in the process he developed a close working relationship with Voloshin, who soon became Chief of Staff for Boris Yeltsin and subsequently for Putin. Voloshin, who subsequently was accused of profiting from a series of such shady transactions, helped Berezovsky gain access to the Yeltsin family and staff.[44] Berezovsky's influence was further enhanced after he made Yeltsin's son-in-law the president of Aeroflot.

Given his influence it seemed only natural that Berezovsky would take the lead in rallying support for the reelection of Boris Yeltsin in the 1996 presidential campaign. Using his control over ORT, the main TV network, he helped shift public opinion from the one-time frontrunner, Communist candidate Gennady Zyuganov, to the incumbent (but often drunk and incapacitated) Boris Yeltsin. That transformation was not so easy. After the December 1995 Duma election, which the Communist Party won, Yeltsin's standing in the polls was less than 10 percent. Fearing that a Communist victory would result in the confiscation of their property and even their imprisonment or death, the oligarchs put aside their feuds and rallied around Berezovsky to finance and publicize Yeltsin's campaign. Those most involved included seven of the oligarch bankers–Peter Aven, Boris Berezovsky, Mikhail Fridman, Vladimir Gusinsky, Mikhail Khodorkovsky, Vladimir Potanin, and Alexander Smolensky–who as we described in Chapter 1 came to be called the *Semibankirshchina*. Using their control of the most important television channels and newspapers, they helped transform the public perception of Yeltsin, so that in June he won the election with 53.8 percent of the votes cast. Reveling in what he saw as the influence of this small group, Berezovsky boasted (falsely) that these seven oligarchs controlled 50 percent of the country's wealth. If the number had been increased to perhaps twelve oligarchs, including those discussed in Chapter 6 who came to control the country's oil and gas enterprises, he would have been closer to the mark.

As a reward for his efforts, Berezovsky was appointed Deputy Secretary of the National Security Council by Yeltsin and, later, the Executive Secretary of the Organization for Coordinating the Commonwealth of Independent States (CIS). Though Yeltsin ultimately fired him from both positions, he continued to have intimate contacts inside the Yeltsin Kremlin, especially with Yeltsin's daughter, Tatyana Dyachenko, and staff. He viewed himself as a king-maker and on occasion he was a major force in the ousting of senior government officials including Sergei Kiriyenko, the Prime Minister, in August 1998.[45] Alert to the danger, Kiriyenko's successor Evgeny Primakov moved to neutralize Berezovsky. As part of an anti-corruption campaign, Primakov had several Berezovsky loyalists from Aeroflot, Sibneft, and ORT fired, and he sent in tax inspectors and auditors to intimidate those who remained.[46]

Primakov's attack on Berezovsky was made possible in part because of the weakened position of the oligarchs, hurt by the August 1998 economic meltdown. But though weakened, Berezovsky's connections to the Yeltsin family remained intact and, much to Primakov's surprise, it was Primakov who was replaced in office. He was succeeded by Sergey Stepashin, until then the Minister of the Interior and earlier the head of Federal Security Service (FSB, the successor to the KGB) and, to top it off, the charges against Berezovsky were, for the time being, dropped.[47]

But President Yeltsin apparently felt that, while Stepashin as Prime Minister was an improvement over Primakov, he needed an even more forceful leader to succeed him. After a bare three months, from May to August, Stepashin was also fired. With Berezovsky's help, Yeltsin replaced him with Vladimir Putin, then head of the FSB. This was done, according to Yeltsin, with the clear intention of preparing Putin to run for president in the 2000 election.[48] As a quid for this quo, Putin eventually agreed to a guarantee of immunity from prosecution for Yeltsin and his family. However in early 2001, the Duma passed legislation intended to restrict such protection. This was in part a response to the multitude of rumors implicating Yeltsin and, more particularly, his daughter in payoffs that were said to be have been made to Pavel Borodin, who had served as the manager of Kremlin property under Yeltsin. This was no small responsibility. According to some estimates, Borodin's portfolio of property amounted to a massive $600 billion.[49] There was particular concern over Borodin's expenditure of $800 million for the refurbishing of government properties such as the Kremlin, the Belgrade Hotel, the Palace of Congresses in the Kremlin, and Yeltsin's presidential airplane. Swiss government authorities found evidence that the two Swiss firms, Mabetex and Mercata, which did the work kicked back $25 million from the contract for Borodin and his friends, some of whom were said to have been Yeltsin's daughters.[50]

The accusations against Borodin indirectly affected Berezovsky since the two had earlier been close collaborators and important members of what was referred to as "the Family." It was "the Family" that was said to have put forward Putin. In fact, after Putin found himself jobless in St. Petersburg, it was Borodin who brought Putin to Moscow in 1996 to work under him as Deputy Director of the Kremlin Property Division.[51] From there, Yeltsin appointed Putin head of the FSB, then Prime Minister, and finally, Acting President. Berezovsky claims that he was involved at each stage of Putin's Moscow promotion process.[52] This must have made it all the more painful when Putin turned on him, threatened him with imprisonment for various illegal acts, and eventually forced him to yield control of ORT, the country's main television network.

How Berezovsky came to run ORT was always a bit of a mystery. The state owned 51 percent of ORT's stock and at most Berezovsky was said to control only 19 percent. But because Yeltsin and "the Family" seemed content to let Berezovsky hold sway, that was enough for him to determine the makeup of the network's management. In fact, as Paul Klebnikov notes, control of management, not necessarily the absolute ownership of a majority of the stock, was the secret to Berezovsky's success. In this way he could spread his influence and capital over a wider circle of enterprises.

By late 2000, amid unrelenting pressure from Putin, Berezovsky decided to resign from the Duma seat he won in 1999 and later to flee Russia. Among the accusations against him, both Russian and Swiss prosecutors charged Berezovsky with diverting as much as $973 million from Aeroflot through Forus Services and Andava, two Swiss firms, and FOK, an Irish firm, all controlled by Berezovsky. These three firms were set up shortly after Berezovsky took over control of Aeroflot in 1995. His deputies at Aeroflot, Alexander Krasnenker and Nikolai Gluskov (subsequently arrested by the Swiss), then ordered that all the foreign currency earned by Aeroflot from ticket sales be sent to Andava and Forus. FOK was then hired to collect Aeroflot's foreign debts from Andava. For this FOK was paid $38 million. As Yulia Latynina, a columnist for *The Moscow Times*, pointed out, Aeroflot was borrowing its own money and paying a finder's fee for the privilege.[53] This behavior was typical of the way the oligarchs enriched themselves at the expense of the partially privatized state enterprises. In this particular instance, Berezovsky justified his actions by explaining that some of these funds were used to finance Yeltsin's 1996 presidential election campaign and later Putin's 2000 campaign.[54]

Of all the oligarchs, **Anatoly Chubais** had the least experience as a businessman. Until 1998 when he became the president of UES, the electricity monopoly, most of his work had been as an academic, political reformer, and government bureaucrat. A native of Leningrad, he was born in 1955 to a father who was a military man, a "convinced communist," and a true believer in socialism.[55] His older brother, however, was a radical dissident who, but for his father's influence, would have been jailed after protesting the Russian invasion of Czechoslovakia in 1968. As for Anatoly, he was too young for such protests and so graduated from the Leningrad Engineering Economic Institute without incident.

Under the influence of his family and communist indoctrination, Chubais acknowledges that in his younger days he was very anti-business. Subsequently, however, he organized several economic discussion groups that debated the outlines of the possible economic reforms and he became more and more supportive of a move to the market. With the coming of Gorbachev's *glasnost* and democratization, he joined the political reform movement and was elected to the Leningrad city council. Subsequently, he joined the reform administration of Mayor Anatoly Sobchak.

When Yegor Gaidar, who had organized similar reform discussion groups in Moscow, was asked to draw up a reform program for Boris

Yeltsin he brought in Chubais as a participant. In late 1991 Chubais was put in charge of the State Committee on Privatization. He designed and helped implement the voucher program and the subsequent privatization of state enterprises. Throughout all of this, at least until 1993, Chubais managed to survive Yeltsin's purges of other reformers. Gradually he rose through the bureaucracy to become Deputy Prime Minister, a post he filled from 1992 to 1993 when Yeltsin fired him as well. Yeltsin rehired him in 1994, but he was again fired in late 1995 because of the widespread criticism of the privatization process and blamed for the Communist Party victory in the 1995 Duma election. In 1996 however, he resurfaced to lead Yeltsin's successful campaign for reelection as President, and as a reward was put in charge of Yeltsin's administrative staff. Like a jack-in-the-box who keeps popping up, he was appointed a third time as Deputy Prime Minster in 1997 but then once more fired in 1998.

Because of Chubais' contact with Western leaders (including Stanley Fischer, the Deputy Director of the IMF, and Larry Summers at the US Treasury,) Kiriyenko, then the Prime Minister, called on Chubais in mid-1998 to negotiate for a loan from the IMF. Just before the August 17, 1998 financial crash, Chubais managed to convince the IMF to provide Russia with $4.8 billion in loans, double what had been expected. He later acknowledged however that he "misrepresented" Russia's economic health in order to persuade the IMF to grant that loan. When asked about Chubais' negotiations with the Fund, Stanley Fischer acknowledged that, "The central issue is, Were we lied to? ... The answer ... is unfortunately 'yes'."[56]

Chubais initially built up his personal wealth by providing services for some of the oligarchs. Shortly after Yeltsin fired Chubais in December 1995 as Deputy Prime Minister, Alexander Smolensky provided him with a $3 million interest-free loan, which as of the time of writing this has still not been repaid. Other bankers, as we saw earlier, also provided him and some of his associates with rather large advances for a book which, after some delay, was published in 1999.[57] Though Chubais insisted there was nothing wrong with such arrangements, given that those who provided the advance had profited enormously under Chubais' watch, his arguments were not entirely persuasive.

After having been in and out of government so often, Chubais decided the best way to provide himself with a financial and political base was to join the ranks of the oligarchs. In the spring of 1998, he arranged to have himself appointed CEO of UES, Russia's dominant electrical utility. Given the country's economic difficulties, many UES customers had developed the habit of not paying their bills. To pressure them, Chubais began to turn off their electrical supplies.

Subsequently Chubais came in for further criticism because of a plan he put forward to reorganize UES. Under his proposal, many of UES's electric generating plants would be spun off and sold while UES and Chubais would retain ownership of the transmission lines. This scheme upset many UES stockholders, especially foreign investors who complained that the generating plants would likely be sold for too cheap a price, thereby benefiting the new–not the old–owners.[58] In other words the stock value of the original stockholders would be watered down. Angered by what he saw as repeated instances of Chubais' shady behavior, one Russian complained, "well in 1993–1994 we Russians learned that Anatoly Chubais was a swindler; in 1997–1998, the IMF and the U.S. Treasury learned that Chubais was a swindler. And now, finally in 2000, foreign investors are learning that Chubais is a swindler. But he's an entertaining swindler."[59] Such criticism notwithstanding, with the help of his banker friends and his administration of UES, Chubais gradually provided himself with a nice financial cushion. Nonetheless, as of early August 1998, Chubais was the poorest of the oligarchs discussed in this chapter.

Mikhail Fridman, along with **Peter Aven**, founded the Alfa Group Consortium, a holding company which today controls the Alfa Bank, Alfa Capital, Tyumen Oil, several construction material firms (cement, timber, glass), food processing businesses, and a supermarket chain. In 2001 they also toyed with the possibility of buying a Swiss trading company created by Marc Rich, the American in exile who received the controversial pardon from President Bill Clinton. Alfa is also a major holder of tea and sugar plant processors. One of the youngest of the newly rich presented here, Fridman, the son of an academic father, was born in 1964 in Lvov and graduated from the Moscow Institute of Steel and Alloys. From 1986 to 1988 he worked as an engineer in the Electrostal factory.

Fridman began work as a private entrepreneur while a student. He washed windows on the side as a *del'ets*, a form of activity, as we noted earlier, that was officially illegal. With some classmates, he also organized a discotheque and became an early devotee of American jazz, also frowned upon by Soviet officials at the time. Fred Starr, the leader of the Louisiana Repertory Jazz Band, which performed in several Soviet cities, reported that Fridman would appear at almost every concert. Fridman and his classmates also sold theater tickets and arranged small construction projects.

Thus, when it became legal to open cooperative and private concerns in 1987, Fridman was well prepared. He set up *Kur'yer*, a cooperative which arranged for courier delivery of goods, window-washing, and apartment rentals. He also imported Western cigarettes, perfume and Xerox machines, and even bred white mice.[60] In 1988 he set up his own photo cooperative, Alfa Foto and then ALFA/EKO, a commodities trading firm, and AlfaKapital. He also resold computers, one of the most profitable activities in the late 1980s. With the capital he had built up from these various activities, especially from trading commodities, he established the Alfa Bank in January 1991 in Moscow. That required 6 million rubles–at the time the equivalent of $100,000.[61] The bank was the precursor of the Alfa Group Consortium. Shortly thereafter in 1992, Fridman brought in Peter Aven, a one-time academic who left his post (Gaidar says he was fired) as Minister of Foreign Economic Relations to head the bank. Together they purchased Indian and then Russian debt securities that shortly thereafter rose in value, earning them several million dollars in profit.[62] In July 1997, he and Aven made their most important acquisition when they bid $810 million to acquire 40 percent of Tyumen Oil, which they now own jointly with Access, an American-based investment group run by Russian émigrés.[63] Today Fridman and Aven own half of one of the country's richest oil companies and are not accountable to thousands of shareholders and owners.

While Fridman and Aven are often considered to be among the more enlightened oligarchs (especially by reform political figures such as Boris Nemtsov and Grigory Yavlinsky), their Alfa Group has come in for its share of criticism. For example, one of its subsidiaries, Crown Resources, an offshoot of Alfa's Swiss company called Trading Resources, made a practice of chartering the cheapest oil tankers it could find to ship its petroleum. One of them, *Prestige*, broke up off the Spanish coast in late 2002 and created a massive oil slick.

Alfa and its subsidiary, Tyumen Oil, have also been among the more notorious users of the Russian bankruptcy courts. It used them to seize assets from several Western investors including BP/Amoco and Norex, a Canadian firm. In suing Tyumen Oil to recover its assets, Norex notes that Tyumen has not only used bankruptcy courts to strip it and Sidanko of their assets, but it has also stripped companies such as Rospan, Rospan Nosta, Black Sea, NNG, and Tagmet.[64]

As for BP, it now has a good working arrangement with Tyumen Oil (TNK), but as we saw in Chapter 6, there were times when relations were very nasty. TNK was eager to gain control of Chernogorneft's oil fields because they were adjacent to TNK's Samotlor field in Nizhnevartovsk in the Tyumen region of West Siberia. However Chernogorneft was owned by Sidanko, which in turn was owned by Vladimir Potanin, who in turn in 1997 had sold a 10 percent share of Sidanko to BP/Amoco for $484 million.[65] (Other reports put the investment at $571 million.)[66] Other investors in Sidanko included George Soros, Harvard University, and the EBRD.[67]

To BP/Amoco's amazement, in October 1998 a minor creditor sued Chernogorneft for an unpaid bill of a mere $50,000. Other suits followed and in December 1998 Chernogorneft was suddenly declared bankrupt by a regional judge appointed by Leonid Roketsky.[68] But as noted, Roketsky also just happened to be Chairman of TNK at the time. Try as they might, under the then bankruptcy code there was no way for either Sidanko or BP/Amoco to step in to pay off the overdue bills.[69] Fearful for their lives, BP/Amoco wrote off $200 million of their investment and the company faced the prospect that it might have to write off the rest as well.[70] BP/Amoco's concerns were precipitated by the discovery that in the wake of the bankruptcy proceedings, Chernogorneft was about to be put up for sale to the highest bidder. But we have seen how in Russia, the highest bidder is not always forced to bid high and the winners of the auction are not always who we think they are.

It might be assumed that Sidanko would enter a bid to protect its interests. However because it was badly hurt by the financial collapse of August 17, 1998, Sidanko did not enter a competing bid. At the same time BP/Amoco was uncertain how to respond. Making it even more difficult for Sidanko, TNK arranged for a straw subsidiary to purchase 60 percent of Chernogorneft's debt. Ownership of this debt along with the connivance of Governor Roketsky and his judges gave TNK effective control of the bankruptcy proceedings.[71] As a result TNK ended up bidding a mere $176 million for what was considered a $1 billion property, and BP/Amoco for all intents and purposes was out.[72] TNK tried to find a compromise but BP/Amoco refused.[73] For its part, TNK rejected belated offers by Sidanko to pay off all of Chernogorneft's overdue bills.

To an outside observer this all seems illegal. But in an interview with Simon Kukes, the CEO of TNK, and later with Peter Aven of Alfa Bank, who with Mikhail Fridman owns 50 percent of TNK, both insist that what they did was perfectly legal.[74] As Peter Aven put it, "We did indeed make aggressive use of the bankruptcy law" (that is, until the law was amended in 2002, those with an existing share of ownership in a company declared bankrupt had no automatic right to pay off the debt and thus preserve their equity interest), "but we did nothing illegal." In our analogy, they were hard-riding jockeys determined to make the best of the lame horses or flawed initial conditions then existing.

Frustrated and angered by what they regarded as the uneven and opaque rules of corporate behavior in Russia, BP/Amoco decided to use its political clout in the United States where it knew the rules and customs to frustrate and embarrass TNK. Aware that TNK had turned to the U.S. Export Import Bank for a $198 million loan to upgrade its Ryazan refineries and a second loan for $292 million to help develop its Samotlor oil field, BP/Amoco began a PR effort to force the Eximbank to revoke its loan.[75] Its PR firm Andreae, Vick and Associates then began to battle with

Fleishman-Hillard, Tyumen's PR firm. The loan became a natural target, especially for Republican Congressmen, many of whom had always wanted to close down the Eximbank. Others doubted the wisdom of financing credit for Russian companies, especially a petroleum company, even if the proceeds of the loan were to be used to pay the U.S. companies Halliburton and ABB Lummus Global for the Ryazan and Samotlor work. Sensitive to the issues involved, especially when Russia resumed its attack on Chechnia, Secretary of State Madeleine Albright and the Clinton administration called for cancellation of the loan.[76] After a temporary cancellation on December 21, 1999 the loan was ultimately approved a few days later, helped in part by lobbying of the administration and Congress by, of all people, Richard Cheney. He had a personal interest. He was then the CEO of Halliburton and only later would he be chosen by George W. Bush to be his presidential running mate.

It also helped that at almost the same time BP/Amoco and TNK managed to resolve their difficulties and enter into what seems to be a pragmatic working relationship. The Chernogorneft field was returned to Sidanko. For this TNK was given an equity ownership in Sidanko equal to 25 percent plus one share. BP/Amoco was given the same voting rights but kept its ownership at 10 percent.[77] In 2002, BP put in another $375 million so that it now owns 25 percent of Sidanko.

Not everything has been controversial. Fridman and Aven have also moved into the telecom business, purchasing major shares of Golden Telecom and Vimpelcom. Because they anticipated the instability of Russia's economic situation, in 1998, Alfa Bank cashed in many of its rubles and bought dollars.[78] As a result, of the various banks controlled by the oligarchs, Fridman's bank was the least affected by the August 1998 financial crisis. Also to their credit, Alfa Bank was one of the few, if not the only, bank associated with the oligarchs that stood by its depositors and investors and did not default on its obligations.

Unlike Alexander Smolensky, Fridman and some others, who in their youth made their way by defying the Soviet state and central planning, **Mikhail Khodorkovsky** initially was the very model of the young communist bureaucrat. Born in 1963, he rose from a poor family in a communal apartment in Moscow to power and wealth and inclusion in the Forbes Five. He began in the Komsomol, the Young Communist League, and graduated from the prestigious Mendeleeva Chemical Technical Institute in 1986, one year after Gorbachev came to power. He also studied law for two years and took courses on finance at the Plekhanov Institute.[79] In December 1987 he, along with twelve Mendeleev classmates, opened a coffeehouse and a discotheque, and shortly thereafter formed the Intersectoral Center of Scientific Technical Progress, whose initials in

Russian were Menatep. It was a catch-all cooperative which sought to finance the work of thirteen fellow graduates of the Mendeleeva Chemical Technical Institute. They offered their skills in scientific research, particularly in chemistry, automation and computerization. Like Fridman, one of their main sources of profit stemmed from the buying and selling of computers. They also lent money to their classmates and operated much like a credit union.

In August 1988, the cooperative was reconstituted into the Interbank Organization for Scientific Technical Progress, with the same initials. As we saw in Chapter 5, Menatep officially received a charter for the Commercial Innovative Bank on December 29, 1988, which was a joint venture of Menatep and the Soviet Bank Zhilsotsbank. Its founding capital was 2.5 million rubles, equivalent to about $4 million at the time.[80] According to some reports, the early deposits of the bank may have included funds provided by the Komsomol Central Committee and perhaps the Communist Party itself.[81] Khodorkovsky has acknowledged that on occasion he sought help from the State Committee on Science and Technology to ward off some harassment from the police, and of course this particular state committee worked closely with the KGB.[82]

In 1990 the Commercial Innovative Bank was rechartered as Menatep, a joint stock company, and Khodorkovsky became chairman of the board of directors. This was the first time in seventy years that individuals could openly buy stock in such an entity. To attract investors, Khodorkovsky also made stockholders members of the Menatep Stockholders Club, which was created in August 1991.[83]

When the state began the campaign to privatize state enterprises, Menatep saw this as an opportunity to expand beyond banking. It set up a market for the vouchers issued by the state and used these vouchers to gain control of several enterprises that had just been privatized. To do so, in 1992 the bank created Rosprom as a holding company to manage its industrial portfolio. While Menatep directly controls some businesses, particularly metallurgical and paper manufacturers, most of its forty or so industrial holdings are divided into six categories: chemicals, construction, textile, consumer goods, mining, and oil.[84] Among them, its most successful and controversial holding is YUKOS, which has grown to become the country's largest oil company. Until his purchase of YUKOS, Khodorkovsky's involvement with the petroleum business was limited to his brief stint as Deputy Minister of Fuel and Energy in 1993. Menatep gained control of 78 percent of YUKOS for a mere $309 million in December 1995 during one of the notorious Loans for Shares auctions.[85] Not a bad bargain. By 2002, YUKOS had a capitalized value of approximately $15 billion.[86]

In May 1997, Khodorkovsky changed his title to become Chairman of the Board of Rosprom. This allowed him to devote more time to the bank's industrial holdings. He also assumed the presidency of YUKOS. Some of his actions have generated considerable criticism, particularly from minority stockholders who held shares in some of Rosprom's subsidiaries. Amoco, the former United States oil company now owned by BP/Amoco, was one of his harshest critics.[87] Foreign banks in Japan, Germany and South Africa have also complained that YUKOS diluted the collateral that it had originally pledged on loans the banks had provided.[88] Similarly Russia's Federal Securities Commission was asked to investigate the propriety of an $800 million loan that YUKOS took out by putting up collateral assets in Samaraneftegas, one of its subsidiaries. Minority stockholders in Samaraneftegas also complained that their oil company was sold at a steep discount to YUKOS, thereby transferring the profit on the transaction to YUKOS with the result that Samaraneftegas operated at a loss.[89] In another instance, Rosprom was ordered to give back to the government two large factories, the Volzhsky Pipe Factory and Apatit, a chemical company that it privatized in 1994. Rosprom was charged with failing to make the investments in the companies that were a condition of the purchase from the state.[90]

Menatep's operations have been equally controversial. In 1994, the U.S. Federal Reserve Bank, for example, ordered an investigation by the CIA to determine whether the bank was engaged in illegal activities in the United States, including organized crime.[91] While the report was said to warn that "the majority of Russian banks are controlled by the dreaded Mafia," apparently the only bank mentioned explicitly was Menatep.[92] These charges resurfaced when Menatep was alleged to be involved along with the Bank of New York in Russian money laundering, charges which Khodorkovsky denied.[93]

During the August 17, 1998 financial crisis, with hands quicker than Houdini's, Khodorkovsky managed to protect himself at the expense of his depositors and creditors. Like most of Moscow's large banks, Menatep had invested heavily in the Russian government's GKOs. When the government announced that it would no longer pay interest or redeem these notes, Menatep became insolvent and was forced to close its doors, effectively nullifying the deposits of thousands of businesses and individuals. Menatep also defaulted on a $236 million loan from Western banks.[94] Some say that Mr. Khodorkovsky, along with some of the other Russian oligarchs, had advance warning of the government's pending decision to cease support of the ruble, which gave him time to convert his rubles into dollars. In addition, Mr. Khodorkovsky moved quickly to switch the few assets in Menatep that remained viable to a "new" bank, renamed

Menatep St. Petersburg, thus preventing their seizure by his creditors.[95] He also shuffled shares of some oil subsidiaries to reduce the value of the YUKOS shares held as collateral by the Western lenders.[96]

Because the banking crisis ran so deep, there were not many assets left in Menatep for Khodorkovsky to strip. What helped him more than anything else was the significant climb in oil prices in 1999 that pushed up the value of YUKOS. Given a second chance, Khodorkovsky decided to disassociate himself from his previous business strategy, and began instead to posture himself as a crusader for stockholder and investor rights. In that guise he launched a PR offensive to convince Western investors that YUKOS, with a stock price earnings ratio hovering around one or two, would be a good investment. To show he was serious, he brought in several Western executives as well as a Western accounting and a PR firm and appointed five foreigners to his Board of Directors, including Sarah Carey, a Washington lawyer, Raj Kumar Gupta, a former vice president of Phillips Petroleum, and Michel Soublin, the treasurer of Schlumberger.[97] To show how public-spirited YUKOS had become, it donated $1 million to the U.S. Library of Congress and set up an Open Russia Foundation with, among others, Henry Kissinger as a member of the board of trustees.[98] This strategy also meant settling some earlier stockholder suits instituted by some of the banks like ING Barings and Credit Lyonnais. He also offered to compromise with individual investors such as Kenneth Dart. Dart had claimed he had been defrauded of millions of dollars when Khodorkovsky stripped assets from oil subsidiaries invested in by Dart but ultimately controlled by YUKOS and Khodorkovsky.[99] As part of the compromise, YUKOS had to suspend its PR campaign that pictured Dart as the asset stripper and YUKOS as an innocent victim.[100]

What remains to be seen is whether or not Mr. Khodorkovsky, previously one of the most notorious abusers of Western corporate governance procedures, has managed to overcome his conditioned response to unethical opportunities and instead adhere to those codes of behavior that have heretofore been so alien. The challenge is to determine whether or not he has truly reformed, or if he has simply concluded that having stolen all he can within Russia he must now look overseas. As recently as 1999 Khodorkovsky switched the location of the shareholders' meeting without advance notice to minority stockholders. He moved it to a location 160 miles from Moscow, making it impossible for them to attend a session and vote against the sale of YUKOS' assets to an offshore company assumed also to be under Khodorkovsky's control.[101] In January 2002, the government's audit chamber charged that YUKOS had engaged in stripping assets from Eastern Oil.[102] Similarly, in a PR gesture to show YUKOS' support for American efforts to reduce its reliance on Saudi Arabian oil, and incidentally to draw attention to YUKOS stock–in June 2002 YUKOS delivered a tanker full of petroleum to Houston, Texas. However, because YUKOS is apparently not yet a fully compliant corporate citizen, the tanker shipment was seized by Dardana, a Houston oil services company that charged YUKOS with failing to pay its bills.[103] Dardana claims YUKOS owes it $17 million, awarded to Dardana in 1988 by a Swedish arbitration tribunal.

Whether YUKOS has in fact turned over a new leaf or not, investors, including many in the West, believe that it has. In 2001 and 2002, they have bought YUKOS stock and in the process lifted the price earnings ratio of YUKOS' stock to even eight and, on occasion, ten. This has meant a four-fold increase in Mr. Khodorkovsky's net worth, which in June 2002 he acknowledged was $7.6 billion.[104]

Not all of the oligarchs are products of the pre-market era. One of the youngest was **Roman Abramovich**. For some time, he was probably the least well known–almost a "stealth" oligarch. Few people even knew what he looked like; the newspaper *Versiya* in 1999 offered a reward to the first person to find his photograph.

While he may have been the new man on the block, Abramovich's rise was rapid and his politics adroit. It was only in 2000, for example, that his name was listed among the ten most influential Russian businessmen. He, as well as everyone else, agreed that he owed most of his success to Boris Berezovsky. Under Berezovsky's patronage, Abramovich managed to win the confidence, first of Yeltsin's daughter Tatyana Dyachenko, then Yeltsin, and, in a maneuver common to the oligarchs who survived, the support of Yeltsin's successor, Vladimir Putin. It was not by chance that Tatyana Dyachenko's husband, Alexei, headed East Coast Petroleum, an oil trading company that sold oil purchased from a refinery owned by Sibneft, a company created by Berezovsky and later controlled by Abramovich.[105]

Sibneft was one of the private petroleum companies created out of the Ministry of Energy. On August 24, 1995 a presidential edict called for the formation of a Siberian oil company. Five days later, President Yeltsin issued a subsequent decree announcing the formation of what came to be called Sibneft, Russia's sixth largest oil company. At one of the early Loans for Shares auctions in December 1995, 51 percent of Sibneft's shares was offered for sale.[106] Finansovaia Neftyanaia Kompaniia (FNK/Financial Oil Company), heretofore an unknown company, won control of Sibneft for the rather paltry bid of $100 million, plus a promise of future investment.[107] At the time Sibneft was said to be worth at least $600 million.[108] Ninety-five percent of FNK was controlled by ALKION Securities, which was owned 100 percent by the bank SBS Agro, controlled by Alexander Smolensky, who in fact was said to be acting on behalf of Berezovsky.

However, the so-called "auction" that was conducted under the Loans for Shares program was run by the Neftyanaia Finansovaia Kompaniia, or NFK (note the similarity in names), which was closely affiliated with Boris Berezovsky.[109] Yeltsin's former bodyguard, Alexander Korzhakov, not exactly a fan of Berezovsky, reported that Berezovsky asked the Kremlin to set aside Sibneft for him, as a personal slush fund, so that he could finance the operation of the TV network ORT.

Abramovich arrived on the scene at Sibneft the following year. While some of his subsequent associations relate more to politics than petroleum, Abramovich's training and prior work experience was as a petroleum specialist. Born on October 24, 1966 in Saratov, orphaned at age four, Abramovich was brought up by his grandparents in the Komi region. He graduated from the Gubkin Institute of Oil and Gas in Moscow.[110] After graduation, he entered the oil business and by 1992 he was trading commodities, especially petroleum. Although in that same year he was accused of using false papers to sell Siberian oil, the lawsuit was switched from Moscow to a provincial jurisdiction where the charges were dropped.[111] Continuing to trade oil and other commodities, he became head of the Moscow office of Runicom, a Swiss trading company that operated in the same fashion as the Russian trading companies described earlier. In a second Loans for Shares auction for the remaining shares of Sibneft in 1996, Runicom bought 12.2 percent of the shares offered.[112] Given the number of shares under Abramovich's control through Runicom, he was made a member of Sibneft's Board of Directors, and later put in charge of Sibneft's Moscow office. By 2000, he was reported to control over 40 percent of Sibneft's shares.[113]

As for Berezovsky, after what seemed to be his initial success with Putin, he misstepped, probably by allowing the ORT TV network to criticize the way Putin responded to the sinking of the submarine *Kursk*. As a result, Berezovsky soon found himself on the out with Putin and, for that matter, out of Russia itself. After several investigations and threats of more to come, Berezovsky, as we saw, resigned from his seat in the Duma and took refuge in England, France and the United States. By contrast, as of 2002 Abramovich seemed to be one of the few oligarchs still part of the Putin entourage. More than that, when Berezovsky decided he had better cash out of some of his investments, he sold his stock in the television network ORT for $80 million to Abramovich. In turn Abramovich dutifully transferred his voting rights to the state, thus assuring Putin control of the country's largest TV network and at the same time removing yet another critic.[114]

Abramovich seemed to insulate himself from these intrigues. In a further show of government favoritism, Putin and the anti-monopoly authorities stood by silently in March 2000 as Abramovich expanded his empire to form

RUSSAL (Russian Aluminum), a Russian aluminum monopoly, with another oligarch, **Oleg Deripaska**, who was only 32 at the time. Each owns 50 percent of the company's stock.[115] RUSSAL controls 80 percent of Russia's aluminum output and ranks second in world production. It also owns 25 percent of GAZ, the automobile manufacturer, which produces the Volga automobile and the Gazelle light truck.[116] Though Russian Aluminum, Deripaska, and another of his partners, Mikhail Chernoi, were sued in a New York court in late 2000 for, among other things, money laundering, extortion, and attempted murder, Abramovich was not named in the suit.[117]

Nonethless Abramovich has not escaped criticism. Interviewed in *Le Monde*, Dzhalol Khaydarov, a former partner of Chernoi, charged that both Abramovich and Deripaska bring together two clans, the Administrative Clan (Abramovich) and the Criminal Clan (Deripaska– whose request for a visa has been denied by the U.S. government).[118] This alliance, Khaydarov says, operates under the patronage of the Kremlin. That, he asserts is also a factor in explaining why almost no one has been able to stand up or challenge the alliance. Those who have tried in the past invariably find themselves physically threatened; or in other cases the judges or officials involved succumb to bribes.

Abramovich has also been criticized for some of his oil dealings. In a complicated move that some feel was an attempt to disadvantage minority stockholders, in October 2001 Abramovich shifted control of Sibneft and most of his other properties to a London-based entity that he called Millhouse Capital.[119] Almost overnight Millhouse ended up with 88 percent of Sibneft's shares, 50 percent of Russian Aluminum and 26 percent of Aeroflot as well as a stake in some electric generating plants, diesel engine plants, the GAZautomobile and truck plants, and the Ust Ilimsk pulp and paper processing factories. (Ust Ilimsk has been the subject of a bitter and violent dispute. Deripaska tried to seize control by sending in armed agents.) Millhouse was said by a financial analyst for the investment firm Troika Dialog to be worth $5 billion and to generate between 3 and 4 percent of Russia's GDP.[120]

In September 2001, before transferring Sibneft and his other enterprises to Millhouse, Abramovich pulled one of his tricks that have made foreign investors so leery of investing in Russian companies. Only two months after he praised Sibneft for instituting a new corporate governance code that would "treat investors right," Sibneft's president, Eugene Shvidler, revealed that Sibneft had resold 27 percent of its shares back to the same "core shareholders" from whom it had purchased those shares for $542 million in December 2000.[121] There were rumors that the repurchase price was considerably less than $542 million. What angered outsiders even more, however, was that immediately after that secret repurchase by these insider shareholders, Sibneft announced a huge $612 million dividend to its stockholders (primarily Abramovich who is said to control 87 percent of the company), in a sense stripping Sibneft's cash in order to finance that repurchase for Abramovich and his friends.[122]

Abramovich did not restrict his energies to business. Entering the political field, Abramovich won a seat in the 1999 election for the Duma. In addition to the prestige that a Duma post provides its members, it also grants them immunity from lawsuits. In 2001, Abramovich also ran for and won the post of Governor of Chukotka, a remote Far Eastern region which earlier had elected him to his seat in the Duma.

Abramovich may need some immunity. Based on accusations of Swiss investigators, Runicom allegedly played a major role in winning construction contracts for Western firms in Russia, which involved kickbacks and money laundering stemming from the reconstruction of the Kremlin, the Russian White House, the Yeltsin presidential airplane, and the Hotel Belgrade.[123]

According to several reports, Abramovich controls three firms besides Runicom. They are SINS, Rifain Oil, and Financial Oil Company, or FNK, the company that won control of Sibneft at a bargain price in December 1995. As of mid-April 1999, these firms were said to control 91.6 percent of Sibneft.[124]

Under Abramovich's wing, Sibneft continued to win favors from the Yeltsin and then Putin governments. For example, Abramovich pressured the Ministry of Petroleum to include Sibneft as one of the companies allowed to export a share of Iraqi oil being sent to Russia as a form of debt repayment. This reversed an earlier decision, which assigned that right to the Transneftexport Company.[125] Abramovich's Runicom was also made the sole trader for Slavneft, a state-owned oil company.

Sibneft, however, has not been spared government harassment. Sibneft offices were raided by the tax police in August 2000, though that seemed to be aimed more at Berezovsky and his involvement in negative stories about Putin on ORT television news than at Abramovich.[126] The raid may also have been in response to press reports that of all the oil companies, none of whom were thought to be paying their fair share of taxes, Sibneft paid the least. Reflecting Berezovsky's and Abramovich's influence, it was found that Sibneft paid taxes at the rate of 49 rubles per metric ton of oil extracted or refined, whereas LUKoil, then the largest company and one with its own political ties, paid over 135 rubles per ton.[127]

II

The emergence of a business oligarchy seems unique to Russia. There are rich men in other transition countries, but they are fewer in number and do not exercise the influence within the economy and the government that the Russian oligarchs do. Nor were members of the *nomenklatura*, factory directors or entrepreneurs in other transition economies able to or allowed to seize so much control of industrial ministries, factories or natural resources.

There is no single explanation as to why the Russian reforms evolved in this way. The fact that other countries lacked Russia's natural wealth certainly was one factor. The "initial conditions" were different in Eastern Europe as well as in China; there was less to steal, which meant that it was virtually impossible to develop such an ensemble of raw material, oil, nickel, natural gas, aluminum and steel magnates.

But the "jockeys"–those designing Russia's privatization policies–were also responsible for the difference. The determination in Russia to privatize state enterprises so quickly meant that, because existing government regulations were designed for an era of central planning and state ownership, there were no laws regulating private businesses. Thus there were virtually no restraints within the government on what could be done–corners were turned, rents were sought, eyes were blinked, assets stripped, and favors rendered. And again, as distinct from elsewhere, startup businesses were discouraged, not encouraged. As a result, the newly privatized state enterprises encountered little competition from other businesses. Without restraints from the government or from economic rivals, there was nothing to stop members of the *nomenklatura* from seizing industrial ministries, such as the Ministry of Gas and the Ministry of Petroleum. Who else knew better how to run Gazprom or LUKoil? At the same time, the decision to do away with economic crimes and legalize private activity unleashed a whole class of energetic and resourceful operators, who until then had operated beyond the fringe of what was legal and acceptable within society. With the end of central planning, their skills had become legitimized. They had gone from being pariahs to plutocrats. Those determined and able enough to make their way through the chaos of the transition from communism to the market found that, once they had learned how to survive, there were almost no limits to what they could do and what they could accumulate.

Nevertheless, whether it be President Boris Yeltsin, his daughter, their staff, Vladimir Putin or local governors, each oligarch needed to cultivate a good relationship with a senior government official or his relatives. Intrigue, connections and payoffs count for more than talent. This was especially true in the early years of the transition period. Just as in the days of the czar, it was necessary to have a patron at court either in Moscow, St. Petersburg or the provinces to provide protection from bureaucrats, tax police and prosecutors. As Gusinsky and Berezovsky would eventually discover, without such a high-level patron, or *krisha* (roof), it was virtually impossible to remain in control. Even under Putin, rule of law in Russia is still less important than rule of in-laws.

The economic oligarchy took form despite the fact that the Russian economy was in a continuous state of decline. Until 1998, at least, the oligarchs seemed to be thriving while most of those around them were suffering and the economy appeared to be contracting. Yet, with the exception of Gusinsky's independent media, it is hard to see that the oligarchs as a class created much in the way of value added or wealth shared with society as a whole.

Given the public's disdain for the oligarchs, as well as Putin's background in the KGB, it was widely anticipated that Putin would crack down on the oligarchs. Indeed, Putin insisted several times that he would eliminate the oligarchs as a class. As he said in a December 2000 interview, "In our country representatives of big business who try to influence political decision making while staying in the shadows have been regarded as oligarchs. There must be no such group of people."[128] While there indeed should be big businessmen, "I cannot imagine anywhere near me, people trying to bring influence to bear from the shadow."[129] Or, as Putin said earlier on February 25, 2000 when he was running for President, "It is asked, what then should be the relationship with the so-called oligarchs? The same as with anyone else. The same as with the owner of a small bakery or a shoe repair shop."[130]

While these sentiments may express Putin's behavior when it comes to oligarchs who are also his critics, such as Gusinsky and Berezovsky, they do not reflect his treatment of the oligarchs as a whole. Not only has Putin continued to meet with a small, select group of oligarchs, as did Yeltsin, he has also done nothing to restrain favorites such as Abramovich or Khodorkovsky, who continued their practice of acquiring more assets and gaining new monopoly control over several industries. In an echo of Berezovsky's 1997 exaggerated declaration that seven oligarchs controlled 50 percent of the Russian economy, by early 2001, under Putin, five of the oligarchs controlled 95 percent of the country's production of aluminum, 18 percent of its oil, 40 percent of its copper, 20 percent of its steel, and 20 percent of its automobile production.[131] Only four of Putin's modern-day boyars, Mikhail Fridman, Vladimir Potanin, Peter Aven and Mikhail Khodorkovsky, were on Berezovsky's original list; the others were crippled by the August 1998 financial crisis or harassed out of the country by Putin. But as we shall see in Chapter 11, they were replaced by Putin's own team. The only difference between Putin and Yeltsin and their interaction with influential oligarchs is that Yeltsin seemed just a bit more tolerant of their criticism than his KGB-bred and -trained successor, and less revengeful.

8 FIMACO, the Russian Central Bank, and money laundering at the highest level

Oligarchs were not the only ones to take advantage of the transition to enrich themselves. Government officials did just as well, some at the very highest levels. Take for example Pavel Borodin, Yeltsin's assistant in charge of Kremlin property, and Mikhail Kasyanov, who as Finance Minister came to be called "Misha Two Percent" for the rake-off he received for providing financial information in advance.[1] But in a throwback to the Soviet era, there were also a small number who sought to enhance their institutions even more than themselves and, by extension, the scope of Russia's national influence. They operated as if the Soviet Union had never disintegrated. This meant acting to promote Russia's political and strategic interests even if such acts had negative economic and financial consequences. Such behavior is what leads business leaders to rank Russia as a finalist if not a winner in rankings of the most difficult and corrupt countries in the world in which to do business. This reflects not only the dishonest practices of private businessmen, but the sometimes deviant behavior of government officials and their recurrent resort to extortion.

The use by Gosbank and its successor, the RCB, of a secret entity called FIMACO (Financial Management Company) to hide billions of dollars from international courts and lenders is a prime example of such malfeasance. It is not simply a case of outright theft or plundering of the state treasury that is common to some countries in Africa, Asia, or Latin America, but a much more sophisticated example of the abuse of domestic and international trust involving state-sanctioned money laundering. Admittedly, the decision to hide assets with FIMACO may have been honorable and well intentioned in the beginning. But as we shall see, eventually senior managers of RCB became more intent on laundering the Bank's reserves and international loans for their own purposes than on instituting an honest and effective commercial banking system. But if the director of the RCB engaged in money laundering at the highest level, how could he be expected to serve as a role model for the rest of the country?

The RCB's deceit and its use of FIMACO is intriguing not only because it may have facilitated more than one run on the ruble, but also because FIMACO may have been used, at least indirectly, to funnel money to Boris Yeltsin and his 1996 campaign for president. All of this involved use and misuse not only of Russia's funds and RCB reserves, but of IMF loans. If the RCB's actions were not always strictly illegal under Russian law, they certainly were not ethical.

In what follows, we will try to explain what the RCB officials did and how they came to do it. In particular, how did the various directors of the RCB, at least those who served until 2002, become so adept at manipulating Western market institutions such as FIMACO? Remember that all of their initial training and experience had been in the state-owned and centrally planned economy of the Soviet Union. Where did they learn techniques that some of the most sophisticated Western banking specialists have trouble understanding, much less tracing?

I

Russia's post-communist central bankers came by their deviousness honestly. Along with the Nazis, Soviet-era bankers dealing in international banking and foreign trade were among the first in modern times to engage in money laundering. Among other schemes, they designed intricate procedures for funneling undocumented funds illegally to foreign communist parties.

The post-Soviet central bankers in Russia simply followed in the footsteps and traditions of their communist-era predecessors. Indeed, many post-Soviet Union central bank officials were holdovers in the posts that they had occupied in the Soviet era. The best example of this continuity is Viktor Gerashchenko (see Box 8.1). Born in 1937, his father Vladimir Gerashchenko had been a Deputy Director of Gosbank, the Soviet state bank, and a financial commissar who participated in the 1945 Potsdam Conference with Stalin, Churchill and Truman. He also served as the Soviet representative at the Bretton Woods Conference, which drew up the proposals for the creation of the World Bank and the IMF.[2] Following in the "family business," Viktor eventually outdid the father and went on to become Chairman of Gosbank, a position he held from 1989 to 1991.

With the collapse of communism and the Soviet Union, Gosbank was divided up among the fifteen former Soviet republics. While central banking functions in Russia were delegated to RCB and so remained under government control, some but not all divisions of what had been Gosbank were spun off as commercial and investment banks, and

Box 8.1: Viktor Gerashchenko, résumé

Born		December 21, 1937
Father		Deputy Chairman, Gosbank
Education		Graduate 1960, Moscow Financial Institute
Work	1960	Bookkeeper, Gosbank
	1961	Inspector and ultimately Section Head, Vneshtorgbank
	1965–1967	Moscow Narodny Bank (MNB), London
	1967	Assistant Manager, MNB branch, Beirut, Lebanon
	1972	Assistant Manager, Vneshtorgbank, Moscow
	1974	President, Ost-West Handelsbank, Frankfurt
	1977	President, MNB branch, Singapore
	1982	First Assistant President, Vneshtorgbank, Moscow (1985 became Vneshekonombank)
	1989–1991	Chairman, Gosbank
	07/1990–08/1991	Member of Central Committee of Communist Party
	1991–1992	Chief, Credit Money Department, Mezhdunarodny Fund for Economic and Social Reform
	07/17/1992	Acting Head, RCB
	11/04/1992	Confirmed as Chairman, RCB
	10/14/1994	Fired from RCB
	1994–1998	Chairman, IMB (Moscow International Bank)
	09/11/1998	Chairman, RCB
	03/15/2002	Pressured to resign as President of RCB

eventually several were privatized. Then, after Gregory Matyukhin, Chairman of RCB, resigned in July 1992, Gerashchenko succeeded him on July 17. He served as Acting Chairman and then, in November, as Chairman, until he was fired from his post a few days after the collapse of the ruble on Black Tuesday, October 11, 1994. Gerashchenko then became Chairman of the Moscow International Bank, a private bank that he ran for four years. After the ruble collapsed yet again, on August 17, 1998 (this time it was called Black Monday) Gerashchenko was reappointed, on September 11, 1998, as Chairman of the RCB. In other words, the same man who had run the Soviet Union's Gosbank went on to serve two separate terms as the head of the market-era RCB. Not surprisingly, Gerashchenko reintroduced many of the Gosbank-era policies, some of which were originally designed more to mask Soviet political objectives than to implement the legitimate monetary policies of a central bank.

II

Because it contradicted the Soviet image as a crusader against economic imperialism and foreign colonial exploitation, little was made known at the time about Soviet economic activity beyond the borders of the USSR. The fact that the USSR had become the world's largest importer of grain and a major exporter of oil and growing quantities of natural gas did not seem to clash with the ideological precepts of communism. What was akward was that in addition to normal import and export activity, the Soviet Union also had a modest but effective network of multinational corporations and banks placed strategically around the world that few even in the USSR were aware of at the time.[3]

Ostensibly, the function of these multinational entities was to facilitate the Soviet Union's foreign trade. NAFTA-B in Belgium and NAFTA-GB in Great Britain, for example, were the largest Soviet external companies in terms of sales volume, and handled a substantial portion of the USSR's petroleum exports. That brought them billions of dollars a year in revenue. Other operations encompassed automobile assembly, repairs, and sales: Konela in Finland and Scaldia-Volga in Belgium, and Belarus Equipment Ltd. in Canada. There were also Soviet-owned offices, warehouses, and repair and assembly facilities for machinery, laboratory equipment, timber, chemicals, diamonds, computers, food, shipping, and insurance. There were also extensive sales operations dealing with Soviet military hardware. Almost all of these operations were staffed by personnel officially described as representatives of branches of the Ministry of Foreign Trade. With some frequency, however, a steady stream of these agents would be arrested for espionage, which evidently was often also one of their responsibilities.[4]

Ownership of these Soviet foreign enterprises was obscured by a maze of interlocking directorates. Some were joint stock companies with shares held by local partners, but in most cases actual ownership and control resided in a Foreign Trade Organization (FTO) belonging to the Soviet Ministry of Foreign Trade. Sometimes shares were also held by several of the Soviet Union's other multinational overseas businesses, which, in turn, were owned by their fellow corporations. In other words, they each theoretically owned shares in each other, but the real owner was the Soviet

Ministry of Foreign Trade. Except that few if any of these corporations ever made a profit, there was little else that would indicate to the outside observer that they were Soviet-owned entities.

It was even harder to identify the branches of the overseas Soviet-era banking network (see Figure 8.1). Given its name, the Moscow Narodny Bank of London (88.9 percent of its shares were held by Gosbank and then the RCB) may have signaled to customers that it had ties to the Soviet Union (but, then again, the Hong Kong Shanghai Bank in Hong Kong had no ties for many years with Shanghai or China). Originally established in 1917 in London by a pre-Revolutionary Moscow cooperative bank, the Moscow Narodny Bank was claimed by the newly established Soviet government in 1919, which eventually subordinated the London bank to the Vneshekonombank affiliate of Gosbank. The other banks in the network, such as Banque Commerciale de l'Europe du Nord or Eurobank in Paris (77.8 percent of its shares were held by the RCB), the Ost-West Handelsbank in Frankfurt (82 percent of its shares were held by the RCB), the Wozchod Handelsbank in Zurich, the Donau Bank in Vienna (49 percent of its shares were held by the RCB) and the East-West United Bank of Luxembourg (49 percent of its shares were held by the RCB) were much more a part of the local environment and therefore much less identifiable. In one case, the Banque Commerciale de l'Europe du Nord was the tenth largest bank in France.[5] But just as with other enterprises in the Soviet multinational network, ownership was hidden in a morass of interlocking directorates. The net effect of such strategies was that the subordination of these entities to Moscow was not always readily apparent. They not only engaged in conventional Western banking, but Eurobank was widely credited with creating the Eurodollar market in the late 1950s.[6]

Situated in the capitalist world, these multinational banks had to compete with capitalist entities in Western markets. I often wondered how they prepared their Soviet-born and -trained staff to operate in a capitalist world when heretofore their education had been limited to Soviet universities and institutes. Thus until they were sent overseas, most of their bank officials had focused almost entirely on ways to fulfill a five-year plan. Attending a conference in Moscow in December 1978 with the then chairman of Gosbank, Vladimir Alkhimov, I asked how his representatives could operate so well in this unfamiliar environment. "Simple," he responded. "Before we send staff members outside the Soviet Union, we tell them that from now on they should do just the opposite of what they had been taught to do at home."

At the same time, being abroad provided on-the-job learning and training in the ways of the Western world. Viktor Gerashchenko had

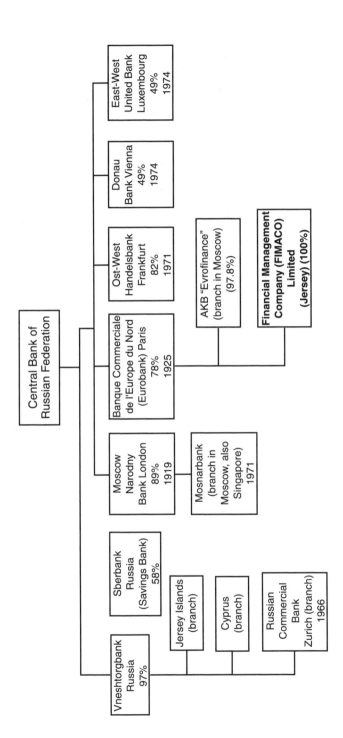

Figure 8.1 Russian Central Bank and related affiliates (shareholdings in %)

Source: PriceWaterhouseCoopers report on relations between the Russian Central Bank and the Financial Management Company (FIMACO), August 4, 1999.

several such opportunities. He was sent to London, where from 1965 to 1967 he worked at the Moscow Narodny Bank.[7] After that initial exposure, he also spent time, in 1967, at the Soviet Union's Beirut bank as its assistant manager and later manager before being sent to the Frankfurt office, where he served from 1974 to 1977. Rising through the ranks in Frankfurt, he ultimately became that bank's president. From there, he was sent to the Singapore branch, where he was assigned to clean up his predecessor's fraud and embezzlement. In between, he served in increasingly senior posts in Moscow at Gosbank's Vneshtorgbank (later to be called Vneshekonombank; Vneshtorgbank was reconstituted in 1990 and put in charge of Russia's overseas banks).[8] And by 1989, well known at home and in the West, and with an understanding of banking in both political systems, he was made chairman of the parent Soviet Gosbank.

Beyond espionage and facilitating and financing foreign trade, the Soviet overseas network of businesses and banks had yet a third task. Soviet multinational banks and corporations were also charged with funding the national communist parties around the world.[9] This involved diverting funds from their ostensible purpose: in other words, money laundering.

I was made aware of this phenomenon in the late 1970s. One of my uncles managed a firm that catered for the athletes every four years at the Olympic Games. Since the 1980 Olympics were scheduled for Moscow, he asked me to help him secure the contract while I was teaching in Moscow as a Fulbright lecturer in 1977. I made a series of inquiries and gained some information, but not much more than that. For a time, my uncle fared no better. Refusing to give up, he eventually received an invitation to dine with the Soviet officials in charge of the Olympics, arranged for him by the US–USSR Trade and Economic Council. Much to his surprise, my uncle was told outright that if his firm wanted to continue its record of catering to the Olympics, he would have to kickback $400,000 plus 3 to 5 percent of the gross paid to him by the Soviets. This money was to be turned over to David Karr, an American expatriate in Paris who also happened to be at the dinner. Because under American law such an arrangement was illegal, my uncle refused.

Who was this David Karr? At one time he was a writer for the American Communist Party newspaper, *The Daily Worker*. A supporter of Communist causes, Karr eventually became an agent for Soviet industrial ministries in their dealings with Western corporations. He also served briefly as a partner in the French investment-banking house, Lazard Frères.[10] By the time he died in mysterious circumstances in July 1979, he had become a multi-millionaire. Among other projects, he held a concession for the sale of specially minted Moscow Olympic coins. He also controlled the license for the use of Mishka, the toy bear that served as the Moscow Olympic mascot.

What was less well known was that Karr was also the conduit for the transfer of funds from his erstwhile profits and kickbacks to the local communist parties throughout Europe. Karr and agents like him laundered funds on behalf of the Soviet government to communist parties around the world. Profits were also skimmed from the export earnings of Soviet products, especially oil and gas, as well as military equipment and, in this case, from concessions associated with the 1980 Olympics. On the way, these funds passed through the Soviet-controlled banks. Therefore, money laundering by organs of today's Russian government and business is nothing new. Their predecessors, the Soviet authorities, long ago had become adept at using legitimate foreign business entities to carry out questionable practices.

III

The acquisition of FIMACO, an offshore company located on Jersey in the Channel Islands, is another instance of the Soviet-era practice of masking questionable conduct. The initial decision to acquire FIMACO with the help of the Royal Bank of Scotland Trust Co., Incorporated (Jersey) (RBSTC) may not have been colored by Soviet-era behavior.[11] Incorporated at the initiative of Eurobank in Paris on November 11, 1990 and registered with the Royal Court of Jersey, FIMACO was apparently intended to duplicate similar offshore entities already established by competing French banks.[12] According to a report prepared by the C.I. Law Agency, a research firm, the date of registration was actually November 17 1990. Since French law at the time restricted investment trust activities of French headquartered banks, many of these banks circumvented such restrictions by establishing offshore entities (often in the Channel Islands) that could then buy and sell assets for the Paris banks in order to provide the parent bank with extra liquidity.[13] Following that practice, FIMACO provided trust management for Eurobank's sovereign debt portfolio, including credit supplied by some Arab countries until at least 1999.[14] Reflecting its virtual nature, FIMACO provided financial management but had no premises, equipment, or employees of its own.

On March 27, 1992, after the collapse of the USSR, FIMACO became a 100 percent subsidiary of Eurobank. In the beginning, shares in FIMACO were held by the RBSTC, on behalf of a mysterious entity called Lavoisier Trust. Then two seemingly obscure corporations, Ogier Nominees Ltd. and Ogier Secretaries Ltd., took control of FIMACO on December 15, 1992 from Lavoisier. FIMACO had a listed capital of a mere $1,000.[15] Of the 1,000 shares of stock issued, Ogier Nominees received 997 shares as a registered stockholder and Ogier Secretaries received the remaining three.[16] Both Ogier entities were 100 percent owned by the Jersey law firm Ogier and LeCornu and operated more or less as a mail drop. Under the December 15, 1992 deed of trust, they served as nominee shareholders of FIMACO and also fiduciary trustees on behalf of Eurobank.[17] All of these maneuvers were designed to be opaque, not transparent–very much in the way Gosbank was run in the Soviet era.

When the USSR dissolved on December 25, 1991, so did Gosbank. This meant shifting not only Gosbank's domestic but also its international operations, including its network of overseas banks and affiliates, such as FIMACO, to other entities. As we just saw, to simplify matters, Eurobank (heretofore a subsidiary of Gosbank) took over direct ownership of FIMACO. Thus, with the agreement of the trustees, Eurobank paid $850,000 to the Royal Bank of Scotland for its previous help. That was not bad compensation for what one critic described as "two years of secretarial and administrative work on behalf of a company that had no employees."[18] The proceeds, apparently, were then redistributed to what were said to be five charitable foundations, four of which were Russian.[19]

Under the new banking arrangement completed on December 25, 1992, FIMACO became a front for Eurobank. As reported by a PriceWaterhouseCoopers (PWC) audit, under this agreement Eurobank agreed to provide staff, office accommodations, and keep the books for FIMACO. Moreover, Eurobank selected FIMACO's board of directors. In fact, FIMACO was a financial management company, but with no employees nor any premises. More important, Eurobank also determined FIMACO's investment moves and managed its funds. All of this was done free of charge for FIMACO until 1995, when it was decided retroactively to pay Eurobank a fee of 500,000 French francs for its previous work.

Initially, FIMACO's relationship with Eurobank was more or less typical of the way French-based banks operated. Moreover, after the demise of Gosbank, Eurobank continued to serve as the investment arm for the RCB. In that capacity it was mostly responsible for investing the first installment of the IMF's initial loan to the Russian government which was announced in August 1992. The money was then disbursed by the IMF on November 23, 1992 to the Ministry of Finance. The proceeds of the loan, $832 million and 267 million German marks, were in turn transferred by the Ministry of Finance to its agent, the RCB. Following standard practices, which the IMF was aware of, the RCB then sent the funds to Eurobank for investment. There was no deception or money laundering at this point: Eurobank had invested RCB funds this way many times before and there was no indication that FIMACO was involved. For example, the PWC audit made no mention of FIMACO in this transaction.

FIMACO's relationship with Eurobank, however, changed dramatically in mid-1993, when Russian banking officials decided to use FIMACO to hide and launder funds. This was a decision taken under Viktor Gerashchenko, who was brought back into central banking in July 1992 as chairman of the RCB by Acting Prime Minister Yegor Gaidar and President Boris Yeltsin. Gerashchenko, as we saw, was well versed in the Soviet Union's practice of disguising or laundering funds to mask their existence from public view. At Gerashchenko's suggestion, Yuri V. Ponomarev (formerly a senior official and board member of Vneshtorgbank who was then working in a supervisory capacity at Eurobank) ordered the transfer of the IMF funds from the RCB to Eurobank. Under an agency agreement, Eurobank then promptly transferred the funds to FIMACO, which then invested them on Eurobank's behalf. Since FIMACO had no staff of its own, the staff of Eurobank made the investment choice.[20] On the face of it, this seems to have been an unnecessary intermediation. Why was FIMACO brought into the transaction?

The decision to assign FIMACO a more significant and more devious role was a consequence of Russia's dire economic circumstances and Vneshekonombank's default and inability to return its depositors' money.[21] In December 1991, because it ran out of its own money, Vneshekonombank froze $6–8 billion worth of customer deposits. The ensuing general financial collapse affected not only private depositors, but also the Russian government, which found that it could not pay its import bills or foreign debts.

Chaos best describes Russia's financial situation at the time. Remember, the official reserve in the RCB had fallen to under $2 billion.[22] Vneshekonombank's inability to pay cash to its depositors, however, did not necessarily mean that Russians had run out of convertible currency or gold. On the contrary, there were funds, but they had been purloined or privatized by almost anyone who had access to them. Among those with access were senior officers of the Communist Party, Komsomol, state banks, KGB, and even the military. In late 1991, Yegor Gaidar, soon to become acting prime minister, hired the US firm Kroll Associates to track down missing state funds.[23] After four months they found that thousands of mostly offshore bank accounts, real estate holdings and offshore companies had been set up to launder and shelter these funds and what had been the Soviet Union's gold reserves. Every day, the planes arriving from Russia in places such as Cyprus, Canada, the United States, Switzerland, and Israel disgorged "New Russians" with suitcases brimming with $100 bills. No one knows exactly how much capital fled the country or was laundered, but many estimate that by the year 2000 the total exceeded $150 billion. No wonder the Yeltsin government had trouble paying its bills.[24]

Nessim Gaon, a Swiss trader, was one of those caught by the financial squeeze. Through his trading company, NOGA Commodities (Overseas), Inc., he decided as early as 1989 to take advantage of the Russian people's hunger for Western consumer goods. Cut off from Western products for seventy years, Russia's consumers were eager to avail themselves of anything coming from the West. Gaon recognized the potential and sought to find financial support to underwrite the purchases. Working with Deputy Prime Minister Gennady Kulik, Gaon arranged for Soviet officials to borrow money to buy tomato seeds and fertilizer for use in the Crimea.[25] The loan was to be repaid when the ripened tomatoes were sold. But the crop failed, and Gaon found himself $1 million in debt. Undeterred, he continued to work with Kulik, a man not known for his integrity. Beginning in April 1991, Gaon began to barter Western consumer goods and food for Russian oil. Reportedly, almost $1.5 billion in goods were involved, financed in part with loans obtained through Gaon's good offices.[26]

Suddenly Gaon discovered that his barter operation was no longer in balance. By spring 1993, Gaon claimed that his erstwhile Russian partners were $250–300 million behind in deliveries, the bulk of which Gaon had to finance with bank loans. For their part Russian officials justified their refusal to ship more oil by charging that Gaon and the original Russian negotiators had agreed on prices very much distorted in Gaon's favor.[27] The deal in fact did have a questionable odor about it. But the fact was that the Russian government was short of convertible currencies.

Seeking help, one of Gaon's assistants called me for advice in May 1993:

 – "Seek an attachment on Russian assets," I replied.
 – "That won't do any good. How can we take assets out of Russia?" he responded.
 – "You don't have to. Just seize some of the property the Russians hold in Europe–their banks, for example."

This was a revelation, since few, either Russians or foreigners, were aware that the Soviets and the Russians, who took over their interests, had such holdings.

Moving quickly, Gaon's staff asked me to prepare a memorandum for the court explaining why Vneshekonombank's default and the seizure, or privatization, of what were state assets by private individuals increased the likelihood that Russia's businessmen would be unable to pay their bills. My memo was sent on June 1, 1993, and in less than three weeks a judge ordered the seizure, or "arrest" of $250 million of assets of the Russian-owned East-West United Bank in Luxembourg.[28]

Panic ensued at the RCB. From his years working at the Russian banks in the West, Gerashchenko, now the chairman of the RCB in Moscow, knew full well that once a court allowed one creditor to seize overseas Russian assets, others would undoubtedly seek the same redress. All nine or so of Russia's overseas banks were vulnerable. Moreover, as we saw, they had just moved most of the $1 billion November–December 1992 IMF loan to Eurobank in Paris. The Russians had to keep some money in the West, but how could they do so and protect themselves from further seizures, especially of this very tempting money the IMF had just provided them?

Because the existence of the Russian-owned banks had become public, the solution was to hide their funds in even deeper cover and secretive accounts. Eurobank, with its $1 billion of IMF proceeds, was particularly vulnerable. But fortunately for Eurobank, it had that unpublicized offshore hideaway, FIMACO. This offered a safe, secretive haven. According to the PWC audit, initially it was decided to transfer the funds to Evrofinance, another murky agency located in Moscow, 97.8 percent of which was owned by Eurobank.[29] Eventually, however, on July 15, 1993, FIMACO was put in charge, but as before Eurobank remained the actual decision-maker.

Whether it was his idea or not, given the size of the money at risk, Gerashchenko had to be aware of what was happening and approve of it. RCB officials acknowledge as much. As Sergei Alexashenko, the former First Deputy Chairman of the RCB put it, instead of criticizing Gerashchenko for trying to disguise these assets, Russians should applaud him. "In my view Viktor Vladimirovich Gerashchenko deserves a monument for saving the currency reserves of the RCB in 1993 from being arrested."[30] If he deserves credit, he must have been involved in the subterfuge. Gerashchenko remained as head of the RCB until he was fired on October 14, 1994.

IV

Without the specter of numerous creditors like Gaon demanding repayment, FIMACO might well have remained a relatively unimportant and innocuous agency of Eurobank and the RCB. Once Russia's central banking officials, however, saw how useful FIMACO's masking activities could be, they involved it increasingly in their daily central banking work, not always in ways that were beneficial to the country. In a growing number of instances, FIMACO was used to the disadvantage of the country as a whole. But as we shall see, what was bad for the country was seldom bad for the bankers themselves, especially the senior staff such as Alexashenko, Gerashchenko, and his successor Sergei Dubinin.

After FIMACO was "outed," investigators discovered that the attempt to deceive creditors was just one of the ways that FIMACO was used to hide, misuse, or divert RCB funds. To be fair, it did engage in some legitimate dealings. But among its other questionable practices, FIMACO was used to weaken rather than strengthen the ruble, mask the true size of the RCB reserves from the scrutiny of the IMF and other lenders, subsidize unprofitable activities of RCB entities as well as favored private commercial banks, and provide unreported bonuses to senior RCB officials. According to some, it also secretly financed Boris Yeltsin's presidential campaign.[31] Most disturbing of all, it did all this with impunity for more than half a decade.

Only in early February 1999 did the public at large learn of FIMACO's existence. Then it was the result of a surprise revelation by the controversial Procurator General of Russia, Yuri Skuratov. Hounded by a video showing someone resembling Skuratov in bed with two prostitutes, Skuratov decided to bring others down with him. So he submitted reports of his investigation on the RCB to the Duma and then resigned. He charged that since July 1993 the RCB had transferred as much as $50 billion in RCB reserves and funds to FIMACO for it to manage.[32] In response, Gerashchenko acknowledged that FIMACO was used to generate high profits on investments and avoid the payment of taxes on those profits.[33] He did this because the Russian government had begun to levy various new taxes, one of which imposed a 50 percent tax on RCB's profits earned in Russia. (The comparable tax on the profits of the U.S. Federal Reserve Bank is 90 percent.)[34] But by using FIMACO, the RCB was able to earn its profits outside of Russia, and thus avoid these new taxes owed the Russian government and, as many suspect, use the extra proceeds instead to pay extra bonuses to senior staff.[35]

Certainly the RCB treated its staff well. The number of employees in the RCB empire inherited from the days of the Soviet Union vastly exceeded that of the central banks in Great Britain and the United States. Moreover its payroll was comparable or even larger. This is despite the fact that the Russian GNP is a fraction of that of England, not to mention that of the United States, and that average Russian salaries are much lower than comparable salaries in the West. In 1999, the RCB had a staff of 86,000, as compared to 3,000 at the Bank of England, or 23,000 at the Federal Reserve Bank.[36] The RCB's payroll in 1997 was $1.4 billion, although it fell a trifle to $1.2 billion in 1998, after the financial crisis. In 1998, Gerashchenko and Sergei Dubinin, who preceded him as the chairman of the RCB, were paid 70 percent more than Alan Greenspan, the US Federal Reserve Bank chairman.[37] In addition, Gerashchenko and at least four other senior RCB officials also served as "supervisory board members" of Russia's various overseas banks.[38] That meant another $95,000 in fees from the Ost-West Handelsbank for Gerashchenko. The other subsidiary banks presumably paid comparable amounts. Since the RCB did not have to obtain Duma approval each year for its budget, executives at the RCB could use the profits from their subsidiaries' trading activities in Europe and through FIMACO in any way they wanted and, apparently, they did.[39]

The use of what should have been government revenue and taxes for the enrichment of the bank staff is a legacy of the fuzziness inherited from the Gosbank days of the USSR when there was often confusion in delineating between what belonged to the state and what belonged to the individual. Gerashchenko's behavior epitomizes this fuzziness. In addition to the cavalier use of Gosbank and the RCB overseas subsidiaries, RCB officials also used RCB resources to help capitalize at least one private commercial bank. Thus, after he was removed as RCB Chairman in 1994, Gerashchenko went to work at the International Moscow Bank (IMB). Taking advantage of the RCB's international contacts, IMB bank officials tapped the resources of a large network of foreign banks and encouraged them to become investors. Among those contributing capital were Creditanstalt-Bankverein of Austria, Bayerishe-Vereinbank AG of Germany, the Industrial Bank of Japan, Ltd., Kansallis-Osake-Panki of Finland, and Komit Holding International of Luxembourg, each of whom held a 12 percent share.[40] The remaining shareholders, Eurobank of Paris and Promstroibank, Vneshtorgbank, and Sberbank, all of Moscow, each had a 10 percent share and were owned directly or indirectly by the RCB. In other words, Gerashchenko's colleagues used the RCB to fund their own private bank. Gerashchenko did nothing to redress this situation. Despite such practices and Jeffrey Sachs' complaint that Gerashchenko was the "worst central banker in the world," Gerashchenko in 1999 was named by the magazine *Euromoney* as the RCB Governor of the Year in Central and Eastern Europe.[41] Certainly, he was the most brazen.

V

In an effort to downplay his misuse of RCB and IMF reserves, Gerashchenko has insisted that the most RCB transferred to FIMACO at any one time was $1.4 billion, not the $50 billion alleged by Skuratov.[42] However, whether $1.4 billion or $50 billion, such practices hid those assets, not only from creditors such as Gaon, but from members of the Paris Club and London Club; that is, the consortium of Russia's unpaid government and commercial creditors. These creditors and bankers would have been less amenable to a write-down of the money owed to them if they had known that Russia had at its disposal this extra $1.4 billion in reserves. The need to hide reserves, according to Gerashchenko, also explained why the RCB's investment activity had to be handled by a trust-worthy Russian-owned entity, not a professional foreign investment house that might have earned an even higher return.

Gerashchenko neglected to defend other questionable FIMACO actions. In 1996 the RCB again re-routed funds lent to it by the IMF to FIMACO, which then used them to buy speculative Russian government securities. Despite the fact that it no longer had those funds at its disposal, the RCB counted some $1.2 billion of those dollar funds as if they still remained available not only to the RCB in Moscow, but to FIMACO. In effect, the RCB double-counted the money as reserves and made it appear that it was operating with greater liquidity than was actually the case.

Using FIMACO in this way accomplished two objectives for the RCB. On the one hand, FIMACO's purchase of $1.2 billion of the RCB's direct holdings of Russia's government debt took them off the RCB's balance sheet and, even though what FIMACO owned also belonged to the RCB, it made it look like the RCB's holdings of Russian securities were less than they actually were. This, then, gave the impression that less credit had been created by the RCB and that the RCB was meeting its promise to the IMF not to generate large inflationary pressures. In fact, this Russian domestic government debt was held by a RCB subsidiary and the purchase of this debt by a subsidiary of the central bank was an inflationary act.

On the other hand, when RCB reported that it "sold" those Russian securities for dollars (to FIMACO) the RCB made it look like these funds had come from an outside source, not from a RCB subsidiary. By doing this, they created the impression that their convertible currency reserves were higher than they actually were, thus keeping its other promise to the IMF that it would remain liquid. The RCB accomplished this sleight-of-hand because it double-counted the IMF loan. FIMACO did not reduce the number of dollars on its balance sheet when it purchased the RCB's government debt. Thus the RCB listed as its reserves the dollars sold to it by FIMACO as well as those same dollars which continued to appear on FIMACO's (its subsidiary's) balance sheet.[43]

When IMF officials eventually learned of this duplicity, they denounced "Russia's lies to the IMF about the level of its reserves." IMF officials declared they would have refused a subsequent loan if they had realized that the RCB's reserves in Moscow were lower than reported and invested in part in such speculative paper.[44] The proceeds of IMF loans were supposed to be held in non-speculative funds such as U.S. government securities. Instead, as early as May 18, 1993 the RCB had invested, through FIMACO, some of those IMF funds (which were supposed to bolster RCB reserves) in Russian government treasury bills, or GKOs.[45] Initially, it was claimed that such purchases by RCB subsidiaries were made to underpin the market for these newly issued GKOs. The RCB's purchases made it appear that there was a larger demand for these securities from the private sector than there actually was. Later, in 1996, when it became legal for foreigners to invest in the GKO market, similar purchases were made by the RCB. Again, that was done to prop up the market so unknowing investors would gain the impression that such investments had wide support.[46]

Some RCB officials denied that IMF funds were used for such purposes. Indeed, Sergei Dubinin disputed PWC findings that the RCB diverted IMF funds to FIMACO. According to Dubinin, the proceeds of the IMF loan went to the Ministry of Finance. So at that point, technically, the money became Russian, not IMF, money and remained that way after it was sent to the RCB and from there on to FIMACO.[47] Others with less sophistry insist there was no reason to be upset. The IMF had always been aware that the RCB was reinvesting its IMF funds in the West; in fact, it would have been foolish not to put the money to work in secure investments, such as U.S. government treasury bills. On occasion, the RCB did just that. What the IMF did not know about, however, was the existence of FIMACO and its role in reinvesting in the considerably less secure GKO market.[48]

What embarrasses the IMF is that while Russians used IMF money to speculate and/or inflate the value of those securities, it did not use the reserves the IMF provided to bolster the ruble, the original justification for the IMF loan. There are numerous allegations that instead of using RCB reserves and IMF loans to provide support for the ruble before the Black Tuesday 27 percent collapse of the ruble on October 11, 1994, the RCB did just the opposite. The RCB should have used IMF dollars to ward off speculators by converting those dollars into rubles, which would have strengthened the ruble. Instead, the RCB sheltered those dollars by shipping off $300–400 million, and probably more, to FIMACO a month earlier.[49]

While the RCB periodically backed away from supporting the ruble, they seemed less hesitant about propping up their European subsidiaries and a select number of commercial banks. Thus, when Eurobank bought $500 million of OFZ or short-term Russian government notes, on December 29, 1995, and sold them on January 5, 1996 at a loss of $400,000, the RCB came to its rescue, so that Eurobank was able to record a profit on the deal of $688,000.[50] Simultaneously, the RCB recorded a

$3.8 million loss. In somewhat similar fashion, the RCB pumped in $800 million to its overseas banks to insure their solvency after many of them suffered badly in the August 19, 1998 crisis.[51] Fortunately for the RCB and its senior staff, most of its other transactions were profitable, so it could afford such support.

Several commercial banks received similar underpinning. For example, in February 1996, Sergei Dubinin, then Chairman of the RCB, ordered FIMACO to allocate $300 million in RCB funds to a few favored Russian commercial banks.[52] After Black Monday, the August 1998 crash, Gerashchenko provided similar support. (These 1998 loans, however, may have come directly from the RCB vaults in Moscow and not FIMACO.)[53]

SBS/Agro in particular received several credit infusions, all to no avail. Owned at the time by the self-made oligarch Alexander Smolensky, SBS/Agro ultimately went bankrupt. In a related scandal, U.S. federal authorities have revealed that Smolensky had also been a principal share-holder in the Sobinbank and Flamingo banks, both of which were deeply involved in laundering money through their accounts at the Bank of New York.[54]

The flow of funds through the Bank of New York, which amounted to $7 billion over three and a half years, also involved quite complex proce-dures. A substantial portion of the $7 billion (no one knows exactly what percentage) by most measures would be considered as ordinary capital flight. Although the Russian government decreed that all Russians who held bank accounts outside the country had to register them first with the Russian government, it was not automatically illegal to move funds outside the country. It was reported, however, that some of the funds flowing through the Bank of New York were proceeds of ransom fees paid to kidnappers as well as money earned from prostitution and the sale of drugs.[55]

The Bank of New York was not the only nor even the preferred destina-tion of the bulk of the dollars sent out of Russia each year. Among other destinations, Russia used a number of the island havens in the Caribbean as well as places such as the remote and otherwise almost unknown island of Nauru in the Pacific. With a population of only 12,000, Nauru nonetheless is home to 450 offshore banks, all registered to a single govern-ment post office box.[56] Those banks are accused of laundering about $70 billion.

Because of its beaches, warm weather and Greek Orthodox Church, Cyprus is another special favorite. That explains why when some of the oligarchs decided to reinvest some of their funds back into Russia, Cyprus became the second largest source of foreign investment funds, second only to the United States.

Traditionally, the easiest way to move money outside of a country was to take it out as cash, usually in suitcases. This in itself need not necessarily be an illegal act. Assuming the carrier with the cash declares that act to the customs official, it is perfectly legal, for example, to bring more than $10,000 in cash into the United States.

The next most common practice was to instruct those who purchased goods exported from Russia to send their payments not to Russia but to accounts in other countries. Since Russian companies export tens of billions of dollars worth of oil, gas and ferrous and non-ferrous metals each year, this is thought to be the main source of the $1.5 billion or so sent out of Russia each month. Alternatively, payments may be made to Russian exporters in Russia for goods purchased there but at prices much lower than the normal world price. Russian oil producers, for example, were often criticized for selling oil for as low as $1 per barrel to trading firms or foreign importers who would then resell that petroleum overseas at world prices, which have ranged anywhere from $10–30 per barrel.

Even payment for services can be used to disguise the flight of capital. The TASS News Agency, for example, for a time instructed its foreign clients in Moscow and Russia such as *The New York Times* to pay for its services by sending the monthly fees to the TASS account in Frankfurt, Germany.

Of course, money transfers or money laundering can often be more complex. In what might be regarded as graft, Swiss authorities have charged that some Swiss contractors set aside a portion of their fees for refurbishing the Kremlin in overseas accounts for some of President Boris Yeltsin's administrative staff. Allegedly, some of this money was also diverted to some members of the Yeltsin family. Specifically, a Swiss prosecutor charged that Pavel Borodin, Chief of Staff for Boris Yeltsin and the Chief Property Manager for all the property belonging to the Kremlin, and those around him received at least $11 million in the form of kickbacks.[57] This money came from Mabetex, a Swiss firm, in exchange for $300 million of the $823 million spent on refurbishing the Kremlin.[58] It was also alleged that Mercata, also a Swiss contractor, paid out $60 million in kickbacks (including $25 million for Borodin) for sharing in that same contract.[59]

Even importers engage in capital flight and money laundering. At first glance, this might seem contrary to logic. It is easy to understand how exporters could engage in the flight of funds outside the country, but how does an importer do it? This is not like shipping out exports which foreigners will then pay for with funds that are automatically kept outside the country. By contrast, importing involves the payment by buyers within Russia to somebody outside for goods.

Importers, however, can engage in capital flight in a variety of ways. In the simplest version, the importer issues false purchase orders. They order goods from suppliers who have no intention of actually shipping the goods. Acting as if this were a normal, above-board transaction, the Russian importer sends payments to his own foreign bank account. On the surface, this looks like a payment for actual imports, when in fact they are phantom goods.

Importers who do in fact import goods may also engage in the questionable funneling of funds. They do this by using straws with accounts at the Bank of New York in order to reduce import taxes. It works this way: the importer declares that the value of the goods being imported is less than it actually is. The lower the value, the lower the customs tax. But the importer still must compensate the foreign shipper for the remaining costs of the goods. The importer does so by placing other import orders with phantom firms which have no intention of actually shipping any goods to Russia. This way the actual shipper outside Russia will receive money and then be fully paid but no extra goods are shipped. In the meantime, the Russian importer pays a lower percentage of the customs tax on the understated value of the goods that he receives. Of course this procedure can be used not only to pay the foreign exporter the full share but also to put a little aside overseas for the Russian importers as well. This is a form of tax evasion in one form or another, which some in the U.S. Congress want to include in the definition of money laundering.

Practices of this sort are not unique to Russia. Similar schemes are sometimes used in other over-regulated or less than lawful economies. There are few instances, however, where the Central Bank of another country or its affiliate like FIMACO has also been engaged in money laundering, as has the RCB.

But the RCB and FIMACO's questionable activities go beyond money laundering overseas. As mentioned earlier, one of the most sensitive accusations about the misuse of funds by FIMACO and the RCB is that some of the high returns in 1996 were earned from leveraging IMF and other loans used to fund Boris Yeltsin's campaign for president.[60] The RCB sale of the Russian debt to FIMACO occurred one week before the runoff election for president between Yeltsin and Gennady Zyuganov. Then, as we saw, the RCB sold $1.17 billion in ruble-denominated government securities to FIMACO, which the RCB bought back in July after the election.[61] It is charged that the $38 million or so in profits from the initial sale of these securities went to finance the last stage of Yeltsin's campaign.[62] Reportedly, Gerashchenko admitted that the bank's gold and hard currency reserves were used for this purpose.[63] Gerashchenko's candor may have been due to the fact that he was not the head of the RCB at the time the transaction was made. However the money was used, there was good reason to suspect that something was amiss, because although the RCB reported the sale, the whole transaction (both the sale and the buy-back) was not reported on either FIMACO's or Eurobank's books.[64]

VI

Despite protests to the contrary, the revelation about FIMACO and the misuse of RCB reserves and IMF loan proceeds reveals a sorry misunderstanding of how a central bank should function. The nefarious behavior of former Soviet-era state-owned banks in overseas markets helped shape present-day Russia more than any translated U.S. or West European manual on how to run a central bank in a market environment. RCB authorities have not made transparency an operating principle. When caught in a questionable act, the typical first response by bank officials such as Gerashchenko and Dubinin is still denial.[65] Mr. Dubinin, for example, did exactly that in a letter he sent to me on March 14 2000, in which he was bitterly critical of a draft of this chapter.

Although not the only one responsible, Gerashchenko clearly set the tone for the way the RCB has performed. In retrospect, it seems evident that he was unable or unwilling to shed the operating practices he absorbed while on assignment at the Moscow Narodny Bank and other overseas affiliates of the Soviet-era Gosbank. The guiding credo then was to extend the influence of the USSR in the outside world through any means, and if corners had to be cut, so be it. Thus, Gosbank and all its affiliates, as well as the other overseas multinational corporations, focused more on political machinations than on above-board and efficient bank operations. Above all, Gosbank and its executives had virtually no notion of what a central bank's role should be in conducting conventional monetary policy–that was of no matter in a centrally planned economy.

In fairness to our evaluation of the RCB, it is necessary to remember that central bankers in other countries do not always publicize their intentions or their operations. Nevertheless, it is hard to imagine that a member of the Board of Governors of the Federal Reserve Bank or a Director of the Bundesbank would not be informed about their respective banks' operations outside their country. Some of the members of the Board of Directors of the RCB were not so informed.[66] For that matter, few if any other central banks have such affiliates. Moreover, if any central bank in the West purposely set out to defraud the country's tax officials by transferring profit opportunities to offshore tax havens while using those same profits to fatten their bonuses and perks, it is hard to believe that there would be no public protest from the respective parliaments or international agencies. Again, this seems a legacy of the way Gosbank was run in the Soviet era. There was little concern with delineating the interests of the individuals managing the bank from what in the West would be considered good central banking operations.

Perhaps the biggest surprise is not the behavior of the RCB and its officials, but the reaction from international agencies such as the IMF. After all, it was their funds that were being used. Granted, some officials in the IMF complained about being lied to, but there was very little public criticism of the other acts described above, all of which were questionable and many of which would be considered illegal in any other country.[67]

The IMF should also have made a public protest when PWC was denied access to documents for an audit that the RCB had promised it would make available. Once the incomplete audit was released, the RCB often referred to the IMF report to justify various practices. Since PWC had never had complete documentation however, there was no way of knowing whether the RCB and its subsidiaries were properly run. For its part, PWC also deserves criticism for not making more of a public protest about such unacceptable practices.

Given the ingrained practices of Russian banking authorities, it is unrealistic to expect far-reaching improvement. It took two and a half years after he was appointed prime minister before Putin, on March 15, 2002, decided to pressure Gerashchenko to resign, five months before his term in office was due to expire. Putin should have acted much sooner, yet to his credit, until the last minute, many believed that, if anything, Putin would reappoint Gerashchenko. His firing was probably a reaction not only to Gerashchenko's failure to reform the country's banking system, but to his outspoken resistance to any efforts to make the RCB more accountable to the government and to calls for central bank reform, including the selling off of RCB subsidiaries such as Sberbank and the foreign subsidiaries.[68]

As much as it is to be applauded, it will take more than a replacement for Gerashchenko for change to occur. The discovery that Ukrainian Central Bank officials also engaged in similar sleight-of-hand maneuvers in disguising bank reserves reinforces the notion that the legacy of the Soviet era is not one that can easily be discarded.[69] As long as the RCB behaves in the way it does, it is unrealistic to expect that ordinary Russian commercial bankers, not to mention oligarchs, will set a different example. In the meantime, foreign lenders and Western bankers should insist on rigorous accounting procedures and refuse to approve additional loans and grants until those responsible are punished. Given past practices by both the Russians, their overseas Western banking counterparts, and even their Western auditors, those looking for a new beginning in Russian banking may have some time to wait.

9 Corruption, crime, and the Russian Mafia

Because moving to the market opens the door to so many temptations, corruption and Mafia-like crime are hard to avoid. Much to our chagrin, even the United States, Germany and Japan have discovered they are not immune. But as serious as the problem has been in the West, in Russia it has been even more so. What follows is an attempt to explain the economic factors underlying the endemic spread in post-communist Russia of these social maladies. It is not that the Soviet era was free of crime and corruption, but that both have subsequently become so blatant and all-encompassing. As Stephen Handelman in his book on the Russian Mafia so ably demonstrates, criminal groups long predate the Gorbachev era.[1] In fact for a time in the late 1970s to early 1980s, crime, and by extension corruption, seemed to pervade Soviet society. Under Leonid Brezhnev, communist morality all but disappeared. It did not help that Brezhnev's daughter was having an affair with a circus clown who was also a diamond smuggler while her husband, Yuri Churbanov, Deputy Head of the national police, was on the payroll of the Uzbek Mafia.[2] Even more amazing, the head of the Uzbek criminal organization paying Churbanov was Sharaf Rashidev, who in his day job was the Secretary, or leader, of the Uzbek Communist Party. No wonder few of the efforts to attack crime in the waning days of the communist era were successful.

But it is what has occurred since that is noteworthy. The subsequent level of penetration of crime in Russia is probably unprecedented in Russian history. An article on the front page of *Izvestiia* on January 26, 1994, for example, reported that the Russian Mafia controlled 70 to 80 percent of all private business and banking. Though subsequent reports suggest that the pervasiveness of the Mafia has diminished, Handelman asserts that that at one point the Russian Mafia may have been even more pervasive than the Sicilian Mafia.[3] Even if only 40 percent of Russian business was under its control, the Russian Mafia's power would still be enormous. And while fear of the Mafia may be less important today than fear of dishonest bureaucrats, crime in Russia as recently as 2001 remained a serious matter. Moscow for example, with about 1,700 murders in 2001, had about 1,000 more murders than New York City. Whereas there were about 15,000 murders in 1986 throughout the whole Soviet Union, by 2000 the number in Russia alone had more than doubled to 31,829.[4] Russia was second only to South Africa in terms of murders per 100,000 people, and crimes connected to organized crime were up 36 percent in 2001.[5] Most important, the Russian Mafia and crime in general have been a major impediment to Russia's economic recovery.

The pervasiveness of corruption is just as bad. Russia consistently ranks near or at the top in lists of the most corrupt places to do business. The 2001 Opacity Index prepared by PriceWaterhouseCoopers for example gave it the worst rating. According to one survey, "almost one quarter of the national budget disappeared into the pockets of 'decision makers' each year."[6] This abuse reflects not only the shenanigans of Pavel Borodin and his $2 billion Kremlin remodeling projects but plans for a 10 km railroad bridge linking Sakahlin to the mainland, as well as Moscow Mayor Yuri Luzhkov's Manezh Shopping Center and his highway building program.[7] Even the Russian Orthodox Church claimed its share. To help it out, Boris Yeltsin agreed to allow the church to import cigarettes duty free and export petroleum as part of the established export quota. This brought the church hundreds of millions of dollars.[8]

Few institutions remained immune. Not atypical was the scheme by the Navy Chief of Staff and the Pacific Fleet Commander to pass off two Pacific Fleet warships as scrap. The ships sold for $4.5 million despite the fact that the sale included hundreds of kilometers of non-ferrous metal cable as well as fuel and crates of new weapons.[9] Nor was it reassuring when Vladimir Putin appointed "Misha Two Percent" Mikhail Kasyanov to replace himself as prime minister.[10] Admittedly, the Italians have shown that a strong Mafia and widespread corruption do not preclude economic growth. But they distort that growth. The transaction costs are high. Too much is spent on protection, bribes and security, and not enough on breaking up monopolies and opening up markets.

The growth of the Mafia and corruption also illustrates the problems that must be dealt with when reconfiguring a society subjected to seventy years of communism and overly strict control. It brings to mind the fish that live in the bottom of the deepest part of the ocean. When they are brought to the surface they explode. They explode because they have not had a chance to decompress. The East Europeans and the Chinese were able to avoid some of Russia's problems with the Mafia because they moved gradually or they already had existing market-type institutions in place. But Russia suddenly and quickly began its reconfiguration without allowing enough time to build up the institutions it would need to cope with the market processes that were suddenly unleashed.

Some have said this outbreak of crime and corruption was inevitable in the move to a market economy. Michael Scammell, writing in *The New York Times* on December 26, 1993, asserted that the emergence of a Mafia and the growth of crime invariably accompanied robber-baron capitalism. But what took place in Russia is different. That is not to say that we in the United States have been immune to the Michael Milkens of the 1980s, the Kenneth Lays of 2002 or the robber barons of the nineteenth century. Equally important, while there has been an increase in crime in other transition economies such as China, Hungary, Poland, and the Czech Republic, the pattern that developed in these countries is very different. In none of these countries has the pervasiveness of a Mafia been on the scale that it is in Russia and the former Soviet Union. By contrast, the Mafia in the post-Soviet period has come to control not only traditional criminal activity, such as prostitution and drugs, but a large part of ordinary economic activity as well.

Important lessons are to be learned from such a comparison. What is there about the Soviet legacy and the reform process that have exacerbated the problem? Did the nature of Russia's reform help expand Mafia activities? Is what occurred in Russia unique to Russia?

I

The Stalinist state had a strong government as well as centralized control of the economy. Because of its inflexibility there was a need to compensate for the oversights of the central planners. Since Stalin focused on heavy industry and neglected consumer goods, an illegal informal market developed which provided the goods and services that the state sector considered unimportant and did not produce in sufficient quantities. This in turn gave rise to the underground economy. The Russians referred to this phenomenon as "*nalevo,*" everything to the left. Engaging in such market activities was classified as an economic crime, and economic crimes were punishable by death. That dissuaded a lot of people, but not everybody. True, the penalties were severe, but because so few people dared to risk arrest, the potential rewards were enormous.

After Stalin's death, punishment and regulations gradually became less draconian and less strictly enforced. Prior to Brezhnev's death in 1982, enforcement and oversight became more lenient and tolerant. Yet, while legal enforcement was relaxed, officially the underlying economic structure remained inflexible. As laws were unenforced and disorder ensued, Mafia-like groups sought to establish their own kind of order.[11] This explains why the Mafia influence at the time was at a high point–at least until the Yeltsin era.

There was another factor at work. Because of the pervasiveness of the state in the Soviet era, both politically and economically, it became socially and morally acceptable, politically correct if you will, to cheat the state. That was not new for Russia. Such practices predate communism. They go back to the nineteenth century and earlier. As one of my Russian friends said, "What is intolerable today in Russia is not corruption – that's historic; it is the violence." Gogol and Tolstoy reveal the corruption of the *chinovniki* (the bureaucrats) in their works. In *The Inspector General*, for example, Gogol plays on the acceptance of this kind of corruption. Throughout Russian history there has been an underlying ethic that all but lionized those who cheated the state. The difference in today's post-Soviet Union is the pervasive fear that violence may also become part of the ethic.

When Brezhnev died in November 1982 he was succeeded by Yuri Andropov, who as head of the KGB knew about the pervasive criminality and had a rigid sense of legality. Consequently he began to crack down on Mafia-like groups. But since his rule lasted for only eighteen months or so, his effort was interrupted and not resumed during the subsequent Chernenko period. When Chernenko died in March 1985, and Andropov's protégé, Mikhail Gorbachev, was made General Secretary, Gorbachev cracked down again. He also launched a campaign to limit vodka and alcohol consumption. While the restrictions on producing and serving vodka, just as Prohibition in the U.S., seemed to reduce drunkenness at least initially, before long it also opened a vast opportunity for moonshiners and bootleggers and led to a substantial increase in lawlessness.

More significantly, Gorbachev announced his program of *perestroika* and *glasnost*. At least in the beginning, he had no clear conception of what such programs should encompass. He sought to reform the Soviet system, not destroy it. That is easy to say, hard to do.

Neither the crackdown on drinking nor the *perestroika* campaign was intended to increase crime: to the contrary. But that was the effect. The alcohol campaign increased controls and *perestroika* relaxed them. And when a leader shakes up an economy which for seven decades has been very rigidly controlled, it can unravel quickly. Altering the initial conditions, Joe Berliner's horse, requires extra care. In the process of transition from centralized to weakened controls, lines of authority are likely to be disrupted, producing almost certain confusion. The radical abandonment of the centrally planned system risks plunging the whole system into turmoil.

This is what happened when Gorbachev, Joe Berliner's jockey, began his *perestroika* of the Soviet system. He moved slowly at first. The radical changes began in May 1987 when for the first time Gorbachev legalized private trade, and private businesses and cooperatives. Those in charge of maintaining control, such as the police, did not know what to do. Prior to this, when the police saw buyers or sellers on the street, the odds were that the parties were engaged in illegal practices. After May 1987, it was difficult to determine whether a business was legal or illegal. The confusion was compounded by the fact that only the year before, in 1986, Gorbachev had taken the opposite stance, banning all private trade. Then, to sell a product, the seller had to prove that he himself had produced it. But how can anyone prove that he had produced the tomatoes he was selling? Trade was disrupted. In that short time, the police cracked down with great glee. But after a few months when Gorbachev reversed his course, those working illegally underground came out blatantly into the open. Suddenly they were legitimate. This, as we saw in Chapter 7, was precisely what Smolensky and some of the other oligarchs did. No wonder law enforcement authorities were paralyzed.

II

What is intriguing of course is that both before and simultaneously with Russia, some other Eastern European countries as well as China were also making a transition, but with less trauma. In large measure this was the result of the fact that when the Chinese, Poles, Hungarians and the Czechs began their reforms, one of their first priorities was to remove barriers to entry. Anyone who wanted to could open up their own business. This is something the Russians have had trouble doing.

In another contrast with Russia, the Chinese also began with agricultural reform. They allowed the peasants to break away from the collective farm (the communes) and cultivate their own farms. By 1982 almost every farmer in China was operating his own farm on long-term leases. The communes gradually disappeared. In the cities, anyone could set up his own enterprise even if it were no more than a corner-stand. Other economic controls were relaxed only gradually. There was no shock therapy in China.

The East Europeans chose a different strategy, primarily because throughout the communist era most East European countries had tolerated some small-scale private business activities. In Poland, for example, 80 percent of the farms had never been collectivized because the peasants had strenuously resisted. Though Polish peasants were not particularly efficient, their farms remained private and competitive. The private trade sector was not as large but an estimated 15–20 percent of the trading activity was in the hands of private traders. Moreover, when Poland began its shock therapy in 1990, everyone who wanted to go into business was allowed, even encouraged to do so. There were few restrictions.

This was very different from Russia. When Gorbachev allowed private and cooperative business for the first time in May 1987, he initially did so with limits. Fearful that the introduction of private business might lead to the collapse of the state sector, he proceeded by stages. In the beginning, he limited the private sector to pensioners and students, and only gradually allowed the rest of the population to participate. This was gradualism, but the wrong kind. To an economist, this was a restriction of entry; and restriction of entry usually leads to problems.

Gorbachev's strategy inadvertently spawned a surge in the influence of the Mafia. The decision to retain centrally fixed prices in state stores while allowing only partial freedom of entry generated great opportunities for arbitrage. (Arbitrage occurs when prices differ in two or more regions. Arbitragers then buy the goods where the prices are cheapest and take them to sell where the prices are higher.) There were enormous disparities between prices authorized by the state and the prices determined by market pressures. This meant there was lots of money to be made by simply procuring goods in a state store (legally or illegally out the back door) and reselling at the higher prices private sellers could charge. As a result, the small number of entrepreneurs able to open their own businesses often became millionaires overnight. For example, since state planners generally regarded pantyhose as too unimportant to manufacture, a small group of people decided to produce it themselves. Taking advantage of the enormous unsatisfied demand, the new manufacturers became so rich that after just six months of production they closed down their operations for fear that nobody would believe they had made their money honestly. Nonetheless, they and others like them began to spend their new income. Having been deprived access for seven decades to Western consumer goods, they began to buy all they could.

Groups of thugs, racketeers, weight lifters, boxers and even some former policemen soon realized that with a little muscle they could share some of this wealth. Before long, Mafia-like groups began to move in. According to the Directorate for the Fight Against Organized Crime of the Russian Ministry of Internal Affairs, by late 1994 there were 4,352 organized criminal groups with 18,000 "leaders" and approximately 100,000 members.[12] By the time Gorbachev and then Yeltsin decided to open the private sector up to everybody, the Mafia already had a stranglehold and grew faster than the private sector.

The combination of limited entry and inherited shortages was made to order for Mafia-type groups. The use of strong-arm methods at the Avtovaz factory in Tolyatti is a good example. Eight different criminal groups managed to take control of the plant's cars as they came off the assembly line.[13] Sometimes they gained this access after violence, sometimes after bribes or joint working arrangements with senior management. Payment to the factory for the cars was usually belated and below cost of manufacturing, which guaranteed a handsome profit on sales to a public eager to pay almost whatever they were asked. This was much the way Berezovsky operated. Efforts to clean up such crime in Tolyatti, at least as of the time of writing, have not met with much success. Several journalists have attempted to mobilize public support for a crackdown. While they did indeed increase awareness of what has happened, the end result was that three of the journalists were assassinated.[14] The voting public did oust the mayor, Sergei Zhilkin, of Tolyatti, who was blamed for the disappearance of $30 million from the city budget.[15] But his successor, Nikolai Utkin, was alleged to have organized his own scams.[16] In the meantime, five organized crime groups still control the city and apparently Avtovaz. As late as September 1998, it was thought that 80 percent of the factory's output was seized by such gangs.[17] It will be instructive to see how General Motors deals with such groups as it operates its joint venture with Avtovaz to produce its jeep-like recreational vehicle.

As the Mafia's presence increased and spread, prospective entrepreneurs discovered that the more public and transparent their enterprise became, the more vulnerable they were to crime and extortion. As an example, a husband and wife in Yaroslavl that I interviewed began trading Russian ball bearings to customers in Belarus. After a moderate amount of success they decided to advertise in the local paper offering a similar service to other manufacturers. Their first call came from a representative of the local Mafia. When I met these erstwhile entrepreneurs in June 1996, they were desperately looking for ways to prevent this particular group from seizing their business, but to no avail. They were ultimately forced to make a "protective agent" a part owner.

Such a climate also discouraged businessmen from putting large sums of money in private banks. Just like Willy Sutton who robbed banks because, as he said, that was where the money was, so various Mafia groups early on penetrated or even assumed control of almost one-half of Russia's largest banks.[18] But unlike Sutton, they did not do it so much for the assets, as for the records of deposits. With these lists, they could then persuade those with money deposits of the need for protection. Thus in order to avoid such potentially violent confrontations, many businessmen turned to barter, rather than money, which would end up as a bank deposit. This way they could operate under the radar screens of criminal groups. That was another reason why banks had trouble attracting deposits and lending out those deposits.

Before long businesses sought to hide their earnings and deposits not only from criminal groups and banks but also from the Russian government. This made it hard for the government to collect the tax revenue they needed, which forced the government to raise taxes even more, which made businessmen even more determined to hide their earnings. In the Soviet era, because virtually everyone worked for the state, tax collection was not a concern. Personal income taxes were deducted from workers' pay envelopes so that most workers never knew that they paid income taxes in the Soviet Union. Similarly, since all businesses were owned by the state, profit taxes were deducted from state enterprises and turned over directly to the government. But with the privatization of state enterprises and the legalization of new private businesses, it became difficult to impose compulsory wage deductions. In addition, those who were self-employed and those who had a second job were supposed to file their own tax returns. But without a tradition of voluntary tax collection, fewer than 3 million Russians out of the 70 million in the workforce filed returns in 2000.[19] (Some say the actual figure was fewer than 2 percent of the workforce.[20]) Moreover, when a self-acknowledged billionaire such as Boris Berezovsky reported that his income in 1997 was less than $40,000, there was reason to worry about the accuracy of the returns that were filed.

Similarly, there was little compliance within the business community. According to a study conducted by the Prosecutor General's Office, out of the 2.7 million companies that should have paid taxes, 33 percent neither paid taxes nor filed tax declarations.[21] Of those that did pay taxes, one-third used barter as a form of mutual settlement.[22] Another survey found that only one-fifth of Russian businesses even filed a tax form. Consequently, until Putin decided that higher taxes were counterproductive, the state not only had difficulty collecting business taxes, it also had trouble collecting even those withholding deductions already made from the salaries of employees.

Because of its trouble collecting taxes, until 2001 the state sought whenever feasible, and even in some cases where it was not feasible, to increase the number and range of taxes. What it could not collect with a few taxes, it hoped to collect with a wider variety. Thus starting with about four profit-based taxes in 1991, oil companies faced forty-two different taxes, and most, if not all of them, were based not on profits but on revenues.[23] Until 2000, taxes seemed to change on a weekly basis. When I asked a foreign businessman in Moscow about his taxes, he replied, "What day is this?" Some critics in the oil industry have estimated that if they paid all the taxes then on the books, their taxes would have exceeded 120 percent of their profits.[24] Other businesses reported that when local and regional 1998 taxes were included, they were responsible for paying 200 different taxes, which meant of course that few did.[25] More and more businessmen found that if they wanted to continue to operate, they had to seek out connections, cheat, or set up secret accounts. Such practices left them open to blackmail. That also explains the Mafia's interest in taking over the banks. Strange as it may be, those who failed to pay off the Mafia ran the risk that the Mafia would call in the tax police.

The tax police in Russia have virtually unlimited power to force compliance with the law. As we saw, among their weapons they have the power to freeze business bank accounts.[26] A Western firm that neglected to convert its currency on a day-to-day basis from dollars into rubles, and instead did it weekly, ran into trouble with the tax police because the law says it must be done daily. As a consequence, the tax police seized the company's $900,000 bank account. St. Petersburg's most luxurious hotel, the Grand Europa, had a similar experience. It was sued for $28 million because instead of converting dollars into rubles it deposited hotel fees in a bank in Scandinavia. The solution was to work out a "special accommodation" with some of the city authorities. It was only in 2001, when Putin's appointee as Minister of Economics, German Gref, began to simplify and reduce the number and rate of taxes that tax collection revenue began to increase. The tripling of petroleum prices after 1998 also helped.

Even after the 2001–02 tax reforms, however, many Russians did not pay their taxes. Evading taxes, escaping state controls and deceiving state authorities is a practice that predates the Soviet era.[27] In one of the most quoted instances, to prove to Empress Catherine the Great that the peasants and lands under his jurisdiction were thriving, Prince Gregory Potemkin in 1787 arranged for the empress to drive through a make-believe setting of waving peasants standing in front of false village facades. These Potemkin villages typify the ingenuity Russians have used to mislead the authorities. Under President Yeltsin and to some extent under Putin as well, avoiding taxes became an art. Businesses not only under represent income, they adopt financial procedures to avoid accumulating bank deposits for fear not only of the Mafia, but the Russian tax police who regularly seize business accounts.[28] Nevertheless, until 2001 Russia kept in place a large number of taxes that were absent in most other countries, such as a tax on advertising, medical expenses, and property tax.[29]

As if the economic and political turmoil following the dismembering of the USSR was not disruptive enough, the breakup of the republics was accompanied by the further collapse of the economic infrastructure; Gosplan, the ministries and the wholesale operations simply disappeared, creating an institutional vacuum. In addition, there was no accepted code of market business behavior. Russia suddenly found itself with the makings of a market but without a commercial code, civic code, effective bank system, effective accounting system or procedures for declaring bankruptcy. What was left was the legacy of cheating the state.

Because Russia is such a large country, establishing institutions and regulations would have been difficult no matter how honest and committed its bureaucrats and businessmen may have been. Russia's huge geographic size placed a special burden on the country's communication system. Thus even if Russia had an effective banking system, it would have been difficult to organize the effective flow of money, especially in a period of rapid inflation. If it takes twenty to thirty days, for example, to move money between banks, as it usually did at the time in Russia, the creditors lose part of their real earnings. This also gives rise to enormous corruption and more confusion.

Russia's main problem in the early 1990s, however, was that its market system did not function as it should have. Because of traditional interference by Russian bureaucrats and the absence of a market infrastructure, the market could not perform the functions that are taken for granted in a market economy. This led to even more government interference and more opportunities for bribes and extortion.[30] For example, many Russian government officials, particularly at local and regional levels, continued to insist that the government control the proper disposition of land. Zoning laws exist in market economies, but a prospective buyer of land in Russia had first to deal directly with a government authority because until 2001 the government owned most of the land and could arbitrarily set both the rent and the price of the land. By contrast, in a market economy it is assumed that the market will allocate most of the nation's real estate to private owners and that property will be sold at the market, not at an artificially low price. To the extent that the market carries out such functions and there is no rent control, there is less room for bribes and corruption. Though it is probably impossible to eliminate all corruption (even market economies must have regulatory officials such as building inspectors), generally the price of the property is determined relatively freely and fairly by the buyer and the seller. Thus there is less reason or incentive to offer bribes or under-the-counter payments.

III

Another consequence of Russia's reforms was that it was hit by inflation in a more extreme form than other transition economies. Its high inflation was due in part to the fact that Russia did not have enough competitive independent agricultural, service and manufacturing enterprises in place when it privatized state industries. As a result, the privatized state industries were able to act as monopolies with few competitors around to force them to keep prices low. Thus, in 1992, prices rose twenty-six-fold. By contrast, when shock therapy was adopted in Poland in 1990, prices went up a more moderate five times because Poland had private farms, food processors and sellers and shops that after a brief hesitation were responsive to market forces. In Russia, without competitive enterprises to undercut higher prices, greater inflation ensued. As late as 2001, Russian inflation exceeded 20 percent. In turn, higher inflation created more opportunities for arbitrage by the Mafia.

Given that the Mafia was performing many functions that elsewhere were performed by the state, many Russians adopted a somewhat tolerant attitude towards the Mafia. Some even had a legitimate fear that if the government regained some of its powers, it might lead to a return to an abusive government, something Russia has experienced all too often in the past. Consequently, there was some resistance in June 1994 when Yeltsin announced a series of measures designed to make it easier to target and arrest Mafia suspects. Nevertheless, continuing and unresolved crimes have induced a growing desire among the population for a stronger government. Only with that, some argued, would stability be achieved. This rising consensus helps to explain why Yeltsin appointed a succession of three former KGB heads as his prime minister and why Putin and his emphasis on a more orderly and rigid government had an incredible 80 percent approval rating in 2002.

IV

Without a concerted effort to suppress it, the Mafia continues to encroach on business activity. It demands 10 to 20 percent not just of a business's profits, but its revenue. Whether or not a firm makes a profit is immaterial; the Mafia insists on its money even when there are losses. This means the costs of doing business are increased at least 10 to 20 percent more than they would otherwise be.

In the early 1990s, the Russian Mafia grew faster than businesses did. Under Yeltsin the Mafia often seemed stronger than the government. When there were commercial disputes, the parties were more likely to go to the Mafia for help because the government's enforcement abilities were usually ineffective. As one example, while the government had difficulty collecting its taxes, the Mafia seldom had any such trouble.

Since the Mafia had a strong interest in maintaining disequilibrium in the economy, it sought to restrain markets, maintain national and local monopolies, and obstruct economic reform. These monopolies, which distorted the economy, and kept prices up and entry down, served to increase the Mafia's impact. Various Mafia groups have even been able to restrict many of the country's private farmers from access to farmer's markets, thus limiting supplies. Even though only 5 percent of the country's farms are private, these farmers are viewed as a threat to the Mafia's monopoly control. Frustrated by their inability to find outlets for their output, a growing number of these newly privatized farms have closed down. Beginning in late 1994, the number of private farmers giving up farms exceeded those opening new ones. This is another instance where the misguided use of shock therapy, the failure to move against the Mafia, and inattention to building or reconstituting the institutions destroyed under communism has obstructed rather than facilitated the reform process.

The Mafia also extended its activities to foreigners. During the Soviet era foreigners were off limits. The KGB kept ordinary Russians away from foreigners to prevent espionage. An incidental byproduct of this paranoia, however, was that in keeping Russians away from foreigners, the KGB ended up protecting foreigners from theft and intimidation.

In the aftermath of the collapse of communism, there is a certain amount of irony in the way foreigners in Moscow regard the police and bureaucratic restrictions. At one time foreigners in Moscow wanted to get out of the compounds (ghettos) in which they had been forced to live. With a police officer on guard to make sure that only Russians on official business were admitted, many foreigners viewed their housing as a kind of prison. In the post-Soviet era, foreigners are allowed to live wherever they want. But many foreigners now prefer the ghettos precisely because of police protection. Outside it can be dangerous.

What is most disturbing of all for some expatriates is that the cost for contract murder is so low. As they see it, if the cost were higher there would be fewer murders. The low price of about $800 reflects not only the large number of those willing to kill, but the fact that almost none of the gangland-style murders of the last few years have been solved. Under the circumstances there is little fear of arrest, much less of punishment.

V

Because crime and corruption are so pervasive, curbing it will be very difficult. The general public may become so angry that it will rise up and demand action from its government. So far, except for general disgruntlement about the Mafia-like atmosphere, the Russian population has been relatively passive on this issue. In part this is the effect of their long legacy of repressive governments: Russians tend to be relatively patient and more tolerant of abuse than many other nationalities.

So what can be done? Appointing a special commission and paying the bureaucrats and the police more money may help. But neither act will solve the problem. To obtain results, something must be done to eliminate the underlying economic stimulus to crime. This is how the United States curbed the influence of the mob in the 1930s. It reduced Al Capone's power by confronting him with more competition. It ended prohibition and legalized the sale of alcohol. Almost overnight, there were too many outlets to control.

In a similar way that was exactly what happened in Poland and China. The state allowed and encouraged traders, startup ventures and farms so that in short order there were hundreds of thousands doing business. There was little or no restriction of entry making it very difficult for any Mafia group to seize control. There simply were too many parties involved. Yeltsin almost adopted this approach. On January 29, 1992 he said anyone who wanted to could sell anything they wanted on the country's street corners. Soon Moscow streets were filled with new and mobile entrepreneurs around the Bolshoi Theater and Detskii Mir Department Store standing shoulder to shoulder selling a bottle of shampoo, a bottle of vodka or a piece of silverware. So many sellers suddenly appeared that the Mafia could not control them. This made them angry because it looked like they might lose their control of the markets. By contrast they were able to maintain control over the more established but fewer sellers on the street corners who returned to the same location each day and sold from card tables. The Mafia had no trouble forcing them to pay tribute. The two dozen vendors that I interviewed in Moscow and St. Petersburg answered candidly that the average "tax" was $50 per month. If their display required two tables, the fee was doubled. When I asked several of them selling from card tables in St. Petersburg how the Mafia was able to keep track of them, I was told that the Mafia sent out checkers twice a day to conduct a census to be sure they were paid their fee.

If the sellers have no card table and sell from their coat pockets or knapsack they can more easily melt into the crowd, making control harder for the Mafia. To regain control, the Mafia had to find some way to close down these day traders and force them off the streets. Their solution was to create a public backlash by arranging to leave these outdoor markets and the adjacent streets uncleaned. The city authorities went along with this plot because the street vendors paid no taxes. It is also possible that the officers in charge received some kickbacks. The end result was that in short order the streets around Moscow's cultural center, the Bolshoi Theatre, came to resemble an unsightly flea market. Even ordinary Russians found this intolerable. Allowing sellers there was *nekul'turno* (uncultured). As a consequence in May 1992, the controls were reinstated, the traders were driven off the streets, and once more prospective sellers had to obtain licenses which put them back into the hands of the bureaucracy and Mafia. The same thing happened to the kiosks that appeared periodically throughout Moscow in 1993. Mayor Yuri Luzhkov decreed that they were unsightly and ordered that selling be largely restricted to stores located in buildings. In mid-1994, and again in 2000, he and the city council ordered the closing of about half of Moscow's outdoor kiosks.[31] That is one reason why many entrepreneurs report that it is harder today to open up a private business than it was two or three years ago.

Putin's economic advisors have come to understand the problem and have begun an attack on Russia's bloated bureaucracy and its excessive regulation. In 2001 the Minister of the Economy, German Gref, proposed a drastic cut in the red tape businesses have to deal with. Until then, a prospective entrepreneur had to obtain the signatures of at least 250 officials, visit between twenty and thirty different offices, and obtain fifty to ninety clearances.[32] On average, this process would take about six months. Even then, because there were so many laws to satisfy, it was almost inevitable that one law would conflict with another. Jewelry stores for example were obligated by the police to have barred windows, which however violated the fire laws.[33] The most common solution was to pay off a government official or ask the Mafia to intervene. No wonder the number of small businesses in Russia until 2001 never seemed to exceed 880,000. Such restrictions on entry only strengthened Mafia control.

VI

To break these straitjacket barriers and encourage the opening of a large number of new businesses and competitors, Putin should do as Yeltsin did in January 1992 and decree that anyone who wants to can begin selling without formal approval. With some major exceptions where there are such things as health considerations, those who want to sell should be allowed to register by merely sending in a postcard to the regulating authorities. Undoubtedly there will be resistance. Remember, even Prime Minister Viktor Chernomyrdin, viewed as a supporter of business, insisted in January 1994 that "Russia will not become a bazaar economy."[34]

Fortunately, Chinese officials did not adopt such a restrictive stand. If they had, China would probably be where Russia is today. Instead, non-central government startup factories now account for more than 60 percent of China's annual growth of 7 to 10 percent. Chinese private and semi-private factories more often than not began with a trader hawking someone else's goods on a street corner. This required little in the way of startup capital. The next stop was to a table and then to a store and on to a wholesale operation and finally manufacturing. They began, however, with a bazaar economy. If it is beneath Russia's dignity to begin to move to the market that way, the process will take longer and is more likely to give rise to malignant institutions such as the Mafia.[35]

Allowing anyone who wants to sell to individual consumers is a first step, but as in China other measures must follow if there is to be a move to a market economy. One of these measures is to generate competitive wholesaling. After Gosplan was abolished, Russia found itself without wholesaling institutions, opening another arena to Mafia control. If the state had encouraged wholesalers dealing in similar products to locate near one another, it would have facilitated competitive markets. In most large Western cities for example there is a district for furniture, automobile parts, tire, and even flower wholesalers. Clustering wholesalers this way is not a perfect solution to the functioning of a free and unfettered market. In some cases it may lead to collusion and even easier targeting by the Mafia, but more often than not being near to each other seems to generate more competition as well as make it easier to unite to hold off predators.[36] The construction of Belaya Dacha, a $4.5 million food distribution center in Moscow financed by the EBRD, is one attempt to provide just such an environment.[37]

Hungarian authorities reacted in just this way when in 1991 local racketeers began to encroach on wholesaling activity in Budapest. As an experiment Hungarian authorities established a new wholesale district for various suppliers of food products. This district now handles one-half of the country's fruit and vegetables. The traders use TV screens to show what is being requested and offered and at what price. This, as economists say, "is an effort to create a more perfect market." The result is lower costs and prices.[38]

Cartels usually fail, and so sooner or later the Russian Mafia will probably also fail. But to speed up the process, wherever possible an effort must be made to show that the Mafia can be made vulnerable. For example, for a long time the Mafia established effective control over much of Sheremetevo Airport. Among other practices, they kept out all but a favored few taxis. That explains why transportation from the airport into Moscow used to cost anywhere from $40 to $100. The public bus route was inconvenient and it did not go directly to the center of Moscow. New management at the airport, however, eventually decided to challenge the Mafia by arranging additional bus services to downtown Moscow which served to undermine the Mafia's monopoly. The increased competition precipitated a cut in taxi fares to $20 and less.

Government must also introduce effective anti-crime and corruption measures. As indicated earlier, this in itself will not be enough but it can help. Implementation of existing regulations does not necessarily mean increasing government controls. In fact, as Minister of the Economy Gref is trying to do, licenses and permits should be reduced to a minimum. Building regulations invite the open palms of building inspectors.

Foreign companies are also vulnerable. After Coca-Cola built and opened a brand new bottling plant near the St. Petersburg airport, the local fire chief warned the company that unless a new fire station was built in the neighborhood, Coke would not be able to continue its operation there. He could not possibly close his eyes to such a fire hazard. Similarly, Gillette was told it would have to fund the building of additional electrical facilities in that same St. Petersburg industrial park before it could open. It is hard to determine just what did happen, but sure enough there is now a new fire station just around the corner, along with new electrical cables.

The authorities' power to set prices is another limiting factor. Markets should determine prices and government subsidies and arbitrary allocation of state resources should be eliminated. If the government wants to privatize or sell some property there should be open bidding.

Another way to thwart the Mafia is for foreign firms and international organizations to issue strict orders to reject Mafia pressure. That is easier said than done, particularly if threats are made against one's family. Out of "necessity" some Western businesses have decided that dealing with the Mafia is the only way to do business in Russia. They do this in the guise of hiring local security "consultants." This is most unfortunate. To their dismay, some foreigners have discovered that allowing the Mafia to intervene for them in Russia may lead to similar demands for intervention in other foreign markets. When the Mafia makes such demands, the safest strategy is to go home, a move which several firms including Assi Doman of Sweden have decided to take.[39]

Another strategy for undermining the Mafia is to encourage various regions of Russia to compete for foreign investment. One criterion for potential foreign investors should be whether or not the Mafia has a strong presence in the region. Competition for investors should provide an incentive for local authorities to crack down on the Mafia. Many businesses looking for new factory sites use somewhat similar inducements in the United States to win concessions from different states. For example, Alabama tries to compete with Illinois for investment by offering to build roads and provide infrastructure. The competition in Russia should be expanded to see which region can do the most not only to provide infrastructure but to reduce crime and corruption. Such competition in Russia is not as far-fetched as it first might seem. In Kostroma Oblast for example, the traffic police are notorious for not taking bribes and officers in Karelia and Yaroslavl are regarded amongst the least corrupt in the country.[40] Similarly, as an incentive for those looking for a place to set up their businesses, the governor of Novgorod holds up his region as one where the Mafia is less pervasive than elsewhere.

VII

Because the Russian Mafia has become so ubiquitous it will not be easy to dislodge. There have been times, as in 1995, when there was real reason to fear that criminal groups might come to dominate the political scene. Because Russian law provides immunity from criminal prosecution for elected members of legislative groups, approximately eighty candidates with criminal records ran for seats in the national Duma in the December 1995 elections. Victory, for most of these dubious candidates, was achieved either by buying off or physically threatening others off the ballot. In some cases, corrupt government officials, including the head of the tax police, persuaded even incumbent office holders that they would be well advised to allow their opponent to run unopposed, especially if that opponent was an oligarch (such as Roman Abramovich) favored by the Russian president.[41]

The frequency with which government officials, including the prosecutor's office as well as the police, involve themselves as agents of one business group or another is a serious problem. It has become common practice for uniformed police to supplement their low pay by hiring themselves out to business groups who choose to settle disputes with physical force rather than judicial restraint. The seizure of the headquarters of Slavneft in June 2002 by an ousted management group is one such instance.[42] Some call it the privatization of government or even of the KGB. There are also more and more instances where organized crime in Russia today is controlled by a "government syndicate" that is made up of officials from the Ministry of the Interior and the FSB (KGB) and nongovernmental security forces, all working with the Mafia. The problem is particularly serious in the provinces where the local governors often link up with local oligarchs. In 2001, 80 percent of organized crime groups in the former Soviet Union were said to have had ties with local police and law enforcement agencies.[43] Like an old-fashioned western movie, when the sheriff becomes a handmaiden of the largest rancher in town, few appeal or challenge such abusers of the law. Occasionally, an honest U.S. Marshal appears in the scene to produce a happy ending, but, so far, no one comparable has appeared in Russia.

Some argue that as perverted as the law has often become in post-communist Russia, it is still an improvement over the Soviet period. The present-day Mafia and privatized KGB may be wanton and perverse, but conditions in Russia today do not compare with the violence and disregard for existing laws that characterized the brutality of the KGB and Party purges that underpinned seventy years of Communist Party rule.

Still, the intermingling of the Mafia with a partially privatized KGB and government bureaucracy complicates any effort to control Russia's crime and corruption scene.[44] This intermingling may also explain Vladimir Putin's failure to move immediately against the Mafia and corruption when he became prime minister and president. As the former head of the FSB, the KGB's successor, he knew where to find the various Mafia leaders and the corrupt officials. An immediate crackdown on them would have demonstrated that he was a man of action who could address one of the country's most serious problems, but it would also have meant going after some of his former comrades. He may yet choose such a course of action, but so far he has only acted selectively and usually only against those who criticize him. Until he decides to act in a more decisive and blanket way, the dominance of crime and corruption and Misha-Two-Percent bureaucrats will continue to cast a shadow over any effort to regularize Russian economic, as well as social, life.

In the meantime, economic reform in Russia will continue to be handicapped and distorted. Eventually some of the dominant Mafia groups, like some of the oligarchs, may seek to opt for a more regularized, even legitimate life according to GAAP (Generally Approved Accounting Principles) and Roberts Rules of Order. Alternatively they may seek to pass on their gains to their children by sending them to the West for university training (laundering their children, so to speak) and setting up legitimate business fronts. Such a process may reduce violence and create a semblance of stability, but it will take a long time. In the interim, because the Russian Mafia's grasp has been so deep and so prolonged, and corruption become so deeply imbedded in daily life, it will be difficult for Russia to attract the investment, especially that requiring a long pay-back period, enjoyed by less afflicted transition economies.

10 Who says there was no better way?

No one thought that privatization would be painless but many of the proponents of reform assumed that the costs, even crime and corruption, would be mitigated by the economic and managerial restructuring which was touted to be an ensuing byproduct of privatization in Russia.[1] While belatedly there has been some restructuring, after more than a decade what there has been has been limited and slow in coming. Since factory directors ended up as owners or as large shareholders, most hesitated to put themselves out of a job.

That the privatization effort would be less than successful should be no surprise. Even when Margaret Thatcher began to privatize industries that had been nationalized during the years the Labour government was in power, there were abuses, despite the fact that England was a market economy. Yet even when compared with other European transition economies, except for Ukraine and Belarus, Russia has fared much worse. Here we will examine two other cases of privatization, one in Czechoslovakia, where the results were also unsuccessful, and Poland, which stands as a model of a successful reform program.

I

Czech privatization, while complicated, largely revolves around the role of two individuals. The first was Vaclav Klaus, the Finance Minister of Czechoslovakia in 1992 and soon to become its prime minister. The second was a former undergraduate of Harvard University, Viktor Kozeny, who soon became a multi-millionaire and the target of numerous charges of financial manipulation and fraud.

At the time of its privatization in the early 1990s, it looked as if the Czech Republic, both when it was a part of Czechoslovakia and after late 1992 when Slovakia broke away from it, would be one of the most successful of all the East European countries in terminating state control of industry. Before World War II, Czechoslovakia was considered one of the most advanced market economies in Central Europe. Thus not only were its Western institutions deeply grounded, its Finance Minister, Vaclav Klaus, was fervently committed to undoing communism and privatizing Czech industry. He was one of the most devoted adherents of a free, private market in all of Europe, West or East.

Even before the collapse of communist rule in Czechoslovakia, the country had slowly begun to allow some private activity. As far back as 1981, private farmers were allowed to sell their produce directly to the public.[2] In January 1988, private citizens could legally sell their services to the public as well. In 1990, insiders as well as outsiders were allowed to privatize small shops and restaurants, and the privatization of small businesses was officially launched in January 1991.[3] By late 1993, some 22,000 small businesses were privatized for an estimated 30 billion Czech kronas, or about $1 billion.[4]

Major problems appeared with the decision to privatize the country's large businesses. Adopting ideas written and proposed in 1976 by Milton Friedman and refined later in 1988 by two Polish economists, Janusz Lewandowski and Jan Szomberg, the Czechs decided that the best way to share the bounty of privatization with the public was to issue a book of vouchers to each Czech citizen willing to buy one.[5] These vouchers in turn could be exchanged for stock in the various 2,285 Czech corporations selected for the first round of privatization (this number was later reduced to 1,491).[6] Initially these state-owned companies were turned into private corporations and their shares transferred to the National Property Fund, an organization set up specifically to hold these shares prior to their sale or exchange for vouchers.[7] Each share was valued at 1,000 Czech kronas.

As described by Jan Mladek, an economist at Central European University, each voucher book contained 1,000 voucher points and cost 1,000 Czech kronas for the registration stamp and 35 Czech kronas for the booklet itself, altogether a total of about $34.50.[8] That sum was equivalent to about 25 percent of the average monthly wage. The voucher points could then be used to bid for company shares at as little as one hundred voucher points per company share. This procedure allowed individuals to diversify their investments and exchange their voucher points either for stock in one of the corporations being privatized or in an investment privatization fund (IPF). These IPFs were to operate much as mutual funds. By combining the stock from thousands of investors and managing the fund on a full-time basis, theoretically at least, the IPF would be able to make more informed decisions, return greater profits, and be more influential in the operation of Czech corporations than if individuals invested on their own. However, because by Czech standards the vouchers were relatively expensive, had no monetary value attached to them, and could only be exchanged for stock, by December 1991, only a half million Czechs and Slovaks had exercised their option to obtain vouchers. The program appeared destined to fail.

At this point, an unlikely entrepreneur intervened. After working briefly for Robert Fleming, a British investment firm, Viktor Kozeny, a 1989 Harvard graduate, decided in 1990 to return to his native Czechoslovakia. Arriving in 1990 in Prague, he became a consultant to the Ministry of the Interior. This was just about the time that the government had begun to draw up plans to privatize the economy and issue the voucher booklets.

Kozeny calculated that the value of the stock of the state enterprises that was to be exchanged for each book of vouchers significantly exceeded the 1,035 Czech kronas ($34.50) charged for each booklet. As he explained it, he made a calculation and realized that the sale of 8 million voucher booklets would yield the state approximately $280 million ($35 times 8 million).[9] Yet the voucher holders would be able to divide up state industrial property worth approximately $11 billion.[10]

Kozeny did not need a Harvard degree to see the possibilities. With only $3,000 in his pocket, he created a company he called Harvard Capital and Consulting (much to the chagrin of the Harvard administration, which takes a tough stand on the use of its name for commercial purposes). Making what he reasoned to be a sure bet, he promised voucher holders that if they turned over their booklets to him so he could buy up stock in Czech corporations, he would guarantee at least a ten-fold return on the cost of their voucher booklets after a year and a day for those who wanted to redeem them. For the Czech investor, that would mean obtaining 10,350 Czech kronas, or $345 for a $34.50 investment. In the interim each Czech investor received stock in Harvard Capital and Consulting.[11] As Czech investors took him up on his offer, Kozeny accumulated 820,000 vouchers at virtually no up-front cost to him.[12]

His was no easy accomplishment. Before most skeptical Czechs would turn over their vouchers, he had to convince them that they had nothing to lose and much to gain by handing their vouchers to a man without existing resources or a track record. To do this, in early January 1992 he launched a massive television campaign. Within two weeks, the number of Czechoslovaks registered to buy vouchers quadrupled from a half million to 2 million, and again to 8 million by the end of the month.[13] Eventually, 77 percent of those Czechs eligible bought vouchers, and over 70 percent of them turned the vouchers over to Kozeny or one of the other 400 IPFs that sprang up in the wake of Kozeny's success.[14] This campaign also suited Vaclav Klaus, Finance Minister, who had staked his career on the success of the voucher program. Since his name was on each booklet, the public's initial acceptance of the voucher program undoubtedly helped him win the election for prime minister that year.

Kozeny acknowledges that he was successful beyond his wildest dreams. Not only did he rescue the voucher program from what looked like failure, he also gained control over those 820,000 voucher booklets which he then used to acquire stock in and control of a portfolio of Czechoslovak corporations.[15] The downside of his effort was that if all those who consigned their vouchers to him decided to take him up on his offer to cash in their Harvard Capital and Consulting stock, he would be liable for $250 million. But by his reckoning, for a time he controlled nearly one half of the country's privatized industrial assets.[16] That would be more than enough to honor his commitment. (It is hard to judge just how precise Kozeny's estimate is. According to official data, two other IPFs controlled by banks in Prague–Ceska Sporitelna Praha and Ivesticni Banka Group, Praha–ended up with more vouchers in the first wave of privatization than did the Harvard group.)[17]

Whatever the exact proportion of Kozeny's stock, his large accumulation made the country's leaders nervous; they began investigations of his past. Ultimately, the government set a limit of 20 percent ownership as the maximum one investor could own in any one corporation. To skirt these restrictions, Kozeny transformed his IPF in 1995 into a holding company where he could exercise unlimited control and management. In this way, he took over effective ownership of fifty of the country's largest firms.[18]

Even his critics acknowledge that without Kozeny, few Czechs would have exercised their option to take out vouchers. By 1993, however, those who listened carefully could already hear an ever larger number of Bronx cheers mixed in with the applause for Kozeny and the privatization process. In late 1992, for example, Kozeny complained to the Ministry of the Interior that he was being blackmailed by a former espionage agent, Vaclav Wallis. In turn, Wallis explained that Kozeny had come to him for inside information about some of the corporations up for purchase through vouchers. Wallis was arrested and Kozeny was accused of bribery and soliciting secret government documents. Soon after, Kozeny left the country, obtained Irish citizenship, and eventually moved to the Bahamas. The case against Kozeny was closed, then reopened again, and in July 1995 dropped once again.

The accusations and counter-accusations did nothing to improve investor confidence. Initially, shares in Harvard Capital and Consulting did splendidly. From May 1, 1992 to December 16, 1994, the investment fund reported an average return of 350 percent and its shares hit $33.[19] No dividends, however, were paid in 1995. Soon there were reports that

Kozeny had stripped most of Harvard's assets and used them to take over direct control of several of the most valuable Czech companies. By 1996, although his shares in Harvard had lost most of their value, Kozeny was said to be worth $200 million.[20] He was fined $6.8 million for improperly spending investors' money on advertising and consulting fees. Instead of a hero, he became known as the "Pirate of Prague."[21] Later, in 1997 he once more convinced others to invest with him in Azerbaijani oil fields and was subsequently charged with defrauding a long list of sophisticated investors, including a subsidiary of an insurance company, an investment fund run by Columbia University, former Senator George J. Mitchell, and Leon Cooperman, a Wall Street fund manager.

While Kozeny warrants a large portion of the blame for the discrediting of the Czech privatization effort, some of the blame also falls on Vaclav Klaus, then Finance Minister. He was so committed to the market that he rebuffed any attempts to implement strict government supervision.[22] He fought off efforts to create an institution such as the Securities Exchange Commission until April 1998. Even then, he restricted its regulatory powers and held down its budget.[23] Moreover, he was one of the strongest advocates of the issuance of the voucher booklets. His backing was one of the reasons why the Czech plan at least initially appeared to be more popular than the Polish reform program.[24] But this backfired. Because Klaus had been such a strong proponent of the reforms and the privatization process, and so opposed any restraint on the market's functioning, he became a natural target for criticism when the reforms went sour. This also helps explain his failure to win reelection as prime minister.

At best, privatization in the Czech Republic has to be considered a partial, if not a substantial, failure. On the plus side, in the course of two privatization waves, 4,700 large enterprises came under private control, including 1,800 that were privatized using vouchers.[25] The IPFs that were established in the process however have been severely criticized for taking advantage of ordinary citizens. While a few portfolio managers such as Kozeny ran off with the proceeds, the public was left with near worthless pieces of paper. Moreover, many of the other IPFs are now run by Czech banks, which, until recently at least, were controlled by the state. This meant that the businesses they controlled were still, in effect, owned by the state, even if indirectly. This, in part, explains why relatively little industrial restructuring and change of managers has occurred in Czech industry. In sum, while Czech privatization has not resulted in the massive corruption and distortion that characterizes Russian privatization, the public at large has not benefited. The Czech model turned out to be very different from the fair and just privatization that its advocates envisioned.

II

While the Czech model may confirm the views of those who argue that privatization after several decades of communism inevitably leads to abuses, the Polish path to privatization, and for that matter its whole transition effort, demonstrates the opposite. Admittedly, some of the Polish success is due as much to luck as to a carefully thought-out strategy.

Poland's economic transition stands in dramatic contrast to that of Russia's. It is not just that in the aftermath of the transition Russia's GDP fell by 40 percent from 1991 to 1998, including a 5 percent decline in 1998, or that from 1992 to about 2000, Poland's GDP grew at an average of 5 to 6 percent a year, making it one of the more robust economies in Europe.[26] It is also significant that Poland has been spared pervasive economic and social institutional distortions such as Mafia dominance, pervasive corruption, crony capitalism, and the massive theft of state property, all of which characterize today's Russia. Poland may not be immune to such blights, but compared to Russia its problems are minor.

Given that both countries were communist as well as neighbors and both began to move to the market and political reform about the same time (Polish political reform began in 1989 and its economic reform in 1990), why have the results been so different? No one simple set of factors can explain everything. Certainly Poland's proximity to Western Europe, especially to West Berlin, the fact that communism was imposed on it by the Soviet Union, and that communism lasted only forty-five years in Poland, unlike Russia's seventy years, have shaped the outcome.

Poland's adjustment to the market was also facilitated by the small but legitimate number of private businesses tolerated throughout the Polish communist period. Again, nothing comparable was permitted in the USSR. Thus, after the collapse of communism in 1989, it was easier for the Poles to accept the notion of private business as a legitimate activity. Small in number as they were, entrepreneurial Poles were able to build on that base and government authorities and the public accepted it. Therefore, the Polish government as well as the public had fewer qualms about the emergence of independent businesses. Even before the collapse of its communist regime, Poland passed the 1982 Law on State Enterprises and introduced a 1988 Law on Economic Activity that allowed every Polish citizen to engage in private business, be it service, sales, construction, or manufacturing.[27] Suddenly, especially in 1990, vendors appeared in the main market squares and on street corners, selling whatever they could find. The proceeds from a day's sales were promptly used to procure more goods to sell the next day. Beginning with the barest in the way of initial capital, about 2 million new businesses were registered in five years' time, and about 3 million within the decade.[28] In the course of ten years, some of the new startups had grown into substantial businesses.

One example is Roman Kluska, who founded the Polish computer firm Optimus from scratch in 1988. Kluska had a scientific bent, which was nourished at the Krakow School of Economics where he studied in the Department of Cybernetics and Information Technology. He succeeded not by taking over an existing state company, but by creating his own from scratch in his home. Moreover Polish authorities restrained themselves by not muscling in on his success.[29] He was also helped by the fact that Polish banks were willing to provide loans and Mafia groups, especially those which deal with software, were essentially non-existent. When Kluska sold some of his shares in 2000, the capitalized value of options amounted to almost $500 million.[30]

A survey of the richest one hundred Polish businessmen revealed that, unlike Russian oligarchs who became wealthy by taking over control of state assets, most of the Poles had built their fortunes from startups.[31] This stands in sharp contrast to Russia where more often than not, new business startups were likely to be frustrated, discouraged or thwarted, and where bank loans to new small business startups or, for that matter, even to existing small businesses are a rarity.[32]

In addition, because at least 80 percent of the Polish farms were never collectivized, they continued to function as independent entities. That does not mean, however, that with the post-communist period, they were efficient and productive. They were not. But at least Polish farmers were spared the sense of collective stupor and lethargy that characterizes post-Soviet agriculture.

Another major difference was the way that Poland eventually privatized its state enterprises. Initially their approach was similar to that of Russia's. Both countries decided early on that it was essential to privatize not only small businesses, but large state factories. The differences lay in the way they each carried out privatization. The Poles at first declared that once the January 1990 price reform was implemented they planned to privatize the state sector immediately. But because of bureaucratic and political wrangling, they could not argree on how to proceed. In fact, it took five years to launch a meaningful program. In 1990 they did sell off shares in five state companies and disposed of 1,142 smaller businesses to private owners, most of which had operated these businesses under state ownership.[33] But as of September 1995, only 148 large-size enterprises had been privatized. Even though the Law on National Investment Funds and their Privatization was passed in April 1993, it took until December 15, 1994 to put it in operation.

The delay proved to be fortuitous because it gave the Poles time to reflect and design a new and innovative process of privatization. When its extensive program of privatization was finally launched in 1995, it facilitated the restructuring of those former state industries with a minimum of scandal, corruption and outright theft. They had time to improve "the initial conditions."

Drawing on some ideas he had helped formulate in 1988, Janusz Lewandowski, a member of the Union of Freedom Party and the Minister of Privatization from 1991 to 1993, offered a blueprint for privatization shortly after Solidarity regained control in 1991.[34] Working in conjunction with Leszek Balcerowicz, the Minister of Finance and later Deputy Prime Minister, Lewandowski's proposed programs sparked heated political debate, which prevented implementation of the program. By early 1995, when the government was able to move forward, Lewandowski's plan was redesigned to incorporate safeguards that precluded the seizing of those assets by a few rich, aggressive individuals or factory directors. This spared Poland many of Russia's problems. Had the privatization effort been carried out earlier, the only bidders for state enterprises would have been those who had seized government assets for themselves, or Mafia-like criminal groups who literally stole the money. In the immediate aftermath of the breakup of the Polish communist system, there were very few who had legitimately built up a capital stake.

Lewandowski deserves enormous credit for understanding the likely consequences of an unstructured privatization process. He set forth several goals.

• He sought to prevent factory directors from gaining direct or indirect control of state-owned enterprises. Therefore, he arranged for control by outside ownership, so as to insure that factory directors did not block the restructuring of the enterprise or efforts to improve productivity. This meant that, where necessary, outside owners could make changes in personnel, including the firing of the factory director himself, as well as closing down or selling off parts of the enterprise.

• He also understood that foreign specialists and advisors should have a role in providing guidance to Polish managers who might have difficulty at first in operating in a market economy.

• At the same time, he also wanted to maintain Polish ownership of those assets.

• Finally, he also sought to ensure that the average Polish citizen, including the workers in the factories being privatized, derived tangible benefits from the privatization process. This meant not only providing the public with an initial stake in the about-to-be privatized enterprises, but assuring that it would share in any increase in value from the future operation of the enterprises.

The Lewandowski proposals involved several steps. As in Czechoslovakia and Russia, vouchers were sold to the public at large. In

1991, each citizen was entitled to buy one voucher for 20 zlotys (or about $6.20). Out of an eligible 27 million, 25,900,000 Poles, exercised that option. Lewandowski's next task was to select which of Poland's 8,441 state enterprises he wanted to privatize, and how. From an initial 600, he narrowed the list to 512. He then decided to package the 512 businesses together because if privatization went one firm at a time, the process would take too long and be too hard to supervise. He excluded another 3,000 enterprises from the immediate privatization process: 1,100 of these because they were too small and the rest because they were weak and needed to be dissolved or liquidated. Another 1,500 were turned over to local authorities to be privatized under their auspices. As of 1997, this left about 4,000 large enterprises still owned by the state, primarily in key economic centers such as telecommunications, finance, chemicals, raw materials, steel and energy. Because of their size and their importance, most of these 4,000 were to be privatized one by one. However, because many were essential utilities, the state retained ownership of the railroads, the electrical grid, and the post office.

So far the Polish privatization program does not seem to be much different from those in Russia and the Czech Republic. It was the next phase, however, where Lewandowski was so creative. Under his guidance, fifteen National Investment Funds (NIFs) were opened. The NIFs in effect operated as mutual funds. The vouchers that were distributed to the Polish public in the first phase of the privatization project were then made exchangeable for one share in each of the fifteen NIFs. They could buy and sell these shares or retain them and collect dividends from the NIFs.

What distinguished these NIFs and their stock holdings from mutual funds in the Czech Republic or Russia was that Lewandowski understood that if the shares of enterprise stock controlled by the NIFs were divided up into fifteen equal parts, the factory director would most likely continue to control the factory as before and operate it as the *de facto* owner. When power is diffused among many different partners, the odds are that no one entity is able to muster effective control. To prevent this, the Polish privatization authorities divided the 512 companies being privatized into fifteen groups of thirty-four companies each. In an effort to gain control over what they considered the most promising of the thirty-four enterprises in each group, the NIFs then bid against each other in a manner similar to the National Football League's draft for football players. The authorities then allocated a 33 percent share of stock in each of those thirty-four companies to that one NIF. As a result, each of the individual 512 factory directors became accountable to one dominant outside overseer (NIF). The other fourteen NIFs were then provided with 1.9 percent shares of stock in the remaining 478 enterprises that were in the privatization pool (see Box 10.1).

Box 10.1 The Polish Mass Privatization Program (MPP)

I   *National Investment Funds (15 NIFs)*

   A   *Supervising board*
       1   Responsibility: determine general policy
       2   Membership: all Polish
   B   *Management company*
       1   Responsibility: day-to-day management
       2   Membership
          a   Polish banks
          b   Foreign investment funds
             i   20% Polish ownership
             ii 80% foreign ownership

II *Typical NIF portfolio (512 privatized companies)*

   A   34 companies   with 33% of each of 34 companies'
       shares
   B   478 companies   with 1.9% of each of the 478 compa-
       nies' shares

III *Ownership of each company's stock*

A	Principal NIF	33%
B	Remaining 14 NIFs	27% (1.9% each)
C	Staff and management	15%
D	State-owned shares	<u>25%</u>
		100%

Together with their 33 percent holdings in 34 companies and 1.9 percent in 478 companies, the NIFs would control 60 percent of each of the enterprises' stock. Of the remaining shares, 15 percent would be distributed to the employees and directors of the enterprises, and 25 percent would remain with the state. The state, in turn, put 15 percent of its shares into social and pension funds. This move was intended to insure that in addition to the shares each Polish citizen received in the NIFs, the public at large benefited in an ongoing way from the privatization process.

When shares in the fifteen NIFs were listed on the Polish Stock Exchange on June 12, 1997, the NIFs came to operate much like closed-end mutual funds. The price of the NIF shares reflected the underlying asset value of each of their holdings and the NIF could sell or buy additional shares in the individual enterprises at their discretion. In turn, Poles could buy and sell shares in each NIF.

While the dominant NIF with 33 percent equity in an enterprise would not by itself have enough authority to oust management, the assumption was that it would keep a close enough eye on the thirty-four companies that constituted its largest holdings. In most instances that would mean providing guidance and bringing in outside consultants when needed, but on occasion it might also mean seeking support from some of the other NIFs if it became necessary to force a management change. Recognizing that after forty-five years of communist control most Polish managers ,including their supervisors, were ill prepared to compete in a capitalist environment, the Polish privatization officials also proposed that at least one foreign investment firm be represented among the fund managers in each of the NIFs. As Table 10.1 indicates, all but one of the fifteen NIFs had a representative from at least one foreign investment bank.[35] Altogether, there were nine firms from Great Britain, seven from the United States, four from France, three from Austria, and one each from Italy, Hong Kong, Switzerland, and Japan.

The fund managers in turn reported to a purely Polish-controlled Supervisory Board so as to ensure that Polish groups remained firmly in control of the former state-owned enterprises. While this two-tiered supervisory structure made sense politically, administratively it created the potential for conflicts, especially between the Supervisory Board and the foreign members of the funds' managerial groups. Two such conflicts of interest occurred early on. In the second instance the Supervisory Board of Fund 13 threatened to terminate its managerial contact with Regent Pacific and Yamaichi, the Hong Kong and Japanese management teams.[36] However it was the Polish Supervisory Board that was dismissed. In an earlier case, Wasserstein Perella and the New England Investment Company, both American companies, were fired by their partners in Management Fund 11 in April 1996. Except for these two cases, such conflicts were rare.

Generally, the performance of the fifteen NIFs and their 512 newly privatized enterprises can be regarded as a success. Virtually no scandals or charges of insider dealing, and certainly few, if any, instances of crony capitalism or theft of state property are associated with them. Equally important, when the NIFs began to operate in 1995 and 1996, the Poles already had set up two million or so new businesses. This created a viable market infrastructure with competition and a form of checks and balances. When the 512 newly privatized businesses began their operations, they did so in a reasonably well-developed competitive structure. Moreover, despite repeated assertions in Russia that failure to privatize would result in massive asset stripping, the delay in implementing privatization in Poland

Table 10.1 The National Investment Funds (NIFs)*

Name (short form)	Supervisory Board Chairman	Prinicipal participants in the fund manager	Fund manager
First National Investment Fund	Mr. J. Jezak	Bank Rozwoju Eksportu (Poland); GiroCredit (Austria)	BRE/GiroCredit Management Sp. Z.o.o.
Second National Investment Fund	Mr. M. Trocki	UNP International (Poland); Bank Gdanski (Poland); Murray Johnstone (UK)	Hevelius Management Sp. Z.o.o.
Third National Investment Fund	Mr. S. Golonka	Barclays de Zoete Wedd (UK); Bank Polska Kasa Opieki (Poland); Company Assistance (Poland)	Trinity Management Sp. Z.o.o.
Fourth National Investment Fund	Mr. A. Ryttel	Raiffeisen (Austria); WS Atkins (UK)	Konsorcjum Raiffei Atkins; Zaradzanie Funduszami SA
Fifth National Investment Fund	Mr. J. Rymarczyk	Kleinwort Benson (UK); Polski Bank Rozwoju (Poland)	Polskie Towarzystwo Prywatyzacyjne-Kleinwort Benson Sp. Z.o.o.
Sixth National Investment Fund–Magna Polonia	Mr. A. Koprowski	Chase Gemina (US/Italy); Wielkopolski Bank Kredytowy (Poland); Nicom Consulting (Poland)	Chase Gemina Polska Sp. Z.o.o.
Kazimierz Wielki Fund	Mr. J. Borcz (Acting Chairman)	Lazard Frères (France); GICC Capital (US); Bank Gospodarstwa Krajowego (Poland)	Kazimierz Wielki Fund; Management Co. Sp. Z.o.o.
Eighth National Investment Fund	Mr. J. Matyska	Barents Group (US); Bank Handlowy w Warszawie (Poland); Paine Webber (US); York Trust (UK); Kennedy Associates (US)	KP Konsorcjum Sp. Z.o.o.

Name (short form)	Supervisory Board Chairman	Prinicipal participants in the fund manager	Fund manager
Eugeniusz Kwiatowski Fund	Mr. Z. Szeloch		
Tenth National Investment Fund	Mr. H. Skawinski	Banque Arjil (France); Agencja Rozwoju Przemystu (Poland); Warszawska Grupa Konsultingowa (Poland)	Fidea Management Sp. Z.o.o.
Eleventh National Investment Fund	Mr. J. Kedzierski	KNK Finance and Investment (Poland); Wasserstein Perella (US); New England Investment Company (US)	KN Wasserstein Sp. Z.o.o.
Twelfth National Investment Fund–Piast	Mr. P. Swiderski	Banque Nationale de Paris (France); Polski Bank Inwestycyjny (Poland)	BNP-PBI Eurofund Management (Polska) Sp. Z.o.o.
Thirteenth National Investment Fund	Mr. M. Bryx	Yamaichi International Europe (UK/Japan); Regent Pacific (UK/Hong Kong); ABC Consulting (Poland)	Yamaichi Regent Special Projects Limited
West Investment Fund	Mr. L. Kociecki	Bank Zachodni (Poland); Central Europe Trust (UK); Charterhouse (UK); Crédit Commercial de France (France)	International Westfund Holdings Limited
Fifteenth National Investment Fund	Mr. Z. Piotrowski	Creditanstalt (Austria); St. Gallen Consulting (Switzerland)	Creditanstalt–SCG Fund Management S.A.

Source: Program Powszechnej Prywatyzacji (National Investment Fund Program), *Information Relating to the Universal Share Certificate*, Ministry of Privatization, Warsaw, November 1993, p. 4.

*The principal investors are those who have an economic interest of 10 percent or more in the activities of the Fund Manager firm. The full names of such participants have not necessarily been given and intermediate holding companies are generally ignored. Their principal place of business, rather than country of incorporation, is stated.

resulted in relatively little such stripping. Poland's well-functioning reform program contrasted sharply with Russia's malfunctioning reforms.

III

As we saw earlier, while the Poles waited five years to implement their privatization program, the Russian authorities moved immediately in 1992 to privatize up to 70 percent of the country's state enterprises. Ready or not, this included not only the smaller shops and services as in Poland, but most of the other enterprises, including some of the very largest. Anatoly Chubais, at that time the Minister of Privatization, was in a hurry. Ready or not, this led to the immediate distribution of shares in state-owned companies to the public at large. Once the public had an equity in their factories, Chubais reasoned that they, along with both factory management and workers, would oppose efforts by communist leaders to return to state controls.[37]

While responding to these political concerns, Chubais ended up short-changing the effort to stimulate managerial efficiency and restructuring. Thus, unlike Lewandowski, Chubais did little to restrain factory directors from asserting control of their factories. There was no discussion about outside board supervision of the sort introduced in Poland, much less about a role for foreign specialists or restructuring. On the contrary, Chubais agreed, even if reluctantly, to changes in the regulations giving more power to management that were demanded by lobbyists for those same factory managers. As a result Russian factory managers were extended special purchasing and borrowing rights so that they could assume *de facto* ownership of their factories.

Ideologically, Chubais and his Western advisors at the IMF, and Maxim Boycko, Andrei Shleifer, and Robert Vishny believed that private ownership was always preferable to state ownership.[38] For that matter, they argued that the slower Polish approach was bound to fail. "From the efficiency viewpoint, it was (and still is) by no means clear that foreign-run mutual funds in Poland could successfully achieve depoliticization. It was hard to imagine some 35-year-old British or American investment banker telling a Polish manager to sack 3000 people ... .The Polish funds were designed to be too large and too political to be real engines of depoliticization."[39] Russian privatization, they were convinced, was a success. As they saw it, even if because of the immediate privatization in Russia corrupt officials or members of the Mafia ended up as the new private owners, later, but probably sooner, such individuals would be flushed out in proxy fights by the other stockholders.

Such reasoning made sense in a society where the laws and the initial conditions provided for proxy fights, and property rights were enforced as a matter of course by the courts. Boycko, Shleifer and Vishny understood this.[40] Nonetheless, they pursued their reform proposals even though Russia at the time had almost no administrators with practice or experience in dealing with such matters, much less effective laws (that is, in Joe Berliner's words, neither effective jockeys nor horses).

Another important difference between the Polish and Russian privatization programs was that Poland's was implemented in tandem with the reconstruction or introduction of institutions and property rights designed to restrain or sublimate the primeval acquisitive instinct. By contrast, as exemplified by the way Tyumen Oil manipulated the bankruptcy law in Russia, the comparable institutions and limited property rights that came into being were not only not positive and constructive, they served to distort normal market processes and behavior.

Economists generally hold the credo that property rights are necessary in order to protect oneself against government encroachment.[41] But Russia's experience demonstrates that the premature exercise of property rights may actually be counterproductive and undermine the whole reform effort. Henceforth economists may have to reformulate one of their basic axioms. Enforceable property rights can be a stimulus to economic growth and political stability. But if property rights are introduced in the absence of a market and competitive infrastructure and without a system of economic as well as political checks and balances (with poor initial conditions and inexperienced, incompetent or corrupt administrators), those rights may preclude the development of a healthy competitive market, and may even threaten democratic processes and, in an extreme case, the existence of the state.

Using their property rights (excluding land ownership), Russian oligarchs quickly built on the control of their newly seized assets to acquire more property, including media outlets. This in turn allowed some, particularly Boris Berezovsky, (for a time at least), to influence the election process and the makeup of the government. The nexus between the oligarchs, the press and political power is even more evident in the provinces.

Such criticism of Russia's premature privatization effort does not necessarily mean that a more gradual, many-sided approach of the sort adopted by the Poles would have spared Russia the grotesque form of thievery and crony capitalism that ensued. Yet Poland's more equitable, less corrupt, and more gradual privatization program undoubtedly helps explain why the notion of property rights including land ownership is more widely supported in Poland, whereas for substantial numbers in Russia it continues to be cursed.

11 Confidence or con game
What will it take?

Thus far, the reform process in Russia can be considered to be at best only a partial success. Among its other shortcomings, the reforms created a climate in which neither businessmen nor government officials had any serious interest in adhering to the rule of law, much less to conventional Western business codes. Such practices have not brought about the collapse of the economy (although there have been some near misses), but they have led to enormous abuse, waste, missed opportunities and economic distortions. Nonetheless not everything is disheartening. The economy did begin to grow in 1999 and there have been occasional signs that some can–and have–made it honestly and profitably.

To conclude our study we will consider both the hazards and realizable opportunities that exist in the Russian economy. Despite the ubiquitous culture of deceit and corruption we shall examine instances where some businesses, both Russian and foreign, and government officials in the regions have attempted to operate in a reasonably transparent and ethically acceptable way. We will then consider some of the more notable abuses. What remains to be seen is whether the success stories are the exception or the first hint of a trend. Finally we will consider what can and should be done to enhance such opportunities.

I

Efforts to instill market business practices are even more difficult now than they were at the beginning of the reform process because the abuses caused by Russia's reforms are a further hindrance to a market economy. There are still far too many in Russia today who believe that it is naïve to deal honestly and fairly with creditors and minority stockholders. Not that Americans can be as confident these days that American CEOs can always be counted on to act responsibly, nonetheless corporate governance in Russia in the reform process has, more often than it should, become akin to authorized larceny. Appendix 11.1 (though by no means inclusive) lists a number of such practices. Some of these cases, such as the RCB, Tyumen Oil, YUKOS and Gazprom have already been examined in some of the preceding chapters. But there are other examples. As indicated in the Appendix, which provides a good summary, such practices are certainly not exceptional. Hardly a sector of the economy has been spared such behavior and in many cases these practices have become standard operating procedure. They include:

• asset stripping (Gazprom is the most blatant but by no means unique example);
• share dilution of minority shareholders (YUKOS, Sberbank, Norilsk Nickel);
• abuse of bankruptcy procedures (Tyumen Oil, Kondpetroleum, Chernogorneft);
• shell games with public bank deposits (Menatep, SBS/Agro);
• Mafia ejection of legal owners by force, threat or murder (Subway Sandwich franchise in St. Petersburg; Norex Petroleum in Siberia; Sawyer Research Products in Vladimir; the aluminum industry–Krasnoyarsk Aluminum Smelters);
• official intimidation, ejection or threat of imprisonment by senior government officials (Far Eastern Shipping Co.; Media-MOST; TV-6);
• arbitrary seizure of mobile telephone frequencies (MSS Saratov);
• hiding assets from IMF (the RCB);
• rigged bids (LUKoil, Severnaia Neft, Loans for Shares program).

Who knows how many other cases there are that remain to be uncovered.

Businesses and investors in Russia must worry not only about the businessmen they deal with, but about government officials who theoretically are there to insure the adoption of fair codes, but who in fact use their posts to extort. Thus, when asked in 2002 whether laws regulating business are implemented, 59 percent of the enterprise managers questioned said no and only 27 percent said yes.[1] Because they usually have less clout, small businesses have been especially vulnerable to heavy-handed businesses, corrupt officials, and the Mafia.[2]

That helps explain why most Russian businessmen that I interviewed insisted that it became more difficult to open a small business in 2002 than it was at the beginning of the Yeltsin reforms a decade earlier. The number of small businesses officially registered hit a peak of 896,900 in December 1994 but fell to 877,300 in 1995.[3] Though additional new businesses were opened in subsequent years, others closed. The financial collapse on August 17, 1998 did not help. Estimates are that as many as 30 percent of the then existing small businesses were forced to close their doors, 10 percent of them permanently.[4] As of December 2000, the total of officially registered small businesses was only 891,000, still below the 1994 peak.[5] Of course there are many unregistered businesses, but the low number of those officially registered again contrasts sharply with Poland, a country one-third the size of Russia, where in 2001 there were almost 2 million registered small businesses.[6]

Blame for the relatively small number of businesses can be attributed in large part to the persistent disdain toward small businesses that has long characterized Russian culture. That was true even before the 1917 revolution and the enmity intensified during the communist era. Traditionally, in both the czarist and Soviet eras the emphasis was on large-sized business.

As part of that culture then and now, big business and gigantimania-type enterprises invariably had protective patrons that put their entities beyond the reach of ordinary bureaucrats, inspectors, generals and extortionists. As compensation, these petty harassers were allowed free rein to feed themselves on the country's small and medium-sized businesses. This is very different from the West, where small business, if not favored, at least is not more closely regulated than larger businesses. Data collected by the Yabloko Party compare the world of small business in Russia and the West. Whereas in Russia small business generates only about 10 percent of the GDP,(some say as little as 6 percent) in the West it accounts for more than 50 percent.[7] Small business startups also generate jobs. In Poland, the Czech Republic and Hungary, businesses opened since 1990 now employ 50 percent of these countries' workforce, far above the comparable figure in Russia.[8] Russia has only 6 small and medium-sized businesses per 1,000 people; the United States, for example, has 74 per 1,000, and in the European Union the ratio is 45 per 1,000.[9] Even Anatoly Chubais confesses that before he became head of the privatization effort, he had a deep-seated antipathy toward, as he put it, "trade ... buying and selling."[10] Unlike Poland where reform and privatization unleashed a revival of small businesses and an ongoing stream of startups, Russia's privatization, from 1992 to at least 2001, resulted in relatively few startups. Nor does it help when officials such as Mayor Luzhkov in Moscow periodically order the destruction of privately run kiosks on the street and ban street vendors.[11]

Anyone seeking to open his own business faces formidable obstacles. It took six months, for example, to obtain permission to open a Patio Pizza Restaurant.[12] The owner persisted, but he needed permission from the "Health Department, Fire Inspectorate, Environmental Department, two architectural departments and two levels of government administration." In 1999 President Putin himself complained that there existed fifty-one official bodies with the right to check on businesses. In Moscow, to open and register a business, it is necessary to comply with fifty different legal acts, visit between twenty and thirty government offices, and obtain the agreement of fifty to ninety different officials.[13] A U.S. agency for international development study found that it takes an average business 49 person-days and $357 to register as a business and then another 47 person-days and $576 to license said business.[14] One hundred and fifty-seven certificates were required before General Motors could open its joint venture with Avtovaz.[15] According to Alfa Bank President Peter Aven, Alfa Bank requires a staff of ten who do nothing else but deal with its forty inspections per year.[16] According to a survey conducted by Timothy Frye and Andrei Shleifer, it takes four times longer to set up a business in Russia than it does in Poland.[17] This is illustrated dramatically in Figures 11.1 and 11.2, prepared by Grigory Yavlinsky and his Yabloko Party. Figure 11.1 outlines the procedures necessary for opening a business in Germany. Figure 11.2 shows the comparable steps required in Russia as of 2000. Whereas in France, licenses are required for approximately twenty different types of businesses, in Russia the figure until 2001 was closer to 2,000.

Such a large number of government regulations and regulators invites interference and more corruption. As one observer put it, "This is the institutionalized Mafia, but they don't carry guns–they withhold certificates."[18] An OECD-sponsored study in 1996 found that Russian businessmen could expect weekly or even daily visits by extorting government inspectors; in Warsaw, such visits also occurred, but were considerably rarer.[19] In that same February 1996 survey of 887 Russian managers, 57 percent of them regarded "extortion based on threats of violence" to be a common occurrence. Of them, 50 percent experienced "similar extortion from government officials." With so much red tape it is inevitable that most businessmen will not be able to comply with the laws. It was no surprise therefore when a report prepared by the Auditing Chamber (the Russian equivalent of the General Accounting Office) of the Russian Duma found that as many as 90 percent of the Russian businesses that were privatized were found to be in violation of the law.[20] In an oft-cited statement, Boris Berezovsky boasted that because of the helter-skelter nature of the Russian legal code, everyone in business in Russia must of necessity violate the law. In a survey of business managers, 81 percent agreed, saying that it was impossible to operate a business without violating the laws. Only 15 percent said they could operate legally.[21] Remember our earlier example, where the police authorities require that all jewelry stores install bars on their windows but the fire authorities have decreed that for fire safety, windows must not be barred.[22] There is no honest solution.

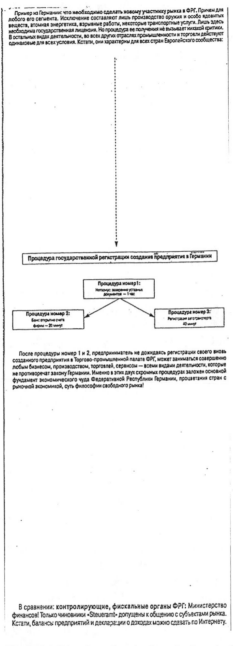

Figure 11.1 Procedures for opening a business in Germany

Source: Grigory Yavlinsky.

Бюрократическая хозяйственная паутина России, куда обязан попасть любой инвестор, желающий начать здесь свой бизнес. Она держит предпринимателя в своем дьявольском плену. **1346 — одна тысяча триста сорок шесть мучительных дней**, — именно такое время необходимо предприятию потратить, чтобы официально получить все разрешительные документы, позволяющие начать бизнес в России. Впрочем, есть и альтернатива — взятка! Она, как волшебная палочка, поможет сократить этот дьявольский срок вдвое, втрое, вчетверо! Но не все пользуются этим приемом — другие, а их большинство, сохраняют свои финансовые ресурсы в оффшорах и ждут изменения инвестиционного климата в стране.

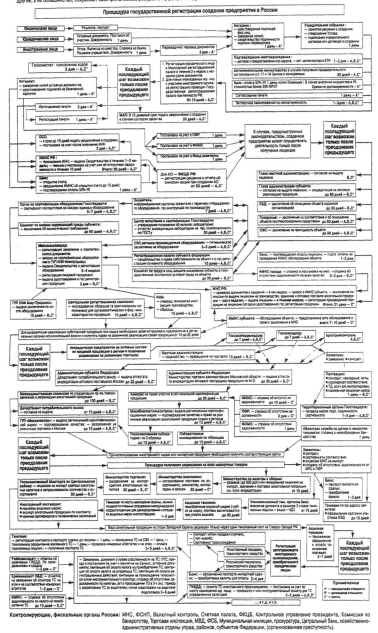

Figure 11.2 Procedures for opening a business in Russia

Source: Grigory Yavlinsky.

II

What will it take to make Russian investment-friendly not only for Russian businessmen big and small but also for foreign investors? Given Putin's KGB background, some expected that immediately he would crack down on crime and institute the rule of law or, as he stated ominously, institute "a dictatorship of the law." He has done just that in curbing the powers of the governors of the various oblasts and in attacking those seeking independence in Chechnia or those criticizing his policies in the media. He has also resumed KGB (FSB) wire-tapping and restraining contact between the Russian Academy of Science and foreign scholars. The Russian public loves it. In 2002, Putin had an 80 percent approval rating, up 72 percent from the year before.[23]

What he has not done is move to crack down on the Mafia. With his experience in the KGB, that should have been one of his first targets. Nor has he moved effectively against the oligarchs. He took a few tentative steps to limit some of the most egregious instances of business theft, such as removing Rem Vyakhirev as Chairman of Gazprom's Board of Management and Viktor Gerashchenko as Chairman of the RCB. But otherwise, except for his moves against Vladimir Gusinsky and Boris Berezovsky, he has rarely moved against the other oligarchs or done much to create an atmosphere of integrity in the business community.

Publicly he has announced, as we saw in Chapter 7, that the oligarchs would no longer be able to expect special treatment (that is, loans for shares) from the government. Because this was to mark a departure from past practice, his words warrant repeating. "It is asked, what then should be the relationship with the so-called oligarchs? The same as with anyone else. The same as with the owner of a small bakery or a shoe repair shop."[24] He went on, "As far as the economy is concerned, this implies a tough policy aiming to ensure equal competitive opportunities for everyone … as well as the lack of exclusive privileges and special regimes for specific businessmen."[25] But his attacks on Vladimir Gusinsky and Boris Berezovsky were more out of anger at criticism of him by their media outlets than the beginning of an effort to rein in the oligarchs. As long as an oligarch keeps a low political profile, he is allowed to function. More to the point, in addition to the oligarchs from the Yeltsin era who painlessly switched fealty from Yeltsin to Putin, Putin now includes in his circle his own favorite oligarchs, some of whom he had worked with in St. Petersburg and some whom have actually made it on their own and are engaged in entrepreneurial activities or manufacturing.

But as with Yeltsin, accusations of ethical misconduct or monopolistic behavior do not appear to be cause for disqualification. For example, in 2001 the new oligarchs Oleg Deripaska and Roman Abramovich were allowed to create a monopolistic aluminum conglomerate. Similarly, two old Putin buddies from St. Petersburg, Leonid Reiman and Valery Yashin, were allowed to join their company Telecominvest with Telia, a Swedish company. Few seemed to be disturbed by the fact that Reiman became the Minister of Communication, or that another of their subsidiaries was granted a GSM phone frequency license for Moscow, again without the nicety of a tender.[26] The Russian government then gave them phone licenses that covered two-thirds of Russia.[27] In addition, without having to bid or offer a tender, another Telecominvest subsidiary was awarded a phone license for a large region along the Volga River. Finally, licenses earlier awarded to other competitors after a competitive tender were revoked and given to Telecominvest instead.[28] On the surface, natives from St. Petersburg such as Reiman and Yashin who knew Putin certainly seemed to have had an unfair advantage. (Reflecting Putin's promotion of so many friends from the KGB and St. Petersburg, the Russians tell the following joke: A man about to board a train in Moscow suddenly is approached by another man who promptly steps on his foot and keeps it there. After about five minutes, the first man asks the second man, "Tell me, are you from the KGB?" "No," comes the answer. "Are you from St. Petersburg?" "No." "Well, then why are you standing on my foot?")

Having rid himself of Gusinsky and Berezovsky in June 2001, Putin asserted that he had eliminated the oligarchs as a class. "The oligarchs represent the big firms who have been abusing their position in society to influence political decision-making .... I do not think they exist anymore."[29] Despite his assertion, according to a calculation by the newspaper *Vedomosti*, as of late 2000, five industrialists close to Putin controlled 95 percent of Russia's production of aluminum, 18 percent of its oil, 40 percent of its copper, 20 percent of its steel and 20 percent of its automobile production. Similarly, economists at Troika Dialog Bank have asserted that seventy large financial and industrial groups controlled 40 percent of the country's GDP.[30] This was not quite the 50 percent of the Russian economy that Berezovsky in 1996 boasted his seven oligarchs controlled, but Boris Nemtsov estimates that indeed the existing oligarchs today do control about 50 percent of the GNP.[31]

Putin also did not terminate the government's special relationships with the oligarchs. For example, in February 2001 he casually suggested to members of the Russian Union of Industrialists and Entrepreneurs (RUIE), the very oligarchs he supposedly had already "eliminated as a class," that they just might want to contribute to a fund created by Putin to help families of military personnel killed in military conflicts, especially the war in Chechnia.[32] In ten days Putin had collected $52.7 million from "voluntary" contributions. True, he did not invite those who made a financial contribution to spend a night in the Lenin Bedroom in the Kremlin. However there is no reason to believe that contributors to Putin's fund will be treated no better than the "owners of a small bakery or shoe repair shop," if for no other reason than Putin has never scheduled regular meetings with bakers or shoe repairmen the way he does with members of the RUIE.

Though they were more stewards of state property than oligarchs and owners of their companies, Putin also moved quickly to make his St. Petersburg friends the CEOs of the most important state-controlled business entities. In addition to Alexei Miller at Gazprom, Putin appointed Nikolai Tokarev as general director of Zarubezhneft, the Russian oil company operating in Vietnam and Iraq. He also appointed Andrei Belianinov as director of Rosoboroneksport, the Russian military weapons sales agency, another very lucrative business.

His pious promises to the contrary, Putin behaved as if dealing with the oligarchs and other reprehensible types was not much different than it had been during the Yeltsin era. While Putin did remove Pavel Borodin from his post as Chief of Staff of the President's Office, he offset that by making him the Chairman of the Belarus–Russian Union. Given that it was Borodin who brought Putin to Moscow from St. Petersburg, some may feel that his removal as Chief of Staff was enough of a humiliation. But if Putin wanted to signal that he would crack down on kickbacks and corruption, the least he could have done was to agree to the reopening of the case against Borodin under which the Swiss authorities indicted him for theft. As we saw, the Swiss authorities reportedly wanted to pursue charges that Borodin had skimmed $25.6 million from a $492 million and a $335 million contract to refurbish the Kremlin Palace of Congresses, the Kremlin Residence, the White House, Yeltsin's yacht and airplane and the Belgrade Hotel, among other projects.[33] These contracts were issued by Borodin to two Swiss companies, Mercata Trading and Mabetex. The Swiss also wanted to investigate rumors that one of Yeltsin's daughters, and in some versions even Yeltsin himself had benefited from some of these payments.

Reflecting the climate of corruption in the Yeltsin years, such rumors spawned the following story. Ivan drove his car into the Kremlin and parked it. A militia man quickly ran up to him and shouted, "You can't park there, that's right below Yeltsin's office." "Don't worry," Ivan replied. "I locked the car."

Explaining that there did not seem to be enough solid evidence to pursue the Borodin case within Russia, Vladimir Ustinov, the Prosecutor General under Putin, decided that unlike their Swiss counterparts, Russian authorities no longer had any reason to investigate such charges.[34] NTV, however, then still under Gusinsky's control, launched an attack on Ustinov, asserting that his benefit of the doubt for Borodin was more a matter of appreciation for the illegal gift of a $500,000 apartment from the Kremlin property holdings administered by Borodin than a result of judicial review.[35] (Some cynics argue that NTV's criticism of these relationships was why Ustinov pursued Gusinsky so relentlessly.)

Putin seemed relatively restrained when Borodin was arrested at Kennedy Airport in New York City in January 2001 on his way to a Presidential Inauguration party organized by one of George W. Bush's financial contributors. But when the Russian Ministry of Foreign Affairs posted a $3 million bond in bail to the Swiss government which had asked the United States to extradite Borodin to them for interrogation, this was read as a clear sign that Putin was standing by his man no matter how much it undercut his well-publicized commitment to the dictatorship of the law. Success or failure in Russia under Putin still seems to be more a case of whim of man, in this instance Vladimir Putin's, than rule of law.

III

While falling far short of his initial commitment to institute new codes of behavior in the Russian business community, Putin has nonetheless made some small, yet meaningful reforms. Among other measures, he worked to simplify Russia's tax structure. By working with the Duma to institute a flat 13 percent tax, he restored some credibility to the legislative process. This represented an increase from the previous minimum 12 percent rate established by Yeltsin, so the poor do not regard this as a positive step because for them, taxes have increased. But now, in what economists would call a supply-side response, more of the rich who paid no taxes at all when the rate was 30 percent are now paying the 13 percent rate. There is less to be gained by cheating. For the same reason, in 2001 Putin also promoted a drop in the business tax from 35 percent to 24 percent. Boris Yeltsin had tried several times without success to do the same thing. Russia under Putin now has some of the lowest tax rates in the world. Yet making it easier for Russian businessmen is not simply a matter of cutting taxes. According to a report in *Transitions*, a World Bank periodical, businessmen had to prepare twelve different tax forms in 2000, sixteen forms in 2001, and in 2002, the year of tax reduction, twenty-four forms.[36]

Putin also moved to introduce land reform that would make it possible for Russians to buy and sell land. After considerable efforts by Putin, the Duma agreed to allow the sale of land in the cities, about 2 percent of all land, and in 2002 it also consented to the sale of agricultural land. The

Communist Party in particular stubbornly opposed such sales. Its members worried that land would be bought for speculative purposes by foreigners or urban Russians. For that reason the Duma banned the sale of farmland to foreigners. They fear that the land will be taken from the peasants just as the factories were taken from the workers. This is not an idle concern. Several oligarchs including Potanin have already put together massive holdings of leased land that they expect to purchase.[37] The peasants fear either that the land they will end up with will be too small to farm efficiently or that they will be forced to lease or sell what they have. Such feelings about peasant landholdings and opposition to land speculation are deeply rooted in the relationship between Russian peasants and the land that dates back to the czarist era.

These fears persist despite the fact that the purchase and sale of land would be an important step toward making it possible for peasants to obtain mortgages and thus the investment funds needed to reinvigorate agriculture. Whatever the fears in the countryside, instituting clear land titles in the cities should help to expand the construction of housing, office buildings and factories.

Putin has also attempted to institute more realistic charges for the costs of providing and maintaining housing. He understands that the poor state of the Russian housing stock has in large part been a consequence of shortchanging the funds needed for repairs and maintenance. With varying degrees of enthusiasm, he has also undertaken to modernize the country's labor and corporate governance laws, reform the pension system, institute commercial as well as central bank restructuring, strengthen the judicial system, and reduce the amount of barter trade.

From an economist's point of view, two of Putin's initiatives are particularly important: his attempt to increase commercial bank lending to small business and his effort to reduce the number of government regulations needed to open and operate private business. According to a study prepared for the Russian State Council, 75 percent of the capital invested in small business comes from private individuals. This limits access to credit and capital and makes it very difficult to open a new small business. This contrasts with the United States where 75 percent of businesses rely instead on outside commercial credit.[38]

His effort to reduce the number of government regulations needed to open and operate private business is equally important. With Putin's encouragement, in 2001 German Gref, his Minister of Economics, began a campaign to pare down the number of businesses that require licenses. He also tried to shrink the Russian civil bureaucracy which by 2000, had come to exceed the level reached for the whole Soviet Union during the planned economy era, when the USSR consisted of a population almost double the size of Russia.[39] Such a large bureaucracy is not only a burden on the budget; it all but guarantees the promulgation of continuous red tape. The bureaucracy inevitably will lobby for more inspectors and regulations to justify its existence. If efforts to shrink the bureaucracy and red tape while expanding the bank credit available to small business succeed, it would become easier to start up new businesses and in the process expand the size of the middle class.

Admirable as it is, in his effort to shrink the bureaucracy Putin must realize all bureaucrats, particularly Russians, know how to protect themselves. In what initially seemed to be a victory, Putin managed to persuade the Duma in 2001 to reduce the number of businesses that require licenses from 2,000 to 104.[40] It is humbling to note, however, that a similar effort was made in 1995 when the number of businesses requiring licenses also just happened to be 2,000. Under President Yeltsin, the order was issued to cut the number of licenses to 500.[41] But as we just saw, within five years the number bounced back up again to 2,000. Will the Russian bureaucrats under Putin (especially since they grew from 800,000 for the whole Soviet Union in 1982 to almost 1.2 million in 2001 in Russia alone) be any more willing this time to accept a shrinking of their influence?[42]

Based on some preliminary surveys, it does not appear as if the bureaucrats will go quietly. A July 2002 World Bank study of 2,000 small businesses reported that these "firms see little improvement to date."[43] To the contrary, the study concluded that "the situation is getting worse on some administrative barriers." If they ultimately fail in this effort, Putin and Gref would certainly not be the first to discover how enduring the Russian bureaucracy has been. As Gorbachev was said to put it, "My initiatives quickly became lost in the Byzantine channels of Soviet bureaucracy where they gradually suffocated as if in layers of cotton wool."[44]

Those efforts to facilitate business startups are a prerequisite for developing a broad-based coalition dedicated to fighting government abuse and oligarchic control. There will only be an effective check on wanton oligarch and government abuse when there is a critical mass of property owners, businessmen, and an independent middle class determined to protect themselves and their property from arbitrary seizure or extortion by the state, monopolistic oligarchs and criminal groups. Laws alone, without public pressure to enforce them, will seldom be effective.

IV

While there are many cases where government bureaucrats and policies have frustrated such efforts, there are also instances where local leaders have sought to facilitate and even stimulate independent economic growth. The governor of Veliki Novgorod is a good example. Governor Mikhail

Prusak has made a special effort to encourage foreign businesses to open factories in his oblast. He does so by assigning a senior aide to assist and shepherd investment projects through the bureaucracy and by promising to punish bureaucrats who obstruct or extort. Governor Konstantin Titov in Samara has tried much the same thing.

Prusak's story is told very well by Blair Ruble, Nancy Popson, and Nikolai Petro.[45] Recognizing that the Soviet-era electronics industry in the region was not competitive with foreign and especially Asian manufacturers, Governor Prusak and his staff curbed the existing subsidies the region had been providing and instead began to solicit foreign investment. In addition, they embarked on a program of improving the region's infrastructure, especially the telephone system and hotels. They also eliminated much of the region's red tape and bureaucracy while moving convincingly against corruption.[46] Finally they offered to provide tax holidays on regional and local taxes until investors earned a profit. Such incentives were made available not only to foreign investors but to small and medium-sized Russian businesses as well. The measure of Governor Prusak's success is indicated by the fact that by 2000, one-quarter of the region's working-age population was employed in small business, a figure more than double the national average.[47]

The results were impressive. Ruble and Popson report that while in 1992 Novgorod was ranked sixty-third out of Russia's eighty-nine oblasts for its investment potential, by 1997 it had risen to sixth place and ranked second in terms of per capita investment rates.[48] The region has attracted companies from Denmark, Great Britain, Germany, Austria, Finland, and the United States, and foreign investment has been directed to the food, chemical, forest and timber industries. As of 2000, foreign direct investment amounted to $800 million. The U.S. government has also included Novgorod in its regional investment initiative designed to stimulate domestic business development.[49]

In a similar way the EBRD set aside $540 million from 1995 to 2001, which it loaned to some 35,000 small businesses.[50] Some of the loans were as small as $30 but most averaged $5,000 to $10,000. Until the August 17, 1998 crash, the rate of repayment was almost 99 percent, and even after the crash it fell only to 97 percent. The goal of the EBRD is to facilitate the growth of small business. The U.S. aid program has the same goal but limits itself to only a few oblasts. It selects those where the governors offer to do the most to promote a business-friendly climate by eliminating the obstacles to opening up a new business or approving a foreign investment. German Gref, Putin's Minister of Economics, and a few of the more forward-thinking governors have even tried to establish one-stop approval centers to simplify and expedite the process.[51]

Unfortunately not all the bureaucratic mismanagement originates on the Russian side. The Defense Enterprise Fund (DEF), for example, which was funded by the U.S. government to facilitate the conversion of Soviet-era producers of military equipment into producers of peacetime machinery and consumer goods is a case study in what can go wrong. Funded with an initial grant of $66.7 million, the administration of the DEF diverted $35.6 million, more than half of its allocation, to itself for administrative expenses.[52] More than that, many of its investments failed, so by 2001 its portfolio value and available cash had shrunk to one-quarter of its original size and amounted to only $15 million.

As the DEF scandal illustrates, not everything must or should be a government initiative. In an effort to encourage good business practices, Citibank together with *The Wall Street Journal* awarded prizes in 1998 to those corporations in Eastern Europe and the former USSR that were judged to be particularly innovative, productive, well-managed and socially responsible. Similarly, the Troika Dialog Bank, a privately owned Moscow investment bank that opened in 1991, has established an investment guide that rates Russian companies according to their transparency, accounting practices, investor relations and financial discipline. Even more surprising, its evaluations seem reasonably fair and candid. Gazprom, for example, in one of the Troika Dialog evaluations was rated low in its degree of transparency and accounting, and only adequate in its investor relations and financial discipline.[53] Standard and Poors, the credit rating agency, has also begun to rank Russian companies on a ten-point scale that covers many of the same criteria.[54] However Standard and Poors' reports are prepared and paid for by the individual companies which can then decide whether or not to release their findings.

In an attempt to generate outside pressure, the World Economic Forum in Geneva and Davos, Switzerland has created what it calls the Corporate Governance Initiative. It sets out eight criteria for judging the five dozen or so companies listed on the Russian stock market (RTS).[55] The criteria range from disclosure of the ownership structure to emphasis on long-term financial returns. The companies are then rated according to risk–high, moderate, or low. In its first attempt in July 2001, the World Economic Forum listed fourteen Russian companies as low risk and eight such as Gazprom and Avtovaz as high risk. The investment bank Brunswick UBS Warburg conducts similar studies and has come up with similar findings.[56]

Recently similar efforts were initiated by some Russian officials and businessmen themselves within Russia. In October 1999 for example, Dmitri Vasiliev became the head of the Institute for Corporate Governance and Corporate Law. This is an organization dedicated to protecting minority stockholder interests and instituting Western models of corporate governance. Together with the EBRD, in 2001 it drew up a model corporate governance and business conduct code intended for adoption by Russian business.[57] It publishes a list periodically that ranks Russian companies based on their corporate behavior.[58] Vasiliev had been the first Director of the Russian Federal Securities Commission, the counterpart of the U.S. Securities Exchange Commission. He successfully challenged some corporate misbehavior but when faced with the Yeltsin government's reluctance to support his efforts, he decided to resign. He had been particularly concerned about the willingness of the government to allow YUKOS Oil to dilute if not erase the equity of minority investors, including that of Kenneth Dart. He was also angered when it looked for a time like Boris Yeltsin would do nothing to prevent the renationalization of the Lomonosov Porcelain factory in St. Petersburg.[59] In his private capacity, Vasiliev has continued his efforts to create a public body to oppose investor abuse while working with the International Finance Corporation of the World Bank. He has also lobbied to convince the Duma to pass reform legislation.

In a similar way, another group of businessmen formed a self-uplift organization which they call Club 2015. Unlike the RUIE, which basically lobbies to grab more for itself from the state, Club 2015 tries to indoctrinate members with the notion that, in the long run, the best way to maximize profits is to create a healthy business environment, or in their words, a "Productive Society."[60] They have set out a year-by-year strategy for achieving their aims. Such private initiatives are especially important in Russia because all too often the state regulating authorities that supervise businesses, such as the Russian Securities Exchange Commission, particularly after Vasiliev's departure, have proven to be only partially effective at best and sometimes are alleged to have violated their own regulations.[61]

V

Despite such hazards, there are instances of both Russian entrepreneurial and foreign investment success. Anatoly Karachinsky's IBS Group is one that is frequently cited. This is not only because he created something out of nothing (rather than take over an existing state enterprise as did almost all of the oligarchs), but because IBS is an information technology conglomerate, not a repeat of an old and traditional Soviet heavy industry. Founded in 1987, but unable to operate as a private business until 1992, IBS has become the leader of Russia's computer industry. It has designed software systems for the RCB as well as Sberbank, Gazprom, YUKOS and LUKoil. Other customers include Boeing and IBM. It has also become the sole supplier for Dell PCs in Russia.[62] Leader it may be, but reflecting how constrained startup businesses in Russia are, IBS sales in 1999 were only $180 million and as of late 2001 it employed only 1,500 people.[63]

Wimm-Bill-Dann is another success story of a sort and for that matter a much larger enterprise, although its products–juices, milk and processed foods–are hardly high technology. Its name, which is intentionally designed to sound Western (Wimbledon), was selected to take advantage of the Russian consumer's pent-up demand for Western goods. The firm opened in 1995. Wimm-Bill-Dann started small by producing soft drinks at a leased bottling and packaging facility in Moscow. Next it began to produce fruit juices packaged as J-7. Those familiar with the sad collection of carbonated drinks available until then will agree that J-7 answered a need. It soon outsold foreign juices and became the leading brand in Russia with a substantial market share. Its product line now ranges from milk products to beer, and it has operating plants spread throughout the country. Its sales exceeded $200 million in 1999 and rose to $480 million in 2001.[64]

Reflecting how difficult it is to sift the good from the bad, the story of Wimm-Bill-Dann may not be as positive as it first seems. Having written the preceding paragraph in an early draft, I discovered that some of those associated with the company have serious criminal records. While seeking authorization to list its $150 million to $230 million American Depository Shares on the New York Stock Exchange, lawyers for Wimm-Bill-Dann acknowledged that its largest stockholder, with 26 percent of the company's shares, was Gavril Yushvaev.[65] Yushvaev, it turns out, had been convicted of a violent crime in 1980. He also dominates the ownership group that has the power to appoint the company's managers and most of the board of directors. At the same time, some of the other directors of the company have links to Trinity, an automobile sales company that has allegedly been connected to several organized crime turf battles.[66] In Russia, even the innocuous (a company producing milk and juice) can turn out to be incriminating if not intimidating.

VI

Some foreign firms have also been successful. One of the best known is McDonald's, which was also one of the first success stories. It is quite a story, and is very much tied up with the persistence of one man, George Cohon. Born in Chicago, Cohon moved to Canada in 1967 to manage McDonald's' operations in the eastern part of the country. By 1976, when Montreal was host to the Olympics, he had come to manage the whole Canadian operation.[67] As a consequence, when the Russians sent a delegation to Canada during the games to seek advice about how to prepare for their own event scheduled for 1980, the Canadian Department of

External Affairs asked Cohon for advice and for the use of McDonald's' custom coach to move the Russian delegation about town. This provided an opening for Cohon to meet the Soviet officials and take them to a McDonald's restaurant. From then on, Cohon's goal was to open a McDonald's restaurant in Moscow.

Beginning in 1976, Cohon sought first to win permission to open a McDonald's restaurant in order to serve visitors to the Moscow Olympics. After months of frustration he failed. The communist leadership at the time was simply unprepared and unwilling to allow foreign owners to operate restaurants, or for that matter any business or industry. But it was just as well because after the Soviet invasion of Afghanistan in December 1979, the United States called for a boycott of the Games. Despite his frustration and the loss of both the time and the millions of dollars spent trying to win approval, Cohon resolved to keep trying.[68] Like other Western businessmen at the time, Cohon assumed that if he was persistent enough, sooner or later Soviet authorities would change their minds and allow McDonald's to open. Few understood that it was ideology and not the right sales pitch that was the obstacle; in the communist USSR at the time, only the state could own the means of production and distribution. Foreign businesses and joint ventures were not allowed. To do otherwise would have been Marxist heresy.

It was only when the recently appointed General Secretary of the Communist Party, Mikhail Gorbachev, decided that it was time to reevaluate the role of ideology and move to more pragmatic ways of operating the economy that a joint venture with a capitalist partner could even be considered as a possibility. At that point, Cohon's persistence and gregariousness began to pay off. Cohon had befriended Alexander Yakovlev, who at the time was Soviet Ambassador to Canada. Yakovlev, who was one of the first Soviet exchange scholars to be sent to study in the United States, was well acquainted with Western business practices and the fast food business. He also recognized that food service in the USSR was a disgrace and that while McDonald's might open a door to capitalism, it would also be something that the Soviet people would enjoy while improving the quality of their lives. It could very well also serve to show Soviet restaurant managers the procedures they might follow to improve their operations, not the least of which might be to clean up their toilets.[69]

Sensible as such a step might have been however, until Gorbachev came to power Cohon and Yakovlev could only fantasize. Yakovlev was fully aware of the fact that he had fallen out of favor in Moscow and his assignment to Ottawa as Ambassador in the late 1970s was the Soviet version of exile, not prestige. His enemies in Moscow criticized him because he was thought to be too liberal and too supportive of capitalism.

So off to Canada Yakovlev was sent. But in his post he renewed his acquaintance with Gorbachev who went to Canada on a visit, and the two began a series of discussions about the Soviet Union of the future. In 1983, once he was in a position to do so, Gorbachev arranged for Yakovlev to return to Moscow, and in 1986 Yakovlev was promoted to membership in the Secretariat of the Central Committee of the Communist Party, the body second only in power to the Politburo. Cohon now had a friend at a very high court.

In 1987 the Soviet Union officially authorized the formation of joint ventures with foreign partners and a few months later in April 1988 McDonald's formed just such a venture. [70] McDonald's was allowed a 49 percent interest, the maximum at the time, and its partner Glavobshchepit, the food service operator for the city of Moscow, held the remainder. While this was a critical breakthrough for Cohon even then his negotiating partners in Moscow ordered their subordinates to sabotage the whole effort. "We do not want these restaurants in our city," Valerie Saikin, the chief negotiator, told his staff. [71]

Through it all, including a shortage of sand and gravel needed for construction, and inadequate supplies of electricity, Cohon persevered. By starting so early and refusing to be put off, he had a jump start on his competitors. By the time Wendy's, Pizza Hut and Burger King decided to try and find their way through the Russian bureaucratic maze, Cohon had already worked back from the dead ends and found the exit. This included the realization that McDonald's would have to build its own processing plant to prepare not only its meat patties but its milk, buns and pies. It had never had to do this elsewhere in the world because there were always well-established, high-quality contractors around that it could count on to purvey the supplies it needed. In Moscow at the time, no such suppliers were available, so it decided to build its own facility for $40 million in the nearby suburb of Solntsevo. [72] Also, by partnering with the City of Moscow, Cohon ended up with a very high *krisha* (roof), or protector. The effort was worth it. The restaurant was opened in great triumph on January 31, 1990. Over 30,000 people were served on that first day, a world record. [73] Clearly it was a conceptual as well as an entrepreneurial success.

Financially it left much to be desired, however. While the worldwide publicity generated for McDonald's at the time was worth millions of dollars, all the sales at the restaurant were in rubles, which in 1990 were not convertible into dollars. This was actually a point of pride for McDonald's since all the other foreign restaurants, along with the Russian restaurants that catered to foreigners, sold at least a portion of their food only for dollars. McDonald's assumed correctly that before long the ruble would be made convertible, at which time it could convert its ruble earnings into dollars. These dollars in turn would then offset the purchase of imported ingredients that McDonald's could not obtain within the Soviet Union. In the meantime, the Russian people would come to appreciate the fact that sales were not in hard currency but in their own rubles.

As McDonald's anticipated, by July 1, 1992 regular currency auctions were authorized and gradually by the end of 1992 the ruble had become convertible.[74] What they did not plan for, however, was that there would be a devastating twenty-six-fold inflation that same year. An inflation of this magnitude had the effect of wiping out the value of the ruble, particularly its value relative to the dollar. Since the ruble/dollar exchange rate in 1990 had been set arbitrarily by the government at approximately $1 = 0.77 rubles, this meant that 1,000 rubles converted at that time would have yielded McDonald's $1,333 (the black market rate of approximately 2–3 rubles to the dollar was not as favorable). By August 1992, however, the 1,000 rubles would have yielded McDonald's only $5.60.[75] Since it was the dollar and not the ruble that mattered to McDonald's, this meant that despite the record number of customers served, McDonald's ended up with a claim on far fewer dollars, which meant that it operated at a loss.

Undeterred, McDonald's kept expanding. Before long it did indeed become a profitable undertaking, not so much because the dollars it earned from selling its Big Macs increased enough to make its operation profitable, but because it began to profit from the real estate it came to control. Its partner, the Moscow municipality, authorized it to open a new McDonald's on Gazetny Pereulok opposite the Central Telegraph Office. More important, it agreed that McDonald's could build a new glass office tower above the restaurant. In a Moscow that was still desperately short of first-class office space, this landlord status brought in a windfall for the company. The Tokyo-level rents that it charged made it too expensive for McDonald's itself to become a tenant in its own building. Moreover, the tenants sent their rent checks to a McDonald's account outside of the country, thus avoiding the problem of having to deal with the RCB in order to convert the rubles into dollars.

Eventually inflation waned and the ruble/dollar exchange rate became somewhat more stable. McDonald's kept opening new outlets and after a time its food operation also became profitable. Building on its success, in 1996 McDonald's began to move outside of Moscow. At the same time it arranged with its Moscow City Hall partner to buy 31 percent of the city's shares so that McDonald's increased its equity to 80 percent. It avoided joint ownership outside of Moscow and is the sole owner of the other restaurants it operates.[76] However, like most foreign investors in Russia, McDonald's was hurt by the August 17, 1998 economic crisis and yet another currency devaluation. This resulted in a halt to their ambitious expansion policy though after a few months they resumed the pace. As of 2002, McDonald's had invested over $270 million dollars and had opened over eighty outlets in twenty-three Russian cities, with plans to open thirty new outlets by 2003 throughout the country.[77]

While overall McDonald's has been a remarkable success, it has not entirely avoided the problems that plague other foreign operators in Russia. For example, it still has to import 25 percent of its supplies, mostly for hard currency, which makes it dependent on a stable dollar/ruble exchange rate. It has also had some labor problems. A few workers at its processing plant in Solntsevo near the Moscow Ring Road have tried to form a union. They charged McDonald's with violating Russia's labor codes. That may have been the case, but given the working conditions in most Russian factories, I can testify that the work environment at the McComplex, as they call it, is far superior to what exists in the normal Russian factory. To top it off, McDonald's has always paid its wages on time. The workers may have legitimate grievances but given that life in the McDonald's processing plant seems far superior to life in comparable Russian food processing plants, there is a multitude of theories about why labor unions seem so active at McDonald's and not elsewhere in the country. Some see this as a form of blackmail– McDonald's will settle quickly to avoid unfavorable publicity. Others speculate that since Solntsevo is the center of one of the most active Mafia groups, the Mafia may also be involved. Others suspect that since labor organizations have had great difficulty organizing McDonald's employees in the United States, if they could establish a union in Moscow it might serve as a beachhead for doing the same in America. But despite such problems now and then, and the very difficult obstacles that they have faced in the past, McDonald's has become a very profitable operation.[78]

Some cynics warn that because of Russia's tax laws, accounting habits (how a business allocates costs, capital and depreciation) and bureaucratic harassment, there is no such thing as a business in Russia that by Western standards is truly and honestly profitable. Nonetheless, in addition to McDonald's, Gillette is one of the few companies that reports that it has been consistently profitable and, even more impressive, that it has been that way from the very beginning of its involvement in the Soviet Union. Early profits reflected sales of imported Gillette products that found their way into the USSR and later Russia via suppliers in India and other neighboring countries. By the late 1980s, retail sales reached a level where it began to make sense to consider producing within Russia itself, or "on the ground" as the Gillette people put it.[79] Gillette in fact felt it had no other choice. Russia was the only major country in which it had no presence. Gillette's first task was to find a partner and form a joint venture. Someone with influence and authority was more important than someone with high-quality manufacturing experience. By Gillette's standards, the quality of razor blade production at the time within Russia was below world standards. Quality and know-how was what Gillette would bring to the match; protective covering and expertise in how to deal with local mores would have to come from the Russian partner.

After a careful search, Gillette picked Leninetz, a key member of the military-industrial complex in Leningrad. While producing for the military was its main activity, as a sideline Leninetz also manufactured the Sputnik razor blade. Gillette decided that it was essential to start slow and profit from Leninetz's experience. Together they formed a joint venture called PPI. But since Gillette wanted management control, it agreed to invest $60 million for 65 percent of the equity.[80]

To bring quality up to their standards, the Gillette management understood that eventually they would have to open new production lines with their own equipment. After debating whether or not to reequip the existing Leninetz factory or start afresh with a new "green field" factory, Gillette decided to build anew. This was not an easy decision since Gillette was aware that building a plant in Russia would cost them double what it would cost elsewhere. The higher cost was partly due to the corruption, but also because Gillette would have to finance construction of the roads, water supplies and electricity it needed to operate the factory.[81] Even then, and despite some promises, Gillette was unable to buy the land under the factory and it could only lease the plant for forty-nine years.

Yet that decision to bear the added cost and build afresh turned out to be a key to Gillette's success, even if for unanticipated reasons. Gillette's partner Leninetz decided it would not be worthwhile for it to come up with the $25 million it would have had to contribute to maintain its equity in the factory. So Leninetz asked Gillette to buy out its shares and terminate the joint venture.

Thus was born the "Gillette miracle."[82] Instead of the usual case where the Russian partner demands that the Western partner sell out or quit the joint venture, it was the Russian partner Leninetz, and its director Anatoly Turchak who wanted out, and in an amicable way. Gillette agreed but asked Turchak to stay on as honorary chairman. This was a way of maintaining the impression that Gillette's *krisha* (roof) or protector was still part of the operation.

It was not all luck. Gillette has had considerable experience opening new markets in third world countries. There were of course differences, but if it

could start from scratch in China and India, Gillette reasoned it could probably succeed in Russia as well. As one example, Gillette realized that it
could take some of the fully depreciated machinery it had acquired when it
bought up Wilkinson's Sword Razor Blade Co. in Britain and use that
equipment at least for a few years in its new St. Petersburg factory. This
would not be top-of-the-line technology, but it would be superior to
anything available in Russia. Most important, since the machinery would
have otherwise sat in storage and was already fully depreciated, it was
almost a free good. Bringing it to St. Petersburg made Gillette's production
costs highly competitive. Gillette's low-cost base and its product line, which
retained the Sputnik brand, also allowed Gillette to switch production to its
cheaper brands. This was an important decision since the demand for top-
of-the-line products all but evaporated after August 17, 1998.

But perhaps the most challenging task that faced Gillette was how to
create a marketing and distribution network. Given that in 1991 and 1992
the economy was in a state of near collapse, there was not much to work
with. The state sector was gradually disintegrating and a market system
was only slowly beginning to take shape. In either case, there was no such
thing as an existing network of suppliers and wholesalers there to supply
the tens of thousands of retailers that Gillette relies on to sell its razors and
other products to the public. In the Soviet economy the distribution of
consumer goods was notoriously poor, and in any case Gossnab, the state
supply organization, and the local affiliates of the Ministry of Trade, were
all being disbanded. A new market era was being created from scratch
with virtually no existing distribution networks available for any consumer
product.

Just as McDonald's decided to finesse the absence of the food processors and suppliers it needed by building its own processing "McComplex"
in Solntsevo, so Gillette's managers decided to create their own network of
distributors and wholesalers. But how? Their approach was ingenious.
They sent four-to-five-man teams out to local flea markets throughout the
country in search of retail traders who might be selling Gillette products.[83]
When they found one, they asked the trader from whom he had purchased
his stock. By working up the "razor chain" they ferreted out wholesale
entrepreneurs who had already demonstrated considerable ingenuity.
These erstwhile entrepreneurs were then asked if they wanted to become
official distributors for Gillette on a larger scale, and where necessary they
were also offered limited financing to test their credit-worthiness. I
attended a sales conference for these distributors organized by Gillette in
June 2000 and it was clear that these Russian businessmen were not only
entrepreneurial, but also loyal to Gillette for recognizing their talent and
enriching their net worth.

VII

As successful as both McDonald's and Gillette have been, neither company has escaped a headache now and then. In addition to its labor problems, there was a time when McDonald's trucks were prevented from driving between its restaurants and the McComplex processing plant because the processing plant was on the other side of the outer Moscow Ring Road where special driving permits were needed. Moreover Mayor Yuri Luzhkov of Moscow used the city's partnership with McDonald's to learn how the fast food business is run. Eventually he opened his own network of fast food restaurants. Serving alcoholic beverages as well as food, his Bistros, as the restaurants are called, were designed to be more Russian in character. The main purpose however was to take business away from McDonald's, Moscow's part-ownership of McDonald's notwithstanding.[84] Even Gillette with its high *krisha* has not escaped entirely: one of its drivers was kidnapped.

But by Russian standards, McDonald's and Gillette's problems are trivial. Coca-Cola, for example, one of the most experienced players in the third world market, decided it did not need a Russian partner. With no one to protect it, Coca-Cola was exposed to all manner of pressures. In November 1993, the bottling plant was hit by what was thought to be a rocket-propelled grenade.[85] In St. Petersburg the local fire chief informed Coke officials that if they expected to keep their bottling plant in operation, Coke would have to finance construction of a new neighborhood fire station.[86] Even experienced businessmen can fumble in Russia. After the August 1998 financial crisis and the near-collapse of demand for expensive foreign consumer goods, the Coca-Cola bottler in Russia had to write off at least $100 million of its asset value. Coke also reported a loss of $36 million for its 1998 fiscal year.[87]

By some measures, Coca-Cola got off cheaply. The bank Morgan Stanley had losses of close to $110 million on its operations in Russia. Citibank and Chase Manhattan each lost $200 million and Bankers Trust had a write-off of $400 million.[88] In the most extreme case, Credit Suisse First Boston (CSFB) acknowledged in August 1998 that it had to write off $500 million.[89] Two months later however it reported that its exposure in Russia was closer to $2.8 billion, most of which was in default ($147 million in government and corporate bonds; $1 billion in loans to the government and some larger companies; $571 million in loans to other companies and $1.1 billion in foreign currency contracts to Russian banks, little of which was ever repaid).[90] Some of the other losses were later recovered, but based on conversations with a former CSFB executive, the eventual write-off exceeded $1 billion.

As upsetting as such write-offs were, at least Coca-Cola and the bankers were not physically pushed out of their offices, strong-armed or told they no longer would be able to operate their businesses in Russia. (One Coca-Cola executive reportedly fled Russia after he was physically threatened.) Appendix 11.1 includes several such instances where this happened not only to Russian companies but Western companies as well. The effort to set up a Subway Sandwich franchise in St. Petersburg is an early example. A joint venture between E–W Invest of the U.S. and Vadim Bordug led to the opening of a Subway Sandwich shop on St. Petersburg's main street Nevsky Prospekt in 1994.[91] An earlier due diligence search by former KGB agents failed to reveal that Bordug was a key member of the Tambov mafia.[92] A few months later in the spring of 1995, Bordug suddenly informed his partners they were no longer partners in the company he renamed Minutka. Faced with death threats, they decided to leave and appeal their case at an arbitration hearing in Stockholm, Sweden.[93] The arbitration hearing awarded them $1.2 million but Bordug refused to pay, saying he was only responsible to a Russian court. So the U.S. partners took their case to a local St. Petersburg court where the judgment of $1.2 million was sustained. Bordug again refused to pay so they went to the Russian Supreme Court where the decision was confirmed yet again. Bordug again refused to pay and he continued to operate Minutka without acknowledging any foreign partners. It was only in 2002, after a visit by President George W. Bush to St. Petersburg and complaints to President Putin, that Minutka was finally closed down.[94] It was of little consolation to the U.S. investors, but throughout the struggle at least the Russian courts recognized the Stockholm arbitration decision. In another case involving the Liral Company, the Russian Supreme Arbitration Court refused to recognize a decision of the London International Arbitration Tribunal.[95]

The Subway Sandwich shop theft occurred before Putin became president. Nonetheless despite pledges by Putin and members of the business community to adhere to high standards of corporate governance, the practice of pushing out legal owners either through legal chicanery or strong-arm methods continue on Putin's watch as well. For example, a Canadian company, Norex, joined with Chernogorneft in 1992 to form Yugraneft.[96] Norex took 60 percent of the stock and Chernogorneft the remainder. To show its support, the Canadian government provided several million dollars worth of guarantees for this project. But as we saw in Chapters 3 and 7, in 2000 Tyumen Oil seized control of Chernogorneft. Tyumen Oil then sent Chernogorneft officials to one of those notorious local courts and their accommodating judges to complain that the know-how provided by Norex was not worth the $5.8 million Norex had agreed to provide for Yugraneft. On that pretext the court took control of Yugraneft away from Norex and turned it over to a former Tyumen official who promptly began to sell Yugraneft output to Tyumen at one-third of the prevailing market price. The new CEO of Yugraneft denied that Tyumen Oil was behind all this. Despite protests by Prime Minister Jean Chrétien of Canada directly to President Putin about the shabby way one of his country's corporations had been treated, Norex was left with nothing to show for its investment.

President Putin also did nothing to help the Sawyer Research Product Company. In June 2001 armed guards prevented Sawyer officers from entering the 120-man workshop Sawyer had been running at the Gus-Khrustalny Quartz Glass Plant outside the city of Vladimir. When Sawyer began its operations there in 1997, the plant as a whole was effectively bankrupt.[97] After buying up a part of the plant, investing $7 million and installing new management, this division started to become profitable. At that point, even though the rest of the plant was still shuttered, some local officials began to warn about the foreigners' takeover of some of Russia's most valuable assets. Seizure of the company followed.

VIII

Despite numerous cases to the contrary, the examples of Wimm-Bill-Dann, Novgorod, McDonald's and Gillette suggest that Russians and foreigners can operate successfully and relatively legally in Russia. To do so however requires entrepreneurial spirit, resolute management, luck and a patron angel or supportive *krisha*. So far unfortunately there are still relatively few instances where the government's support comes as a matter of course, not in return for an implicit or explicit under-the-counter payoff. When they have a problem, businessmen, whether they be foreign or Russian, should not have to call upon Governor Prusak to solve their problems. Fighting corruption and extortion should be a routine matter for the police and investigative organs

Just how corrosive all this can be for an economic system is highlighted by what has happened to the two parts of what in the Soviet era was one city. Today the relative prosperity of the Estonian part of Narva stands in sharp contrast to the pronounced poverty of Ivangorod, its twin city across the river in what is now Russia. This poverty is a consequence of foreign and domestic aversion to investing in Russia. As an article in *The Economist* notes, despite wages that average one-tenth of those in Narva, capital refuses to move across the border to take advantage of the lower overt costs.[98] No matter how much cheaper the wages, they are not low enough to offset the cost of dealing with Russia's bureaucracy, taxes, corruption and crime.

As long as foreign investors perceive that their investments will be subjected to more than the usual risk, they will hesitate to invest in Russia. That explains why foreign direct investment in Russia in 2000 was less than $5 billion.[99] By contrast, the comparable figure for China was $48 billion. Even Poland and Hungary generally do better. Per capita such investment in Hungary was $1,166 but only $96 per capita in Russia.[98]

By mistreating foreign investors, the oligarchs also hurt themselves. Because of the reluctance of foreigners to invest in Russia, the value of most Russian companies as measured by the value of their stock is far below what it would be if these companies were located in the West. As an example, the total value of Gazprom's stock in late 2000 and early 2001 was about $4–7 billion.[101] But if a company with similar deposits of natural gas and petroleum were located in the West or the Middle East, the value of Gazprom stock would amount to almost $2 trillion. Rem Vyakhirev's poor stewardship of Gazprom eventually led President Putin to replace him with Alexei Miller, a former colleague of Putin's from St. Petersburg. Because of Miller's health problems as well as more and more revelations about how extensive the looting of Gazprom had become, investors continued to limit their purchases of Gazprom stock.

As Bernard S. Black of the Stanford Law School has shown, concern about inappropriate corporate governance in Russia adversely affects the market value of an all major Russian companies. He goes on to show that an improvement in governance behavior tends to lead to a significant increase in the capitalized value of an enterprise. As an indication of just how far reaching such a change can be, he finds that moving from the worst of fifty-one rated companies to the best will lead to a 600-fold increase in firm value.[102] (While Black's research deals with corporate governance in Russia, investor shock over fraud and theft in U.S. companies such as Enron and WorldCom produces much the same result.) Mikhail Khodorkovsky's effort to make YUKOS transparent and follow, or at least appear to follow, Western practice is motivated by an understanding of how much he stands to benefit from such a move.

Conceivably this could be the Coase Theorem at work, but unfortunately, given Russia's long-standing acceptance of corruption, bribes and strong-arm methods, it will be some time before the rule of law comes to prevail over whim, payoffs and patronage. For example, despite numerous assertions that the grab and cheat mentality of the Yeltsin era is a relic of the past, the state's sale of its 75 percent share of the oil company, Slavnet in December 2002, differed little from the Loans for Shares fiasco of the mid 1990s. With 14 companies (including one from China) seeking to become bidders, it did seem reasonable to expect that the bidding would push the final price to at least $3 billion, far beyond the $1.7 billion state required starting price. In the end, however, only three companies actually placed a bid, so Slavnet sold for only $1.86 billion. In an echo of the good old bad days, the two losing bidders turned out to be straws for the ultimate winning team of Sibneft and Tyumen Oil, both of whom already owned shares in Slavneft. Once again it turned out to be a setup.

Yet without the rule of law, honest judges, government officials and reasonable restraints on the way businesses are operated, investors will continue to look elsewhere. In other words, to attract investment, business executives and government officials as well as the Russian public in general must switch from a short-term to a long-term time horizon. As long as judges can be found who will declare healthy companies bankrupt or in violation of a contract as several have done for Tyumen Oil in its takeovers of Chernogorneft and Norex, or allow companies to strip assets as YUKOS did in its fight with Kenneth Dart, or as long as there are local government officials who can justify the seizure from foreign investors of legitimate investments as happened to Sawyer Research Product Company and almost happened at the Lomonosov Porcelain Plant, foreign investors and even Russians will hesitate to invest in anything that will require several years for a payoff. But that is just the kind of investment Russia must have if it is ever to free itself from overdependency on the extraction and export of its raw materials.

Of course Russia is not the first country that has had to deal with such plagues, and a fair-minded observer has to acknowledge that in many ways the climate and culture in Russia have improved over what existed a decade ago. Yet after so many years of disappointment, some supporters of reform have collectively come to appreciate that underlying change will not come from the mere adoption of nice-sounding laws. That helps, but to be effective, support–and even more, insistence on the enforcement–of such laws and codes must come from the public. The point must be reached where there are enough members of the public who feel that they will be better off if those laws are enforced than if they are ignored. That in turn means the public must have a stake in their enforcement or something to lose if they are not enforced.

It was only when the people of Sicily, for example, came to a similar conclusion that the government there was able to move more effectively against the Mafia. As long as the bulk of the population was poor and had nothing to win or lose from Mafia activities, there was little support for the police and the courts in their struggle. As the population began to accumulate wealth however, they came to realize that there had to be a limit to wanton violence. This realization and the assassination of a popular and honest judge triggered a shift in attitudes and the subsequent arrest of hundreds of Mafia members.

Why do automobile drivers sometimes experience a similar transformation? Drivers seldom support the installation of more stop-and-go traffic lights. However, as more and more vehicles begin to travel through an intersection, a growing number of drivers will eventually come to believe that they would be better off (that is, traffic would move faster and more safely) with a traffic light than without it. In the same way, when more and more Russians begin to establish their own businesses, there will be growing support for the adherence to rules and regulations and a halt to wanton and arbitrary actions by both government authorities and criminal groups.

The challenge then for those supporters of reform in Russia is to encourage the buildup of the middle-class business community as rapidly as possible. This means it is essential to make it easy to start up new businesses. To do this, the needless red tape and cumbersome bureaucracy standing in the way of would-be businesses must be eliminated. Once these obstacles are removed, supportive measures in the form of readily available lenders and easy credit must be accessible for those who need it. This suggests that to be effective, Russian government programs, as well as foreign aid programs from countries such as the United States, should expand their efforts to provide financing for startup firms both in business and farming. That is the best way to create a relatively independent middle class and a constituency that will demand the rule of law and its enforcement from the bottom up.

IX

Retrofitting a project is almost always more difficult than doing it right from the beginning. Trying to encourage new startups, reduce government bureaucracy and establish international standards of corporate governance has become much harder than it was a decade ago, and it was not so good then. Returning to Joe Berliner's analogy, the "horse" was in bad shape then and given the poor "jockeys" that have ridden it since, the horse is in even poorer shape now. The reluctance by Gaidar to implement a currency reform at the beginning of the reforms and the insistence by Chubais on privatizing industry immediately without restraints on factory directors were serious blunders. Nor should the IMF take much comfort in the way it insisted that Russia should focus on macroeconomic stability, including the curbing of inflation and the maintaining of high interest rates and a strong ruble. When it came, the Russian economic recovery in 1999 stemmed largely from the three-fold increase in world petroleum prices, which the IMF and Russian economic advisors had nothing to do with as well as the four-fold devaluation of the ruble, which the IMF, if anything, opposed. This drop from 6 rubles to the dollar to 24 rubles to the dollar was a consequence of the August 17 1998 financial collapse. The reformers, both Russian and foreign, also stand accused of not paying enough attention to the unique economic and business cultures that evolved during the czarist and communist eras and the resulting absence of market-enhancing institutions that existed when Yeltsin came to power. This gave rise to a formidable class of stakeholders in the form of oligarchs and government overlords who quickly came to regard the country's assets as their own. More often than not, such oligarchs and officials used the government's laws and decrees such as Loans for Shares and the bankruptcy procedures to accumulate financial and raw material empires. Thus today, unlike the situation in 1991, there are thousands who have a vested interest in the Russia that has evolved, and most of them have no reason to want it improved or reformed, particularly if by doing so they should stand to lose their special rent-collecting status.

It is impossible to rewind the tape so Russia can start over again, but if there is to be any change something must be done to force those who bene-fited unfairly from the breakup of the state to pay a fair price for what they have acquired. This applies particularly to the beneficiaries of the Loans for Shares auctions. Some of course have already suffered from unwise investment before the August 17, 1998 crash, but others should at least be required to pay their taxes and other payables such as wages and vendor bills. They should also be required to reimburse minority stockholders or bank depositors for the losses they have suffered. The public must also insist that the government sponsor tenders for all contracts above a certain level such as $100,000 and that the bids be made public.

As for other lessons learned from the flawed nature of past reforms, it is probably too late to adopt the Polish model with its NIFs and a new issue of vouchers to the public. But the Russian government still owns significant shares in many partially privatized or wholly government-owned enter-prises. For example, for 2002 it scheduled the sale of 150 wholly owned enterprises and shares in 300 businesses in which it is a partial owner. Overall it wholly owns 9,700 companies and has stock in 4,000 others.[103] There is thus no reason why the public could not be issued vouchers convertible into shares of those companies. The difference with the 1992 vouchers, however, is that an effort should be made to insure that in any future sale of shares of stock held by the government the directors of an enterprise do not become its *de facto* owners. As an experiment the Russian government should consider creating a state-run mutual fund which would take over ownership of the remaining shares. This mutual fund could be like the Polish NIFs or it could be subordinate to Russia's national pension system. In the latter case, shares of stock would be owned by such a state agency and profits would be passed through to the pension system, much the same as CALPERS (the California Public Employees Retirement System) which invests the funds for the retired employees of the State of California. Increasingly, CALPERS has come to monitor corporate management and pressure it to operate in the interests of the stockholders and public at large, rather than in the interests of corporate management itself. Presumably the Russian pension fund could do the same thing.

Reforms of this nature may turn out to be as flawed as those that have gone before it. For such reforms to be effective, the underlying culture must also be changed. How can we guarantee for example that the proposed Russian pension fund will make its decision on a business, not a political or self-enrichment, basis? This is perhaps the greatest challenge of all because many Russians insist that they want no such change–they like their culture as it is.

Granted it is presumptuous for an inhabitant of one culture to tell another that his culture is flawed. Moreover even if all agree that a change in culture is needed, instituting such changes will be very difficult. Building up a large middle class may be the best way to do it, but that will take more than an *ukaz* by President Putin. And while he must be given credit for some of his legislative initiatives such as tax reduction, land reform, bureaucratic reduction, and judicial and legal reform, as long as Putin is seen to be tolerating or favoring his own set of oligarchs at the expense of his critics, and where rule of in-laws remains more important than rule of law, there can be no true change.

Such skepticism may be too harsh but it reflects the cynicism of those Russians who see their situation as somewhat similar to the encounter God had with President George W. Bush, Prime Minister Tony Blair and President Vladimir Putin.

"Tell me, God," says President Bush, "will the American people ever come to believe that I won the 2000 election in Florida and will my National Missile Defense System ever prove to be technologically sound?"

"Yes, my son," says God. "It will take 25 years but you will not be around to see it."

Then Tony Blair asks, "God, will Great Britain ever come to rule the waves again, will England adopt the Euro and will my wife stop having children?"

"Yes," says God. "It will take 50 years but you won't be around to see it."

Finally its Vladimir Putin's turn. "Will Russia ever be able to control the Mafia and state corruption, will the oligarchs adopt international standards of accounting and transparency and will foreign investors ever come to trust their Russian partners?"

God thinks and thinks. Finally he says, "Yes, President Putin, but I won't be around to see it!"

Change may come sooner than that, but not without enormous determination and support.

Appendix 11.1

MANAGEMENT AND STOCKHOLDER DISPUTES

I Gas sector

Gazprom

Transfers assets to ITERA and a host of some of the other 300 companies owned by friends and relatives of Gazprom management, including *Stroytransgaz* (Chernomyrdin's sons, Vyakhirev's daughter), *Wingas* (Vyakhirev's son), and *Sibneftegaz* (Vyakhirev's brother).

II Petroleum

Tyumen Oil

Chernogorneft

Declared bankrupt and bought out from under Sidanko and its partners BP/Amoco.

Kondpetroleum

Declared bankrupt in 1998 and bought by Tyumen Oil subsidiary. Court ruled against Kenneth Dart.

State sale of 51 percent of Tyumen Oil / 10 percent of LUKoil

Only to existing holders.

Onako

Pay $1 bill for a company with one-quarter of the reserves of a Chevron, which is worth $60 billion (actual worth of Onako should be $15 billion).

YUKOS Oil, Avisma Titanium Plant, and Sibneft

Dilute shares of subsidiaries owned by Kenneth Dart and others. These include *Noyabrskneftegaz, Yuganskneftegaz, Tomskneftegaz,* and *Samaraneftegaz*.

Surgutneftegaz

Take over Surgut Holding, its parent company.

With an issue of new stock, minority stockholders are diluted.

Severnaia Neft

Won bid for three fields in Komi for $7 million.

Won the bid over *LUKoil*, which bid $100 million, *Surgutneftegaz*, and *Sibneft*. Decided by *Governor Vladimir Butov*.

Surgut, LUKoil,1 Sibur2

Shares diluted.

Sibneft

Buys stock from Roman Abramovich for $542 million, then sells it back to him only to declare a $612 million dividend, which he can then use to pay for his stock.[3]

Ivanhoe Energy, Vancouver, Canada

Pushed out of Siberian oil venture.[4]

Bitech Petroleum, Toronto, Canada

Battle over legal title to develop oil field in Komi Region.[5]

III Banks

Hide assets after 1998 crash

From	To
Menatep	Menatep St. Petersburg
RCB	IMPEXS Bank
Oneximbank & Interros	Rosbank and Interros Prom
SBS/Agro Bank	Soiuz and First Mutual Society (Pervoie OVK)

Directors self-dealing

Sberbank: dilutes equity, sells new shares at 25 percent of book value

Misuse of foreign loans

IMF Loan to Central Bank of Russia: directed to Eurobank and FIMACO.
World Bank Loan: misappropriation of funds intended to restructure coal mines.[6]

IV Use or threat of violence

Subway Sandwich franchise, St. Petersburg

Minutka ousts U.S. partner.[7]

Norex Petroleum, Alberta, Canada

Its joint-venture subsidiary in Siberia, Yugraneft, seized by armed men with machine guns sent by Tyumen Oil.[8]

Sawyer Research Product Company

Ousted from its control of Quartz factory at Gus-Khrustalny, near Vladimir.[9]

Aluminum industry

Violence and murder of opponents.

Arkangelsk Diamond Corporation (ADC), Canada

Spent $30 million to develop in Arkhangelsk Region. Once diamonds were found its license was revoked and transferred to Arkhangelskgeoldobycha, associated with among others Alrosa and LUKoil.[10]

Bratsk Paper Mill

Effort by minority stockholders associated with Oleg Deripaska and Siberian Aluminum to seize control from a subsidiary of Ilim Pulp.[11]

Segezhabumprom Paper Mill

Plant seized from its owner Assi Doman.[12]

V Telecommunications

Vimpelcom and Mobile Telesystem

Told for a time that their frequencies had been assigned to *Sonic Duo*, which is owned by *Sonera of Finland* and *Telecominvest*, a subsidiary of *Sviazinvest*. Telecominvest was founded by *Leonid Reiman*, now Minister of Communication and *Valery Yashin*, CEO of Sviazinvest.
MSS Saratov (owned by Telecominvest) awarded a license for mobile phones previously held by *SMARTS* in Samara. Awarded to *Saratov* without a bid. Telecominvest and *Telia* (a subsidiary company) now have two-thirds of the country's mobile phone licenses.

VI Miscellaneous

UES

Proposes to sell off producing subsidiaries, many of which are unprofitable under present rate structure.

Norilsk Nickel

A share exchange challenged by the Federal Securities Commission.[13]

Far Eastern Shipping Company (FESCO)

Governor *Yevgeni Nazdratenko* forces *Andrew Fox*, a British investor, to turn over 7 percent of stock or face prison.

Lomonosov Porcelain Factory

Prevents U.S. owners from assuming control although U.S. owners eventually prevail.

GAZ

New purchasers issue 20 billion new shares, swamping 4.5 million previous shares.

Vyborg Pulp and Paper Mill

Twenty-one-month fight by workers to keep a British firm from assuming control.

Transneft

President forced out by police.

Kristal Vodka

Fight between two who claim ownership.

Kachkanar Vanadium Mining Complex

Fight over who is manager with Oleg Deripaska.[14]

Vyksa Pipe Manufacture

Dilute stock.

Dukat Silver Mine

Canadian group fighting for control with Russian groups.

Moskhimpharmpreparaty

Workers fight for retention of old manager.

Karabash Copper Smelting Plant

Armed struggle for control between Urals Mining and Metals, Co. and Kyshtym Electrolytic Copper Plant. Also use of tax police and bankruptcy court.[15]

Primorkhleboprodukt

Despite two court decisions in its favor, the Euro Asian Investment Holding Co. of Seattle has been unable to obtain access to its $12 million investment.[16]

Kuban Knauf

Local government administration in 1995 evicts Kuban Knauf from its joint venture in Krasnodar.[17]

Cargill

Despite the purchase of a controlling stake in a Krasnodar grain elevator, unable to operate.[18]

Pan American Silver, Vancouver, Canada

Invested $60 million in a Magadan silver mine but forced to write off investments after Polymetall challenged its license.[19]

Kinross Gold Corporation, Toronto, Canada

Spent $68 million on shares in gold mine but challenged in court.[20]

Pratt & Whitney

Russian court freezes Pratt & Whitney's 25 percent stake in Aviadvigatel after $10 billion lawsuit by an Aviadvigatel Board of Directors member.[21]

Notes

1 Russia's financial buccaneers: the wild and woolly East

1 *The Financial Times*, November 1, 1996, p. 5.
2 Lecture in Moscow, July 3, 1997.
3 Goskomstat Rossii, *Uroven' Zhizni Naseleniia* (Internet Securities, Macroeconomics), April 30, 1999.
4 *Komsomolskaia Pravda*, March 19, 1997.
5 Interview, February 17, 1999.
6 *The Moscow Times*, October 22, 1995, p. 27; *OMRI*, August 16, 1996, p. 3; *Russia Review*, September 23, 1996, p. 11.
7 *The Financial Times*, July 9, 1997, p. 3; *Russia Review*, August 25, 1997, p. 18.
8 *The Financial Times*, November 30, 1995, p. 2; *The Wall Street Journal*, January 23, 1997, p. A12.
9 *The Financial Times*, December 29, 1995, p. 2; *The Wall Street Journal*, January 23, 1997, p. A12.
10 *The Moscow Times*, January 23, 1997.
11 *The Washington Post*, October 17, 1997, p. A34; October 23, 1997, p. A1.
12 *Izvestiia*, July 1, 1997.
13 *The Washington Post*, October 17, 1997, p. A34.
14 *The Moscow Times*, November 27, 1999.
15 *The Washington Post*, October 17, 1997, p. A34.
16 *Komsomolskaia Pravda*, July 29, 1997, p. 1.
17 Interfax, July 30, 1997, interview.
18 The "plus one share" is necessary because 25 percent alone was not enough to guarantee the owner a voice in management.
19 *The Washington Post*, October 26, 1997, p. A1; *Obshchaia Gazeta*, July 31–August 6, 1997, no. 30, p. 1; *Current Digest of The Soviet Press*, September 3, 1992, p. 7.
20 *Obshchaia Gazeta*, July 31, 1997, no. 30, p. 1.
21 *Segodnia*, July 28, 1997.
22 *Komsomolskaia Pravda*, August 16, 1997, p. 1; *The Moscow Times*, September 17, 1997, p. 1; NTV, *Segodnia*, September 14, 1997.
23 *Izvestiia*, October 15, 1997.
24 *Moskovskii Komsomolets*, August 19, 1997.
25 *The Times of London*, August 13, 1997; Alexandr Korzhakov, *Boris El'tsin ot Rassveta do Zakata*, Moscow: Interbuk, 1997, p. 283; Chrystia Freeland, *Sale of the Century*, Toronto: Doubleday, 2000, p. 283.
26 *Forbes Magazine*, December 30, 1996, p. 90.

27 *The Financial Times*, August 2, 1997, p. 6.
28 *The Wall Street Journal*, April 30, 2001, p. A15; *The New York Times*, June 22, 2001, p. W1.
29 Joseph Berliner, "The Soviet Past and the Russian Transition," prepared for a conference on the Soviet economy, Zvenigorod, Russia, June 22, 2001.

2 Setting the stage: the Russian economy in the post-communist era

1 Freeland, p. 283; Paul Klebnikov, *Godfather of the Kremlin*, New York: Harcourt, 2000; Peter Reddaway and Dmitri Glenski, *The Tragedy of Russia's Reforms: Market Bolshevism against Democracy*, Washington: The U.S. Institute of Peace Press, 2001; David Hoffman, *The Oligarchs: Wealth and Power in New Russia*, New York: Public Affairs Press, 2002.
2 Berliner.
3 Yegor Gaidar, *Days of Defeat and Victory*, Seattle: University of Washington Press, 1999, pp. 112–13; Economic Commission for Europe, *Economic Survey of Europe in 1992–1993*, New York: United Nations, 1993, p. 122; IMF Staff Country Report, no. 95/107, Washington: International Monetary Fund, October 1995, p. 44.
4 This is not a perfect comparison because there were severe shortages in 1990. Thus, possessing rubles was not the same thing as being able to spend those rubles.
5 Rose Brady, *Kapitalizm: Russia's Struggle to Free Its Economy*, New Haven: Yale University Press, 1999, p. 19. For those who made such predictions see Anders Aslund, *How Russia Became a Market Economy*, Washington: Brookings, 1995; Richard Layard and John Parker, *The Coming Russian Boom*, New York: Free Press, 1996.
6 Martin Feldstein, *The Wall Street Journal*, September 8, 1997, p. A18.
7 *Russia Review*, September 22, 1997, p. 8; *The Financial Times*, September 3, 1997, p. 2.
8 *Izvestiia*, July 28, 1999; *Jamestown Foundation Monitor*, October 15, 1997, p. 1; *The Moscow Times*, September 2, 1997.
9 Simon Johnson, Daniel Kaufmann and Andrei Shleifer, "The Unofficial Economy in Transition," *Brookings Papers on Economic Activity*, Fall 1997, Brookings Institution, Washington, D.C.
10 Alexander Gerschenkron, *Economic Backwardness and Historical Perspective*, Cambridge: The Belknap Press of Harvard University Press, 1962, p. 235.
11 *The Moscow Times*, June 10, 1997; *The Financial Times*, March 25, 1997, p. 14; *Reuters*, April 4, 1997.
12 Johnson, Kaufmann and Shleifer, p. 24. See also Anders Aslund, "The Myth of Output Collapse After Communism," Working Papers, Carnegie Endowment, Post-Soviet Economics Project, no. 18, March 2001.
13 Goskomstat monthly report on *Internet Securities*; *The Moscow Times*, June 21, 2001, p. 7.
14 *Foreign Trade*, January–March 1997, p. 37.
15 Russia/CIS Division, U.S. Dept. of Commerce, May 19, 1997, email message; *The Moscow Times*, June 10, 1997.
16 Johnson, Kaufmann and Shleifer.
17 *The Wall Street Journal*, September 22, 1997, p. B18F.

18 Ibid., October 31, 1997, p. R3. In 1999, after the 1998 financial crash, Lexington Troika Dialog became the world's poorest performing fund.

19 *The Financial Times*, November 25, 1996, p. 10.

20 J.M. Keynes, "A Short View of Russia," *Essays in Pessimism; The Collected Writings of J.M. Keynes*, London, 1972, Part 1, X; Daniel Gros and Alfred Steinherr, *Winds of Change: Economic Transition in Central and Eastern Europe*, London: Longman, 1995, p. 404.

21 Interview, St. Petersburg, June 27, 1993.

22 *Izvestiia*, January 26, 1994, p. 1. Other estimates are usually closer to 40 percent; BBC, September 4, 1998.

23 *The New York Times*, July 29, 2000, p. A3.

24 Personal conversation.

25 *Ekonomika i Zhizn'*, no. 51, December 2000, p. 3; *Segodnia*, January 5, 2001; *The Financial Times*, February 25, 2000, p. 2; *David Johnson's Russia List*, February 12, 2000, no. 4103, item 5.

26 Mikhail Gorbachev, *Memoirs*, New York: Doubleday, 1995, p. 250; interview.

27 Interview with provincial authorities.

28 RFE/RL, *Newsline*, July 19, 1997, no. 75, Part 1.

29 Ibid., July 1997, no. 75, p. 1.

30 Maxim Boycko, Andrei Shleifer and Robert Vishny, *Privatizing Russia*, Cambridge: MIT Press, 1995, pp. xii, ix.

31 Ibid., pp. 10, 16 footnote 2.

32 *Newsweek*, special issue, December 1999, p. 58.

33 *The Economist*, September 18, 1999, p. 81.

34 Vladimir Mau, "Rossiiskie Ekonomicheskie Reformy Glazami Zapadnykh Kritikov," *Voprosy Ekonomiki*, November 1999, p. 5.

35 Speech to the Woodrow Wilson International Center for Scholars, New York City, June 10, 1997.

36 Ibid., p. 2.

37 Ibid., p. 5, emphasis added.

38 Reddaway and Glenski, pp. 35, 543; *Johnson's Russia List*, April 26, 2001, no. 5226, item 2.

39 *The New York Times*, February 22, 1994, p. D4.

40 I. Bunin (ed.), *Biznesmeny Rossii: 40 Istorii Uspekha*, Moscow: OKO, 1994, p. 42.

3 The legacy of the czarist era: untenable and unsavory roots

1 Boris Kagarlitsky, "Don't Blame the Laws," *The Moscow Times*, April 27, 2001.

2 *The New York Times*, May 4, 1997, p. 22.

3 *The Moscow Times*, September 9, 1999, p. 8; *The Russian Journal*, November 29, 1999.

4 Richard Pipes, *Property and Freedom*, New York: Alfred A. Knopf, 1999, p. 160.

5 Ibid., p. 161.

6 Thomas C. Owen, *The Corporation Under Russian Law 1800–1917: A Study in Tsarist Economic Policy*, Cambridge, England: Cambridge University Press, 1991, p. 203.

7 Ibid., p. 204.

8 Marc Raeff, *The Well-ordered Police State*, New Haven: Yale University Press, 1983, p. 250.

9 R.M. Guseinov, "Kapitalizma v Rossii ne Bylo Dazhe v Period 'Kapitalizma'," *Ekonomicheskaia Istoriia Rossii: Problemy, Poiski, Resheniia, Ezhegodnik*, vol. 1, Volgograd, 1999, p. 61.

10 Witt Bowden, Michael Karpovich and Abbot Paison Usher, *An Economic History of Europe Since 1750*, New York: American Book Company, 1937, p. 29.

11 Owen, p. 203; Bowden, Karpovich and Usher, p. 298.

12 Owen, p. 215.

13 Ibid.

14 Peter I. Lyashchenko, *History of the National Economy of Russia to the 1917 Revolution*, New York: The MacMillan Company, 1949, pp. 327–30.

15 Owen, p. 203; Bowden, Karpovich and Usher, p. 298.

16 Jeffrey D. Sachs and Katharina Pistor (eds.), *The Rule of Law and Economic Reform in Russia*, Boulder: Harper-Collins, Westview Press, 1997, p. 44.

17 Owen, p. 55.

18 Sachs and Pistor, p. 44.

19 Natalya Evdokimova Dinello, "Forms of Capital: The Case of Russian Borders," *International Sociology*, vol. 13, no. 3, September 1998, p. 296.

20 *The Financial Times*, August 24, 2000; Putin's annual address to the Duma, April 3, 2001; BBC Monitoring, April 3, 2001; *Nezavisimaia Gazeta*, December 26, 2000; *Johnson's Russia List*, July 12, 2000, no. 4398, item 2.

21 Dinello, p. 304

22 Jonathan A. Grant, *Big Business in Russia: The Putilov Company in Late Imperial Russia 1868–1917*, Pittsburgh: University of Pittsburgh Press, 1999.

23 Owen, p. 207.

24 Lyashchenko, p. 649.

25 Ibid.

26 Irina Arkhangelskaya, "While Russia Sleeps," *Delovie Lyudi*, February 1995, p. 56.

27 Owen, pp. 202–3.

28 Lyashchenko, pp. 490, 716.

29 Ibid., p. 708.

30 Ibid., p. 714.

31 Ibid., p. 716.

32 Owen, p. 213.

33 Ibid.

34 Ibid.

35 Ibid., p. 210.

36 Ibid., p. 198.

37 Ibid., p. 196.

38 Ibid., p. 203.

39 Ibid., p. 215.

40 *The Financial Times*, February 17, 2001, p. IX.

41 Ibid.

42 Lyashchenko, p. 704.

4 It's broke, so fix it: the Stalinist and Gorbachev legacies

1 *John Bartlett's Familiar Quotations*, Boston: Little Brown, 1980, 15th edition, p. 719.

2 Ragnar Nurkse, *Problems of Capital Formation in Underdeveloped Countries*, Oxford: Basil Blackwell, 1955.

3 Marshall I. Goldman, *USSR in Crisis: The Failure of an Economic System*, New York: W.W. Norton, 1983, pp. 34–5.
4 Berliner, p. 16.
5 *The Boston Globe*, February 23, 1999.
6 Joseph A. Schumpeter, *Capitalism, Socialism and Democracy*, New York: Harper & Brothers, 2nd edition, 1947, p. 81.
7 U.S. Department of Defense and The Central Intelligence Agency, *The Soviet Acquisition of Militarily Significant Western Technology: An Update*, Washington, D.C., September 1985; Anthony Sutton, *Western Technology and Soviet Economic Development 1917–1930*, Stanford: Hoover Institution Publications, 1968; Anthony Sutton, *Western Technology and Soviet Economic Development, 1930–1945*, Stanford: Hoover Institution Publications, 1971.
8 Ibid.
9 Since there have been many other studies that have focused on the economic policies of Mikhail Gorbachev and Boris Yeltsin, we will present only the highlights, considering whether those actions were appropriate for Russia and how those actions helped distort the privatization program. See Goldman, *Gorbachev's Challenge: Economic Reform in an Age of High Technology*, New York: W.W. Norton, 1987; Goldman, *Lost Opportunities: Why Economic Reforms in Russia Have Not Worked*, New York: W.W. Norton, 1994.
10 Visit in June 1997.
11 *Pravda*, December 10, 1990, p. 1; interview with Gorbachev, December 15, 1997.
12 See *Ural Business News*, May 16, 2000; *Internet Securities*; *Moscow Times*, February 24, 2000; *The Wall Street Journal*, April 14, 2000, p. A21; interview with Dr. Vitaly V. Shlykov of the Council on Foreign and Defense Policy, and formerly a senior official in military intelligence, Soviet Army, Harvard University, March 12, 2000.
13 Interview with Mikhail Gorbachev, December 15 and 16, 1997, Northeastern University.
14 *Ekonomika i Zhizn'*, February 1999, no. 7, p. 1.
15 *Pravda*, October 28, 1988, p. 4.
16 Goskomstat Rossii, *Rossiiskii Statisticheskii Ezhegodnik 1998*, Moscow: Goskomstat, 1998, pp. 413, 414.
17 Interview, January 26, 2000, Wellesley College.
18 Janine Wedel, *Collision and Collusion: The Strange Case of Western Aid to Eastern Europe, 1989–1998*, New York: St. Martin's Press, 1998, p. 47.
19 *The Boston Globe*, June 27, 2002, p. B1.
20 Wedel, "Tainted Transactions: An Exchange," *The National Interest*, Summer 2000, no. 60; Wedel, *The National Interest*, Fall 2000, no. 61, p. 117.
21 Interview, January 26 2000, Wellesley College; Gaidar, pp. 73–4.
22 Interview, ibid..
23 Stanley Fischer, Ratna Sahay and Carlos Avegh, "Stabilization and Growth in Transition Economies: the Early Experience," *The Journal of Economic Perspectives*, vol. 10, no. 2, Spring 1996, p. 46.
24 ITAR-TASS News Agency, October 10, 2000; BBC, "Russia from A to Z," October 11, 2000; *Novosti*, 1998, p. 128; *The Wall Street Journal*, March 21, 2000, p. A23, October 12, 2000, p. A21.
25 United Nations Development Program, *Transition 1999: Human Development Report for Europe and the CIS*, United Nations, 2000.
26 Anatoly Chubais (ed.), *Privatizatsiia Po-Rossiiski*, Moscow: Vagrius, 1999, p. 33.

27 Andrei Shleifer, Simon Johnson and Daniel Kaufmann, *Brookings Papers on Economic Activity*, no. 2, 1997, Brookings Institution, Washington, D.C., p. 12; Aslund, "Tainted Transactions," *The National Interest*, Summer 2000, p. 100.
28 See also Fabrizio Coricelli, *The Journal of Economic Literature*, vol. XXXVI, no. 4, December 1998, p. 2194.
29 Clifford G. Gaddy and Barry W. Ickes, "Russia's Virtual Economy," *Foreign Affairs*, September 1998, p. 53; Goldman, "The Barter Economy," *Current History*, October 1998, p. 319.
30 Gaidar, p. 129.
31 Boycko, Shleifer and Vishny.
32 Ronald Coase, "The Problems of Social Class," *The Journal of Law and Economics*, no. 3, 1960, p. 1.
33 Layard and Parker; Aslund, 1995; Chubais, p. 65.
34 Sachs, "Tainted Transactions: An Exchange," *The National Interest*, Summer 2000, p. 98.
35 Interview, Moscow, September 6, 1999; See also Padma Desai, "A Russian Optimist: Interview with Yegor Gaidar," *Challenge*, May–June 2000 p. 16.
36 Desai, p. 16.
37 Timothy Frye and Andrei Shleifer, "The Invisible Hand and the Grabbing Hand," *American Economic Review*, May 1997, p. 354.
38 Ibid., p. 356.

5 Privatization: good intentions, but the wrong advice at the wrong time

1 Chubais, p. 29.
2 Gaidar, pp. 78–9.
3. The U.S. Government General Accounting Office's report says, for example, "No aspect of Russia's economic transition has been more controversial than the privatization of enterprises." The U.S. Government General Accounting Office, "Report to the Chairman and the Ranking Minority Member," Committee On Banking and Financial Services, House of Representatives, *Foreign Assistance: International Efforts to Aid Russia's Transition Have Mixed Results*, GAO-01-8, Washington, D.C.: United States Government, November 1, 2000, p. 90.
4 For a more complete presentation of their thinking, see Gaidar's and Chubais' books written about the reforms: Gaidar, pp. 74–76, 216–17; Chubais, pp. 24–30.
5 Gaidar, pp. 74–5.
6 Chubais, pp. 28–30.
7 Gaidar, p. 17.
8 Boycko, Shleifer and Vishny, p. viii.
9 Ibid.
10 Coase, p. 1.
11 Boycko, Shleifer and Vishny, p. 9.
12 Robert J. Schiller, Maxim Boycko and Vladimir Korobov, "Popular Attitudes Toward Free Markets: The Soviet Union and United States Compared," *American Economic Review*, no. 81, 1991, pp. 385–400.
13 Boycko, Shleifer and Vishny, p. 10.
14 Ibid.
15 *The Financial Times*, March 15, 2000, p. xvii.

16 Boycko, Shleifer and Vishny, p. 10.
17 Ibid., p. 25.
18 Douglass North, "Economic Performance Through Time," *American Economic Review*, vol. 84, no. 3; Stefan Hedlund and Niclas Sundstrom, "Does Palermo Represent the Future for Moscow?" *The Journal of Public Policy*, no. 16, p. 2.
19 Daniel Kaufman and Paul Siegelbaum, *Privatization and Corruption in Transition Economies*, Winter, 1996.
20 Andrei Shleifer and Robert Vishny, *The Grabbing Hand: Government Pathologies and Cures*, Cambridge: Harvard University Press, 1998, p. 11.
21 Joseph Stiglitz, "Quis Custodiet Ipsos Custodes? (Who is to Guard the Guards Themselves?)," *Challenge*, November–December 1999, p. 55; Stiglitz, *Globalization & Its Discontents*, New York: W.W. Norton, 2002, pp. 163, 164.
22 Georgy Skorov, "Highlights of Privatization à la Russe," mimeographed, Paris, May 25, 1996, p. 6.
23 *Izvestiia*, January 26, 1994, p. 1; *The New York Times*, January 30, 1994, p. 1.
24 *The Wall Street Journal*, July 26, 2002, p. A9.
25 Personal interview, June 23 and 27, 1993, Leningrad Oblast.
26 See Joseph R. Blasi, Maya Kroumova and Douglas Kruse, *Kremlin Capitalism: Privatizing the Russian Economy*, Ithaca: Cornell University Press, 1997, pp. 182–3.
27 John Vickers and George Yarro, *Privitization: An Economic Analysis*, Cambridge: MIT Press, 1998, p. 157.
28 *The Moscow News*, no. 33, 1988, p. 8; no. 7, 1988, p. 13; no. 11, 1989, p. 3.
29 *Transition*, vol. 6, nos. 1–2, p. 15.
30 *Izvestiia*, October 27, 1985, p. 2; May 28, 1986, p. 2; November 20, 1986, p. 5; *Pravda*, July, 1986, p. 3; Foreign Broadcasting Information Service (FBIS), November 26, 1986, p. S11.
31 Blasi, Kroumova and Kruse, pp. 18, 21, 25.
32 Susan J. Ling and Gary Krueger, "Russia's Managers in Transition: Pilferers or Paladins?" *Post-Soviet Geography and Economics*, October 1996, p. 419; Roman Frydman, Andrzej Rapaczynski and John S. Earle, *The Privatization Process in Russia, Ukraine, and the Baltic States*, New York: Central European University Press, 1993, p. 22.
33 *Sovetskaia Rossiia*, July 17, 1991.
34 Chubais, p. 44. For an excellent description of the various laws, decrees and institutions, see Morris Bornstein, "Russia's Mass Privatisation Programme," *Communist Economies and Economic Transformation*, vol. 6, no. 4, 1994, p. 425 and Michael Kaiser, "Privatization in the C.I.S.," *Post-Soviet Business Forum*, London: The Royal Institute of International Affairs, p. 11.
35 *Rossiiskaia Gazeta*, January 10, 1992.
36 U.S. Government General Accounting Office, "Foreign Assistance: The Harvard Institute for International Development's Work in Russia and Ukraine," Washington: GAO/NSIAD, 97–27, November 27, 1996.
37 Lynn D. Nelson and Irina Y. Kuzes, *Property to the People: The Struggle for Radical Economic Reform in Russia*, Armonk: M.E. Sharpe, 1994, pp. 125–6; Chubais, p. 55.
38 Goldman, 1996, p. 137.
39 Bornstein, p. 435.
40 Andrei Shleifer and Daniel Treisman, *Political Tactics and Economic Reform in Russia*, Cambridge: MIT Press, 2000, p. 28.
41 Bornstein, p. 436; Blasi, Kroumova and Kruse, p. 41; Chubais, p. 55.

42 Boycko, Shleifer and Vishny, p. 78; *Ekonomika i Zhizn'*, 1994, no. 1, p. 14.
43 Bornstein, p. 435.
44 Lecture in Moscow, September 6, 1999.
45 Gaidar, p. 164.
46 Nelson and Kuzes, p. 127; Chubais, p. 56.
47 Blasi, Kroumova and Kruse, p. 41.
48 Goskomstat, *Narodnoe Khoziaistvo 1996*, Moscow, 1996, p. 702; Chubais, p. 38.
49 For two insightful studies of the problem, see Joel Scott Hellman, *Breaking the Banks: Bureaucrats and the Creation of Markets in a Transitional Economy*, submitted in part for the fulfillment of requirements for the degree of Ph.D., Graduate School of Arts and Sciences, Columbia University: New York, 1993 and Mark S. Nagel, *Supplicants, Robber Barons, and Pocket Banks: The Formation of Financial-Industrial Groups in Russia*, Department of Government, Cambridge: Harvard University, April 26, 1999.
50 Hellman, p. 132.
51 Ibid., p. 133.
52 Ibid.
53 Konstantin Borovoi in I. Bunin, p. 42.
54 Hellman, p. 138; David Lane (ed.), *Russian Banking*, Northampton, Mass: Edgar Elgar, 2002 p.13.
55 Ibid., p. 139.
56 Ibid., p. 140; *The Financial Times*, November 27, 2000, p. III.
57 Nagel, p. 209.
58 Freeland, p. 116; Nagel, p. 212.
59 Nagel, p. 212; Steven L. Solnick, *Stealing the State*, Cambridge: Harvard University Press, 1998; pp. 119–20, Freeland, p. 117; Hellman, p. 233.
60 Klebnikov, *Godfather of the Kremlin*, New York: Harcourt, 2000, p. 100.
61 On-site visit to Lutch in Podolsk, June 24, 1994.
62 Hellman, pp. 145–6, details an extensive list of other banks underwritten this way, including Tokobank, which was financed by Gossnab, Neftekhimbank, financed by the Petroleum Ministry, and Avtovazbank, financed by Avtovaz.
63 Ibid., pp. 146, 169, 172, 174, 242, 280; Nagel, p. 290.
64 Bornstein, p. 427; U.S. Government General Accounting Office, 2000, p. 91; *The Moscow Times*, August 15, 2002.
65 Nelson and Kuzes, p. 62.
66 *Komsomolskaia Pravda*, April 26, 2000; Chubais, p. 37.
67 The World Bank Report, "Investment Funds in Mass Privatization and Beyond," no. 23, p. 3.
68 *Ekonomika i Zhizn'*, February 1999, no. 7, p. 3.
69 Bornstein, p. 437.
70 *Ekonomika i Zhizn'*, February 1999, no. 7, p. 3; Bornstein, p. 445; Katharina Pistor and Andrew Spicer, "Investment Funds in Mass Privatization and Beyond: Evidence from the Czech Republic and Russia," Cambridge: Harvard Institute for International Development, Harvard University Development Discussion Paper no. 565, December 1996, p. 8.
71 Brady, p. 110; Pistor and Spicer, "Investment Funds in Mass Privatization and Beyond," *Between State and Market: Studies of Economies in Transition*, Washington D.C.: World Bank, no. 23 1997, p. 101.
72 *Argumenti i Fakti*, March 1995, no. 9.
73 Blasi, Kroumova and Kruse, p. 83.
74 *Ekonomika i Zhizn'*, February 1999, no. 7, p. 3.

75 Freeland, p. 58.
76 Ibid., p. 58–63.
77 Ibid., p. 58.
78 Brady, p. 73.
79 Freeland, p. 59; *Nezavisimaia Gazeta*, December 31, 1997.
80 Brady, p. 75.
81 Nelson and Kuzes, pp. 54–6.
82 Government of Russian Federation, "Small-Scale Privatization in Russia: The Nizhny Novgorod Model Annexes," March 1992.
83 Nelson and Kuzes, p. 55.
84 Boycko, Shleifer and Vishny, p. 110.
85 *The Moscow Times*, March 5, 1999; July 17, 1999.
86 Freeland, pp. 159, 242; Virginie Coulloudon, "Moscow City Management: A New Form of Capitalism?" mimeographed, 1999, p. 5.
87 *The Moscow Times*, January 29, 1995, p. 15; February 26, 1995, p. 27.
88 Boycko, Shleifer and Vishny, p. 2.
89 Stiglitz, 2002, p. 163.
90 Goskomstat, *Narodnoe Khoziaistvo 1992*, Moscow: Nar Khoz, 1993, p. 66; 1996, p. 702.
91 *Izvestiia*, December 2, 1992, p. 2.
92 German Federal Statistical Office, *Statistical Yearbook of West Germany*, 1991; IMF, *A Study of the Soviet Economy*, 1991.
93 *The Financial Times*, March 29, 1997, p. 2.
94 Skorov, "Highlights of Privatization", May 26, 1996, p. 9.
95 *The Moscow Times*, October 31, 2000; *The Wall Street Journal*, October 24, 2000, p. 821; *The Moscow News*, August 16, 2000, p. 5.
96 *Ekonomika i Zhizn'*, June 1999, no .23, p. 5.
97 Ibid., November 1999, no. 46, p. 29; *Russtrends*, July–September 1997, no. 22, www.securities.com.
98 Coulloudon, "Privatization In Russia: Catalyst for the Elite," *The Fletcher Forum of World Affairs*, vol. 22:2, Summer/Fall 1998, p. 47; *Russtrends*.
99 *Segodnia*, February 18, 1995, p. 3.
100 *The Financial Times*, September 6, 1996, p. 10.
101 Blasi, Kroumova and Kruse, p. 193.
102 *Ekonomika i Zhizn'*, September 1999, no. 37, p. 27.
103 *The New York Times*, October 20, 2000, p. B2.
104 *The Moscow News*, August 16, 2000, p. 5; *World Link*, July–August 2000, p. 41; *The Financial Times*, July 17, 2000; August 11, 2000, p. 3; October 20, 2000, p. 3; *The Wall Street Journal*, October 24, 2000, p. A21.
105 Daniel Treisman, "Blaming Russia First," *Foreign Affairs*, November–December 2000, p. 148; Solnick, p. 229; Simon Johnson and Heidi Kroll, "Managerial Strategies for Spontaneous Privatization," *Soviet Economy*, no. 2, 1991, p. 281.
106 Treisman, p. 128. See also Aslund (ed.), *Economic Transformation in Russia*, New York: St. Martin's Press, 1994, p. 7.
107 Boris Nemtsov, discussion, Arden House, April 11, 2002.

6 The *nomenklatura* oligarchs

1 *Forbes Magazine*, July 6, 1998, p. 192.

2 In its 2001 compilation, *Forbes* listed eight Russian billionaires: *Forbes Magazine*, July 9, 2001, pp. 116–22.
3 *The Washington Times*, December 5, 1994, p. 1; *Moskovskaia Pravda*, December 17, 1994, p. 5; *Izvestiia*, January 26, 1994, p. 1.
4 *The Wall Street Journal Europe*, April 11, 1995; *The Wall Street Journal*, April 11, 1995, p. A2; April 13, 1995, p. A14.
5 Interview and lecture, Nizhny Novgorod, June 8, 1995.
6 *The Wall Street Journal*, January 16, 1997, p. 6; *The Washington Post*, May 21, 2001.
7 *The Financial Times*, May 25, 2001, p. 24; *The Los Angeles Times*, May 23, 2001.
8 *The Independent*, April 15, 2001; *BusinessWeek*, June 4, 2001; *The Times of London*, June 21, 2001.
9 www.polit.ru/documents/414213.html.
10 *The Financial Times*, May 25, 2001, p. 24; May 11, 2001, p. 34 supplement; *The Guardian*, April 18, 2001; *BusinessWeek*, June 4, 2001; *The Moscow Times*, November 22, 2001.
11 *The Moscow Times*, June 4, 2001.
12 Martin McCauley, *Who's Who in Russia Since 1900*, London: Routledge, 1997, pp. 63–4.
13 Peter Rutland, "Russia's Natural Gas Leviathan," *Transition*, May 3, 1996, p. 12.
14 *Ogonek*, December 1995, no. 7, pp. 22–3; *The Wall Street Journal*, October 7, 1996, p. A19.
15 *Transition*, June 1997; *Forbes Magazine*, July 6, 1998, p. 192.
16 *The Economist*, July 5, 1997, p. 65; *Jamestown Foundation Monitor*, December 23, 1997, p. 2.
17 *Johnson's Russia List*, June 2, 2001, no. 5280, item 13; *The Moscow Times*, June 4, 2001, states that Gazprom was privatized in March 1993.
18 *The New York Times*, May 12, 2001, p. B2; *The Wall Street Journal*, January 16, 1997, p. 1; *The Financial Times*, May 15, 2001, p. 22.
19 *The Moscow News*, May 25, 1999, p. 13.
20 *The Financial Times*, June 21, 2001, p. 19.
21 Ibid., June 27, 2002, p. 30.
22 *Johnson's Russia List*, February 19, no. 60872002, item 8.
23 Ibid., no. 6149, March 21, 2002, item 11.
24 *BusinessWeek*, December 4, 2000, p. 62 E4.
25 Figure 6.1 source: *The Financial Times*, June 14, 2001, p. 19; Boris Fedorov, "Gazprom–The World's Largest 'Non-Profit' Corporation," mimeographed, October 2000, p. 5.
26 *The Moscow Times*, November 11, 2000.
27 Interview, April 12, 2000.
28 *The Financial Times*, July 2, 1998, p. 3.
29 *The Moscow Times*, January 30, 2002; August 21, 2002.
30 Ibid., May 21, 2001; *The Financial Times*, May 22, 2001.
31 *The Moscow Times*, May 21, 2001.
32 Ibid., July 2, 2001; *The Financial Times*, July 5, 2001.
33 *The Financial Times*, March 14, 2001, p. 17; March 30, 2001, p. 23.
34 *Johnson's Russia List*, April 24, 2001, no. 5220; RFE/RL, April 24, 2001.
35 *The Financial Times*, August 11, 2000, p. 3.
36 Ibid., March 14, 2001, p. 17; *The Wall Street Journal*, March 7, 2001, p. A23.
37 *The New York Times*, March 27, 2002, p. W1.

38 *The Moscow Times*, November 11, 2000.
39 *The Wall Street Journal*, October 24, 2000, p. A21.
40 Ibid.
41 *The Financial Times*, May 25, 2001, p. 24.
42 International Group of Companies, ITERA, Jacksonville, Florida, press release.
43 *The Wall Street Journal*, October 24, 2000, p. A21; *BusinessWeek*, December 4, 2000, pp. 62, E6; *The Moscow Times*, April 3, 2001.
44 *Novaia Gazeta*, April 19, 2001.
45 *The Wall Street Journal*, October 24, 2000, p. A21.
46 *BusinessWeek*, December 4, 2000, pp. 62, E6; *The New York Times*, October 28, 2000, p. B2.
47 *The Moscow Times*, November 11, 2000.
48 *The Wall Street Journal*, January 21, 2002, p. C1.
49 *The Moscow Times*, November 9, 2001, p. 5.
50 Ibid., November 28, 2001; *The Financial Times*, December 8, 2001.
51 *The Moscow Times*, December 18, 2001.
52 *The Financial Times*, April 11, 2001, p. 20.
53 Ibid., April 10, 1997, p. 2.
54 *The Wall Street Journal*, January 25, 2001, p. A6.
55 *The Financial Times*, April 11, 1996, p. IX.
56 *The Wall Street Journal*, February 20, 2002, p. A16.
57 Interview, June 21, 2001.
58 Boris Fedorov, "Svoboda ili Prodazhnost' Pressy?" mimeograph, June 2001.
59 *The Financial Times*, May 16, 1997, p. 3; May 26, 1997, p. 1; May 22, 1997, p. 18; *Russia Review*, July 2, 1997, p. 23.
60 *The Moscow Times*, May 29, 2001.
61 *The Wall Street Journal*, February 20, 2002, p. A16.
62 Ibid., May 30, 2001, p. A19.
63 *The Moscow Times*, July 5, 2001.
64 *The Wall Street Journal*, June 30, 2000, p. A10; *The Financial Times*, July 1, 2000, p. 2.
65 *Johnson's Russia List*, December 1, no. 5573, 2001, item 11; *The Russian Journal*, November 30, 2001; *The Moscow Times*, November 22, 2001.
66 *The Financial Times*, September 17, 2001, p. 24; *The New York Times*, January 10, 2002, p. W1; *Johnson's Russia List*, no. 6013, January 9, 2002, item 2.
67 *The Moscow Times*, January 30, 2002; March 6, 2002; March 12, 2002; March 26, 2002.
68 Ibid., March 26, 2002.
69 *The Wall Street Journal*, April 4, 2002, p. A14; *The Moscow Times*, April 3, 2002.
70 *The Wall Street Journal*, May 23, 2002, p. A12.
71 *The Moscow Times*, August 22, 2002.
72 *Johnson's Russia List*, June 2, 2001, no. 5280, item 13.
73 *The Financial Times*, November 28, 2002, p. 16.
74 Peter Rutland, "Russia's Energy Engine Under Strain," *Transition*, May 3, 1996, p. 6.
75 *The Moscow News*, May 5, 1995, p. 7.
76 *The New York Times*, July 25, 2002, p. W1; *The Wall Street Journal*, July 16, 2002, p. A12; *The Moscow Times*, July 29, 2002.
77 *The Financial Times*, July 31, 2002, p. 18; *The Moscow Times*, July 29, 2002.
78 *The Financial Times*, April 27, 1998, p. 1.

79   *The Moscow Times*, November 26, 2001.
80   *Johnson's Russia List*, October 21, 2000, no. 4592; *The Russian Journal*, October 4, 2001, p. 15; November 30, 2001.
81   Interview, August 5, 2002, and correspondence.
82   *Forbes Magazine*, March 18, 2002, p. 125.
83   *Russia Review*, November 3, 1997, p. 16.
84   Ibid., February 26, 1996, p. 26.
85   Freeland, pp. 174–5, 177–8.
86   *The Moscow Times*, November 1, 2001.
87   *The Washington Post*, August 22, 2001; Freeland, p. 175.
88   *The Moscow Times*, November 1, 2001.
89   *The Wall Street Journal*, March 8, 1999, p. A1.
90   Ibid., February 9, 2000, p. A21.
91   JSB Inkombank, ADR Level-1 Program Presentation, arranger, C.A. Atlantic Securities, Boston, May 12, 1997, p. 21.
92   *Russia Review*, November 3, 1997, p. 13.
93   *The Moscow Times*, December 15, 1998; April 1, 1999; May 12, 1999.
94   *The Moscow Times*, December 4, 2001.

7 The upstart oligarchs

1   *The Washington Post*, October 17, 1997, p. 1; *Ekonomicheskaia Gazeta*, no. 8, February 1997, p. 32; *Rossiiskaia Gazeta*, March 14, 1995, p. 1.
2   *Ekonomicheskaia Gazeta*, no. 8, February 1997, p. 32.
3   *The Washington Post*, October 17, 1997, p. 1; Hoffman, p. 35.
4   Seminar, Davis Center for Russian Studies, Harvard University, February 21, 2001; *The Moscow Times*, April 12, 2002.
5   *The Washington Post*, October 17, 1997, p. A34.
6   *The Wall Street Journal*, October 4, 2000, p. A.
7   *Izvestiia*, July 1, 1997.
8   Ibid., September 7, 1997.
9   *The Wall Street Journal*, October 4, 2000, p. A10.
10   *The Moscow Times*, June 8, 2001.
11   Ibid., April 6, 2001; April 10, 2002.
12   Ibid., December 11, 2001.
13   Ibid., February 12, 2001; *The Wall Street Journal*, February 14, 2001, p. A16.
14   *The Wall Street Journal*, February 14, 2001, p. A16.
15   *The Economist*, April 22, 1995, p. 69.
16   Ibid.; *The Washington Post*, April 7, 1995, p. D4; David Remnick, *Resurrection: The Struggle for a New Russia*, New York: Random House, 1997, p. 186.
17   *Rossiiskaia Gazeta*, March 7, 1995, p. 1.
18   *The Moscow News*, November 11, 1994, no. 45, p. 3; *The Moscow Times*, July 2, 1995, p. 37.
19   *The Washington Times*, December 5, 1994, p. 1.
20   *The Washington Post*, April 7, 1995, p. D4; interview, New York, May 16, 1999.
21   Interview, New York, May 16, 1999.
22   *Rossiiskaia Gazeta*, November 19, 1994, p. 3; March 7, 1995, p. 1; *The Moscow News*, February 10–16, 1995.
23   Interview, Vitaly Tretyakov.
24   Korzhakov, p. 285.
25   *The Moscow Times*, April 11, 2000.

26 *The Financial Times,* January 22, 2001; *The Moscow Times,* January 26, 2001, p. VI.
27 *The Moscow Times,* December 19, 2000; February 23, 2001; *The Russian Journal,* February 17, 2001.
28 *The Russian Jewish Congress Annual Report,* 1998, p. 43.
29 *Izvestia Press Digest Russiska Izvestia,* September 19, 2000.
30 *Sovershenno Sekretno,* no. 12, December 2000.
31 *The New York Times,* April 3, 2001, p. C11.
32 Ibid.
33 Interview, May 11, 2001.
34 Interview, May 12, 2001.
35 *Forbes Magazine,* July 6, 1998, p. 192; *Forbes Magazine,* December 30, 1996, p. 90.
36 Klebnikov, 2000, p. 37.
37 *The New Republic,* October 9, 2000, p. 34.
38 Ibid.
39 *The Guardian,* December 21, 2000.
40 *BusinessWeek,* April 13, 1998, p. 46.
41 Klebnikov, 2000, p. 12.
42 Ibid., pp. 140–1.
43 Ibid., p. 141.
44 *Novaia Gazeta,* March 26, 2001; *Johnson's Russia List,* March 27, 2001, no. 5171.
45 *The Washington Post,* August 25, 1998, p. A12; August 28, 1998, p. A18; *The Moscow Times,* June 5, 1999.
46 *The Moscow Times,* April 8, 1999; December 11, 1998; December, 6, 2000; *The Financial Times,* September 25, 1999, p. 4; *The New York Times,* February 4, 1999, p. A3.
47 *The Wall Street Journal,* June 1, 1999, p. A17.
48 Boris Yeltsin, *Midnight Diaries,* New York: Public Affairs, 2000, p. 284.
49 *Jamestown Foundation Monitor,* May 16, 2001; *Johnson's Russia List,* May 16, 2001, no. 8; *The Moscow Times,* June 24, 2000.
50 *The New York Times,* April, 13, 2001, p. A4.
51 Vladimir Putin, *First Person,* New York: Public Affairs, 2000, p. 125.
52 TV-6, April 25, 2001; *St. Petersburg Times,* July 17, 2001, p. 3.
53 *The Moscow Times,* November 15, 2000.
54 Ibid., December 8, 2000; November 15, 2000; Klebnikov, 2000, p. 89; *The Guardian,* December 21, 2000.
55 Chubais, p. 4.
56 *The Moscow Times,* July 30, 1999; August 4, 1999; *The Financial Times,* July 30, 1999, p. 2.
57 Chubais.
58 *The Financial Times,* May 31, 2001, p. 18; *The Wall Street Journal,* May 21, 2001, p. A15.
59 *The Russian Journal,* October 12–18, 2001.
60 *The Moscow Times,* November 1, 2001.
61 Interview, December 5, 2000.
62 Interview, February 7, 2002.
63 *World Link,* January–February 2000.
64 Seminar, Arden House Conference on Russian–U.S. Relations, April 14, 2002.
65 *The Financial Times,* May 19, 1999, p. 19; *The New York Times,* August 13, 1999, p. C1; *The Wall Street Journal,* July 20, 1999, p. A18; February 9, 2000, p. A21.

66 *The New York Times*, December 17, 1999, p. A14.
67 *The Wall Street Journal*, December 20, 1999, p. A10.
68 Ibid., February 9, 2000, p. A21; *The Moscow Times*, January 30, 1999, p. 8.
69 *The Financial Times*, August 27, 1999, p. 21.
70 *The New York Times*, August 13, 1999, p. C1.
71 *The Wall Street Journal*, September 16, 1999, p. A26; February 9, 2000, p. A21; *The Financial Times*, October 20, 1999, p. 25.
72 *The Wall Street Journal*, February 9, 2000, p. A21.
73 Interview with Simon Kukes, October 22, 1999.
74 Interview, October 22, 1999 and February 8, 2002.
75 *The Moscow Times*, March 31, 1999; July 8, 1999; *The Wall Street Journal*, May 29, 1999, p. A21; December 22, 1999, p. A10.
76 *The New York Times*, December 21, 1999, p. A14; *The Wall Street Journal*, December 22, 1999, p. A10.
77 *The New York Times*, December 22, 1999; *The Wall Street Journal*, December 22, 1999, p. A10.
78 Interview, February 7, 2002.
79 Bunin, p. 169.
80 Russian Research Center, *Economic Newsletter*, January 13, 1989; Bunin, p. 171.
81 Nagel, p. 211.
82 *The Moscow Times*, April 12, 2002.
83 *Kommersant Daily*, September 2, 1991, p. 13.
84 *Russia Review*, November 3, 1997, p. 14.
85 *The Wall Street Journal*, December 24, 1996, p. A6; Freeland, p. 178; Paul Klebnikov, "The Oligarch Who Came in From the Cold," *Forbes*, March 18, 2002, p. 114.
86 *Forbes Magazine*, March 18, 2002, p. 114; Klebnikov; 2002, p. 114.
87 *The Wall Street Journal*, September 11, 1997.
88 Ibid., June 4, 1999, p. A12.
89 Interfax, February 7, 1998; *Financial Times*, July 16, 1998, p. 2.
90 *The Moscow News*, March 19, 1998.
91 *The Wall Street Journal*, August 26, 1999, p. A1; September 3, 1999, p. 2.
92 *Moskovskaia Pravda*, December 17, 1994, p. 5.
93 *The New York Times*, August 28, 1999, p. A6.
94 *The Wall Street Journal*, August 15, 2000, p. A23; *The Moscow Times*, September 22, 1999.
95 *The Moscow Times*, February 17, 2000.
96 *The Wall Street Journal*, June 4, 1999, p. A12; Klebnikov, 2002, p. 110; *Forbes Magazine*, March 18, 2002, p. 114.
97 *The Wall Street Journal*, July 1, 2002, p. A5.
98 *The Moscow Times*, November 9, 2001; *The Guardian*, December 15, 2001.
99 *The Financial Times*, December 20, 1999, p. 17; *The Moscow Times*, December 21, 1999; January 16, 1999.
100 *Ekonomika i Zhizn'*, December 1998, no. 52, p. 29; *The Moscow Times*, August 15, 2000.
101 *Johnson's Russia List*, March 21, 2002, no. 6149, item 8.
102 *The Moscow Times*, January 21, 2002.
103 *The Wall Street Journal*, July 2, 2002, p. A12.
104 *The Financial Times*, June 21, 2002, pp. 13, 18.
105 *The Moscow Times*, June 1, 1999.
106 Ibid., April 4, 2000.

107 *The Moscow News,* June 2–8, 1999, no. 20, p. 2.
108 *The New York Times,* December 20, 1999, p. C2.
109 *The Moscow Times,* April 11, 2000.
110 *The Financial Times,* January 6, 2001, p. I; *The Washington Post,* March 2, 2001; *Johnson's Russia List,* March 19, 2001, no. 5159.
111 *Moskovskii Komsomolets,* June 2, 1999, pp. 1–21; *Ha'aretz,* August 29, 1999, p. B4.
112 *The Moscow Times,* April 11, 2000.
113 *The Financial Times,* November 9, 2000, p. 24.
114 *The Washington Post,* March 2, 2001.
115 *Izvestiia,* February 1, 2001.
116 *Johnson's Russia List,* January 10, 2001, no. 5018, item 8.
117 *The Financial Times,* December 20, 2000, p. 3.
118 *Le Monde,* November 28, 2002.
119 *The Moscow Times,* October 25, 2001; November 1, 2001.
120 *The Moscow Times,* November 1, 2001.
121 Ibid., August 7, 2001; October 29, 2001; October 30, 2001; November 1, 2001.
122 Ibid., October 29, 2001; *The Financial Times,* September 17, 2001, p. 24.
123 *The Wall Street Journal,* August 24, 2000, p. A19; *The New York Times,* December 28, 1999, p. C2.
124 *The Moscow Times,* June 1, 1999; November 17, 1999; April 11, 2000.
125 *The Moscow News,* June 9–15, no. 21, 1999, p. 3.
126 *The Wall Street Journal,* August 11, 2000, p. A11.
127 Ibid., July 28, 2000, p. A13.
128 *Nezavisismaia Gazeta,* December 26, 2000; *Johnson's Russia List,* December 25, 2000, no. 4709.
129 Ibid.
130 *Izvestiia,* February 25, 2000.
131 French Press Agency, January 10, 2001; *Johnson's Russia List,* January 10, 2001, no. 5018, item 8.

8 FIMACO, the Russian Central Bank, and money laundering at the highest level

1 *The Moscow Times,* January 11, 2000; April 4, 2000; April 22, 2000; *Johnson's Russia List,* July 2, 2002, no. 6336, item 1.
2 *The Moscow Times,* December 22, 1998.
3 Marshall Goldman, *Détente and Dollars,* New York: Basic Books, 1975, pp. 298–300.
4 *The New York Times,* September 23, 1971, p. 1; April 7, 1983, p. 1; September 15, 1985, p. 1.
5 *Foreign Trade,* February 1974, p. 40; *Moscow Narodny Bank Bulletin,* March 13, 1974, p. 7.
6 *The New York Times,* October 2, 1972, p. 55.
7 *The Moscow Times,* September 22, 1998.
8 Ibid., November 19, 2001.
9 Ibid., August 4, 1999; *The New York Times,* August 30, 1973, p. 3; January 7, 1976, p. 4; March 25, 1976, p. 8.
10 *The New York Times,* October 5, 1979, p. D1; *The Washington Post,* October 6, 1978, p. D15.

11 *Kommersant Daily*, July 13, 1999, p. 1; *The Moscow Times*, August 17, 1999, p. XXII. Most of what follows is from the PricewaterhouseCoopers (PWC) audit performed for the Russian Central Bank, August 4, 1999.

12 BBC Broadcast, March 22, 1999; PWC, p. 3.

13 *The Moscow Times*, August 17, 1999, p. XXII.

14 *Kommersant Daily*, July 13, 1999, p. 1; *The Moscow Times*, March 1, 1999; August 17, 1999, p. XXII.

15 *The Moscow Times*, February 23, 1999; August 17, 1999.

16 Ibid., August 17, 1999.

17 PWC audit report.

18 *The Moscow Times*, August 17, 1999, p. XXII.

19 PWC audit.

20 *Kommersant Daily*, July 13, 1999, p. 1.

21 *The Wall Street Journal*, June 16, 1992, p. A12.

22 IMF Staff Country Report, p. 44.

23 *Internet Securities*, July 10, 1999.

24 *Ekonomika i Zhizn'*, December 1999, no. 51, p. 3. By 2002, estimates of accumulated capital flight amounted to as much as $300 billion: *The Wall Street Journal*, June 26, 2002, p. A7.

25 *The Moscow Times*, February 23, 1999; Oleg Odnokolenko, *Itogi*, July 30, 2002, p. 12.

26 *The Moscow News*, March 17, 1999, no. 10, p. 4; *The Moscow Times*, December 8, 1998.

27 *The Moscow Times*, February 23, 1999.

28 *The Financial Times*, June 24, 1993, p. 1. Those funds were eventually released. Unwilling to give up, Gaon obtained another court judgment on May 18, 2000. This time a French court ordered the seizure of assets of Eurobank, the Russian Embassy in Paris, overseas assets of Slavneft, Rosneft, and Vneshekonombank, which are partially owned by the Russian government. Part of the judgment was overturned on June 13, 2000; *The Moscow Times*, June 14, 2000.

29 *The Moscow Times*, August 17, 1999, p. XXII; PWC audit, section 12.2.

30 Press conference, February 16, 1999, Kremlin Package, Federal News Service, Internet Securities.

31 *Kommersant Daily*, August 3, 1999, p. 1; *The Moscow Times*, July 2, 1999.

32 *The Moscow Times*, February 17, 1999.

33 Ibid., February 6, 1999.

34 Ibid., November 28, 2001.

35 Ibid., August 17, 1999, p. XXII; October 19, 1999.

36 Ibid., October 19, 1999.

37 Ibid., August 17, 1999, p. XXII.

38 Ibid., October 19, 1999.

39 Ibid.

40 *Russika Izvestia*, July 7, 1998.

41 *Central European*, April 1999, p. 22.

42 *The Moscow Times*, February 6, 1999; February 23, 1999.

43 PWC, pp. 14–15; Randall W. Stone, "Russia and the IMF," *Lending Credibility: The IMF and the Post-Communist Transition*, section 21.17, mimeographed, pp. 26–7.

44 *The Financial Times*, September 27, 1999, p. 12; *The Moscow Times*, August 3, 1999.

45 *The Moscow Times*, March 2, 1999.
46 Ibid., July 6, 1999.
47 Ibid., August 17, 1999, p. XXI.
48 Ibid., February 17, 1999.
49 *Kommersant Daily*, July 13, 1999, p. 2.
50 *The Moscow Times*, November 2, 1999; PWC, section 21.
51 *The Moscow Times*, October 19, 1999.
52 PWC, sections 21.2, 21.3, 21.4; *The Moscow Times*, August 3, 1999.
53 *The Moscow Times*, November 5, 1999; February 8, 2000.
54 *The New York Times*, February 17, 2000, p. A1; February 18, 2000, p. A1.
55 Ibid., February 17, 2000, p. A6.
56 Ibid., December 6, 2001, p. A5.
57 *The Financial Times*, June 1, 2000, p. 2, *Johnson's Russia List*, February 18, 2000, no. 4119, item 1; June 13, 2000, no. 4366, item 11; *The Moscow Times*, June 9, 2000.
58 *The Financial Times*, January 29, 2000, p. 2.
59 Ibid., June 1, 2000, p. 2 Intercom Daily Report on Russia, February 18, 2000; *Reuters*, February 18, 2000.
60 *Kommersant Daily*, August 13, 1999, p. 1; *The Moscow Times*, July 2, 1999.
61 *The Moscow Times*, November 2, 1999.
62 *Newsweek*, March 29, 1999, p. 39; *Echo* Radio Program, March 22, 1999; *The Moscow Times*, July 2, 1999; *The Washington Post*, July 1, 1999; *Moskovskii Komsomolets*, June 3, 1999, p. 1; *The Moscow Times*, November 2, 1999.
63 *Kommersant Daily*, August 3, 1999, p. 1.
64 PWC, sections 21.7, 21.16, 21.17, 21.18, 21.19; *The Moscow Times*, November 2, 1999.
65 *The Moscow Times*, August 3, 1999; August 17, 1999, p. XXI; November 2, 1999; Interfax, September 19, 1998.
66 *The Moscow Times*, July 30, 1999.
67 *The Financial Times*, September 27, 1999, p. 12; *The Moscow Times*, August 3, 1994.
68 *The Moscow Times*, March 21, 2002.
69 *The Financial Times*, February 11, 2000, p. 1.

9 Corruption, crime, and the Russian mafia

1 Stephen Handelman, *Comrade Criminal: Russia's New Mafiya*, New Haven: Yale University Press, 1995. This is one of the most thoughtful and carefully researched studies of crime in Russia.
2 Ibid., p. 95.
3 Ibid., p. 338; *The Moscow Times*, February 12, 2002.
4 *The Moscow Times*, February 12, 2002.
5 *Jamestown Foundation Monitor*, December 3, 2001.
6 *The Moscow Times*, October 18, 2001; *Rossiiskaia Gazeta*, July 20, 2001.
7 Ibid., October 10, 2001; discussion with Moscow bankers, October 28, 2001.
8 *The Washington Post*, May 23, 2002.
9 *The Moscow News*, January 23–29, 2002, pp. 1–2.
10 *The Moscow Times*, January 11, 2000; April 22, 2000; April 4, 2000; *Johnson's Russia List*, July 3, 2002, no. 6336, item 1.

11 Susan Rose-Ackerman, "Corruption and Competition," mimeographed, January 28, 1994; Shleifer and Vishny, "Corruption", *The Quarterly Journal of Economics*, August 1993, p. 599.
12 *Moskovskaia Pravda*, December 17, 1994, p. 5.
13 *The Moscow Times*, March 22, 2002.
14 *The New York Times*, May 16, 2002, p. A4; May 2, 2002, p. A6.
15 *The Moscow Times*, May 24, 2002.
16 Ibid.
17 Ibid.
18 *The Washington Times*, December 5, 1994, p. A1; *Moskovskaia Pravda*, December 17, 1994, p. 5.
19 *The Financial Times*, January 2, 2001, p. 3; *The Moscow Times*, May 8, 2001.
20 *The Financial Times*, April 15, 1998, p. VIII.
21 Ibid., p. II.
22 ITAR-TASS, February 20, 1998.
23 *U.S.–Russia Business Journal*, "Russia After the Election," July 26, 1996, p. 19; *Russia Review*, August 14, 1998, p. 24.
24 *The Moscow Times*, March 14, 2000.
25 *Ekonomika i Zhizn'*, May 2000, no. 21, pp. 4–5; *Russia Review*, June 16, 1997, p. 20.
26 BBC Report, RIA, July 7, 1998; BBC Report, July 1, 1998; *The Moscow Times*, February 28, 1998.
27 *Business Review*, January 1999, p. 35.
28 ITAR-TASS, August 6, 1998; *The Moscow Times*, November 6, 1999; November 19, 1999; February 12, 1995, p. 42.
29 *The New York Times*, August 1, 2000; March 8, 1998, p. 3; *The Moscow Times*, July 25, 2000; August 14, 2000.
30 *Johnson's Russia List*, January 3, 2002, no. 6005, item 2.
31 *The Moscow Times*, September 18, 2001; March 3, 2000; *The New York Times*, May 13, 1993, p. A4.
32 *The Moscow Times*, March 26, 2001; *Johnson's Russia List*, March 24, 2001, no. 5168.
33 *Argumenti i Fakti*, March 2001, no. 12, p. 3.
34 *Nezavisimaia Gazeta*, December 16, 1992, p. 2; *Moscow News*, no. 31, 1992, p. 2.
35 Maxwell Street on Chicago's west side for many years served just such a purpose. As grubby as the district was, many successful businesses got their start there.
36 Such markets cannot guarantee immunity from the Mafia. Hunts Point and the Fulton Fish Market in New York have had periodic bouts with various American Mafia families, but sooner or later government authorities have managed to restore order.
37 *The Moscow Times*, April 5, 2002.
38 *The Financial Times*, March 9, 1994, p. 26.
39 Ibid., July 22, 2002, p. 7.
40 *Rossiiskaia Gazeta*, July 20, 2001; December 12, 2002.
41 *The Moscow News*, December 19, 2000; *The Moscow Times*, December 19, 2000; *The Washington Post*, March 2, 2001.
42 *The New York Times*, July 2, 2002, p. W1.
43 *The Moscow Times*, January 30, 2002; February 5, 2002; *Johnson's Russia List*, January 31, 2002, no. 6050, item 17; February 5, 2002, no. 6059, item 15.
44 *The Russian Journal*, December 3, 2001, business p. 3.

10 Who says there was no better way?

1 Boycko, Shleifer and Vishny, p. 125.
2 John S. Earle, Roman Frydman, Andrzej Rapaczynski and Joel Turkewitz, *Small Privatization*, Budapest: Central European University Press, CEU Privatization Reports, vol. 3, 1994, p. 43.
3 Ibid., p. 49.
4 Ibid., p. 65; Jan Mladek, "Voucher Privatisation in the Czech Republic and Slovakia," OECD, Center for Co-operation with the Economies in Transition, *Mass Privatization, an Initial Assessment*, Paris: Organization for Economic Operation and Development, 1995, p. 61.
5 Jan Winiecki, "Polish Mass Privatisation Programme: The Unloved Child in a Suspect Family," in Center for Co-operation with Economies in Transition, p. 48; Janus Lewandowski and Jan Szomberg, "Propertisation as a Foundation of Socio-Economic Reform," paper for the seminar of "Transformation Proposal for Polish Economy," Warsaw, mimeographed, November 17–18, 1988.
6 Mladek, p. 66; Josef C. Brada, "Privatization is Transition, Or Is It?" *Journal of Economic Perspectives*, vol. 10, no. 2, Spring 1996, p. 72.
7 Mladek, p. 66.
8 Ibid., p. 67.
9 Viktor Kozeny, Davis Center for Russian Studies Seminar, Harvard University, October 9, 1996.
10 Davis Center for Russian Studies Seminar, October 10, 1996; *Newsweek*, July 3, 1999, p. 40; Mladek, p. 69.
11 Mladek, p. 68.
12 *BusinessWeek*, December 11, 1995, p. 58.
13 Ibid.
14 Pistor and Spicer, 1997, p. 101; Pavel Meitlik, "Post-Privatization Restructuralization of Property Rights in the Czech Republic," Economic Commission for Europe, Spring Seminar, 1998, Geneva Paper 5, pp. 2–3.
15 Davis Center for Russian Studies Seminar, October 9, 1996.
16 Ibid.
17 Mladek, p. 76.
18 Pistor and Spicer, 1997, p. 103.
19 *The Wall Street Journal Europe*, July 12, 1996, p. 4.
20 *The New York Times*, December 22, 1999, p. F4.
21 Charles Wallace, "The Pirates of Prague," *Fortune*, December 23, 1996, p. 79.
22 *The Financial Times*, March 20, 2000, p. 3.
23 Ibid.
24 Winiecki, p. 54.
25 *The Boston Globe*, June 23, 1996, p. 4.
26 Interfax, November 30, 1998.
27 Earle *et al.*, p. 195; Roman Frydman, Andrzej Rapaczynski and John S. Earle, *The Privatization Process in Central Europe*, Budapest: Central European University Press, 1993, p. 162.
28 *The Financial Times*, July 12, 2000, p. 16.
29 *The Warsaw Voice*, "Polish and Central European Russia," April 1998, p. 13.
30 Ibid.; *The Financial Times*, March 14, 2000, p. 3. Vladimir Gusinsky was one of the few who created something from scratch in Russia.
31 100 Najbogatszych Polakow, *Wprost*, June 18, 2000.
32 *The Moscow Times*, November 12, 2001.

33 *Poland: Fundamental Facts, Figures, and Regulations*, The Polish Agency for Foreign Investment, Warsaw, January 1996, p. 29.
34 Interview with Ewa Freyberg, the Under-Secretary of State of the Polish Ministry of the Treasury July 7, 1997, Warsaw, Poland; OECD, Centre for Co-operation with the Economies in Transition, p. 48; Janusz Lewandowski, "The Political Context of Mass Privatization in Poland," in *Between State and Market: Studies of Economies in Transition*, no. 23, World Bank, Washington, 1997, p. 35.
35 See Table 10.1 for note.
36 *The Financial Times*, June 4, 1996, p. 3.
37 The details of this process are spelled out in Goldman, 1996, pp. 122–45.
38 Boycko, Shleifer and Vishny, p. 11.
39 Ibid., p. 83; Chubais, p. 59.
40 Boycko, Shleifer and Vishny, p. 11.
41 They do this even though a new study shows that private ownership is not always more efficient. See Roman Frydman, Marek Hessel, Andrzej Rapaczynski and Cheryl Grey, "Ambiguity of Privatization, Private Ownership, and Corporate Performance: Evidence from the Transition Economies," undated.

11 Confidence or con game: what will it take?

1 *Ekonomika i Zhizn'*, May 2002, no. 21, p. 1.
2 *Bisnis Russia*, U.S. Department of Commerce, Development of Small and Medium-sized Business in Russia, December 7, 2001.
3 *OECD Economic Summary 1997–98*, Russian Federation, Paris: OECD, 1997, p. 136.
4 Vadim Radaev, "Russian Entrepreneurship After the 1998 Crisis," *Programs in New Approaches to Russian Security, Policy Memo Series*, no. 78, October 1999, p. 50.
5 *Ekonomika i Zhizn'*, April 2001, no. 15, p. 27, says there were only 879,300; *Bisnis Russia*.
6 *The Financial Times*, December 19, 2001, p. 2.
7 *The Wall Street Journal*, March 21, 2000, p. A23; *The Moscow Times*, December 20, 2001.
8 *The Financial Times*, January 16, 2002, p. 3.
9 *The Wall Street Journal*, October 12, 2000, p. A21.
10 Chubais, p. 22.
11 *The Financial Times*, May 2, 2001, p. 2; *The Moscow Times*, January 30, 2002.
12 *The Moscow Times*, October 21, 2000.
13 *Argumenti i Fakti*, March 12, 2001, p. 3; *The Financial Times*, December 17, 2001.
14 *Transitions*, World Bank, March–April 2002, p. 15.
15 Interview with John Mylonas, Director for General Motors in Tolyatti, September 6, 2002.
16 Seminar, September 10, 2002, Moscow.
17 *OECD Economic Surveys, 1997*, Paris, Russian Federation, p. 36.
18 *The Moscow Times*, February 5, 2002.
19 *OECD Economic Surveys, 1997*, p. 137.
20 ITAR-TASS/*Johnson's Russia List*, March 21, 2001, no. 5163, item 1.
21 *Ekonomika i Zhizn'*, May 2002, no. 21, p. 1.
22 *Argumenti i Fakti*, March 12, 2001, p. 3.
23 *Johnson's Russia List*, June 27, 2001, no. 5326, item 11; *The Moscow Times*, November 29, 2002.

24 *Izvestiia*, February 25, 2000.
25 *Rossiiskaia Gazeta*, June 15, 2000.
26 *The Moscow Times*, November 22, 2001.
27 *BusinessWeek*, December 4, 2000, p. 56.
28 Ibid., December 2, 2000, p. 58.
29 *French Press Agency*, January 10, 2001; *Johnson's Russia List*, January 10, 2001, no. 5018, item 8.
30 *Academy of Management Executive*, November 2001, p. 20. See also *The Moscow Times*, August 9, 2002.
31 *The Financial Times*, November 1, 1996, p. 5; lecture, Arden House Conference, April 13, 2002.
32 *The Moscow Times*, February 7, 2001.
33 *Moskovskii Komsomolets*, January 20, 2001; *Jamestown Foundation Monitor*, December 15, 2000.
34 *Johnson's Russia List*, February 12, 2001, no. 5089.
35 *Segodnia*, February 8, 2000.
36 *Transitions*, World Bank, March–April 2002, p. 15.
37 *The Economist*, June 27, 2002; *The Moscow Times*, November 5, 2001; March 13, 2002; May 17, 2002; *Forbes Magazine*, February 18, 2002.
38 *The Moscow Times*, November 12, 2001.
39 Ibid., August 26, 2000; *The Moscow News*, January 26, 2000, p. 5; *Johnson's Russia List*, June 14, 2000, no. 4367, item 13.
40 *Johnson's Russia List*, November 17, 2002, no. 5552, item 7.
41 *Moskovskie Novosti*, no. 52, December 25–31, 2001, p. 10.
42 *Christian Science Monitor*, February 22, 2002.
43 *The Wall Street Journal*, July 26, 2002, p. A4.
44 *Christian Science Monitor*, February 22, 2002.
45 Blair Ruble and Nancy Popson, "The Westernization of a Russian Province; The Case of Novgorod," *Post-Soviet Geography and Economics*, no. 8, 1998, p. 33; Nikolai Petro, "The Novgorod Region: A Russian Success Story," *Post-Soviet Affairs*, 1999, no. 3, p. 235; Petro, "Creating Social Capital of Russia: The Novgorod Model, A Natural Concept for Eurasian–East European Research," working paper, September 18, 1999.
46 Ruble and Popson, p. 436.
47 Ibid., p. 441; Harry G. Broadman, *Is Russia Restructuring*, World Bank, February 16, 2001, p. 16.
48 Ruble and Popson, p. 438.
49 The United States program of regional support for a select number of oblasts, including Novgorod, Samara and Tomsk, evolved from a series of discussions in 1995 with the then Ambassador Richard Morningstar who was in charge of the U.S. program of foreign aid with the former Soviet Union. These were held at the Russian Research Center (now the Davis Center) at Harvard and focused on how to make U.S. economic aid to Russia more effective; U.S. Government General Accounting Office, 2000, p. 177. Support for this idea was renewed in the administration of George W. Bush by Paul O'Neill, the Secretary of the Treasury; *Johnson's Russia List*, October 31, 2001, no. 5519, item 6.
50 *The Moscow Times*, February 20, 2001; *BusinessWeek International*, July 2, 2001.
51 *The Moscow Times*, March 26, 2001; interview, Novgorod, September 8 2002.
52 Ibid., January 14, 2002.

53 Troika Dialog Research, "Russian Corporate Governance: The Perception and Costs of Corporate Governance Risk," Moscow, February 2001, section 2, p. 9.
54 *The Financial Times*, November 15, 2000, p. 24.
55 *The Moscow Times*, July 3, 2001.
56 Ibid., August 22, 2002.
57 *Johnson's Russia List*, January 2, 2002, no. 6003, item 5. The Federal Securities Commission drew up its own recommended Corporate Governance Code in April 2002. *The Moscow Times*, April 5, 2002.
58 *The Moscow Times*, September 21, 2001.
59 *The Wall Street Journal*, October 18, 1999, p. A37; *The New York Times*, August 18, 2001, p. B3.
60 *Club 2015: A Positive Scenario for Russia Through a Productive Society, Presentation for U.S.–Russia Business Conference*, Washington, D.C., March 21, 2000; *The Moscow Times*, February 27, 2001.
61 *Johnson's Russia List*, December 11, 2001, no. 5593, item 8.
62 *Time*, May 29, 2001.
63 *Forbes Magazine*, December 11, 2000; *World Link*, January 2001, p. 214; *The New York Times*, November 18, 2001, p. A12.
64 *The Financial Times*, July 25, 2001; December 31, 2001, p. 11; *Vedomosti*, September 10, 2001.
65 *The Financial Times*, February 2, 2002, pp. 19, 23.
66 Ibid.
67 George Cohon with David McFarlane, *To Russia With Fries*, Toronto: McClelland & Stewart, 1997, p. 169.
68 Ibid., pp. 20, 35, 119.
69 James L. Watson (ed.), *Golden Arches East: McDonald's in East Asia*, Stanford: Stanford University Press, 1997, pp. 150, 222–23.
70 Cohon, p. 180.
71 Ibid., p. 194.
72 *The Wall Street Journal*, February 11, 1990, p. A6.
73 Cohon, p. 219.
74 *The Financial Times*, July 1, 1992, p. 2; *The Wall Street Journal*, November 5, 1992, p. A8.
75 Paul Gregory and Robert Stewart, *Russia and Soviet Economic Performance*, Boston: Addison Wesley Longman, 2001, 7th edition, p. 348.
76 *The Moscow Times*, November 6, 2001.
77 Discussions with George Cohon; *Johnson's Russia List*, January 20, 2001, no. 5039, item 9; February 3, 2001, no. 5072, item 3; *The Moscow Times*, November 6, 2001; January 22, 2002; discussions with Hamzalot Khasbulatov, Director of McDonald's in Russia, Moscow, September 10, 2002.
78 *The Moscow Times*, January 18, 2001.
79 *Gillette Joint Ventures in the USSR: One Company's View*, 1991.
80 *The Moscow Times*, April 3, 1998; a visit to the St. Petersburg plant, June 5, 2000.
81 Michael Hawley, CEO Gillette, Arden House, March 29, 1998; visit to St. Petersburg plant, June 5, 2000; *The Moscow Times*, April 3, 1998.
82 Discussion with Gillette management, St. Petersburg, June 5, 2000.
83 Michael Hawley, CEO Arden House, March 29, 1998.
84 Evidently Bistro was not successful and the city offered the chain for sale in 2001; *The Moscow Times*, October 1, 2001.
85 *Atlantic Journal/Constitution*, November 13, 1993, p. A11.

86 "Survey Russia," *The Economist*, July 12, 1997, p. 12.
87 *The New York Times*, October 6, 1998, p. C4.
88 *The Moscow News*, September 10–16, 1998, no. 35, p. 7; *The New York Times*, October 23, 1998, p. C1.
89 *The Financial Times*, August 28, 1998, p. 14.
90 *The New York Times*, October 23, 1998, p. C4; *The Wall Street Journal*, February 26, 1999, p. C1.
91 *The Moscow Times*, March 13, 1998; April 25, 1998, p. 13.
92 James Gansinger, Seminar and Interview, Arden House, April 14, 2002.
93 Ibid., October 8, 1998.
94 *The Moscow Times*, May 28, 2002.
95 Ibid., May 31, 2001.
96 Ibid., July 13, 2001, p. 7; *St. Petersburg Times*, July 17, 2001, p. 8.
97 *The Moscow Times*, July 27, 2001.
98 *The Economist*, July 19, 2001.
99 *The Moscow Times*, August 21, 2001.
100 *The Wall Street Journal*, December 5, 2000, p. A22.
101 *The Financial Times*, November 24, 2000, p. 15; *The New York Times*, April 10, 2001, p. W1.
102 Bernard S. Black, *University of Pennsylvania Law Review*, vol. 149, p. 2131; *Emerging Market Review*, vol. 2, p. 89.
103 *Johnson's Russia List*, August 2, 2001, no. 5379, item 6; Interfax.

Appendix 11.1

104 *The Financial Times*, March 28, 2001, p. 18.
105 Ibid., April 19, 2001, p. 23.
106 *The Moscow Times*, October 29, 2001; October 30, 2001; October 31, 2001; *The Financial Times*, September 17, 2001, p. 24.
107 *McLean's Magazine*, May 20, 2002.
108 Ibid.
109 *The Moscow Times*, October 3, 2001.
110 Ibid., April 25, 1998, p. 13; May 8, 1998, p. 13; October 9, 1998; April 30, 1999.
111 *The Russian Journal*, July 6, 2001; *The Moscow Times*, July 3, 2001; July 5, 2001; July 13, 2001, p. 7; July 16, 2001.
112 *The Wall Street Journal*, August 3, 2001; *The Moscow Times*, July 27, 2001; August 2, 2001.
113 *The Russian Journal*, November 30, 2001; *McLean's Magazine*, May 20, 2002.
114 *The Moscow Times*, December 28, 2001.
115 *The Financial Times*, July 22, 2002, p. 7.
116 *The Economist*, February 23, 2001.
117 *The Moscow Times*, August 8, 2001.
118 Ibid., June 20, 2001, p. 10; August 1, 2001.
119 Ibid., June 26, 2002.
120 Ibid., December 5, 2001.
121 Ibid.
122 *McLean's Magazine*, May 20, 2002.
123 Ibid.
124 *The Moscow Times*, July 3, 2002

Bibliography

100 Najbogatszych Polakow, *Wprost*, June 18, 2000.
Academy of Management Executive, November 2001, p. 20.
French Press Agency, January 10, 2001.
Argumenti i Fakti, March 1995, no. 9; March 2001, no.12, p. 3.
Arkhangelskaya, Irina, "While Russia Sleeps," *Delovie Lyudi*, February 1995.
Aslund, Anders, "The Myth of Output Collapse After Communism," Working Papers, Carnegie Endowment, Post-Soviet Economics Project, no. 18, March 2001.
—— "Tainted Transactions," *The National Interest*, Summer 2000.
—— *How Russia Became a Market Economy*, Washington: Brookings, 1995.
—— (ed.), *Economic Transformation in Russia*, New York: St. Martin's Press, 1994.
Atlantic Journal/Constitution, November 13, 1993, p. A11.
BBC, July 1, 1998; July 7, 1998; September 4, 1998; March 22, 1999; October 11, 2000, "Russia from A to Z.".
Berliner, Joseph, "The Soviet Past and the Russian Transition," prepared for a conference on the Soviet economy, Zvenigorod, Russia, June 22, 2001.
Bisnis Russia, U.S. Department of Commerce, Development of Small and Medium-sized Business in Russia, December 7, 2001.
Black, Bernard S., *University of Pennsylvania Law Review*, vol. 149, p. 2131.
Blasi, Joseph R., Kroumova, Maya and Kruse, Douglas, *Kremlin Capitalism: Privatizing the Russian Economy*, Ithaca: Cornell University Press, 1997.
Bornstein, Morris, "Russia's Mass Privatisation Programme," *Communist Economies and Economic Transformation*, vol. 6, no. 4, 1994, p. 425.
Borovoi, Konstantin, in I. Bunin, *Biznesmeny Rossii: 40 Istorii Uspekha*, Moscow: OKO, 1994.
Bowden, Witt, Karpovich, Michael and Usher, Abbot Paison, *An Economic History of Europe Since 1750*, New York: American Book Company, 1937.
Boycko, Maxim, Shleifer, Andrei and Vishny, Robert, *Privatizing Russia*, Cambridge: MIT Press, 1995.
Brada, Josef C., "Privatization is Transition, Or Is It?" *Journal of Economic Perspectives*, vol. 10, no. 2, Spring 1996.
Brady, Rose, *Kapitalizm: Russia's Struggle to Free Its Economy*, New Haven: Yale University Press, 1999.
Broadman, Harry G., *Is Russia Restructuring*, World Bank, February 16, 2001.
Bunin, I. (ed.), *Biznesmeny Rossii: 40 Istorii Uspekha*, Moscow: OKO, 1994.
Business Review, January 1999, p. 35.
Central European, April 1999, p. 22.

Christian Science Monitor, February 22, 2002.

Chubais, Anatoly (ed.), *Privatizatsiia Po-Rossiiski*, Moscow: Vagrius, 1999.

Club 2015: A Positive Scenario for Russia Through a Productive Society, Presentation for U.S.–Russia Business Conference, Washington D.C., March 21, 2000.

Coase, Ronald, "The Problems of Social Class," *The Journal of Law and Economics*, no. 3, 1960.

Cohon, George with McFarlane, David, *To Russia With Fries*, Toronto: McClelland & Stewart, 1997.

Coricelli, Fabrizio, *The Journal of Economic Literature*, vol. XXXVI, no. 4, December 1998.

Coulloudon, Virginie, "Moscow City Management: A New Form of Capitalism?" mimeographed, 1999.

——— "Privatization In Russia: Catalyst for the Elite", *The Fletcher Forum of World Affairs*, vol. 22:2, Summer/Fall 1998.

Desai, Padma, "A Russian Optimist: Interview with Yegor Gaidar," *Challenge*, May–June 2000.

Dinello, Natalya Evdokimova, "Forms of Capital: The Case of Russian Borders," *International Sociology*, vol.13, no.3, September 1998.

Earle, John S., Frydman, Roman, Rapaczynski, Andrzej and Turkewitz, Joel, *Small Privatization*, Budapest: Central European University Press, CEU Privatization Reports, vol. 3, 1994.

Echo Radio Program, March 22, 1999.

Economic Commission for Europe, *Economic Survey of Europe in 1992–1993*, New York, United Nations, 1993, p. 122.

Economic Newsletter, Russian Research Center, Harvard University, January 13, 1989.

Fedorov, Boris, "Svoboda ili Prodazhnost' Pressy?" mimeograph, June 2001.

——— "Gazprom–The World's Largest 'Non-Profit' Corporation," mimeographed, October 2000.

Feldstein, Martin, *The Wall Street Journal*, September 8, 1997, p. A18.

Fischer, Stanley, Sahay, Ratna and Avegh, Carlos, "Stabilization and Growth in Transition Economies: the Early Experience," *The Journal of Economic Perspectives*, vol. 10, no. 2, Spring 1996.

Foreign Trade, February 1974, p. 40; January–March, 1997, p. 37.

Freeland, Chrystia, *Sale of the Century*, Toronto: Doubleday, 2000, p. 283.

Frydman, Roman, Hessel, Marek, Rapaczynski, Andrzej and Grey, Cheryl, "Ambiguity of Privatization, Private Ownership, and Corporate Performance: Evidence from the Transition Economies," undated.

Frydman, Roman, Rapaczynski, Andrzej and Earle, John S., *The Privatization Process in Russia, Ukraine, and the Baltic States*, New York: Central European University Press, 1993.

——— *The Privatization Process in Central Europe*, Budapest: Central European University Press, 1993.

Frye, Timothy and Shleifer, Andrei, "The Invisible Hand and the Grabbing Hand," *American Economic Review*, May 1997.

Gaddy, Clifford G. and Ickes, Barry W., "Russia's Virtual Economy," *Foreign Affairs*, September 1998.

Gaidar, Yegor, *Days of Defeat and Victory*, Seattle: University of Washington Press, 1999.

German Federal Statistical Office, *Statistical Yearbook of West Germany*, 1991.

270   *Bibliography*

Gerschenkron, Alexander, *Economic Backwardness and Historical Perspective*, Cambridge: The Belknap Press of Harvard University Press, 1962.

Gillette Joint Ventures in the USSR: One Company's View, 1991.

Goldman, Marshall I., "The Barter Economy," *Current History*, October 1998.

—— *Lost Opportunity: Why Economic Reforms in Russian Have Been so Difficult*, New York: W.W. Norton, 1996.

—— *Lost Opportunities: Why Economic Reforms in Russia Have Not Worked*, New York: W.W. Norton, 1994.

—— *Gorbachev's Challenge: Economic Reform in an Age of High Technology*, New York: W.W. Norton, 1987.

—— *USSR in Crisis: The Failure of an Economic System*, New York: W.W. Norton, 1983.

—— *Détente and Dollars*, New York: Basic Books, 1975.

Gorbachev, Mikhail, *Memoirs*, New York: Doubleday, 1995.

Goskomstat, monthly report on *Internet Securities*.

Goskomstat, *Narodnoe Khoziaistvo 1992*, Moscow: Nar Khoz, 1993, p. 66; 1996, p. 702.

Goskomstat Rossii, *Uroven' Zhizni Naseleniia* (Internet Securities, Macroeconomics), April 30, 1999.

—— *Rossiiskii Statisticheskii Ezhegodnik 1998* (Russian Statistical Report 1988), Moscow: Goskomstat, 1998, pp. 413, 414.

Government of Russian Federation, "Small-Scale Privatization in Russia: The Nizhny Novgorod Model Annexes," March 1992.

Grant, Jonathan A., *Big Business in Russia: The Putilov Company in Late Imperial Russia 1868–1917*, Pittsburgh: University of Pittsburgh Press, 1999.

Gregory, Paul and Stewart, Robert, *Russia and Soviet Economic Performance*, Boston: Addison Wesley Longman, 2001, 7th edition.

Gros, Daniel and Steinherr, Alfred, *Winds of Change: Economic Transition in Central and Eastern Europe*, London: Longman, 1995.

The Guardian, April 18, 2001; December 21, 2000; December 15, 2001.

Guseinov, R.M., "Kapitalizma v Rossii ne Bylo Dazhe v Period 'Kapitalizma'," *Ekonomicheskaia Istoriia Rossii: Problemy, Poiski, Resheniia, Ezhegodnik*, vol. 1, Volgograd, 1999.

Handelman, Stephen, *Comrade Criminal: Russia's New Mafiya*, New Haven: Yale University Press, 1995.

Hedlund, Stefan and Sundstrom, Niclas, "Does Palermo Represent the Future for Moscow?" *The Journal of Public Policy*, no. 16.

Hellman, Joel Scott, *Breaking the Banks: Bureaucrats and the Creation of Markets in a Transitional Economy*, submitted in part for the fulfillment of requirements for the degree of Ph.D., Graduate School of Arts and Sciences, Columbia University: New York, 1993.

Hoffman, David, *The Oligarchs: Wealth and Power in New Russia*, New York: Public Affairs Press, 2002.

IMF, *A Study of the Soviet Economy*, 1991.

IMF Staff Country Report, no. 95/107, Washington, International Monetary Fund, October 1995, p. 44.

Internet Securities, July 10, 1999.

ITAR-TASS, February 20, 1998; August 6, 1998; October 10, 2000.

Izvestia Press Digest Russiska Izvestia, September 19, 2000.

JSB Inkombank, ADR Level-1 Program Presentation, arranger, C.A. Atlantic Securities, Boston, May 12, 1997, p. 21.

Jamestown Foundation Monitor, October 15, 1997, p. 1; December 23, 1997, p. 2; December 15, 2000; May 16, 2001; December 3, 2001.

John Bartlett's Familiar Quotations, Boston: Little Brown, 1980, 15th edition, p. 719.

Johnson, Simon and Kroll, Heidi, "Managerial Strategies for Spontaneous Privatization," *Soviet Economy*, no. 2, 1991.

Johnson, Simon, Kaufmann, Daniel and Shleifer, Andrei, "The Unofficial Economy in Transition," *Brookings Papers on Economic Activity*, Fall 1997, Brookings Institution, Washington, D.C.

Kagarlitsky, Boris, "Don't Blame the Laws," *The Moscow Times*, April 27, 2001.

Kaiser, Michael, "Privatization in the C.I.S," *Post-Soviet Business Forum*, London: The Royal Institute of International Affairs, p. 11.

Kaufman, Daniel and Siegelbaum, Paul, *Privatization and Corruption in Transition Economies*, Winter, 1996.

Keynes, J.M., "A Short View of Russia," *Essays in Pessimism; The Collected Writings of J.M. Keynes*, London, 1972, Part 1, X.

Klebnikov, Paul, "The Oligarch Who Came in From the Cold," *Forbes*, March 18, 2002, p. 114.

—— *Godfather of the Kremlin*, New York: Harcourt, 2000.

Korzhakov, Alexandr, *Boris El'tsin ot Rassveta do Zakata*, Moscow: Interbuk, 1997.

Kremlin Package, Federal News Service.

Lane, David (ed), *Russian Banking*, Northampton: Edgar Elgar, 2002

Layard, Richard and Parker, John, *The Coming Russian Boom*, New York: Free Press, 1996.

Lewandowski, Janusz, "The Political Context of Mass Privatization in Poland," in *Between State and Market: Studies of Economies in Transition*, no. 23, World Bank, Washington, 1997.

Lewandowski, Janus and Szomberg, Jan, "Propertisation as a Foundation of Socio-economic Reform," paper for the seminar of "Transformation Proposal for Polish Economy," Warsaw, mimeographed, November 17–18, 1988.

Ling, Susan J. and Krueger, Gary, "Russia's Managers in Transition: Pilferers or Paladins?" *Post-Soviet Geography and Economics*, October 1996.

Lyashchenko, Peter I., *History of the National Economy of Russia to the 1917 Revolution*, New York: The MacMillan Company, 1949.

McCauley, Martin, *Who's Who in Russia Since 1900*, London: Routledge, 1997.

McLean's Magazine, May 20, 2002.

Mau, Vladimir, "Rossiiskie Ekonomicheskie Reformy Glazami Zapadnykh Kritikov," *Voprosy Ekonomiki*, November 1999.

Meitlik, Pavel, "Post-Privatization Restructuralization of Property Rights in the Czech Republic," Economic Commission for Europe: Spring Seminar, 1998, Geneva Paper 5.

Mladek, Jan, "Voucher Privatisation in the Czech Republic and Slovakia," OECD, Centre for Co-operation with the Economies in Transition, *Mass Privatization, an Initial Assessment*, Paris: Organization for Economic Operation and Development, 1995.

NTV, *Segodnia*, September 14, 1997.

Nagel, Mark S., *Supplicants, Robber Barons, and Pocket Banks: The Formation of Financial-Industrial Groups in Russia*, Department of Government, Cambridge: Harvard University, April 26, 1999.

Nelson, Lynn D. and Kuzes, Irina Y., *Property to the People: The Struggle for Radical Economic Reform in Russia*, Armonk: M.E. Sharpe, 1994.

The New Republic, October 9, 2000, p. 34.

North, Douglass, "Economic Performance Through Time," *American Economic Review*, vol. 84, no. 3.

Nurkse, Ragnar, *Problems of Capital Formation in Underdeveloped Countries*, Oxford: Basil Blackwell, 1955.

Odnokolenko, Oleg, *Itogi*, July 30, 2002, p. 12.

OECD, Centre for Co-operation with Economies in Transition, *Mass Privatization, an Initial Assessment*, Paris: Organization for Economic Operation and Development, 1995, p. 48.

OECD Economic Surveys, 1997, Paris: Russian Federation, p. 36.

OECD Economic Summary 1997–98, Paris: Russian Federation, 1997, p. 136.

Ogonek, December 1995, no. 7, pp. 22–3.

OMRI, August 16, 1996, p. 3.

Owen, Thomas C., *The Corporation Under Russian Law 1800–1917: A Study in Tsarist Economic Policy*, Cambridge, England: Cambridge University Press, 1991.

Petro, Nikolai, "The Novgorod Region: A Russian Success Story," *Post-Soviet Affairs*, no. 3, 1999.

—— "Creating Social Capital of Russia: The Novgorod Model, A Natural Concept for Eurasian–East European Research," working paper, September 18, 1999.

Pipes, Richard, *Property and Freedom*, New York: Alfred A. Knopf, 1999, p. 160.

Pistor, Katharina and Spicer, Andrew, "Investment Funds in Mass Privatization and Beyond," *Between State and Market: Studies of Economies in Transition*, Washington D.C., World Bank, no. 23, 1997.

—— "Investment Funds in Mass Privatization and Beyond: Evidence from the Czech Republic and Russia," Cambridge: Harvard Institute for International Development, Harvard University Development Discussion Paper no. 565, December 1996.

Poland: Fundamental Facts, Figures, and Regulations, The Polish Agency for Foreign Investment, Warsaw, January 1996, p. 29.

PricewaterhouseCoopers (PWC) audit performed for the Russian Central Bank, August 4, 1999, p. 3.

Program Powszechnej Prywatyzacji (National Investment Fund Program), *Information Relating to the Universal Share Certificate*, Ministry of Privatization, Warsaw, November 1993, p. 4.

Putin, Vladimir, *First Person*, New York: Public Affairs, 2000.

Putin's annual address to the Duma, April 3, 2001, BBC Monitoring, April 3, 2001.

Radaev, Vadim, "Russian Entrepreneurship After the 1998 Crisis," *Programs in New Approaches to Russian Security, Policy Memo Series*, no. 78, October 1999.

Raeff, Marc, *The Well-ordered Police State*, New Haven: Yale University Press, 1983.

Reddaway, Peter and Glenski, Dmitri, *The Tragedy of Russia's Reforms: Market Bolshevism against Democracy*, Washington: The U.S. Institute of Peace Press, 2001.

Remnick, David, *Resurrection: The Struggle for a New Russia*, New York: Random House, 1997.

Reuters, April 4, 1997; February 18, 2000.

RFE/RL, April 24, 2001.

RFE/RL, *Newsline*, July 19 1997, no. 75, Part 1.

Rose-Ackerman, Susan, "Corruption and Competition," mimeographed, January 28, 1994.

Ruble, Blair and Popson, Nancy, "The Westernization of a Russian Province; The Case of Novgorod," *Post-Soviet Geography and Economics*, no. 8, 1998.

Russia/CIS Division, U.S. Dept. of Commerce, May 19, 1997, email message.

The Russian Jewish Congress Annual Report, 1998, p. 43.

The Russian Journal, February 17, 2001; October 12–18, 2001.

Russika Izvestia, July 7, 1998.

Russtrends, July–September, 1997, no. 22, www.securities.com.

Rutland, Peter, "Russia's Natural Gas Leviathan," *Transition*, May 3, 1996.

—— "Russia's Energy Engine Under Strain," *Transition*, May 3, 1996.

Sachs, Jeffrey D., "Tainted Transactions: An Exchange," *The National Interest*, Summer 2000.

Sachs, Jeffrey D. and Pistor, Katharina (eds.), *The Rule of Law and Economic Reform in Russia*, Boulder, CO: Harper-Collins, Westview Press, 1997.

Schiller, Robert J., Boycko, Maxim and Korobov, Vladimir, "Popular Attitudes Toward Free Markets: The Soviet Union and United States Compared," *American Economic Review*, no. 81, 1991.

Schumpeter, Joseph A., *Capitalism, Socialism and Democracy*, New York: Harper & Brothers, 1947, 2nd edition.

Shleifer, Andrei, Johnson, Simon and Kaufmann, Daniel, *Brookings Papers on Economic Activity*, no. 2, 1997, Brookings Institution, Washington, D.C.

Shleifer, Andrei and Treisman, Daniel, *Political Tactics and Economic Reform in Russia*, Cambridge: MIT Press, 2000.

Shleifer, Andrei and Vishny, Robert N., *The Grabbing Hand: Government Pathologies and Cures*, Cambridge: Harvard University Press, 1998.

—— "Corruption," *The Quarterly Journal of Economics*, August 1993, p. 599.

Skorov, Georgy, "Highlights of Privatization," mimeographed, Paris, May 26, 1996.

—— "Highlights of Privatization à la Russe," mimeographed, Paris, May 25, 1996.

Solnick, Steven L., *Stealing the State*, Cambridge: Harvard University Press, 1998.

Sovershenno Sekretno, no. 12, December 2000.

Stiglitz, Joseph, "Quis Custodiet Ipsos Custodes? (Who is to Guard the Guards Themselves?)" *Challenge*, November–December, 1999.

—— *Globalization & Its Discontents*, New York: W.W. Norton, 2002.

Stone, Randall W., "Russia and the IMF," *Lending Credibility: The IMF and the Post-Communist Transition*, section 21.17, mimeographed.

Sutton, Anthony, *Western Technology and Soviet Economic Development 1917–1930*, Stanford: Hoover Institution Publications, 1968.

—— *Western Technology and Soviet Economic Development, 1930–1945*, Stanford: Hoover Institution Publications, 1971.

Transitions, World Bank, June 1997; March–April 2002, p. 15; vol. 6, nos. 1–2, p. 15.

Treisman, Daniel, "Blaming Russia First," *Foreign Affairs*, November–December 2000.

Troika Dialog Research, "Russian Corporate Governance: The Perception and Costs of Corporate Governance Risk," Moscow, February 2001, section 2, p. 9.

TV-6, April 25, 2001.

United Nations Development Program, *Transition 1999: Human Development Report for Europe and the CIS*, United Nations, 2000.

Ural Business News, May 16, 2000.

U.S. Department of Defense and The Central Intelligence Agency, *The Soviet Acquisition of Militarily Significant Western Technology: An Update*, Washington, D.C., September 1985.

U.S. Government General Accounting Office, "Report to the Chairman and the Ranking Minority Member," Committee On Banking and Financial Services, House of Representatives, *Foreign Assistance: International Efforts to Aid Russia's Transition Have Mixed Results*, GAO–01–8, Washington, D.C.: United States Government, November 1, 2000, pp. 90, 91, 177.

—— "Foreign Assistance: The Harvard Institute for International Development's Work in Russia and Ukraine," Washington: GAO/NSIAD, 97–27, November 27, 1996.

U.S.–Russia Business Journal, "Russia After the Election," July 26, 1996, p. 19.

Vedomosti, September 10, 2001.

Vickers, John and Yarro, George, *Privatization: An Economic Analysis*, Cambridge: MIT Press, 1998.

The Wall Street Journal Europe, April 11, 1995; July 12, 1996, p. 4.

Wallace, Charles, "The Pirates of Prague," *Fortune*, December 23, 1996.

The Warsaw Voice, "Polish and Central European Russia," April 1998, p. 13.

The Washington Times, December 5, 1994, p. 1.

Watson, James L. (ed.), *Golden Arches East: McDonald's in East Asia*, Stanford: Stanford University Press, 1997.

Wedel, Janine, "Tainted Transactions: An Exchange," *The National Interest*, Summer 2000, no. 60 and Fall 2000, no. 61.

—— *Collision and Collusion: The Strange Case of Western Aid to Eastern Europe, 1989–1998*, New York: St. Martin's Press, 1998.

Winiecki, Jan, "Polish Mass Privatisation Programme: The Unloved Child in a Suspect Family," OECD, Centre for Co-operation with Economies in Transition, *Mass Privatization, an Initial Assessment*, Paris: Organization for Economic Operation and Development, 1995.

The World Bank Report, "Investment Funds in Mass Privatization and Beyond," no. 23, pp. 35, 101.

World Link, January–February 2000; July–August 2000, p. 41; January 2001, p. 214.

www.polit.ru/documents/414213.html, Russian government website.

Yeltsin, Boris, *Midnight Diaries*, New York: Public Affairs, 2000.

Magazines and newspapers

Atlantic Journal/Constitution
The Boston Globe
Business Review
BusinessWeek
BusinessWeek International
Christian Science Monitor
Current Digest of the Soviet Press

David Johnson's Russia List
Economic Newsletter, Russian Research Center, Harvard University.
The Economist
Ekonomicheskaia Gazeta
Ekonomika i Zhizn'
The Financial Times
Forbes Magazine
Foreign Trade
French Press Agency
The Guardian
Ha'aretz
The Independent
Internet Securities
Izvestia Press Digest Russiska Izvestia
Izvestiia
Kommersant Daily
Komsomolskaia Pravda
Le Monde
The Los Angeles Times
The Moscow News
The Moscow Times
Moskovskaia Pravda
Moskovskie Novosti
Moskovskii Komsomolets
The New Republic
The New York Times
Newsweek
Nezavisimaia Gazeta
Novaia Gazeta
Novosti
Obshchaia Gazeta
Pravda
RFE/RL, *Newsline*
Reuters
Rossiiskaia Gazeta
Russian Journal
Russia Review
Russika Izvestia
St. Petersburg Times
Segodnia
Sovetskaia Rossiia
Time
The Times of London
Ural Business News
Vedomosti
The Wall Street Journal
The Wall Street Journal Europe
The Washington Post
The Washington Times
World Link

Meetings, interviews, seminars, and discussions

Aven, Peter, President, Alfa Bank, Moscow.
Balcerowicz, Leszek, Deputy Prime Minister, Minister of Finance, Warsaw.
Berezovsky, Boris, oligarch and now Co-Chairman of the Liberal Russia Party, Moscow.
Berger, Mikhail, Editor in Chief, *Khronika*, and former editor of *Segodnia*, Moscow, Davos.
Bigman, Alan, Vice-President, Director of Financing, Tyumen Oil, Moscow, Arden House.
Bogomolev, Oleg, Director, Institute for International and Political Studies, Moscow.
Borovoi, Konstantin, Founder Moscow Stock Exchange, Moscow, Davos, Cambridge.
Bushuev, Alexey, Chairman of the Board of Directors, Analytic Center, Yaroslavl.
Cannon, Douglas, Chief Financial Advisor, Jenswold, King & Associates, Inc., Warsaw.
Chernomyrdin, Viktor, Former Prime Minister, Russian Federation, Former Chairman, Gazprom, Moscow.
Chubais, Anatoly, Chairman, UES, Former First Deputy Prime Minister, Russian Federation, Moscow.
Cohon, George, CEO McDonald's Canada, Moscow, Cambridge, Arden House.
Derby, Peter, Dialog Bank, Moscow.
Dobrinin, Peter, General Director, Novosibirsk Low-Voltage Equipment Works, Novosibirsk.
Elisov, Alexei, General Director, Sinar, Novosibirsk.
Ermilov, Aleksey, Vice-President, Siberian Bank, Novosibirsk.
Evdokimova, Valentina, Director, Volga Fashion Design House, Yaroslavl.
Evsiutkin, Alexander, General Director, Vtortsvetmet Nonferrous Metals, Yaroslavl.
Fay, Eric, Vice-President, Bank of America, Warsaw, Cambridge.
Federov, Boris, Former Finance Minister, Russian Federation, Moscow.
Federov, Valentin, Governor, Sakhalin.
Filipiak, Janusz, Professor, Chairman, Telecommunication Department, University of Mining and Metallurgy, Krakow, Poland.
Fraishtout, Revmir, President, Lutch, Podolsk.
Frantzev, Afanasii, General Director, Glavnovosibirskstroi, Novosibirsk.
Freyberg, Ewa, Under-Secretary of State, Ministry of the Treasury, Warsaw.
Fridman, Mikhail, President, Alfa Bank, Moscow.
Gaidar, Yegor, Member of the State Duma (Parliament) of the Federal Assembly of the Russian Federation, Former Prime Minister, Russian Federation, Moscow, Cambridge.
Gansinger, James, Subway Russia, St. Petersburg, Arden House.
Gavrilov, Igor, Director, Accent, Yaroslavl.
Gerashchenko, Viktor, Chairman, Russian Central Bank, Moscow, Davos.
Gorbachev, Mikhail, President, Gorbachev Foundation, Former General Secretary of the Communist Party, Soviet Union, Moscow, Boston, Hobe Sound, Florida.
Gref, German, Minister of the Economy, Russian Federation, Moscow, Salzburg.
Gusinsky, Vladimir, Former Chairman, Media-MOST, Moscow, Davos, Cambridge.
Hawley, Michael, CEO, Gillette, Cambridge, Arden House, Moscow.
Illarionov, Andrei, Economic Advisor to President Putin, Moscow, Cambridge.
Inozemtsev, Vladislas, CEO, Moscow Paris Bank, Moscow.

Jacaszek, Andrzej, Chief Marketing Officer, Agros Holding S.A., Warsaw.
Jenk, Justin, McKinsey & Company, Inc., Warsaw.
Johnson, Gary, CEO, Sawyer Research, Cleveland, Arden House.
Jordan, Boris, General Director, NTV, Moscow, Salzburg.
Kegeles, Alexander, President, Podati, Yaroslavl.
Khasbulatov, Hamzalot, Director, McDonald's Russia, Moscow.
Kirienko, Sergei, Former Prime Minister, Russian Federation, Moscow, Cambridge.
Kostikov, Igor, Chairman, The Federal Commission for the Securities Market, Moscow, Cambridge.
Koziurin, Vladimir, Technical Director, Nizkovoltnoi Apparatur, Novosibirsk.
Kozeny, Viktor, Davis Center for Russian Studies Seminar, Harvard University, Cambridge.
Kukes, Simon, President, Tyumen Oil, Moscow,.
Kulikov, Stanislav, Director, General Manager, Ripel, Novosibirsk.
Kurtsevich, Alexander, General Director, Siberian Leather Goods and Accessories, Novosibirsk.
Lebed, Alexander, Former Governor of Krasnoyarsk Region, Moscow, New York.
Luzkhov, Yuri, Mayor of Moscow, Moscow, Davos.
Margelov, Mikhail, Council of Federation, Arden House.
Margueritte, Bernard, President, International Communications Forum, Warsaw.
Martovaya, Marina, Deputy Director, International Department, Mayor's Office, City of Novosibirsk.
Medvedko, Victor, Director General, Novosibirsk Electrovacuum Plant, Novosibirsk.
Mizulina, Elena, Deputy of the State Duma, Committee for the Legislation and Judiciary Reform, Yaroslavl.
Morozov, Mikhail, Commercial Director, Vershne Volshk Shina, Yaroslavl.
Mylonas, John, Director, General Motors, Russia, Tolyatti.
Nemtsov, Boris, Chairman, Union of Right Forces, Russian Duma, Moscow, Cambridge, Davos, Salzburg.
Obermayer, Michael, Managing Director, Central & Eastern Europe, McKinsey & Company, Moscow.
Odinets, Alexander, Director, Kvanteks, Novosibirsk.
Ossadchy, Alexander, Production Director, Novosibirsk Low-Voltage Equipment Works, Novosibirsk.
Parshikov, Andrei, General Director, Shelesobeton, Yaroslavl.
Petrov, Gennady, General Director, NXBK, Novosibirsk.
Ponomarev, Vladimir, President, Novomir, Novosibirsk.
Primakov, Evgeny, Former Prime Minister of Russian Federation, Moscow, Salzburg.
Prokhorov, Alexander, Financial Manager, Vershne Volshk Shina, Yaroslavl.
Raskina, Isabella, Director, RBS, oil trading, Yaroslavl.
Roketsky, Leonid, Governor, Tyumen and Chairman, Tyumen Oil, Moscow, Davos.
Rotzang, Alex, Chairman, NOREX Petroleum, Calgary, Arden House.
Rozlucki, Wieslaw, President, Chief Executive, Warsaw Stock Exchange, Warsaw.
Ruben, David, Chairman, Transworld Metals, London.
Rychkov, Nikolai, President, Elektro Signal, Novosibirsk.
Shatalin, Stanislav, Economic Advisor to Gorbachev and Yeltsin, Moscow.
Shlykov, Vitaly, Council on Foreign and Defense Policy, Moscow.
Shokin, Alexander, Deputy Prime Minister, Moscow.

Sielicki, Tomasz, ComputerLand, Warsaw.
Sobchak, Anatoly, Former Mayor of St. Petersburg, St. Petersburg, Boston.
Soskovets, Oleg, First Deputy Prime Minister, Moscow.
Stepashin, Sergei, Former Prime Minister of Russian Federation, Moscow, Cambridge.
Swiecicki, Marcin, Mayor of Warsaw, Poland, Salzburg, Cambridge.
Titov, Vadim, General Director, Energoresource, Novosibirsk.
Tolokonsky, Victor, Mayor, City of Novosibirsk.
Trofimov, Valery, President, Invest, Novgorod.
Turchak, Anatoly, Leninets, St. Petersburg.
Tutaev, Vladimir, General Director, Yarsantechmontazh, Yaroslavl.
Vasiliev, Dmitry, Chairman, Investor's Protection Association, Moscow.
Vasiliev, Sergei, President, Leontief Center, Moscow.
Volsky, Arkady, President, Industrial and Entrepreneur Union, Moscow, Davos.
Wroblewski, Andrzej Krzystof, Polityka, Warsaw.
Yakovlev, Vladimir, Governor of St. Petersburg.
Yasin, Evgeny, Economic Advisor to President, Moscow, Davos.
Yavlinsky, Grigory, Chairman, Yabloko Party, Russian Duma, Moscow, Davos, Cambridge.
Yeltsin, Boris, Former President of Russian Federation, New York.
Zagorny, Rafal, President, Piast National Investment Fund, Warsaw.
Zhirinovsky, Vladimir, Chairman, Liberal Democratic Party, Moscow.
Zyuganov, Gennady, Chairman, Communist Party, Russian Duma, Moscow, Cambridge.

Other

Balakna Volga Paper Plant, Nizhny Novgorod.
Farms-Sakhalin.
Gaz Automobile Plant, Nizhny Novgorod.
General Motors–Avtovaz Joint Venture, Tolyatti.
Gillette Razor Plant, St. Petersburg.
Khrunichev Missile Plant, Moscow.
Lutch Laser Factory, Podolsk.
McDonald's Processing Plant, Moscow.

Index